TWENTY-FIRST-CENTURY
British Fiction

A *Gylphi Limited* Book

First published in Great Britain in 2015
by Gylphi Limited

Copyright © Gylphi Limited, 2015

All rights reserved.

A CIP catalogue record for this book is available from the British Library.

ISBN 978-1-78024-021-3 (pbk)
ISBN 978-1-78024-022-0 (Kindle)
ISBN 978-1-78024-023-7 (EPUB)

Design and typesetting by Gylphi Limited. Printed in the UK by imprintdigital. com, Exeter.

Gylphi Limited
PO Box 993
Canterbury CT1 9EP, UK

TWENTY-FIRST-CENTURY
British Fiction

edited by
Bianca Leggett and Tony Venezia

Gylphi

CONTENTS

Part V: Forms

FICTION IN A FICTIONALIZED SOCIETY

Joseph Brooker

Raymond Williams' inaugural lecture at Cambridge in 1972 was entitled 'Drama in a Dramatized Society' (Williams, 1984). Williams' title is resonant for thinking about fiction in the twenty-first century. Its implication is that drama – on the formal stage of the theatre – now takes place in a much more crowded context of dramatic action and representation. For Williams these certainly include cinema and television, which have meant that 'drama, in quite new ways, is built into the rhythms of everyday life' (Williams, 1984: 12). An average person, he reflects in the early 1970s, will now 'watch simulated action, of several recurrent kinds, not just occasionally but regularly, for longer than eating and for up to half as long as work or sleep'; this, Williams asserts, must be 'a new form and pressure' (Williams, 1984: 12). As television viewers we seek word from '"out there"': 'not out there in a particular street or a specific community but in a complex and otherwise unfocused and unfocusable national and international life, where our area of concern and apparent concern is unprecedentedly wide' (Williams, 1984: 14). 'In the simplest sense', Williams avows, 'our society has been dramatized by the inclusion of constant dramatic representation as a daily habit and need' (Williams, 1984: 15).

Williams' thoughts are suggestive for an attempt to describe the world in which contemporary fiction makes its way. Such fiction takes its place in a world already full of fictions, of diverse kinds. The im-

1

mense generalization of textuality and self-expression facilitated by the Internet has altered the reading environment since the mid-1990s. To draw on Williams' lecture to explore this point brings an evident initial irony. Williams was writing forty years ago. By definition, what he describes cannot now be new. But it can give us an emphasis for the contemporary moment, while also cautioning us against reinventing the wheel and imagining that our condition is unprecedented.

New fiction enters a world crowded with fictions. Literature itself is a mine to be quarried. Intertextuality within literature is accepted. Texts bounce off other texts and gain traction from them. The historical novels of A. S. Byatt and Pat Barker depict worlds known partly from the literature of the earlier eras that they reconstruct. David Mitchell, often keen to take things further than his peers, has constructed an intratextual world of his own. Characters from *Ghostwritten* (1999), *number9dream* (2001), *Cloud Atlas* (2004) and beyond cross into each others' books, knitting the writer's hefty novels into a universe of their own. Texts from the past also inform our sense of life now. For many of us, that past includes the early twentieth century. One of the most dynamic areas of criticism in contemporary fiction studies has concerned what David James has dubbed the legacies of modernism. Henry James, James Joyce or Virginia Woolf are part of how we see and how we read: and they also inform how many contemporary novelists write (see James, 2012a, 2012b).

Fictions surround every writer and reader. We see fictional feature films at the cinema, on television, on computers or on other portable devices. Television drama, in its extended American forms, is routinely referred to as the major art form of the twenty-first century, or as having actually beaten the novel at its own game and supplanted it for cultural importance, emotional depth or social insight. Indeed this is a rather surprisingly high-toned rerun of an old rivalry, between page and screen, which would once have more likely centred on the displacement of prose fiction by televisual trash. Television – watched through various technological means – continues to contain such diverse forms of drama. They include comedy, soap opera (now stripped across the British week in a way unthinkable when *East-Enders* was launched in the mid-1980s), cartoons. Taking Williams' sense of drama as an extended practice, reaching across social life, we could go further. The narratives that we consume also include advertisements (which Williams used as an example of the porousness of drama, in an age when an actor on TV might also appear in the commercial break [16]), the news and its analytical and satirical satellites, sport, public opinion.

None of these is straightforwardly fiction. Most of them significantly contain facts. But they are hard to insulate from fiction. It is difficult to say that Sky Sports' Premier League, or discussions of the public perceptions of political leaders, are just stonily factual. They also involve elaboration, narrative, projection. This was perhaps more clearly true of one of the major televisual experiments of the 2000s. Reality television was sold in part as being more real than drama. But it was life manipulated and mediated, rather than an actual slice of life that any of us could recognize. Its participants have fictionalized themselves. Those who were already celebrities, and those who have become celebrated for being on reality TV, have alike collaborated in forming caricatures of themselves. These have in turn been kept afloat week by week in another sea of fiction: the media of gossip and celebrity news.

The author who made the most deliberate effort to integrate fiction and reality, novel and news, was Gordon Burn. His very original book *Born Yesterday: The News as a Novel* (2008), braided together news stories from the summer of 2007 like the disappearance of Madeleine McCann and Gordon Brown's succession of Tony Blair. Burn suggests patterns and narratives in the news, and highlights the way that the media define and construct what is news at all. The best-known novel of the news in the last decade, though, was that peculiarly divisive novel, Ian McEwan's *Saturday* (2005). The book retains interest as an attempt to render the contemporary, or the immediately recent past: an attempt less original than Burn's, but still distinctive. In McEwan, the media is a background noise or mood music, the News 24 screen a pulse or leitmotif as Big Ben was for Woolf's *Mrs Dalloway* (1925).

Digital technology is the factor that has most evidently distinguished twenty-first from twentieth-century life. The sequence now includes the personal computer; the broadband connection; the

3

mobile phone, and latterly the smartphone; the travelling Internet, interactive map, photos that can instantly be despatched around the world. The Internet has meanwhile generated its own textual forms. They include the mailing list; the weblog; the messageboard; the podcast. Then the social network, one after another, perhaps reaching an apotheosis, at the time of writing, with twitter's particular way of covering the world in instant words and pictures. Even in real life – or IRL – new formats of behaviour have accompanied digital development: from flash mobs generated on railway concourses, to the social movements famously coordinated online, in Cairo or San Francisco.

These technologies have not necessarily created novels – though some have done. In that category we can name Jennifer Egan's *Black Box* (2012), published on twitter; and E. L. James' *Fifty Shades of Grey* (2012), an immensely successful sequence that grew from online fan fiction. The Internet has also spurred people to write novels who would not otherwise have done so. NaNoWriMo – National Novel Writing Month – takes place each November, and despite its name is international. Clearly this vastly expands the number of novels and novelists. More precisely, it surely expands the number of *bad* novels. There is a general penchant for quantity over quality here: NaNoWriMo's website proclaims that the word count for 2011 is 3000 million, but has no interest in telling us how many good sentences were produced or what they sound like. But in this instance, at least, the World Wide Web is encouraging not just alternative literary forms but more novels in their own right.

Literary forms and digital technology will continue to interact and combine. The blog can be a way of writing a novel; and the weblog itself, by an individual or many hands, can perhaps be considered a new literary form, insofar as it has stretched the essay or the meditation sideways and lengthways, opening it out laterally across hyperlinks and horizontally through the time of a writer's life. Indeed the temptation is to see older texts and forms on the model of new technologies. Geoff Dyer's *The Colour of Memory* (1989) was written long before weblogs, but could otherwise be one gathered into book form. Ezra Pound's *Cantos* may currently be viewed as a poetic Tumblr account, stuffed with bits he liked and wanted to pass on.

We inhabit, some of the time, a state of speed, of flow, of information and matter too extensive and proliferating ever to be fully imbibed and apprehended. The critic Tom Ewing has talked of that space of contemporary distraction as *the stream*: 'that ceaseless flow of information we access every time we use social media'. He notes that a cultural text might now be 'something you see sandwiched between other status updates, tweets, or posts, fighting for attention with every other picture, stray thought, polemic, or advert'. He further defines a *nanoculture*, which he says 'encompasses the streams we create, curate, and consume online, and the stories that flow through them, and the things we do to that stuff: sharing it, liking it, reviving it, changing it, arguing over it.' (Ewing, 2011).

In a sense much of this material *is* a kind of fiction: not at the level of the novel – but the hit and run scale of avatars, personae, jokes, parodies, and exaggerations. Would such a state, such a world of buzz and background noise, make it harder to focus on novels? If novels are adrift in a stream of generalized textuality, how do they stay afloat? The answer may be structurally similar to one that could be identified in earlier epochs. In the Modernist era of mass literacy, of a new tabloid press, *Tit-Bits* and the first few decades of film, literature can be found seeking an *alternative* to that world, seeking a bulwark or to shore something against the ruins of cultural value. Or, just as plausibly, it can be seen as sometimes participating in that world, forming a continuum with the proliferation of text and media, and, as most famously with *Ulysses* (1922), incorporating it directly into the highest forms of literature itself. We may wish to see contemporary fiction on similar lines. It can be an alternative, an escape, a cabin to hide out from a blizzard of information: the novel as a long form that might maintain our attention span against shorter and shorter, more and more transient forms. Laura Miller, in an insightful piece on fiction and the Internet, characterizes the view thus:

> The further literature is driven to the outskirts of the culture, the more it is cherished as a sanctuary from everything coarse, shallow and meretricious in that culture. It is the chapel of profundity, and about as lively and well visited as a bricks-and-mortar chapel to boot.

> Literature is where you retreat when you're sick of celebrity divorces, political mudslinging, office intrigues, trials of the century, new Apple products, internet flame wars, sexting and *X Factor* contestants – in short, everything that everybody else spends most of their time thinking and talking about. (Miller, 2011: 2)

But the contrary can also be true. Equally, Miller states, the novel can be viewed as ineluctably part of that world, contributing to it, talked about within it, sometimes incorporating new kinds of information from it, and bringing us news.

In the former category, the historical novel is important. Byatt, Sarah Waters and, most imposingly, Hilary Mantel would be cases in point. Compared with Angela Carter's 1899 in *Nights at the Circus* (1984), or John Fowles' nineteenth century in *The French Lieutenant's Woman* (1969), Mantel's latest work seems to represent on one hand a withdrawal from reflexivity and self-consciousness, into a narrative whose diegesis is relatively untroubled by anachronism and winks at the present; and on the other hand, in her deployment of the present tense, a vivid sensory immersion in the past, a sense of the past as present rather than as a period being rewritten now.

On the other side of the equation, how has the novel engaged with the living stream of the contemporary? To stay with the example of technology, Mez Packer has proposed that 'literary fiction' has a poor record of representing the digital communication, which is part of most readers' everyday lives (Packer, 2012). She notes that such technology dates quickly and will stand out in a narrative within a couple of years. Many writers, Packer suggests, effectively flee to a past that cannot date, and are often rewarded for it by being listed for prizes. We need not view the historical novel with such suspicion, but we can wonder, with Packer, how the newest generation of 'digital natives' will write of a technological environment they can take for granted. Science fiction, though, has been a place where not merely contemporary technologies are represented, but as yet inexistent ones are imagined. This is one reason for the growing prestige of science fiction within and without the academy, as hierarchies of value around genre are restructured in contemporary criticism. It is worth asking how the writers discussed in this book are engaging with the experience of twenty-first century life, whether or not they turn to science fiction to try to understand the present.

Digital technology has also had a different, powerful effect, on cultural markets. It has become harder to make substantial money out of culture, because most things, in digital form, can be more easily copied and redistributed for free. Film, television, and especially the press: all are threatened. The music industry has been profoundly challenged. Profit margins from recorded music have plummeted; proceeds from live performance have tended to replace them as a major income stream.

Has something similar happened in literature? Thousands of novels are still printed, but released into a world where the status of print has changed. Print suddenly seems newly expendable, at risk of being a waste of space, about to be superannuated. E-readers are becoming standard. One productive response to this situation has been the reassertion of physical formats. The emergence of the digital offers a space to estrange and rethink the more conventionally material. In music, the obvious case is the relative rebirth, or at least the dogged persistence, of vinyl records. Meanwhile, some writers and designers have explored deliberately elaborate physical media for writing: taking their cue from the earlier example of B. S. Johnson and from the more recent model of *McSweeney's*, the deluxe US quarterly that takes a different form each issue.

Another obvious parallel with music arises. The decline in value of recorded music sales has partially been compensated by a boom in live music, and inflation of prices for concerts and live events. The literary world can tell a related story. Even twenty or thirty years ago, it was newly noticeable that writers were asked to tour and read in public – and hence that they needed to be presentable. This trend has only increased – especially with the importance of literary festivals, from Edinburgh to Hay-on-Wye. More than ever, the book world now sells itself to us as a gregarious, live world. To be a major author you need to be able not just to write good sentences but also to sit in a tent talking to Andrew Marr or James Naughtie over a bottle of mineral water. And if you want to run a bookshop, you cannot just stock books: you probably need to buy some wine and get people in to listen to authors, or at least talk to each other in a book group.

Writers themselves are live in another sense: they are online, running their own websites, responding to fans and critics, tweeting adverts for their own readings or opinions on riots, the coalition or Katy Perry. The figure of the writer has subtly changed this century: perhaps metamorphosing slightly into a member of the public, in a Bakhtinian abolition of the footlights separating performer and audience. Can an author aspire to the same status as 20 or 30 years ago? The first *Granta* list of 1983 contains several names who would still figure on a list of major British writers today. It is hard to picture such long-standing status for the 2013 list – which is no judgement of intrinsic literary quality, but one of cultural status and accelerated turnover.

Twenty-first century fiction subsists in a world of fictions of many kinds, from which it draws and with which it competes. It may offer a refuge from the stream of distraction that floods the contemporary, prompting a slower form of attention or historical insight. But it may also chase the news or seek a way to encapsulate that stream of novelties in prose. It does so as the status of paper and print themselves change, perhaps more radically than for centuries; and at a time when the novelist needs to be freshly resourceful, multitasking between genres and jobs as between tabs in an Internet browser. The first name on *Granta*'s 1983 list, Martin Amis, wrote of a character 'addicted to the twentieth century' (Amis, 1984: 91). Even if we do not feel addicted to the twenty-first century, we are presently dependent on it, unable readily to escape it. The essays that follow describe how a number of the most interesting novelists in Britain today have met its challenges thus far.

Works Cited

Amis, Martin (1984) *Money*. London: Jonathan Cape.

Ewing, Tom (2011) 'Take me to the river', *Pitchfork*, 9 December, accessed 10 May 2013, http://pitchfork.com/features/poptimist/8724-take-me-to-the-river/

James, David (ed.) (2012a) *The Legacies of Modernism*. Cambridge: Cambridge University Press.

James, David (ed.) (2012b) *Modernist Futures*. Cambridge: Cambridge University Press.

Miller, Laura (2011) 'How novels came to terms with the internet', *Guardian*, 15 January, *Review*, p. 2, accessed 10 May 2013, http://www.guardian.co.uk/books/2011/jan/15/novels-internet-laura-miller.

Packer, Mez (2012) 'Techno-phobia and the modern writer', *Writers' Hub*, 5 March 2012, accessed 10 May 2013, http://www.writershub.co.uk/features-piece.php?pc=1380

Williams, Raymond (1984) *Writing in Society*. London: Verso.

What We Talk About When We Talk About Twenty-first-century British Fiction

Bianca Leggett and Tony Venezia

The title of this collection, *Twenty-first-century British Fiction*, serves a dual function. First, it is a discursive space in which an extremely diverse group of texts that share an origin in the same time and place can be brought into dialogue with each other. Second, it is the subject of conversation itself. The new millennium has been a period of rapid change and under this stimulus British fiction has evolved in new and sometimes unpredictable directions. It is the mercurial nature of its subject matter, which makes the study of contemporary British fiction both so dynamic and yet so challenging. New voices, forms and themes sometimes require the discarding of old critical frameworks and the creation of new. With this in mind we have endeavoured to create a truly forward-thinking collection that not only maps the journey of British fiction in the new millennium so far, but which also hints at the path ahead.

We open with Joseph Brooker's foreword in which he asks about the role of 'Fiction in a Fictionalized Society', that is 'a social world in which texts, images and narratives are almost omnipresent'. In the information age, he suggests, the relationship between literary fiction and genre fiction has been reconfigured and the existence of national literary traditions called into question. In this he raises concerns that are considered in greater depth in the survey essays that follow in Part

I ('Engagements'), starting with Bianca Leggett's survey into the British cosmopolitan novel. In this essay, Leggett outlines how the tension between local and global perspectives in cosmopolitan novels is productive, both for British fiction and for the imagining of a cosmopolitan future. Brooker's observation that the academy has become increasingly alive to the literary value of genre texts is demonstrated in Ian Hague's study of 'British Comics in the Early Twenty-first Century'. Hague argues that despite 'painful' pressures from international competitors, commercial forces and the advent of digital publishing platforms, a look at the 'bigger picture' suggests that there are reasons to be cheerful as regards the future of British comics.

In 'Histories' (Part II) we move from considering the future of fiction to the fiction of the past. British historical fiction, long suggested to be one of the British literary tradition's strongest suits, has received particular attention in the wake of historical novelist Hilary Mantel's second Man Booker Prize win. Sara Knox considers the status of the genre and questions of bias and accuracy through a study of Mantel's historical fiction, with particular attention to her most recent to date, *Bring Up the Bodies*. Marie-Louise Kohlke's study of neo-Victorian fiction suggests a genre whose popularity relies, less on its historical accuracy, than in its receptivity to 'reverse-projections' of contemporary consciousness. Authors of neo-Victorian fiction, she writes, 'revive the traumas of the nineteenth-century past within the cultural consciousness of the present, ensuring as much as attesting to their continued afterlife'. It is the somewhat unlikely afterlife of the 1980s, re-played in a nostalgic key rather than as a manifestation of trauma, which is Christopher Vardy's theme in his essay, 'Our neo-liberal childhood: remembering the 1980s in David Mitchell's *Black Swan Green*'. Through a reading of Mitchell's story of growing up in the age of Thatcher, Vardy illustrates the way in which the author both uses, and problematizes, a framework of nostalgic material signifiers to memorialize an age which itself encouraged the commodification of the past. The legacies of Thatcherism are also at the heart of Rhona Gordon's analysis of perspectives on housing reform in the fiction of Gordon Burn, David Peace and Andrew O'Hagan. Gordon shows us that these authors present the home as, not a place that 'shelters daydreaming' as Gaston Bachelard would have it, but which represents the corruption that goes on behind closed doors, both in the private sphere and the public one.

For Part III, 'Spaces', we move to a re-appraisal of the spatial turn in, beginning with Deborah Lilley's essay, 'Contemporary British Fiction and the Pastoral', which considers the permutations of the genre in its neo-, post – and anti-pastoral formulation. By examining a range of texts including Kazuo Ishiguro's *Never Let Me Go* (2005) and Ali Smith's *The Accidental* (2004), she explains how the genre has been reinvigorated by 'questioning its conventions and turning its critical viewpoint in upon itself'. From the countryside to the city, Emma Hayward examines late-capitalist London from the perspective of Lee Rourke's *The Canal* (2010). The novel, she writes, suggests that in a culture where 'the surface no longer veils a strange unknown', the scrutiny of the flâneur must produce different results. Mystery is restored to the London landscape, however, in the 'tropologies of monstrousness, doubling, and alterity', which characterize the fiction of China Miéville's fiction, considered by Tony Venezia. Venezia situates Miéville's fiction within a genealogy of visionary Londons in literature but ultimately argues for its originality in exceeding the 'now limiting purview of psychogeography'.

Venezia's essay opens a conversation about the role of the weird and magical in fiction that is continued in our next section, 'Technologies' (Part IV). The essays that follow chart a degree of ambivalence in British fiction towards the advance of technology and digital culture, which is sometimes perceived as a competing medium that threatens to render the novel an anachronism, while elsewhere it is suggested to be a source of rejuvenation. Neal Kirk finds a 'contemporary fascination with network models of social organization' combined with a 'nostalgic, almost fetishistic' portrayal of the book as a material object in Scarlett Thomas's *The End of Mr. Y*. Kirk presents the ways in which 'Mindspace', a virtual realm reached through the portal of a book, becomes a means by which Thomas considers the possibilities of the Internet and of an increasingly mediatized world. Networks and novels are also at the heart of Marianne Corrigan's analysis of Salman Rushdie's *Luka and the Fire of Life*. Corrigan posits that through an engagement with gaming culture, Rushdie's work 'incorporates links to the narratology, structure and gameplay of audiovisual texts into its narrative framework in order to examine the impact of digital technology on the traditional, linear format of the novel'. Kaja Marczewska suggests that the majority of British authors have, nevertheless, lagged behind their American peers, particularly in failing to adopt what she calls the 'aesthetics of cut-and-paste (un) creativity'. With attention to an anomalous but noble exception – i.e. the work of Jeff Noon – Marczewska argues that contemporary British fiction has failed to heed Mark Amerika's prediction that 'creating a work of art will depend more and more on the ability of the artist to select, organize, and present the bits of raw data'.

Finally, we address the omnipresent question of form; focusing particularly in the ways that experimental form can draw attention to the relationship between describing the world and reformulating it along utopian lines. Tory Young's essay, 'You-niversal Love' considers the artful use of the non-gendered second-person voice in the fiction of Ali Smith. Smith's use of 'you' creating a text in which we are not 'snagged by the identification or failure to identify with a homosexual or heterosexual relationship', but instead are encouraged to consider love as a universal experience. Conversely, it is a message of the limits of language's universality that Dorothy Butchard finds in an analysis of a section of David Mitchell's matroyshka-like text *Cloud Atlas*. Presented as the transcription of an unreliable oral tale, Mitchell invents an idiosyncratic language for his futuristic narrator, which draws attention to the perishability of his story. Butchard argues that Mitchell creates a situation of 'anticipatory remembrance' for his reader that encourages positive action to avoid the realization of the novel's apocalyptic vision of the future.

Like all studies of contemporary fiction, this collection can only claim to be, in Patrick Parrinder's phrase, a 'frozen snapshot of a moving object', or rather, a mosaic-like collection of snapshots. What emerges from this collage, however, is a network of formal, thematic and ideological concerns which make these snapshots cohere into something like a portrait of British fiction as it is now in all its complexity.

Part I

Engagements

THE BRITISH COSMOPOLITAN NOVEL
A SURVEY

Bianca Leggett

It is unwise to speak of the British cosmopolitan novel unless one is prepared to first explain just what it is. Indeed, so complex and multifarious is the debate that it can be hard to leave room to say anything else.

The terms 'British' and 'cosmopolitan' are at present both disputed. In recent decades, it has been argued that the nation is an anachronistic entity in a world that is increasingly transnational, a fact reflected in the increasingly globalized nature of the influences and subject matter of literature in Britain. Cosmopolitanism, on the other hand, is a term with great currency but whose meaning is not wholly fixed. For some of cosmopolitanism's proponents, this is precisely the point: cosmopolitanism is a term that 'cannot be subject to discursive hegemony' (McCulloch, 2012: 185). By placing the terms British and cosmopolitanism in conjunction with each other and applying them as descriptors of a certain kind of novel, further ambiguity arises. In its simplest formulation, the British cosmopolitan novel is one that is written by an author who identifies as British, but whose themes and form engage with a cosmopolitan world-view. If the text itself is to be understood as both British and cosmopolitan, however, the possibility of contradiction emerges. The question arises of whether a novel can be in itself British – in terms of its themes, its perspective or even its character – and yet also described by a term which imagines the world in transnational terms.

The attempt to trace the workings of the relationship between the local and the global, and to improve upon it, is an inter-disciplinary preoccupation that has gathered momentum in the last decade. Britain – a nation which has experienced the acceleration of globalization and devolution simultaneously – is a particularly rich case study. In turn, British fiction – which has traditionally been indicted for its insularity – has itself been enriched by the attempt to meet the formal and ideological challenges of capturing an increasingly cosmopolitan world.

Narrating the End of the Nation?

In the new millennium the study or categorization of literature along national lines has increasingly been subject to challenge. In 2006, Brian McHale and Randall Stevenson published *The Edinburgh Companion to Twentieth-century Literatures in English* in which they argued:

> Once, perhaps, it had seemed unproblematic to speak of the 'literature of England' or of 'America'. Looking back, however, it became clear how violent an imposition these territorial categories had been, how they ignored or absorbed national differences... and linguistic diversity. (McHale and Stevenson, 2006: 3)

In his 2010 book *Global Matters,* American critic Paul Jay considers the transnational turn in literary studies and concludes that we have 'shifted away from scholarly practices and critical paradigms rooted in the nation', which have been 'displaced by a new, more contemporary engagement with transnational spaces, hybrid identities, and subjectivities grounded in differences related to race, class, gender, and sexual orientation' (Jay, 2010: 16). For McHale and Stevenson, 'England', let alone 'Britain', encompasses too broad a field to be valid, conflating local differences, whereas for Jay national paradigms are too confining, shutting off the possibility of recognizing the bonds which transcend borders.

There are few sign that forecasts of these kind are being borne out by the last decade of studies of contemporary fiction in Britain, which have included Peter Childs' *Contemporary Novelists: British Fiction Since 1970* (2005), Philip Tew and Rod Mengham's *British Fiction Today* (2006), Richard Bradford's *The Novel Now: Contemporary British Fiction* (2007), Nick Bentley's *Contemporary British Fiction* (2008) and, of course, this collection. Perhaps the tendency to declare the nation's demise prematurely arises from the feeling held by some critics that we would be better off without it. In *Cosmopolitan Criticism and Postcolonial Literature*, Robert Spencer looks forward to the day when allegiance to the nation, 'a hunk of territory gerrymandered by the former colonial power', gives way to 'a fully global community' (Spencer, 2011: 70). He concedes, however, that for nations which are rediscovering an independent identity after living under colonization, the nation might be an 'essential means for a people to regain a self-confidence and legitimacy', that is, the case is different for Britain than for its once-colonies (Spencer, 2011: 70).

This caveat suggests that even arguments about the need to dispense with the nation-state must, for the time being at least, be made in a national context. If we ignore the role that the nation plays in the present as part of an attempt to construct a post-national future, we risk decontextualizing literature from its national past. In *End of Empire and the English novel since 1945*, Bill Schwarz argues that a national focus 'highlights a set of problems which remain pressing, and which do not easily go away' (Schwarz, 2012: 17). This is recognized in the introduction to Rebecca Walkowitz's *Cosmopolitan Style: Modernism Beyond the Nation* (2007), which focuses exclusively on British authors, albeit those like W. G. Sebald and Kazuo Ishiguro who claim a cultural connection beyond British borders. Walkowitz glosses her decision by saying, 'I speak of Britain in order to emphasize global contexts of citizenship, world war, empire, and decolonization, and to examine rather than obscure the many different experiences, local and transnational, that inform British culture today' (Walkowitz, 2007: 5). Although the nation may be, as Robert Spencer argues, an arbitrary 'hunk of territory', it is also a space whose history, and the bearing of that history upon the present, needs to be taken into account in cosmopolitan projections for the future.

Franco Moretti argues that 'When historians have analysed culture on a world scale (or on a large scale anyway), they have tended to use two basic cognitive metaphors: the tree and the wave', that is 'national literature, for people who see trees; world literature, for people who see waves' (Moretti, 2000). The tree, he explains

> describes the passage from unity to diversity: one tree, with many branches: from Indo-European, to dozens of different languages. The wave is the opposite: it observes uniformity engulfing an initial diversity: Hollywood films conquering one market after another (or English swallowing language after language). (Moretti, 2000)

In reality, he suggests the two work together: 'the wave runs into the branches of local traditions, and is always significantly transformed by them' (Moretti, 2000). British Cosmopolitan literary criticism might be understood as a way of reading that acknowledges that literature is best understood by considering both the model of the tree and the wave; the particular and the universal; the local and the global.

Rooted cosmopolitanism

Cosmopolitanism of a kind which believes identification with local forms of identity or culture is complementary, rather than antagonistic to, the cosmopolitan project is usually described using another arboreal metaphor: rooted cosmopolitanism. The term was first suggested in 1992 by Mitchell Cohen who proposed 'a dialectical concept of *rooted* cosmopolitanism, which accepts a multiplicity of roots and branches and that rests on the legitimacy of plural loyalties, of standing in many circles, but with common ground' (Cohen, 1992: 483). A rooted cosmopolitan novel, then, is one which can be read through the prism of the nation but also depicts the 'multiplicity' of connections beyond the nation which Cohen describes. It is this idea which accommodates the notion of a specifically British cosmopolitanism and which guides my thinking in this essay.

Rooted cosmopolitanism can account for the seemingly contrary forces that are acting upon Britain at present better than can a cosmopolitanism which anticipates the imminent withering away of the nation state. The progress of devolution in the twenty-first century has stimulated the consolidation and celebration of separate national identities within the United Kingdom. Rooted cosmopolitanism not only allows for the rise of national particularization, but suggests it might have an affirmative role to play in the cosmopolitan project. Kwame Anthony Appiah argues that a sense of national belonging is in fact a necessary component of the cosmopolitan project, inspiring the 'partiality' required to galvanize the individual towards enacting 'a general moral good' and teaching him or her to invest emotionally in an 'abstract level of allegiance' beyond their immediate circle (Appiah, 2007: 225, 225, 239).

Consequently, mapping the relationship between individuals and their local community is a cosmopolitan concern. Berthold Schoene includes novels like Rachel Cusk's *Arlington Park* (2007), Jon McGregor's *If Nobody Speaks of Remarkable Things* (2002) and Ian McEwan's *Saturday* (2005) in his study *The Cosmopolitan Novel* because they engage with the problem of anomie and social atomization in neo-liberal, globalized Britain. Even so, what emerges from Schoene's analysis of these texts is their *failure* to embody cosmopolitan principles. In McEwan's work, for example, he complains of an absence of 'cosmopolitan impetus and conviction capable of reconciling the familial with the communal, the local and the global' (Schoene, 2009: 43). Schoene's reading of these texts is enriched by testing them against cosmopolitan ideals, yet his findings group together novels that demonstrate these ideals with those in which they are absent. For my own purposes, cosmopolitan literature is a heterogeneous category but one which describes those novels that engage with cosmopolitan thought rather than evading the challenges it poses.

Devolution and the provincialization of Britishness

The valorization of an 'antidotal protective bulwark' which Schoene finds in McEwan's work, that is a shrinking from the wider world into the domestic sphere, has shades of a criticism often levelled at British culture in general and the British novel in particular (Schoene, 2009: 43). Insidiously insular, provincial in its influences and suspicious of intellectualism and innovation, British literature has been accused of being slow to evolve stylistically and stubbornly narrow in its themes. Bill Schwarz argues that in England, that is the 'centre' of what was once the British Empire, parochialism has developed as a result of colonial history, rather than in spite of it. 'English parochialism and insularity', he argues 'have historically, functioned as screens which have obscured an entire stratum of colonial realities' (Schwarz, 2012: 5). Paul Gilroy has argued that contemporary Britain is in the grip of postcolonial melancholia, unable to acknowledge its grief for the Empire it has lost and so fixated on notions of a nostalgic past and a decaying present. While criticism of 'parochial' novels which exhibit these tendencies might help us to better understand how to work through the impasse, I would argue it is a separate field of study from cosmopolitan literature. What distinguishes cosmopolitan literature is that, like the ethos at its centre, it retains a mood of the subjunctive: it is a vehicle for imagining how an ideal global community might work, rather than purely how it fails to function in the present. If it is true to say that British literature has been caught in a feedback-loop of melancholia, constantly reinforcing an association of itself with paralysis and pessimism in its national literature, cosmopolitan literature offers a way out which does not abandon the notion that the term 'British' remains meaningful.

In the twenty-first century, the advancement of devolution has meant that to speak of Britishness often requires the separate treatment of the nations which make up Britain. Determining what constitutes the effects of devolution upon insular, introspective Britishness is far from simple. Devolution, like decolonization, has had a decentring effect upon Britishness, which has strengthened local 'roots' and promoted a cosmopolitan sense that belonging is made up of plural and overlapping allegiances. Nationalism cannot be straight-forwardly equated with isolationism: in some quarters, enthusiasm for devolution is linked to a pro-European stance, as in the case of the Scottish National Party. Conversely the UK Independence Party, whose supporters are primarily English and anti-devolution, argues that membership of the European Union threatens British culture. As these allegiances might suggest, devolution is often linked in England with a feeling of diminishment and withdrawal where in Scotland, Wales and Northern Ireland it is a release from domination by England and the promise of new bonds. In an article that considers the effect of devolution upon British literature, Robert McCrum predicts that 'without infusions of new blood from Scotland and Ireland, British writing could start to look rather vulnerable' (McCrum, 2012).

As McCrum implies, Scotland is often suggested to be the main beneficiary of devolution in literary terms. In *Cosmopolitanism in Contemporary British Fiction*, Fiona McCulloch analyses two Scottish novels that respond to the context of devolution as a moment in which national identity can be re-formulated along more inclusive lines since 'home ... under-goes relocation, liberated from fixed geo-political positions towards the aspiration of transformative utopian possibilities' (McCulloch, 2012: 11). This optimism is not, however, universally shared. Stefanie Lehner warns that

> The seemingly liberating potential of Scottish devolution... requires caution, as it proves to be imbricated within the wider context of a political and economic restructuring which is ultimately designed to increase convergence with the forces of global capitalism. (Lehner, 2007: 295)

For Lehner, the feelings stirred by independence merely obfuscate the extent to which Scottish fortunes are determined by globalized, not national, forces. Nationalism is another form of screen which hides a more globally interconnected and more troubling reality.

English critics have had concerns along similar lines. Julian Barnes in a short story that follows up on *England, England* (1998) playfully imagines a dystopian future in which the departure of Scotland, Wales and Northern Ireland from 'the Union' have left England merely a 'sulky rump' with whom Europe, tired of decades of English 'carping on the sidelines', has lost all patience and has opted to 'evict' (Barnes, 2012). Neither, Barnes tells us, is there any solace from across the Atlantic: 'The United States had long been looking westward, and now tended to regard England as an embarrassing ancestor, and a case for humane termination' (Barnes, 2012). Initially England greets its new found isolation with enthusiasm: 'There was much excitement, as the country, having become smaller and less influential, had also become more xenophobic' (Barnes, 2012). The euphoria and street parties, however, give way to gloom as the economic infrastructure collapses taking public services with it. The retreat into isolationism is suggested to not only harm international relations, but also to lead to a process of disintegration on the local level. Barnes' story, published to mark National Libraries Day, imagines a future in which the Coalition not only withdraws public funding from libraries but goes on to burn them all down to the ground. Isolationism is linked to anti-intellectualism and to the impoverishment of English literature.

What emerges from these commentaries on devolution is the exigency of understanding, critiquing and improving upon the way in which the symbiotic relationship between the local and the global works, or rather fails to work, in the interest of the people. A distinction emerges between a kind of national self-confidence and communitarian feeling on the one hand and a tendency towards self-congratulation and isolationism on the other. The first functions as a smaller cog within the larger mechanism of cosmopolitanism and exists on the basis that it is neither possible, nor desirable, to function apart from the wider world. The second is merely a set of blinkers which conceals both the colonial past and the globalized present, producing stagnation at the local level. The role of a rooted cosmopolitan novel is to provide an enlarging vision of the interconnected world, which is not always appreciable to the individual, a particularly needful function, it would seem, in the British context.

Imagining the global

The particular virtue of the cosmopolitan novel, as opposed to nonfictional texts, is its ability to, in Barak Obama's phrase, balance our 'empathy deficit' by creating characters and narratives which engage our imaginative sympathy (Obama, 2006). Gayatri Spivak (1998: 329) stated that, 'No one lives in the global village' since its 'an abstraction inaccessible to experience'. The depiction of abstractions along individualized lines is, however, the province of the novel. Its metonymic capability for depicting the whole is what has made it the natural vehicle for the imagined community of the nation, but also fits it for the larger task of imagining the global population.

The difficulty of such an enterprise should not be underestimated. As Rana Dasgupta argues, 'Paradoxically, the more the world becomes interwoven the less it seems possible to tell a single, representative story of it – yet the connections are real and lived.' (Dasgupta, 2005). However real these connections might be in their effects, they often seem to be in themselves inhuman, intangible and too diffuse to trace. The cosmopolitan novel must depict the tangled networks of influence and counter-influence with the complexity it is due, yet also represent cosmopolitanism's utopian belief that the world is improvable and global community desirable, that is that human agency and ethical conduct remain meaningful in this seemingly entropic world. A novel that only depicts the patterns and quirks of the globalized world might be anti-cosmopolitan, recommending a retreat into isolationism or into a mythologized simpler past. In this sense, my view of the cosmopolitan novel is more prescriptive or utopian than some cosmopolitan literary critics would allow. I would argue that while cosmopolitan novels may be pessimistic in its description of the present, they suggest the possibility of better worlds. While there is no consensus as to what precisely this better world should be – and rightly so in an ethos which values pluralism – it is predicated on the idea that the answer lies in greater openness, understanding and generosity to both one's immediate community and the world beyond it.

I draw here on Robert Spencer's idea that cosmopolitan criticism 'can exemplify and engender the critical consciousness and the global solidarities that are required to uphold cosmopolitan political arrangements' (Spencer, 40). Cosmopolitan literature should not only expose the problems which arise from the atomization of individuals and parochialism of nations on the one hand and the juggernaut of global capitalism on the other, but should actively seek alternatives. Whereas Spencer suggests that cosmopolitan criticism can achieve this by studying postcolonial literature, I would argue that cosmopolitan literature is a distinct category in itself. Although it continues to engage with the legacies of Empire, it describes a world in which ideas of centre and periphery have been remapped, and in which the relationship between the global and the local has been critically altered.

Even when cosmopolitanism wishes to criticize the nation state or to locate its subject matter in interstitial, hybrid or transnational spaces, it needs to acknowledge that national context remains pertinent. Experiences of belonging to the global community are wildly disjunctive and determined by where the observer, or in this case author, is located. Readers too exist within particular national contexts and also, crucially for the novel, specific language communities. According to Terry Eagleton, the novel depends 'on the presence of a sizeable community of men and women who speak the same language and share roughly the same cultural assumptions' for its subject matter and for its reading public (Eagleton, 2006). The question is open, then, whether the cosmopolitan novel should attempt to address itself to a cosmopolitan public whose 'cultural assumptions' are more diverse and divergent from each other and whose 'image of themselves' has been formed from a vast array of transnational cultural influences, or rely upon the translatability of its nationally-specific subject matter.

Multilingual novels, like multilingual readers, remain a rarity and as such translation remains the key to a single text reaching multiple language communities. The issue of translation in Britain, both into and from English, raises some interesting questions from a cosmopolitan perspective. According to *The Economist*, 'Only 3% of the books published annually in America and Britain are translated from another language; fiction's slice is less than 1%' (A.C., 2012). This means that in literary terms, Britain is mostly set to 'transmit', broadcasting its literature to different language communities but receiving few incoming narratives from beyond the English-speaking world. For British writers who write in English, the possibilities of reaching beyond a British readership is increased both by their writing in a language which one in four of the world's population can speak (although not necessarily read) to some degree of competence and by the chance of their text being translated, yet the dominance of one global language over its fellows works against the cosmopolitan preference for diversity over uniformity. An author in Wales, for example, must choose between reaching a broader readership by writing in English or preserving the language of a minority culture: local and global are pitted against each other. In cases such as these, the contrary priorities of rooted cosmopolitanism simply cannot be reconciled.

The planetary cosmopolitan novel

Similar tensions are evident when we consider the cosmopolitan novel's approach to topographical space. Berthold Schoene is confident that the zoom lens of the novel is sufficiently broad-angled to encompass a panoramic view of the globe: 'There is nothing that ought to prevent us imagining the world as one community or capturing it inside the vision of a single narrative', he argues (Schoene, 2009: 13). It has become something of a convention in studies of cosmopolitan literature to consider the image of Earth as seen from space, both as an image which often appears on the cover of studies of cosmopolitan criticism, and as an image that is analysed within. For Paul Gilroy and Hywel Dix the earth from space is a hopeful image for promoting global solidarity and ecological awareness: it is an 'emblem or signature of [...] planetary consciousness' (Dix, 2010: 106) and a 'vision of planet Earth as such – a single entity, isolated and precarious, rather than a series of separate and bordered societies' (Gilroy, 2005: 72). It is also an image that is vulnerable to appropriation. Ursula K. Heise notes that since its first appearance the image has been adopted as the logo of Visa, a symbol of globalization rather than what Gilroy, using a term first conceived by Gayatri Spivak, calls 'planetarity' (Heise, 2006: 203; Gilroy, 2005: xv).

As a model for the cosmopolitan novel the image of the world from space is problematic. How can a novel possibly contain a whole world of characters? There is a tension to be negotiated if the novel is not to sacrifice depth of perception for breadth of scope. If the cosmopolitan novel is in some sense an expanded version of the national – featuring more characters, a variety of different national and cultural communities and taking place over greater distances – then this plays against the contemporary British novel's preference for smallness. There is some evidence that following the dissolution of Empire, the British novel has proved suspicious of 'big' novels, particularly when compared to those produced on the other side of the Atlantic. Martin Amis has argued that, 'Nineteenth-century England was the time of our big novels, our centre of the world novels, our time of imperial confidence [...] That has shifted to America' (Bigsby, 2011: 42). While Amis means to criticize the British tradition for its turn to modest miniaturization, if he is right to say that the 'big' novel is a product of 'imperial confidence' then its passing is not, perhaps, to be mourned. Gordon Burn suggests that the 'big, brick-like novels which also double as encyclopedias' of a Don Delillo or a Thomas Pynchon are a product of the 'splurging American century', a culture of excess which is foreign to the contemporary British aesthetic (Burn, 2003). In their 2011 collection *The Good of the Novel*, Liam McIlvanney and Ray Ryan suggest that the literary career of Jonathan Franzen took a turn for the better because, while his first novels tried to 'function as working scale-models of the contemporary American city' which 'overwhelmed their ability to communicate the lives of believable human beings', *The Corrections* represented 'a contraction of scope, but also an enlargement of sympathy' (McIlvanney and Ryan, 2011: xi). Taking their cue from James Wood's attack on the 'big, ambitious novel' which 'knows a thousand things but does not know a single human being', Ryan and McIlvanney suggest a strand of British critical sympathy for the idea that small is beautiful (Wood, 2001).

Nevertheless, the attempt to capture the largeness of a global vision has prompted new experiments in narrative and the writing of some 'big' British novels. Hywel Dix suggests Julian Barnes' experimental *A History of the World in 10 ½ Chapters* (1989) as an early transnational novel. To my mind, the tone of Barnes' novel, which is ultimately pessimistic about the possibilities of altruism beyond the purely personal sphere, cannot be called cosmopolitanism. Even so, its form may well be. The novel is a kind of network, made up of smaller stories set in different times and places which are connected to each other by a linked historiographic enquiry and repetitive tropes. It bears comparison with David Mitchell's *Cloud Atlas* (2004) whose story also encompasses a broad transhistorical sweep, broken down by the use of separate stories and narrators. Mitchell's novel, however, maintains a greater sense of continuity in that each narrator finds the story of the one who precedes him or her and comments upon it. Furthermore, each narrator bears a meteor-like birthmark, a clue that each is host to the same constantly reincarnated soul, suggesting a cosmopolitan sense of connection between those who are separated both by time and space. Rana Dasgupta's *Tokyo Cancelled* (2005) uses an airport as the node through which his disparate stories are connected. In a device that has been compared to *The Canterbury Tales* and *The Decameron*, it features a group of grounded aeroplane passengers who spend the night together in an unnamed airport, swapping stories that fuse myth and magic with commentary on recent world events. As Sarah Crown asserts, in her *Guardian* review, the stories are 'Rich, strange, pulsing with colour, they leave iridescent trails that criss-cross the globe like a flight map' (Crown, 2005). Hari Kunzru's networked-novel *Transmission* (2005) takes the Internet itself as its model. Its separate plots are tangled together by the unleashing of a computer virus that, Frankenstein-like, outwits its mild-mannered creator's attempts to disable it and brings about a technological meltdown in which boundaries of many kinds are distorted and transgressed.

These fragmented novels have the extra merit of challenging its readers to find connections between narratives and the grander narratives that emerge from their sum total. This kind of cosmopolitan reading practice has an extra-literary function, instilling a way of looking at the world that emphasizes the relevance of events beyond our immediate surroundings and is sensitive to the role that the shadowy forces of globalization play on everyday life. These narratives have found ways to depict a truly transnational reality but the picture of the world that emerges is necessarily an impressionistic one.

While the image of the world from space potentially inspires a cosmopolitan sense of global citizenship, few narratives are focalized from space. SF texts have sometimes offered readers this vantage point in order to offer cautionary tales of the future of the Earth, as in Jeanette Winterson's *The Power Book* (2000). The god's eye view of the Earth from space has its problems, however: the author risks universalizing their perspective which is, in fact, one which is both informed and limited by a particular cultural context. The more impressionistic, networked novel has similar risks if it claims to portray a truly global vision. However hectic or sprawling its narrative, it inevitably renders some kinds of global citizen more visible than others in a way which betrays the author's own national and social perspective. *Transmission,*for example, only concerns itself with the world of Internet users, who remain only 32.5% of the world's population (International Telecommunications Union, 2011).

With this in mind, I will look at a different kind of cosmopolitan novel whose scope is more modest, but which is equally engaged in finding a way to tell a story which gives us bi-focal lenses with which to look at the world, keeping both the local and the distant in sharp perspective.

The regional cosmopolitan novel

I begin with a kind of narrative which I term the regional cosmopolitan novel, since the action of the novel is for the most part located within a small and distinct region or area of Britain, whose depiction is as central to the novel as its characters. Like the more familiar form of regional novel they are concerned with capturing the particularity of place and the culture of everyday life within it, proving particularly interested in questions of class and community that determine the relationship between residents.

The regional novel is most readily associated with rural and provincial settings. It traditionally values indigenous folk culture and proves suspicious of the forces of modernity that have the potential to alter historically established ways of life. In this, it shows a cosmopolitan concern as to the effects of globalization upon local ways of life, yet the regional novel has become associated with an 'Anglocentric nativism' and social conservatism which borders on bigotry (James, 2011: 46). The regions are also associated with the regenerative possibilities of the pastoral. Fiona McCulloch praises Zoe Strachan's *Negative Space* (2002) in which the bereaved heroine feels liberated by the 'wild northern hinterland' of the Orkney Islands where, despite the occasional bigotry of some of its citizens, she is able to transform from 'female object to supranational citizen' (McCulloch, 2012: 27–8). By situating a text that focuses on marginalized identity and peripheral places at the heart of the cosmopolitan project, McCulloch's study suggests the way that cosmopolitanism itself might proceed along radically de-centred lines.

For similar reasons, the regional novel's depiction of multicultural community may be a key part of the puzzle. The regional cosmopolitan novel has the potential to both change our understanding of what the regional novel might be and to offer a de-centred perspective on cosmopolitanism. The relative rarity of such texts is in part a reflection of a social reality – that is, that Britain's black and minority ethnic population is mostly concentrated in its cities, especially London – but also the expectations of the reading public which in turn shape the market place. British readers tend to look to London for fictions that depict a multicultural and multi-ethnic community. Notable exceptions do exist, however, like Swansea-born Meera Syal's *Anita and Me* (2002), Orknian Luke Sutherland's *Venus as a Boy* (2004) and Glaswegian Jackie Kay's short fiction *Reality, Reality* (2012). The work of Leeds-born Caryl Phillips, who now lives in the United States, represents a concern with both the cosmopolitan sweep of the legacy of slavery and Empire and a nuanced perspective on the bearing of region upon contemporary British identity. His latest novel, *In the Falling Snow* (2009), moves between the industrial north of England, Bristol and West London in its depiction of the life of a middle-aged Black British council worker, reflecting on the course of his life. In her introduction to *Immigrant Fictions: Contemporary Literature in an Age of Globalization* (2006) Rebecca Walkowitz considers the biographical details of Caryl Phillips which are printed, in variant forms, in the inside cover of his works. 'The language of the biographies varies slightly,' she observes, 'but there are constants: he emphasizes cities and smaller regions rather more than continents, empires, or nations' (Walkowitz, 2006: 535). Phillips' identification with his home city – Leeds – over his home country suggests a conscious shift towards a mode of identity which is both more pluralistic and more provincial. The emphasis Philips places on both the transnational and the local aspects of his own identity as well as that of his characters works together to complicate and de-centre our understanding of his British belonging.

While multicultural London continues to be a dominant literary locus, the sprawl of the metropolis also seems to be subject to a process of provincialization. The depiction of London in post-millennial fiction has often restricted itself to a small, distinct community within the city itself, particularly those that are geographically peripheral and socially marginalized. Like Courttia Newland before her (*The Scholar* [1997] and *Society Within* [1999]), Zadie Smith has taken inspiration from North-West London where she grew up. The locale has book-ended her career to date with *White Teeth* (2000) and *NW* (2012), both of which were particularly praised for their attentive rendering of multiculturally layered demotic speech patterns. Monica Ali's *Brick Lane* (2003), which, like Smith's North-West London, depicts a microculture into which we can read the problems of cosmopolitan community writ small. Monica Ali explores the functioning, and malfunctioning, of bonds between people who share different kinds of community: the family and the extended family of the immigrant community, but also of the shared urban space of Brick Lane and the possibilities of British identity.

Nadeem Aslam's *Maps for Lost Lovers* (2004) occupies similar territory in its story of clashes between the generations, this time in a British Pakistani community in an industrial town in the north of England, referred to only by the name given to it by its residents – Dasht-e-Tanhaii – the desert of loneliness. Aslam defamiliarizes British space by rendering white Britons invisible in an uncanny landscape that blends the natural world of rural England with Pakistani cultural markers. It is a novel that draws on pastoral traditions, but Aslam has said that it is also 'about the classic theme of Islamic literature: the quest for the beloved' and whose influences include '1001 Nights, the Koran, Bihzad' (Brace, 2004). Aslam's regional cosmopolitan novel is not only comprised of a combination of global culture as well as local, but produces a hybrid too thoroughly blended to be separated into constituent cultural parts.

Like *Brick Lane* and *White Teeth* (2000) before it, *Maps for Lost Lovers* calls for a balance between the value of roots, family and community on the one hand and of agency, self-fashioning and freedom of movement on the other. Connections are made between events of the personal sphere and in the wider world. *White Teeth* refers to the Berlin Wall, not only as a pivotal historical moment, but also as a metaphor for the divisiveness of fundamentalism of all kinds. Similarly, in speaking of his writing process, Aslam declares: 'I asked myself whether in my personal life and as a writer I had been rigorous enough to condemn the small scale September 11s that go on every day' (Brace, 2004). The little world of the small local community can be shown to register the seismic movements of the wider world, providing a cosmopolitan commentary on the importance of realizing that no community can truly exist in isolation from the global community in which it is contained.

Conclusion

The diversity of novels that might justly be included under the banner of British Cosmopolitan fiction highlights that the concept remains open and multiple in its definitions: critics remain free to choose which British cosmopolitanism they mean. This is apt. Stuart Hall suggests that the virtue of cosmopolitanism itself is that it equips us with 'the ability to stand outside of having one's life written and scripted by any one community, whether that is a faith or tradition or religion or culture – whatever it might be – and draw selectively on a variety of discursive meanings' (Hall, 2003: 26). Cosmopolitan literature has a hermeneutic function, which can help illuminate the roles that these scripts play in twenty-first-century life, but also a space to imagine new narratives that improve upon them. This impulse towards imagination and innovation is a healthy stimulus upon a national tradition that has sometimes responded to its diminished power by retreating into dejected solipsism. Britain, in turn, has a useful contribution to make to the cosmopolitan novel. Despite its anxieties to the contrary, it remains a place which is densely interconnected to the rest of the world but which is nevertheless learning to think of itself along provincialized lines. As such, in the twenty-first-century British fiction should afford some of the best views of the big, wide, small world.

Works Cited

A.C. (2012) 'Stories From Elsewhere', *The* Economist, 22 July, accessed 15 November 2012, http://www.economist.com/blogs/prospero/2012/07/books-translation

Appiah, Kwame Anthony (2007) *The Ethics of Identity*. Woodstock: Princeton University Press.

Bigsby, Christopher (2011) 'In Conversation with Martin Amis', in Christopher Bigsby (ed.) *Writers in Conversation*, pp. 21–44. Norwich: Arthur Miller Centre

Brace, Marianne (2004) 'Nadeem Aslam: A question of honour', *Independent*, 11 June, accessed 28 May 2012, http://www.independent.co.uk/arts-entertainment/books/features/nadeem-aslam-a-question-of-honour-6167858.html

Barnes, Julian (2012) 'The Defence of the Book', *Guardian*, 3 February, accessed 3 February 2012, http://www.guardian.co.uk/books/2012/feb/03/julian-barnes-defence-of-the-book

Burn, Gordon (2003) 'After the flood', *Guardian*, 15 November, accessed 23 June 2011, http://www.guardian.co.uk/books/2003/nov/15/featuresreviews.guardianreview10

Cohen, Mitchell (1992) 'Rooted Cosmopolitanism: Thoughts on the Left, Nationalism, and Multiculturalism' *Dissent* 39: 483.

Crown, Sarah (2005) 'Narrative Planes', *Guardian*, 29 March, accessed 2 July 2012, http://www.guardian.co.uk/books/2005/mar/29/fiction.sarahcrown

Dasgupta, Rana (2005) 'Narrative Planes', interviewed by Sarah Crown, *Guardian*, 29 March, accessed 2 July 2012, http://www.guardian.co.uk/books/2005/mar/29/fiction.sarahcrown

Dix, Hywel (2010) *Postmodern Fiction and the Break-Up of Britain*. London: Continuum.

Eagleton, Terry (2006) 'What Are We?', *Guardian*, 29 April, accessed 14 March 2012, http://www.guardian.co.uk/books/2006/apr/29/highereducation.news

Gilmour, Rachel and Bill Schwarz (2011) *End of Empire and the English Novel Since 1945*. Manchester: Manchester University Press.

Gilroy, Paul (2005) *Postcolonial Melancholia*. New York: Columbia University Press.

Hall, Stuart (2003) 'Political Belonging in a World of Multiple Identities', in Steven Vertovec and Robin Cohen (eds) *Conceiving Cosmopolitanism: Theory, Context and Practice*, pp. 25–31. Oxford: Oxford University Press.

Heise, Ursula K. (2006) '1970, Planet Earth: The Imagination of the Global', in Brian McHale and Randall Stevenson (ed.) *The Edinburgh Companion to Twentieth Century Literatures in English*, pp. 201–16. Edinburgh: Edinburgh University Press.

International Telecommunications Union (2011) 'Internet Users Per 100 Inhabitants 2001–2011', accessed 21 July 2012, http://www.itu.int/ict/statistics

James, David (2008) *Contemporary British Fiction and the Artistry of Space: Style, Landscape, Perception*. London: Continuum.

Jay, Paul (2010) *Global Matters: The Transnational Turn in Literary Studies*. New York: Cornell University Press.

Lehner, Stefanie (2007) 'Subaltern Scotland: Devolution and Postcoloniality', in Berthold Schoene-Harwood (ed.) *The Edinburgh Companion to Contemporary Scottish Literature*, pp. 292–300. Edinburgh: Edinburgh University.

McCrum, Robert (2012) 'Independence for Scottish Literature', *Guardian*, 26 January, accessed 27 January 2012, http://www.guardian.co.uk/books/booksblog/2012/jan/26/independence-scottish-literature-robert-mccrum

McCulloch, Fiona (2012) *Cosmopolitanism in Contemporary British Fiction: Imagined Identities*. Basingstoke: Palgrave Macmillan.

McHale, Brian and Randall Stevenson (2006) *The Edinburgh Companion to Twentieth Century Literatures in English*. Edinburgh: Edinburgh University Press.

McIlvanney, Liam and Ray Ryan (2011) *The Good of the Novel*. London: Faber and Faber.

Massey, Doreen (1994) *Space, Place and Gender*. Cambridge: Polity Press.

Moretti, Franco (2000) 'Conjectures on World Literature', *New Left Review*, 1 January-February, accessed 12 June 2012, http://newleftreview.org/II/1/franco-moretti-conjectures-on-world-literature

Obama, Barack (2006) 'Obama challenges graduates to address 'empathy deficit', 22 June, accessed 12 December 2012, http://www.northwestern.edu/observer/issues/2006/06/22/obama.html

Schoene, Berthold (2009) *The Cosmopolitan Novel*. Edinburgh: Edinburgh University Press.

Spencer, Robert (2011) *Cosmopolitan Criticism and Postcolonial Literature*. Basingstoke: Palgrave Macmillan.

Spivak, Gayatri Chakravorty (1998) 'Cultural Talks in the Hot Peace: Revisiting the "Global Village"', in Pheng Cheah and Bruce Robbins (eds) *Cosmopolitics: Thinking and Feeling Beyond the Nation*, pp. 329–48. Minneapolis: University of Minnesota Press.

Walkowitz, Rebecca L. (ed.) (2006) Editorial, *Immigrant Fictions: Contemporary Literature in an Age of Globalization*, pp. 527–549. Madison: University of Wisconsin Press.

Walkowitz, Rebecca (2007) *Cosmopolitan Style: Modernism Beyond the Nation*. New York: Columbia University Press.

Wood, James (2001) 'How Does it Feel?', *Guardian*, 6 October, accessed 12 February 2011, http://www.guardian.co.uk/books/2001/oct/06/fiction

British Comics in the Early Twenty-first Century

Ian Hague

British comics seem to need a regular kick up the backside; whether it comes from Japan's long, complex manga comics, cartoon bands like Gorillaz, Alan Moore and company's *Albion* revivals of classic characters, the urban vinyl cult or comics for mobile phones, iPods or whatever comes next, that kick will definitely come.

(Gravett and Stanbury, 2006: 13)

In these closing remarks from the introduction to their book *Great British Comics*, Paul Gravett and Peter Stanbury imply that the British comic book industry in the mid-2000s could best be described as stagnant. Although there were clearly some indications of hope, the scene was characterized by a lack of forward motion and the type of revolutionary change that was needed to keep the industry vital. By 2009, by some accounts, this change had still not appeared. In the first issue of *Solipsistic Pop*, an anthology comic launched that year, editor Tom Humberstone and contributor Matthew Sheret asserted:

It is time for a new paradigm. A new wave of Comics. A new, vague blueprint for Comics to take up. This is a map that lets you fill in the locations and plot your own course. Away from something definitely, without knowing for sure what we're moving towards.

(Humberstone and Sheret, 2009: 2)

This statement was part of a manifesto, 'Declaration of The New Vague', which argued forcefully for the production of high quality comics that were unashamed of their nature *as* comics, did not strive to be anything more, and were read by a wide audience in a variety of contexts. Yet it would seem that even this very explicit argument for a redevelopment of British comics from within the context of their production was not sufficient to provide the necessary 'kick up the backside', and in 2012 Paul Abbott lamented the state of the industry in an article entitled: 'Wanted: A British comic book industry', which concluded that publishers were simply not providing a context for the already-extant wealth of British comics talent to demonstrate their abilities. Other writers were more optimistic. James Hunt responded to Abbott's article directly with 'Offered: One Comic Book Industry (good condition)', while *Herald Scotland* reported on 'The second coming of graphic novels'. James Chapman (2011: 257), in drawing his 2011 cultural history of British comics to a close, noted: 'While comics are no longer the mass medium they once were, there are signs that, finally, they are being taken more seriously both as an art form and as a social practice'.

Clearly then, by the start of the second decade of the twenty-first century, neither the press nor practitioners had reached a consensus on the state of British comics. Indeed, in surveying reportage on the field, it is difficult to know whether one should be wildly optimistic about the strong and lively British comics scene post-2000, or shed tears for a once proud industry in decline. Over the course of this essay, I survey three areas of the British comics scene post-2000 in order to determine the extent to which either of these perspectives is supportable. First, I look at the position of the graphic novel, a format whose status has changed significantly since it first came to public prominence in the 1980s. Next, I consider what appear to be the most precariously situated British comics: periodicals, and discuss how a selection of titles has dealt with the challenges of the twenty-first century. Finally, I discuss the ways in which the comics publishing industry in Britain has been affected by the disruptive rise of digital media, and outline how the landscape looks at present. Although I do present a fairly wide ranging survey in this essay, I make no claims to being comprehensive, since to do so would require a space longer than this book. For ideas of where to get started with wider reading on British comics, I would direct readers to my list of references; good general introductions to British comics (both historical and more recent examples) can be found in the works of: Martin Barker, James Chapman, Mel Gibson, Paul Gravett, Graham Kibble-White and Roger Sabin.

The Graphic Novel Returns

In the mid-1980s, the term 'graphic novel' came to prominence (although it had existed for some time before then) when it was used as a marketing tool to sell three major books (*Maus Volume I: My Father Bleeds History* [1986], *Batman: The Dark Knight Returns* [1986], and *Watchmen* [1987]), the so called 'Big 3' and their imitators to an unsuspecting audience of mainstream bookshop customers 'who may either have felt intimidated by fan shops ... or who may never have otherwise come across them' (Sabin, 1993: 94–5). As Roger Sabin (1993: 96) notes, the popularity of the Big 3 and the rise of the graphic novel as a highly visible marketing category in the late 1980s culminated in an economic bubble that 'eventually burst in 1990–2, precipitating a rapid decline, and leaving public perceptions of the medium largely unchanged'. Even as late as 2000, Thierry Groensteen lamented that 'the legitimating authorities (universities, museums, the media) still regularly charge [comic art] with being infantile, vulgar, or insignificant' (Groensteen, 2000/2009: 3). By the time I interviewed him for the British journal *Studies in Comics* in 2010, however, Groensteen's position had changed somewhat: 'There are less and less people who charge comics with being infantile, vulgar or insignificant – or, if that's what they believe, they do not dare to share that kind of opinion anymore' (Hague, 2010: 360). One of the reasons for this shift, he asserted, was 'the invention of the 'graphic novel' as a new form of literature', which he noted 'has proved very profitable from a strategic point of view' (Hague, 2010: 360). Paul Gravett, writing in a 2005 issue of *Comics International* also noted the return of comics and graphic novels to the cultural mainstream, which he linked to a variety of factors including the massive expansion of the comic-book film and, perhaps more interestingly, an increasingly wide selection of high-quality graphic novels in a range of genres. Rather than a few key titles capturing the attention of a public that was subsequently disappointed and turned off by a flood of substandard imitators, the more recent re-establishment of the graphic novel is characterized by a far more substantial body of good works:

> Now that it's fifteen years later, almost a generation, some truly formidable graphic novels have been completed: *Palestine, Preacher, Cerebus, Bone, From Hell, Locas, Palomar, Jimmy Corrigan, Epileptic, Cages,* for starters. A library of undeniable quality is amassing. Patience is a virtue, because great graphic novels need time to come to fruition and more are slowly ripening. (Gravett, 2005/2006)

While the Big 3 by themselves may not have been enough to sustain a mass market industrial level of production throughout the 1990s, it is fair to say that they were extremely influential because they showed creators, publishers and, critically, retailers, that comics could be high in both quality and profitability, and that there was therefore a reason for including them on the shelves. That it was necessary to call them 'graphic novels' to get them onto those shelves does of course indicate the prejudices that comics faced at that point, but the term nonetheless validated the medium in such a way that the books were stocked by major retailers. Perhaps more importantly, it also established a familiar context into which the later titles (many of which were influenced to some degree by the Big 3) could slip almost effortlessly.

The benefits of this for graphic novels (or comics, whichever term you prefer) were substantial, because rather than fighting an uphill battle to justify their position in bookshops, graphic novels have a section all to themselves. The questions asked now are not so much 'why should comics be sold in this bookshop?' but rather 'which graphic novels should be sold?' and 'how should they be sold?'. Interestingly, retailer responses to these questions appear to imply a more nuanced understanding of what graphic novels are, and attempt to draw qualitative distinctions between texts for the benefits of purchasers. On a visit to the Manchester branch of national bookshop chain Waterstones in July 2012 I was surprised to note that the store had divided its graphic novel selection into two parts: 'Graphic novels' and 'Literary graphic novels'. In the former category were those titles that were perhaps more amenable to an audience drawn to the store by the latest superhero blockbusters and comics-inspired television series: collections from ongoing Marvel and DC serials, but also zombie thriller *The Walking Dead* (2003–), science fiction anthology *2000AD* (1977–), *Watchmen* (1986–7) and *V for Vendetta* (1982–8). The latter seemed to be populated by anything that did not involve superheroes or the supernatural: Alison Bechdel's *Fun Home* (2006), Eddie Campbell's *Alec: The Years Have Pants* (2010), and collections of *Commando* (1961–) war comics.[1]

British creators have proven extremely capable of addressing both sides of the literary/non-literary divide as construed by Waterstones. Veterans of the 'British invasion' of the American comic book industry of the 1980s and 1990s remain prominent, with Grant Morrison and Mark Millar (among others) producing major works at DC and Marvel throughout the 2000s. In fact, around the middle of the decade it was these two figures who seemed to be driving the broader philosophical and conceptual enterprises of the two companies; Millar's *The Ultimates* (2002–2007) and *Civil War* (2006–2007) reasserting Marvel's claims to 'real world relevance' following 9/11, and Morrison's *All Star Superman* (2005–2008) and *Final Crisis* (2008) emphasizing 1960s style silliness and continuity-heavy metafiction at DC.[2] British artists have made major impacts as well, with Bryan Hitch (*The Ultimates* and *Fantastic Four* [both with Mark Millar]) and Frank Quitely (*All Star Superman* and *We3* [both with Grant Morrison]) both producing distinctive artwork that has come in for high praise from critics. British creators remain prominent in Marvel's and DC's titles at the time of this writing. Finally, it would be remiss of me to omit Charlie Adlard, whose work on Image Comics' *The Walking Dead* (2004–) has contributed to it becoming a perennial bestseller in both comic book and collected edition paperback formats.

The 'literary' side of the divide is also thriving in Britain, with established authors such as Posy Simmonds and Bryan Talbot continuing to publish major works throughout the 2000s, and newer voices being heard as well. Simmonds' *Tamara Drewe*, originally serialized in the *Guardian* from 2005–2006, was collected by Jonathan Cape in 2007 and adapted for cinema by Stephen Frears in 2010. Bryan Talbot, meanwhile, is almost an industry unto himself, producing books at a prodigious rate and across a wide range of genres. *Alice in Sunderland*, a lengthy exploration of the history of Sunderland (among other things) was published in 2007, and was followed by the first instalment of anthropomorphic steampunk series *Grandville* in 2009. The sequel, *Grandville Mon Amour*, was released in 2010 and between that and the third volume, *Grandville Bête Noire* (2012), Talbot somehow found time to provide artwork for the Costa Book Award winning *Dotter of Her Father's Eyes* (also 2012), produced in collaboration with his wife, writer Mary M. Talbot. In addition to publishing the works of Simmonds and Talbot, Jonathan Cape (and other imprints of Vintage) has also helped to nurture a growing field of British graphic novelists such as Hannah Berry (*Britten and Brülightly* [2008], *Adamtine* [2012]), Simone Lia (*Fluffy* [2009], *Please God, Find Me a Husband!* [2012]), Julian Hanshaw (*The Art of Pho* [2010], *I'm Never Coming Back* [2012]) and Karrie Fransman (*The House that Groaned* [published by Square Peg, 2012]). Importantly, as well as *printing* the works of these authors, Jonathan Cape helps to situate them within international contexts of creation and consumption. Cape is the British publisher for a number of major comic artists including noted British creator Raymond Briggs (*Ethel and Ernest*), North Americans Alison Bechdel, Charles Burns, Daniel Clowes and Chris Ware, Maltese-American Joe Sacco, and Canadians Guy Delisle and Seth. Given that all of these comic authors are renowned for the production of innovative and broadly addressed graphic novels that appeal to a far wider audience than the latest collection of *Action Comics*, for example, it is encouraging that Berry, Lia and the like are counted among their number. While the graphic novel boom of the late 1980s may have turned to bust for many publishers, it is clear that there does remain an artistic and intellectual tradition of graphic novel production within Britain that is capable of standing alongside the very best examples of international talent.

It is important to avoid suggesting, however, that Jonathan Cape is the only major graphic novel/comic publisher in Britain, and it would seem that the field is, if not booming, at least fairly stable and perhaps even growing. Noted underground/alternative comics publisher Knockabout has continued to put out works by major authors such as Hunt Emerson (*The Festival Ritual* [2005], *Dante's Inferno* [with Kevin Jackson, 2012]) among others. Knockabout has also cultivated productive relationships with other publishers, working together with America's Top Shelf Productions to publish important new works by Eddie Campbell (*The Playwright* [with Daren White, 2010], *The Lovely Horrible Stuff* [2012]) and to finally publish Alan Moore and Melinda Gebbie's completed erotic re-imagining of twentieth century children's fiction, *Lost Girls* (published in America in 2006 but not imported to the UK due to copyright restrictions until 2008 [Millidge 2011: 190]). Newer publishing concerns have also arisen, displaying varying thematic and formal emphases in their catalogues. Nobrow Press and Blank Slate Books are among the higher profile names in this regard, although print runs are still fairly low, with the Nobrow website indicating numbers in the 1500–6000 range depending on the title (Nobrow, n.d.) and Blank Slate Press founder Kenny Penman admitting to *Herald Scotland* that: 'Blank Slate doesn't make money,' but also noting that: 'that was never the point' (Herald Scotland, 2012: n.p.). Importantly, like Jonathan Cape and Knockabout, Nobrow and Blank Slate have demonstrated an interest in international engagement. Not only do they publish comics from outside Britain, they also make serious efforts to distribute their books internationally. This does seem to be having some impact, as a 2012 article by *The Comics Journal* columnist Rob Clough made clear:

> Both [the US and Canada] have strong alt-cartooning traditions. England is a country that historically has seemed way behind the US, Canada, and Europe in terms of publishing and appreciating art comics, but two burgeoning publishing concerns are filling that gap. Nobrow Press and Blank Slate Books bear little resemblance to each other in terms of design and aesthetic focus, but both are playing a role in not only providing a place for young British artists to publish

their work, but also in bringing the work of European artists to English-speaking audiences for the first time. (Clough, 2012: n.p.)

While Clough's comments are surprisingly ignorant of the many significant comics that the UK alternative publishing scene *has* produced, titles such as *Escape* (1983–9), *Deadline* (1988–1995), *Crisis* (1988–1991) and *Revolver* (1990–1), they do perhaps indicate a more sustained engagement on the part of these publishers with producing comics that are *exported to* (rather than only *influenced by*) the American art comics markets. Where it was once the case that the 'British invaders' were viewed largely in terms of superhero-oriented publishers like Marvel and DC (even if some [e.g. Alan Moore] were featured in significant alternative series such as *Raw* [1980–1991]), Clough's comments suggest that British creators and publishers are now starting to gain a foothold in the more diverse alternative comics field as well. If they are successful in marketing titles such as *Nelson* (various, Blank Slate, 2011) and *Hilda and the Midnight Giant* (Luke Pearson, Nobrow, 2011) in the United States, it is to be hoped that these publishers can also stimulate American readers and creators to look into the extensive back catalogue of British alternative comics history.

Engagement has also been an important element in the publishing strategy of what is perhaps the most significant and successful of the post-2000 British graphic novel publishers: Self Made Hero. Launched in 2007, the publisher has latched on to a global fervour for Japanese comics, or manga, in publishing one of its most extensive lines, which adapts the works of the bard into the manga format: Manga Shakespeare. Although there are publishers translating Japanese manga titles (and in some cases producing original English language [OEL] manga) for Western markets, the majority of these titles tend to be imported from America (Malone, 2010: 326–7). Self Made Hero is therefore one of the few, if not the only, publisher of British OEL manga, although importer/licenser Tokyopop did open (and close) a UK branch in the mid-2000s. Interestingly, while the Manga Shakespeare titles are sold in general bookshops and comic shops, Self Made Hero also makes substantial efforts to access the educational market, providing learning and teaching resources through a separate Manga Shakespeare website that offers assurances to teachers and parents both on the quality of their products specifically, and on the educational value of manga in general. Thus while it may appear that the UK has come 'late to the party' (Malone, 2010: 326) as far as the production of original manga goes, it could also be suggested that Self Made Hero's address to the educational market has concealed its contribution to the general field of comics and graphic novels, and to the 'comics scene'. The publisher also emphasizes engagement with other classic texts through comics; their catalogue includes adaptations of various prose works, including *Don Quixote* (2011 and 2013, adapted by Rob Davis), *Heart of Darkness* (2010, adapted by David Zane Mairowitz and Catherine Anyango) and the Sherlock Holmes novels (2009–2011, adapted by Ian Edginton and I. N. J. Culbard). Rather than producing works that sell well in a contracting and highly specialized market, Self Made Hero has instead made an effort to *broaden* the comics market (in Britain and internationally) by selling to the general public in a fashion that is more sustainable than the boom time economics of the late 1980s. Only time will tell how successful this strategy is in the longer term.

The Perils of the Periodical

Although the graphic novel market is showing signs of vitality, there is one area in British comics publishing which has not fared so well in the new millennium: serialized comics. While titles such as *The Beano* (1938 –), *Bunty* (1958–2001), *The Dandy* (1937–2012), *Girl* (1951–1964, 1981–1990) and *Eagle* (1950–1969, 1982–1993) are so iconic as to perhaps be the best known emblems of British comics publishing around the world, like many areas of periodical publishing (e.g. magazines, newspapers) serialized comics have struggled to adapt to an increasingly competitive marketplace that offers a wide variety of entertainment options, printed and digital, to choose from. *Bunty*, having been left 'the last British-originated strip-based publication for girls' (Gibson, 2003: 96) following the collapse of *M & J* in

1997 and *Twinkle* in 1999, folded in 2001. *The Dandy* attempted numerous revamps throughout the 2000s, including a high-profile retitling (the name was changed to *Dandy Xtreme*) and shift to fortnightly rather than weekly publishing in 2007. In 2010, the comic returned to the weekly schedule and dropped the *Xtreme* from its title, but was revamped again to include material featuring popular celebrities such as Harry Hill and Cheryl Cole. By 2012 this too had proven unsuccessful, and sales had slumped to an average of 7489 in the last six months of 2011 (Sweney, 2012). On 4 December 2012, the comic 'celebrated' its 75th anniversary with the publication of its final printed issue; the future of *The Dandy* is digital, it would seem, with the company retaining an online presence for the title in lieu of a place on the newsagent's shelf. Interestingly, DC Thompson continues to publish *The Dandy* annual and merchandise, suggesting that there is an audience for the comic but this may only be the kind of market that can sustain occasional nostalgic/novelty purchases rather than a weekly publishing schedule.

Some comics have managed to maintain sufficient circulations to last longer in the post-2000 market. *Commando* (1961–) and *Viz* (1979–) are still in publication. Panini and Titan continue to publish UK editions of the outputs of Marvel and DC respectively. *The Beano* also continues to be published, and in 2007 it launched a monthly spinoff entitled *Beano Max*, but as an article on *The Economist*'s 'Blighty' blog made clear in 2012, this is not necessarily a sign of rude health:

> Circulation has halved since 2007; it was 38,000 in 2011.
>
> Most children's magazines are taking a hit because of the recession. It seems when parents' incomes are squeezed, less money is spent on them. But the decline in British comics goes back farther than the present downturn. The Beano's circulation was a 'six-figure' number in 2003. (L. S. 2012)

Tellingly, the article goes on to point the finger at computer games and online options such as *Moshi Monsters* as competitors for children's time, but also other (often licensed) publications such as *Simpsons Comics* and *Doctor Who Adventures*. Ultimately, however, it may be that these two elements are only two sides of the same coin: those comics that do well are not standalone objects but elements of an entertainment franchise that offers many different modes of engagement including television programmes, video games and other channels (note that both *The Simpsons* and *Doctor Who* were television shows before they were comics). In this model comics may not be the most profitable element of a particular business but they can offer alternative benefits to the owners of the franchise, such as low cost market research and an ongoing emphasis on brand visibility.

This would seem to be part of the strategy that has sustained *2000AD* (1977–) and its spinoff *Judge Dredd Megazine* (1992–) into the new millennium. While Roger Sabin noted in 1993 that: 'few commentators seriously believe [*2000AD*] will still be here in the year 2000' (Sabin, 1993: 61), it has proven surprisingly resilient, vindicating Sabin's (1993: 61) statement that '[w]e should be wary of writing off *2000AD* prematurely: it has an unequalled record for bouncing back'. In 2000 the title was sold by Fleetway to Rebellion, a game development studio founded in 1992, which made its multimedia intentions clear when it released its first Judge Dredd video game *Judge Dredd: Dredd vs. Death* in 2003, although it did not limit itself to the iconic lawman when developing its properties, publishing a *Rogue Trooper* game in 2006. The year 2012 saw the release of a new film, *Dredd 3D* (dir. Pete Travis), a pared down action thriller that laid the ghost of the poorly received *Judge Dredd* (1995, dir. Danny Cannon) to rest using a mix of relentless violence and very limited character development (an element that the *Guardian* asserted was essential for its success: '[t]he essence of Dredd is that he is almost an anti-character – he doesn't change or learn' [O'Neill, 2012]). The comic titles were not neglected by Rebellion, however, and by the time *2000AD*'s 35th anniversary rolled around in 2012, the company had not only kept it and *Judge Dredd Megazine* on the shelves, it had also printed extensive archives of a wide range of the strips from *2000AD* and the *Megazine*, as well as a substantial history of the magazine by former editor David Bishop (*Thrill Power Overload: Thirty Years of 2000AD* [2007]). This served to emphasize the cultural significance of the magazine that had propelled such luminaries as Alan Moore, Bryan Talbot, Grant Morrison and others to international success.

There have also been some signs of growth (or regrowth) in the British periodical comics market, with new titles appearing that address a variety of audiences. Among the most high profile of these upon launch was Titan's *CLiNT* anthology (2010–), overseen by Mark Millar and sold through general high street retailers such as WHSmith in addition to more specialized comic shops. Interestingly although the magazine was fairly well stocked with comics, the first issue alone including instalments of *Kick Ass 2* (Millar and John Romita Jr.), *Nemesis* (Millar and Steve McNiven), *Turf* (Jonathan Ross and Tommy Lee Edwards), and *Rex Royd* (Frankie Boyle and Michael Dowling), the early covers emphasized films and comedy over and above the drawn content inside (although from issue 7 onwards comics came to the fore on the covers). In fact, the cover of the first issue included a caution for readers: 'Warning! Contains comics!'. While this may appear to be an almost apologetic statement or a clarification for readers who might mistakenly purchase *CLiNT* thinking it was a film magazine, it could also be read as a knowing wink towards the more informed purchaser who was aware of the roots of the *Kick Ass* film (2010, dir. Matthew Vaughn) within the comic book series of the same name. Taken in this way, the warning serves to emphasize the substantial impact that comics have had upon other media and the cultural milieu in general, but also hints towards the notion that comics are subversive and dangerous, something that is made clear if we compare the warning from *CLiNT* #1 to the last page of the first issue of notorious 1970s comic *Action*, which offered the advisory note: '*Warning* to nervous readers – *don't* buy *Action!*' (Kibble-White 2005: 34).[3]

British publishers have not wholly neglected the children's comics market, although the demise of *The Dandy* and the rise of magazines in which comic strips are relegated to a marginal position alongside features, puzzles and other elements (as in *Doctor Who Adventures*) suggest that they are certainly not thriving in the way they once were. One attempt to reverse this trend came in the form of *The DFC*, a weekly anthology edited by David Fickling and published by Random House that launched in 2008 and was targeted specifically at children. Rather than newsagent based distribution, *The DFC* employed a subscription model that was effectively reliant upon parents seeking out the comic and paying for it in advance. For this reason the comic targeted not only children but their parents as well, with a letter that came packaged with issues of the comic emphasizing its aims and, like Self Made Hero's *Manga Shakespeare*, making arguments for the educational value of the work: '[*The DFC's*] mission: to entertain. And to get kids reading!' (DFC, 2008: enclosed letter). Yet although the price of the comic was, as the letter made clear 'less each week than your average take-away coffee' (DFC, 2008: enclosed letter), it was evidently still too high, and the comic folded after less than a year. Following the collapse, some of the strips from the magazine were collected in hardback album format by David Fickling Books, and in early 2012 David Fickling Comics launched a follow-up to *The DFC*, aptly titled *The Phoenix*, which did still offer subscriptions but was also distributed through independent book and comic shops, along with Waitrose supermarkets (Phoenix, n.d.) and, since early 2013, in a digital format on Apple's iPad. Given that Waitrose is often considered to be a middle – and upper-class outlet (see for example Smithers, 2012) this approach by *The Phoenix* perhaps implies that the type of class based social hierarchy that Mel Gibson (2010: 123) has identified in the girls comics of the 1950s still exists today, although it would take more research to find out how rigid class boundaries are in modern British comics. Nevertheless it is clear that *The Phoenix*, like *CLiNT*, has the potential to make a major contribution to the UK comic industry if it is able to sustain itself longer than its predecessor, and to continue offering a space in which established and emerging artists are able to present their work to an engaged audience.[4] Of course issues such as longevity and revitalization have long been of concern for British comics, but as examples such as *2000AD* and *The Beano* demonstrate there is some reason to be hopeful – these issues are challenges to be overcome, not insurmountable obstacles.

Digital Developments

Where it was possible at the start of the millennium to shrug off the threat of digital media as a future concern, by the time Apple popularized the tablet computer with the launch of the first iPad in 2010 it had become clear that comics publishers would have to adapt to a digital landscape or risk perishing, with issues such as digital piracy becoming serious concerns throughout the 2000s.[5] This does not necessarily mean that publishers are *required* to present their comics in digital formats but they do need to make sure that their products offer a reasonable value proposition that takes account of the various possibilities of printed and/or digital media. Responses to this challenge have been many and varied, with the manifesto from *Solipsistic Pop* that I mentioned in my introduction suggesting just one approach to the digital format: specifically, to produce books whose physical properties cannot be reproduced electronically:

> We reject the notion that print is dead
>
> True, the screen promises endless possibilities but we vow to create beautiful work you can hold and beautiful work you cannot. We are committed to producing gorgeous, tactile Comics that readers will cherish. (Humberstone and Sheret, 2009: 2)

Other publishers and creators have also followed this line, with Carlton Books producing titles such as *The Best of Jackie* in a facsimile format to appeal to a generation of readers nostalgic for the reading experiences of the 1970s, and Bryan Talbot's *Grandville* being issued with hard, textured covers in part to make it a desirable object that is worthy of purchase rather than digital theft.[6] Although fairly simple, this mode of publication does incentivise the purchase of the printed version since the size, shape and feel of the book cannot yet be replicated on the computer screen.

Digital comics, meanwhile, have tended to take two forms: the *file* and the *app*. The file based digital comic requires the reader to download a reading application that is able to open files of a particular type on whatever device they are using (computer, tablet, smartphone, etc.), with comics often presented in PDF or comic book archive (e.g. CBR, CBZ) formats. While some reading applications (e.g. ComicRack) are designed solely for the purpose of opening files, others combine retail and distribution elements to provide what is effectively an online comic shop. At the time of this writing in late 2012 the dominant player in this regard is probably Comixology, launched in 2007, a company whose offering allows users to make a single purchase and then download and read comics on a wide range of devices. While there was a degree of competition around this type of service when Comixology launched, the company's securing of distribution rights for a large number of comics publishers (including Marvel, DC, Fantagraphics and Image, as well as British publishers Titan and Com.x) has enabled it to gain a virtual monopoly over the distribution and sale of digital comics, with other companies (such as Graphicly) being forced to restructure their offerings to avoid trying to compete directly with Comixology (The Beat 2012: n.p.). Comixology's monopoly is not total, however, with Dark Horse and some other publishers electing to distribute their own comics, and numerous publishers (e.g. Image, Com.x) distributing through Comixology as well as other services (including Graphicly). Some other comics, for example *2000AD*, are sold as standalone files with the reader responsible for sourcing the software to open them separately. This is perhaps the model that is most amenable to the small press since it requires neither software engineering skills nor editorial oversight, although some distributors (including Graphicly and more recently Comixology) have made commitments to distributing user-uploaded comics.

The alternative to the file-based digital comic is the app-based model. Under this approach the comic is not a file to be opened within a general reading application; rather the comic *is* the application, i.e. the comic is installed on the reading device (computer, tablet, smartphone, etc.) as a separate application. Working in association with Ave Comics, Self Made Hero has published one of its titles, Reinhard Kleist's *Johnny Cash: I See a Darkness*, in the app format for Apple devices (iPhone, iPad, etc.). Translated into English by Self Made Hero, Kleist's comic (originally published in German) was first issued in print in 2009 and released as an app for the iPhone in the same year (the iPad version appeared in 2010). In addition to digitized versions of the images and text from the printed version, the app integrates Cash's music at relevant points within the narrative. If the owner of the iPhone has Johnny Cash's songs in their iTunes library they can listen to them as they read the narrative; if they do not there is the option to purchase them (via iTunes) within the app. Here the benefits of the app-based model become clear. Although the file-based approach is convenient (particularly since all the issues of a comic tend to be contained within a single app), the app model allows creators and publishers a far greater degree of flexibility than something like Comixology, which has a very limited number of display options and transitions that are applied to a wide range of comics. In an app, producers are able to customize interfaces and interactions more specifically for each text, and employ elements such as device hardware very effectively. Other app-based comics include 4th Estate/Robot Comics' *Scott Pilgrim's Precious Little App*: a digital adaptation of Bryan Lee O'Malley's popular *Scott Pilgrim* series that incorporates vibrations, as well as limited musical and other video-game style elements, and like *Johnny Cash*, suggests the possibilities for app-based comics.[7]

This is not to say that the app-based approach is inherently superior, because it does have its own problems. One of the most substantial issues for app creators is ensuring that their products remain compatible with updated hardware and software. Where an app is created for a particular platform, it becomes necessary to update the whole app whenever the platform is updated in order to guarantee that it will remain functional. If a publisher has many apps (i.e. a number of comics) this is likely to be a time consuming and potentially expensive process. Similar problems arise when cross-platform considerations are taken into account. Since an app programmed for the Apple iOS operating system cannot run on Google's Android platform, for example, it must be rewritten to work on the other system, which also adds to the time and cost of production. Contrarily, where a file-based approach is taken, any update to a platform or move to access another platform will necessitate only an update to the reading application that is used to access the files, not a modification of the files themselves (just as one does not need to update every PDF one has when an update is released for Adobe Reader). This has enormous economic benefits for publishers and for this reason it seems unlikely that the app-based model could become the dominant one across the industry in the longer term, but for specific titles of the type discussed above it is clear that it does offer some fascinating possibilities.

One publisher that is endeavouring to bridge the gap between the two approaches is Madefire, which offers creators a far wider selection of elements to work with in the creation of their comics and enables them to choose how the comic progresses. Launched in 2012 with a host of British creators including Dave Gibbons (*Watchmen*), Robbie Morrison (*2000AD*) and Gary Erskine (*Dan Dare*), Madefire comics require the reader to download an app for their Apple device through which they can subsequently download a selection of titles. Although this has the hallmarks of a file-based approach, Madefire comics will only run on the Madefire app (at the time of this writing available only on Apple's iOS operating system), which enables them to be built more specifically for the operating environment that app generates. In addition to standard panel transitions, Madefire enables its creators to integrate multimedia elements into their comics, including sound and limited motion, which offers greater possibilities for the creation of more comprehensively multimodal works.[8]

A Kick up the Backside

In some senses, it could be argued that British comics are still in need of the 'kick up the backside' that Paul Gravett and Peter Stanbury advocated in 2006. Yet to do so would seem somewhat inward looking, given that (as the examples I have discussed here demonstrate) British creators and publishers are working in a variety of genres and contexts and having a great deal of success. Whether it is the very varied outputs of publishers such as Jonathan Cape, Nobrow Press, Blank Slate Press or Self Made Hero (to say nothing of publishers such as Cinebook, Com.x and Myriad Editions or the very vibrant small press scene, which I have not had space to discuss here), the arguably less stable but nonetheless productive periodical field, or the continuing interest in printed material objects as well as the developing move towards engaging digital works, it would seem that British comics are in fairly good health. Having recovered from the slump of the early 1990s, the graphic novel has been refreshed and renewed as a format, with established names such as Eddie Campbell, Hunt Emerson, Posy Simmonds and Bryan Talbot being joined by a new generation of creators who are well positioned to make their marks in the field: Hannah Berry, Julian Hanshaw, Karrie Fransman, Simone Lia, and Luke Pearson, among others. While the periodical market is no more stable than it ever was, it too is demonstrating resilience, expanding and adapting where possible to meet the demands and opportunities of an unstable market in economically difficult times. Stalwarts such as *2000AD*, *The Beano*, *Commando* and *Viz* have been joined by newcomers with new ideas and new creators: *CLiNT* and *The Phoenix*, which have contributed to the vitality and diversity of the field. Similarly, it is now becoming clear that digital production and distribution systems do not necessarily represent a threat to creative processes, and while the possibilities of electronic media have yet to be fully realized in comics, companies such as Comixology, Graphicly and Madefire have made some significant steps towards this goal. Although it is easy to be pessimistic about declining sales and the collapse of titans such as *The Dandy*, the history of British comics would seem to suggest that change, though often painful, is inherent in the field. Thus, before writing any more manifestos calling for 'a new paradigm' in comics or lamenting the lack of a British comic book industry, it is wise to look at the bigger picture and think about whether the existing model is really broken after all.

Acknowledgments

I would like to thank Mel Gibson, Paul Gravett and Roger Sabin for their helpful feedback on a draft of this essay.

Notes

1 Perhaps as a result of *Maus*, anthropomorphic talking animals seem here to be excluded from the category of 'supernatural' since Juan Díaz Cana-

les and Juanjo Guarnido' *Blacksad* (2000) was included in the 'Literary graphic novels' category.

2 For more on Millar and Morrison's respective projects at Marvel and DC in the 2000s (albeit from Morrison's perspective) see Morrison (2011).

3 For more on *Action*, see Barker (1989).

4 For more on *The Phoenix*'s role in cultivating new talent in the UK comic book industry, see: BBC (2011).

5 Book publishing had faced this possibility earlier, with the launch of the first substantially successful ereader (Amazon's first generation Kindle) in 2007. Although there is reason to think this would affect comics too, the Kindle's relative inability to handle images and the lack of colour on the earlier versions meant that for most publishers it was not a major concern (this changed with the launch of the Kindle Fire in 2011). For an interesting article on perceptions of digital comics around the turn of the millennium, see Sabin (2000).

6 I am grateful here to Bryan Talbot, who marked up the importance of materiality as an anti-piracy device in conversation at London's Comica Festival in 2009.

7 For more on *Scott Pilgrim's Precious Little App*, see Murray (2012).

8 Interestingly, Madefire has also offered wider access to the 'Motion Book Tool' used to create comics for the platform (Madefire, n.d.), which suggests there may also be possibilities for individuals and smaller publishers to present titles using the system, although at this point it remains to be seen how successful this will be.

References

Abbott, Paul (2012) 'Wanted: A British comic book industry', *The Spectator*, accessed November 2012, http://blogs.spectator.co.uk/books/2012/07/wanted-a-british-comic-book-industry/

Barker, Martin (1989) *Comics: Ideology, Power and the Critics*. Manchester: Manchester University Press.

BBC (2011) 'The Phoenix comic rises from recession flames', *BBC News*, accessed November 2012, http://www.bbc.co.uk/news/uk-england-oxfordshire-16288067

Beat, The (2012) 'Graphicly gets out of apps and into eBooks', *The Beat*, accessed November 2012, http://comicsbeat.com/graphicly-gets-out-of-apps-and-into-ebooks/

Carlton Publishing Group (n.d.) 'The Biggest Jackie Annual Ever: The Best Thing for Girls – Next to Boys', *Carlton Publishing Group*, accessed November 2012, http://www.carltonbooks.co.uk/books/products/the-biggest-jackie-annual-ever-the-best-thing-for-girls-next-to-boys

Chapman, James (2011) *British Comics: A Cultural History*. London: Reaktion Books.

Clough, Rob (2012) 'London Calling: Blank Slate Books and Nobrow Press', *The Comics Journal*, accessed November 2012, http://www.tcj.com/london-calling-blank-slate-books-and-nobrow-press/

DFC, The (2008) *The DFC*, issue 23. Oxford: Random House Group.

Gibson, Mel (2003) 'What Became of *Bunty*? The Emergence, Evolution and Disappearance of the Girls' Comic in Post-War Britain', in Morag Styles and Eve Bearne (eds) *Art, Narrative and Childhood*, pp. 87–101. Stoke on Trent: Trentham Books.

Gibson, Mel (2010) 'What Bunty did next: exploring some of the ways in which British girls' comic protagonists were revisited and revised in late twentieth-century comics and graphic novels', *Journal of Graphic Novels and Comics* 1(2): 121–135.

Gravett, Paul (2005/2006) 'Graphic Novels: Can You Hear The Trucks?', Paul Gravett (originally published in Comics International), accessed November 2012, http://www.paulgravett.com/index.php/articles/article/graphic_novels2

Gravett, Paul and Peter Stanbury (2006) *Great British Comics*. London: Aurum Press.

Groensteen, Thierry, (2000/2009) 'Why Are Comics Still in Search of Cultural Legitimization?', trans. Shirley Smolderen, in Jeet Heer and Kent Worcester (eds) *A Comics Studies Reader*, pp. 3–11. Jackson: University Press of Mississippi.

Hague, Ian (2010) 'Interview with Thierry Groensteen', *Studies in Comics* 1(2): 359–367.

Herald Scotland (2012) 'The second coming of graphic novels', *Herald Scotland*, accessed November 2012, http://www.heraldscotland.com/books-poetry/comment-debate/the-second-coming-of-graphic-novels.18976233

Humberstone, Tom and Matthew Sheret (2009) 'Declaration of the New Vague', *Solipsistic Pop* 1: 2.

Hunt, James (2012) 'Offered: One Comic Book Industry (good condition)', *New Statesman*, accessed November 2012, http://www.newstatesman.

com/blogs/cultural-capital/2012/07/offered-one-comic-book-industry-good-condition%E2%80%A8

Kibble-White, Graham (2005) *The Ultimate Book of British Comics*. London: Allison & Busby Limited.

L. S. (2012) 'Not so Dandy', *The Economist*, accessed November 2012, http://www.economist.com/blogs/blighty/2012/08/decline-classic-boys-comics

Madefire (n.d.) 'Motion Book Tool: Forge New Myths', *Madefire*, accessed November 2012, http://www.madefire.com/motion-book-tool/

Malone, Paul M. (2010) 'The Manga Publishing Scene in Europe', in Toni Johnson-Woods (ed.) *Manga: An Anthology of Global and Cultural Perspectives*, pp. 315–31. New York and London: Continuum International Publishing Group Inc.

Millidge, Gary Spencer (2011) *Alan Moore: Storyteller*. Lewes: ILEX.

Morrison, Grant (2011) *Supergods: Our World in the Age of the Superhero*. London: Jonathan Cape.

Murray, Padmini-Ray (2012) 'Scott Pilgrim vs the future of comics publishing', *Studies in Comics* 3(1): 129–42.

Nobrow Press (n.d.) 'What's Nobrow Then?', *Nobrow Press*, accessed November 2012, http://www.nobrow.net/?pagename=about

O'Neill, Phelim (2012) 'Dredd – review', *The Guardian*, accessed November 2012, http://www.guardian.co.uk/film/2012/sep/06/dredd-review

Phoenix, The (n.d.) 'Contact Us' *The Phoenix*, accessed November 2012, http://www.thephoenixcomic.co.uk/contact-us/

Sabin, Roger (1993) *Adult Comics: An Introduction*. London and New York: Routledge.

Sabin, Roger (2000) 'The Crisis in Modern American and British Comics, and the Possibilities of the Internet as a Solution', in Anne Magnussen and Hans-Christian Christiansen (eds) *Comics and Culture: Analytical and Theoretical Approaches to Reading Comics*, pp. 43–57. Copenhagen: Museum Tusculanum Press and University of Copenhagen.

Smithers, Rebecca (2012) 'Waitrose Twitter hashtag invites ridicule', *Guardian*, accessed November 2012, http://www.guardian.co.uk/business/2012/sep/19/waitrose-twitter-hashtag

Sweney, Mark (2012) 'The Dandy comic to go online only after 75 years', *Guardian*, accessed November 2012, http://www.guardian.co.uk/media/2012/aug/16/dandy-comic-online-dc-thomson

PART II

HISTORIES

Gothicizing History
Traumatic Doubling, Repetition, and Return in Recent British Neo-Victorian Fiction

Marie-Luise Kohlke

The prominence of neo-Victorianism in British as well as global fiction marked both the closing decade of the twentieth century and the opening decade of the twenty-first. Indeed, if anything, the trend of textually resurrecting the nineteenth century only intensified following the millennial turn, producing a surprisingly long list of major literary prize winners – though evidently not all by British writers – including Mathew Kneale's *English Passengers* (2000), Peter Carey's *True History of the Kelly Gang* (2001), Richard Flanagan's *Gould's Book of Fish* (2002), Valerie Martin's *Property* (2003), Colm Tóibín's *The Master* (2004), Edward P. Jones' *The Known World* (2004), Geraldine Brooks' *March* (2006), Kate Grenville's *The Secret River* (2006), Stef Penney's *The Tenderness of Wolves* (2006), and Lloyd Jones's *Master Pip* (2007). Further public and critical attention for this distinctive strain of historical fiction was garnered by popular bestsellers adapted for television, like Sarah Waters' *Tipping the Velvet* (1998; BBC, 2002) and *Fingersmith* (2002; BBC, 2005) and Michel Faber's *The Crimson Petal and the White* (2002; BBC, 2011). The thing that all these novels share, to some extent at least, is an intensely *Gothicized* sense of the nineteenth century as a deeply disturbing, traumatic 'dark age', fraught with repressed desires and anxieties liable to erupt at any moment into sinister violence and victimization.[1]

What accounts for this Gothicizing of the advent of (post)modernity and today's historical fiction writers' frequent, not to say obsessive, resort to the nineteenth century in particular? In part, it may be attributed to the fact that, as Alexandra Warwick remarks, for most of today's public, 'the Victorian is in many ways *the* Gothic period' (Warwick, 2007: 29, emphasis in original). Hence it is unsurprising for re-imaginings of the nineteenth century to assume Gothic overtones and for contemporary Gothic to be mediated through the period's afterimages. Explained differently, neo-Victorianism both reflects and contributes to Gothic's progressive infiltration and permeation of mainstream culture.[2]

As significant is the point that the Gothicizing of history reflects the influence and impact of Trauma Studies on postmodern literature in the final decades of the twentieth century, as well as an ethical turn/return to the referent in the suffering body/psyche following poststructuralist relativizations of concrete realities, truth values, and moral certainties. In the wake of perceived limit-events, especially the First World War, the Holocaust, and the Vietnam War, Trauma Studies developed psychoanalytical notions of *Nachträglichkeit* (or belatedness), repressed memories, repetition compulsion, and the talking cure to theorize the emergence of an always already fissured, self-alienated subjectivity – either actually or potentially wounded/ woundable – precariously constructed around a metaphorical 'black hole' of constitutive trauma. Mark Seltzer claims that 'the modern subject has become inseparable from the categories of shock and trauma' (Seltzer, 1997: 18), while Roger Luckhurst asserts that 'the public sphere' of culture itself 'is increasingly only conceivable through communalities of trauma' (Luckhurst, 2008: 209). This development has influenced fiction at the level of both content and form, thematically and stylistically (see Whitehead, 2004), with narratives 'incorporate[ing] the rhythms, processes, and uncertainties of trauma within the[ir] consciousness and structures' (Vickroy, 2002: xvi), as well as characterization. Today trauma functions as perhaps *the* privileged trope for conceptualizing personal and collective identity formation and politics; one might think, for example, of the insidious trauma of homophobic discrimination and the rise of gay activism and queer fiction, or trauma's central role in postcolonial literatures exposing the crippling legacies of imperialism and racism. No longer exceptional, trauma has become the norm of both historical and fictional subjectivities, going hand in hand with the proliferation of testimonial/confessional literature focused on suffering and survival, addressing topics from incest and child sex abuse to the horrors of large-scale atrocities. Inevitably, historical fiction writers have projected this contemporary 'traumatophilia' (Luckhurst, 2003: 39) backwards in time to elucidate more distant historical events also.[3] This process is further encouraged by Trauma Studies' and Gothic's shared approach to narrative: one dependent on notions of the concealed, withheld and potentially unrepresentable, thus highlighting the equivocal attractions of shock, revulsion and horror when coming face to face with the unspeakable.

Problematically, neo-Victorian Gothicizations of history implicate readers in dubious desires of gratuitous voyeurism, titillation by spectacles of suffering, and perhaps even racist or sexual sadism. One might think of Faber's *The Crimson Petal and the White* with its typically Gothic tropes of female incarceration, persecution and hysteria, and the transformation of the domestic haven into a site of inescapable trauma, including paedophilia in the case of the one-time child prostitute Sugar, apparent sexual abuse by her doctor and marital rape in the case of William Rackham's wife Agnes, and child neglect and emotional cruelty (and possibly worse) in the case of the Rackhams' daughter Sophie. Or consider Kneales's *English Passengers* with its idealistic quest for the Garden of Eden in Tasmania revealed as little more than a perpetuation of the vicious struggle for racial hegemony in the colonial territories, albeit ironically subverted when the ultimate rationalist and racialist, Dr Thomas Potter, is himself utterly Othered and rendered monstrous: as the paranoid writer of a monomaniacal racist manifesto justifying genocide; as the uncanny double of the criminal Black O'Donnell at the Port Arthur penitentiary (foreshadowing the doctor's later grave robbery of indigenous remains and his piracy of the Manx sailing ship); and finally as an exhibited corpse, misclassified as a *'presumed Tasmanian aborigine'* and likely *'human sacrifice'* (Kneale, 2001: 454, emphasis in original), a member of the lowest of the low in Potter's designated hierarchy of races. Nor are these by any means all of the novel's Gothic motifs, which proliferate at an alarming rate. Besides the already mentioned doublings and grave-robbery, Kneale's text features the brutal rapine and rape of indigenous women; the slaughter of innocents, as when the early white settlers go 'crow-hunting' for sport and massacre a complete tribe, including women and children; the aborigines' betrayal into captivity, exile, and lingering death by their self-professed 'friend' and 'protector' Robson; and images of monstrosity related to the unfeminine 'warrior queen' Walyeric and her son Peevay, the mixed-race child of rape, as well as the latter's eventual murderous vengeance on the white oppressors.[4]

These neo-Victorian Gothicizations of history can only be properly accounted for by recourse to trauma discourse. So closely followed by 9/11 and its aftermath of related conflicts variously described as the 'War on Terror' or the West's resurgent neo-imperialist push for world domination – like some 'evil empire' double of the avaricious Victorian imperial power that once turned the map of the world a bloody pink and red – the millennial cusp marked not a break with the horrors of the twentieth century but rather a repetition and return to trauma, Gothic politics of terror and the paranoia of infiltration and persecution.[5] Trauma's underlying structure, of course, is characterized by belatedness – necessitating the retrospective effort of working-through and integrating into consciousness what was crucially missed in the initial *non*-experience of the rupturing event – as well as the already cited repetition and return, both as uncontrolled flashbacks and willed re-memberings of the fragmented spectral past *called (back) into presence*. These elements link trauma directly to the Gothic mode. For Gothic is likewise dominated by the past's inimical overshadowing of and intrusion into the present, tropes of haunting and spectrality, the terrors of absolute power and powerlessness, the abjection of radical self-estrangement and self-loss, and narrative patterns of repetition and return linked to the wilful infliction of suffering and its attempted transcendence by its victims (or else their hopeless succumbing). As David Leon Higdon remarked as early as 1984, in *Shadows of the Past in Contemporary British Fiction*, since the modernists, '[t]he substitution of discontinuity, sequence, and cycle, for continuity, process, and line' has 'constitute[d] a major reinterpretation of the relationship the culture perceived between past, present, and future' (Higdon, 1984: 5–6), something that still holds true of British neo-Victorian fiction in the twenty-first century.

Unsurprisingly, neo-Victorianism, so often associated with theories of spectrality and/or trauma (see Arias and Pulham, 2010; Kohlke and Gutleben, 2010a; Mitchell, 2010), proves an inherently Gothic mode of working-through and re-imagining or, perhaps more accurately, re-*en*visioning history from the period's future perspectives, producing 'Future Pasts', to borrow another of Higdon's formulations (Higdon, 1984).[6] Described in another way, neo-Victorianism *anticipates* the Victorians' twentieth – and twenty-first-century futures (and beyond) through recourse to the nineteenth-century past as the mainspring of modernity, and hence as the inception of postmodernity's trauma culture and alienated identity, marked by trauma's disruptive/irruptive Othering of self, experience and consciousness. It is no coincidence, for example, that David Mitchell's *Cloud Atlas* (2004) opens and closes with a nineteenth-century setting, which frames the text's multiple, chronologically organized, split narratives set in different historical periods, first arranged projectively and then recursively, with each temporal section in the second half of the novel returning to an earlier traumatic narrative stopped short. Indeed, the *in medias res* interruption of each narrative structurally replicates trauma's interruption of the individual and/or collective self's story. In Mitchell's text, trauma literally renders the subject radically discontinuous, fracturing into pre-traumatic and post-traumatic self, initiated by the proleptic nineteenth-century traumatic moment which, as Celia Wallhead and I argue, '"haunts" the rest of the novel, resurfacing continuously like the return of the repressed or an involuntary flashback to an originary traumatic scene' (Wallhead and Kohlke, 2010: 217). And that moment is itself strikingly Gothic, featuring the naive Adam Ewing's encounter with the vampiric, disgraced surgeon Dr Henry Goose, who is first met collecting teeth from cannibal victims before turning his predatory attentions to Ewing and attempting to poison him for personal gain, all against the historical backdrop of the British assisted genocide and enslavement of the peaceful Moriori by the warlike Māori on the Chatham Islands off New Zealand.

Although Gothic has sometimes been viewed as a form of innocuous escapist fantasy, neo-Victorian fiction's recursive mode is rarely that. On the contrary, it stages a confrontation with some of the most unpleasant aspects of Victorian reality (and often our own time as well), even where it gestures towards trauma's unrepresentability or ineffability. Uplifting tendencies are brutally sabotaged by patterns of Othering, repetition and return, which short-circuit the teleological impetus of much Victorian fiction that conveyed an unspoken belief in notions of historical progress and self and societal development (though sometimes less so with regards to Victorian Gothic texts that only vanquished monstrous evil provisionally or ambiguously, or else dramatized reverse processes of degeneration). Let me offer two specific case studies from the oeuvres of Sarah Waters and A. S. Byatt, namely *Fingersmith* (2002) and *The Children's Book* (2009), which describe more oblique traumatic movements than does Mitchell's novel with its overt, structurally exemplified repetition and return.

At the close of *Fingersmith*, the lesbian narrators Susan (or Sue) Trinder and Maud Lilly are reunited at the Gothic mansion Briar, Maud's childhood home, inherited from her sadistic bibliophile monomaniacal 'uncle', who virtually enslaved her as cataloguer to his pornographic collection, much of it now sold or destroyed by Maud. Some critics read this ending in positive terms as the protagonists' liberation from the Gothic snares of both Christopher Lilly and his mercenary inadvertent handmaiden Grace Sucksby, who switched her daughter Maud shortly after birth with Lilly's real niece Sue, whom she later betrays to gain Maud's (more rightfully Sue's) inheritance. Kate Mitchell, for example, asserts that Maud and Sue move 'beyond the patriarchal gaze and, as such, are free to create a female space that exists outside the order provided by law' (Mitchell, 2010: 140) – and arguably outside of abusive patriarchal history that stretches back to Maud's (actually Sue's) persecuted runaway mother who, following her lying-in at Mrs Sucksby's house, was recaptured by her father and brother and forcibly incarcerated in an insane asylum until her death.[7] Other critics view Maud's resort to writing pornography for a living as a subversive feminist appropriation of a misogynistic genre, doubly so since the lesbian writer will presumably be 'performing' or aping male heterosexual desires as well as her own for profit. Cora Kaplan, for example, suggests that 'this ending can be seen as a celebration and libertarian defence of the sexual and the literary imagination, and its appropriation by women writers today' (Kaplan, 2007: 113). Kathleen A. Miller similarly describes *Fingersmith* as 'a corrective to the inheritance of a male-dominated pornography trade', privileging women's 'own interiority' rather than exemplifying their self-loss as mere objectified bodies, and concludes that Waters demonstrates how 'erotic pornographic literature can be a sexually and socially liberating force for women writers and readers' (Miller, 2007: para. 3–4) – a comment that resonates with the recent popular bestselling sensation of E. L. James' *Fifty Shades of Grey* (2011). According to Miller, Waters' novel depicts a progressive growth in the protagonists' 'female power' and agency, prescribing an end to victimhood, replaced with the promise of 'joy and fulfilment' at the novel's close, where the women's own story truly begins (Miller, 2007: para. 5, 25, see also para. 14).

Considered through the Gothic lens, however, a very different reading emerges, rendering affirmative interpretations deeply suspect. The protagonists' reunion is predicated on the traumatic repetition of the loss of the mother, with Marianne Lilly's death being replicated by that of Mrs Sucksby, who apparently goes to the gallows in Maud's stead for the latter's inadvertent murder of their accomplice Gentleman in a desperate effort to prevent him revealing the true relationship between Mrs Sucksby and herself and Sucksby's treachery to Sue. Likewise, the lovers' new life together involves a return to Briar, the primary site of trauma, and will be financed by another traumatic return – to the pornography industry which Maud was condemned to be part of as a child and adolescent and now, only seemingly freely (since actually choiceless), becomes part of again. For with no other skills or means of income, Maud admits of herself and the dead Lilly, 'I am still what he made me. I shall always be that'

(Waters, 2002: 546). Hence she never achieves the post-traumatic liberated subjectivity posited by Mitchell and Miller. From a Gothic point of view, Maud's future writing career will constitute a continuous re-enactment of her former abjection and quasi-prostitution, just as her offer to teach Sue to read and write, on which the novel ends, draws her lover into the perpetuation of the vicious cycle of traumatic (re-)victimization. As Nadine Muller notes, the imagistic link established between 'ink' and 'poison' throughout the novel leaves unclear 'whether or not Maud poisons rather than liberates Sue by teaching her how to read and write' (Muller, 2009/2010: 122–3). Indeed, Sue replicates Maud's one-time learning to read and recite aloud from pornographic texts that the child could not even understand. As Helen Davies notes, this 'place[d] her in the role of a "dummy" in relation to the ventriloquist roles of both the anonymous pornographers and her uncle ... condemned to act as an unthinking, unknowing vessel for the obscene repetitions', little more than a 'quasi-automaton' (Davies, 2012: 156–7). Although Sue, unlike the child, presumably *does* already understand the subject matter, she too is drawn into the automaton-like unknowing repetition and perpetuation of past trauma as Maud's double, while Maud ends up assuming the unnamed pornographers' and her uncle's Svengali-like ventriloquist roles. Both women thus remain puppets of and victims to the past, their 'future' curtailed before it has even properly begun.

Not coincidentally, Sue remarks upon her return that Briar 'seemed like a house not meant for people but for ghosts' (Waters, 2002: 538).[8] In this sense, the lovers remain irreversibly marked by trauma, not actualized selves so much as lost souls suspended in the haunted purgatory or what might be called the endless Gothic 'traumatopia' of Briar. As much is also suggested by Briar's association with the 'Sleeping Beauty' fairy-tale, evoking its heroine-victim's century-long suspension in sleep, that is, a sort of extended living death. In spite of Waters' tongue-in-cheek inversion of the tale, by having Sue instead of a prince arrive to awaken Maud from her isolation, Sue never manages to rescue her lover from Briar's metaphorical underworld or the literal underworld of pornography. The fairy-tale seems to become conflated with the Eurydice and/or Persephone myths of perpetually repeated loss; during her search of the house, for example, Sue reflects that 'I wept as a ghost would: silently, not minding the tears as they came falling – as though I knew I had tears enough for a hundred years, and in time would weep them all' (Waters, 2002: 540). What binds the protagonists together at the end is as much their remembered traumas as their passion for each other; each woman acts as a constant and indelible reminder to the other of the traumas suffered and inflicted, as underlined by Sue's brief flashes of hatred for Maud during the final reunion scene.

Byatt's *The Children's Book* likewise employs intricate, at times excessive doubling to figure history as the cyclical return of and to trauma, underlined by the novel's temporal setting, which spans the century's cusp from 1895 to the end of the First World War in 1919.[9] Though a structural rupture, trauma paradoxically becomes a mark of uncanny connection between the book's depicted Victorian and post-Victorian periods, much as Mitchell employs trauma in *Cloud Atlas* to link disparate historical pasts and imagined futures. Doubling occurs not only between different characters and situations, but also between individuals' nineteenth-century childhoods and twentieth-century adult experiences. The novel's opening clearly signals its Gothic credentials, as the young Tom Wellwood and his cousin Julian Cain go 'stalk[ing]' the working-class hideaway Philip Warren through the subterranean vaults of the South Kensington (later the V&A) Museum (Byatt, 2009: 5). They follow him down a 'passage [...] roofed with Gothic vaulting, like a church crypt', which issues into a 'funereal chamber', 'a dusty vault, crammed with a crowd of white effigies', whom Tom suspects of 'be[ing] prisoners in the underworld, or even the damned', while his cousin jokingly proposes that the boys 'were lost, no one would find them, rats would pick their bones' (Byatt, 2009: 6). Having escaped the soul-destroying environs of Burslem's industrial working-class slums and gruelling child labour in the potteries, Philip finds refuge first in the Bohemian Wellwoods' country home and later that of the potter Benedict Fludd to whom he is apprenticed. Yet the Gothic implications of his first sanctuary as a symbolic 'crypt' (Byatt, 2009: 6), containing the nineteenth century's repressed forbidden desires, resonates eerily throughout the rest of the novel, not least in the name of the Wellwood's home, Todefright, and the family's labyrinthine kinship ties and closely guarded secrets. (Some of the Wellwood children are actually Humphrey's children by his wife Olive's live-in sister Violet, whom they believe to be their aunt, while 'their' daughter Dorothy is the product of Olive's adulterous affair with the German puppet-master Anselm Stern.) The novel's opening is also recalled in the title of *Tom Underground*, the continuous fiction that Olive, a writer of children's books, composes for her son.[10] Significantly, Tom's story centres on traumatic self-loss and the protagonist's quest to recover his stolen shadow (much like trauma survivors' quests to re-integrate pre- and post-traumatic fractured selves); like an unresolved trauma, the story has been 'constructed to be endless' (Byatt, 2009: 517). This inconclusiveness further relates to the likelihood that Tom's narrative may well constitute an uncanny reiteration and unconscious attempt at working-through his mother's and her sister's own traumatic working-class childhoods in a Northern mining community.[11]

Similarly desperate childhoods were experienced by Philip and his sister Elsie, surviving in overcrowded conditions where premature death from sickness and accidents was commonplace and incest was rife. Intermittent flashbacks to this intolerable existence foreshadows the revelation of one of the Gothic's foundational motifs, namely the tyrannous father's – in this case Benedict Fludd's – incestuous assaults on his daughters. Following the thwarting of his illicit desires, when his eldest daughter Imogen escapes him by marrying Fludd's patron Prosper Cain, Fludd commits suicide by drowning. Again, the family hearth becomes the primary site of trauma, unconsciously re-enacted by Imogen's younger sister Pamona, who sleepwalks in the nude, and figured in the Bluebeardesque locked room where the potter hides away the pornographic art memorializing his transgressions, sculpted pots bearing the images (and explicitly depicted genitalia) of his daughters, hence constituting another form of doubling. (Not coincidentally, the potter's crimes are also foreshadowed in Humphrey Wellwood's earlier propositioning of his purported daughter Dorothy.) Although Pamona, with Philip's assistance, removes and buries the pots after her father's death, they are not physically destroyed but continue to exist 'underground' as it were (see Byatt, 2009: 463). Hence there is something curiously apt about James Wood's critique of what he takes to be Byatt's over-the-top use of ekphrasis, albeit in a different sense to that intended by him: 'the novel quivers in aspic' (Wood, 2009). Art, like Byatt's novel as a whole, quite literally becomes an image of preserved but entombed trauma. Excessive doubling turns Byatt's text into a veritable recessive echo chamber or crypt, so that, to borrow Victor Sage and Andrew Lloyd Smith's formulation, the technique constitutes a 'modern form of haunting; reiteration of narrative manoeuvres and motifs, unholy reanimation of the deadness of the past' (Sage and Smith, 1996: 4) – a past that is not *quite* dead but persistently and traumatically resuscitated. As a spectral absent presence, Fludd's pots shadow the victims' lives, again curtailing any notions of complete liberation from trauma. This is particularly apparent in Imogen's case. Her seemingly happy and freely chosen union with Prosper is ghosted by the spectre of her symbolic father murder as well as connotations of incest and child abuseAs Mark Llewellyn notes, the marriage 'raises further questions about the nature of sublimated cross-generational desire' (Llewellyn, 2010: 146), due to the significant age differential between husband and wife and Prosper's earlier role as a substitute father, welcoming Imogen into his home as a sister to his own daughter.

The puppet and puppet-play tropes, so prominent throughout *The Children's Book*, similarly reiterate the theme of self-loss, paralleling the way that trauma takes over a victim's actions and consciousness akin to an external controlling force. Tom is haunted by his fictional double, until the difference between his 'secret' story and actual life uncannily collapse.[12] At the boarding school, the latest instalment of *Tom Underground* sent him by Olive precipitates his aggravated sexual abuse by older boys in the boiler room where Tom has retreated to read in private, literalizing the terrors encountered underground by his fictional counterpart. Later, his mother's adaptation of the story (without consultation with Tom) for public performance as a puppet play, aptly mixing real actors and marionettes, seems to reactivate the trauma of his shame and humiliation. At the end of the performance he flees the theatre as he fled his school years before and several days later, having walked from London to the sea, leaves 'his theatre-going shoes and coat' with a folded programme of the play in its pocket on the beach and commits suicide by drowning (Byatt, 2009: 532), re-enacting the fictional Tom's descent, albeit underneath the water rather than the earth. Tom's self-destruction also doubles Fludd's death, attesting to the failure of coming to terms with the modern riven traumatized/monstrous sense of self-as-Other, whether as victim or perpetrator.

Yet it also foreshadows another 'drowning' to come. *The Children's Book*'s recurrent traumatic tropes and their inception in the Victorian age pre-figure the cataclysmic collective trauma of the First World War, which consumes or cripples a number of legitimate and illegitimate Wellwoods, Fludds, and Cains from Byatt's extensive cast of characters. Most significant for the purpose of my argument, however, is the scene of Philip's awakening in a French hospital, being tended by Dorothy Wellwood and her cousin Griselda, after having been pulled out of the mud at Passchendaele, in which he nearly drowned after being hit by a shell. In effect petrified, like a rigid puppet, with 'breathing holes and eye holes' cut into the carapace of mud that the girls begin to unpick,[13] Philip remarks laconically, 'When I went under, I thought, it's a good end for a potter, to sink in a sea of clay' (Byatt, 2009: 608). His statement resurrects Gothic images of Fludd's and Tom's deaths in the sea, as well as of *Tom Underground*, in Philip's case literalized in his submersion into the consuming earth or clay.[14] Simultaneously, this *deus ex machina* on Byatt's part returns readers to the beginning of the novel, since it could be read as a further oblique doubling, evoking Tom and Julian's quest through the museum's underground passages in search of Philip; only this time Philip is rescued from 'underground' first by the ambulance men and then by Dorothy and Griselda. In a sense, the mud in Byatt's novel stands in for trauma itself and its monstrous interminability: 'the mud layer was inexhaustible, always renewing itself' (Byatt, 2009: 608). And just in case readers should have missed the imagistic patterning of traumatic return that proleptically incorporates the narrative's future, Byatt's third to last paragraph, a somewhat clumsy example of overkill, explicitly spells it out in the scene of the survivors around the dinner table:

> Ghosts occupied their minds, and crowded in the shadows behind them. They had all done things they could not speak of and could not free themselves from, stories they survived only by never telling them, although they woke at night, surprised by foul dreams, which returned regularly and always as a new shock. (Byatt, 2009: 614)

A Gothic-traumatic patterning of doubling, repetition and return sustains and drives current neo-Victorian fiction and its disturbing recreations of the nineteenth-century as the inception of postmodern trauma culture. Within the constraints of this essay, it is not feasible to pursue the still ongoing theoretical debates about exact definitions and demarcations of the 'neo-Victorian' at any length. Suffice to say that, though I have drawn my main examples from British texts, I do not believe that we can speak of a distinctly *British* strain of twenti-eth- or now twenty-first-century neo-Victorian fiction in isolation from important neo-Victorian work undertaken elsewhere. Admit-tedly, British writers, such as Peter Ackroyd, Beryl Bainbridge, A. S. Byatt, Angela Carter, John Fowles, Graham Swift, and Sarah Waters, have been at the forefront of this kind of writing and have ensured its growing popularity. Yet the extensive overlap between their stylistic approaches and privileged topics (imperial/colonial and racist depre-dations, gender politics and sexual inequities, crime and criminality, transgressive desires, etc.) and those of their non-British contempo-raries working similar veins against nineteenth-century backdrops, among them Margaret Atwood, Peter Carey, Richard Flanagan, Ami-tav Ghosh, Valerie Martin, and Toni Morrison, renders categorical distinctions on the basis of authors' nationalities rather pointless, not to say counter-productive in mapping the field as a whole. I see 'neo-Victorian' very much as an inclusive umbrella term, covering much more than just British fiction or just fiction incorporating Brit-ish nineteenth-century characters and contexts at home and abroad, analogous to the way that the term 'Victorian Studies' effectively equates to 'Nineteenth Century Studies', for example encompass-ing North American literary productions also. Neo-Victorianism is clearly a *global* rather than British phenomenon, albeit one to which British writers have made and continue to make a vital contribution.

My proposed working definition of 'neo-Victorian', then, is as follows: neo-Victorianism is the *inherently Gothic-traumatic* (re-)engagement – by writers of any national affiliation, in texts deploying any geographical settings[15] – with the nineteenth century as:

> a) a virtual storehouse or lumber-room of the cultural imaginary (and cultural unconscious), precipitating an on-going crisis with regards to the period's invasive influence, as much a potential encumbrance, cluttering up and oppressively weighing down collective consciousness, as a source of artistic and intellectual fecundity; and

> b) a virtual space demanding cultural memory-work and testimony, what Christian Gutleben and I have elsewhere called 'after-witness' (Kohlke and Gutleben, 2010b: 7), inviting ethical confrontations with historical accountability for the period's unquiet ghosts and undead traces and its insidious, at times disabling, legacies in the present-day.

Examples of these legacies include the earlier referenced, neo-imperialist political tendencies, as well as welfare and social services, especially as regards approaches to child protection and failing families (*The Children's Book*), or popular gender ideology (*Fingersmith*) still so often inflected by essentializing or re-victimizing propensities. A combination of race politics and the commemoration of Empire constitute a further example. Only recently, the UK has witnessed heated public debate concerning the possible re-naming of the honours awards of CBEs, OBEs and MBEs that all contain the word 'Empire' (as in 'Order of the British Empire'). Queen Elizabeth II's own advisors apparently deem the term 'anachronistic and inappropriate', as it occasions 'unease', particularly among ethnic minorities originating from or descended from immigrants of former colonies, due to the term's problematic association with conquest and oppression (Drury, 2012). Structurally and thematically, twenty-first-century neo-Victorian fiction by British and other writers thus participates in a complex hybridizing process of cultural memory-work, predicated on compulsive repetition and traumatic return – to earlier texts, genres,

Gothic motifs, traumas and ethical crises – to capture if not actual nineteenth-century history, at least its re-imagined 'feel'. Yet arguably that decidedly Gothic 'feel' is also a peculiarly twentieth/twenty-first-century *invention* of history as inherently, indelibly, recursively and hauntingly traumatic.

Kate Mitchell suggests that neo-Victorianism is primarily predicated on 'the emergence of memory discourse in the late twentieth century', with its 'increasing interest in non-academic forms of history', including narrative forms, fictional and otherwise, and assigns the genre a 'creative role' in wider cultural processes of 'historical recollection' (Mitchell, 2010: 4, 11). Analogously, my double-barrelled definition proposes that neo-Victorian fiction inevitably conflates memory and fantasy, since it cannot ever literally recall the nineteenth century. Rather, it must imaginatively reconstruct or *simulate* it through the period's textual and other traces, comparable to trauma survivors' attempted narrativization of the unrepresentable black holes of traumatic crises from fragmentary leftovers and after-images within their consciousnesses. This also accounts for the genre's intense, not to say obsessive self-reflexivity, for example in terms of its extensive, at times repetitive inter- and intra-textuality,[16] its metafictional inflections and tropes of appropriation and adaptation (themselves processes of reiteration and return), and the patchwork 're-memberment' of history (e.g. from multiple contradictory and partial perspectives, as in the case of *English Passengers*). Hence I earlier described neo-Victorianism, both as a form of ambiguous cultural commemoration and painful after-witness, as *inherently Gothic-traumatic*: it hearkens back to an *admired-hateful* past with its momentous technological achievements, scientific advances and social reforms set against the period's socio-political iniquities, imperialist exploitations, gender inequalities and moral hypocrisies (repetition and return), while simultaneously seeking – but never managing completely – to lay that conflicted past to rest and/or transcend it (working-through).

The very process of repetition, return, and working-through, however, necessarily resurrects/recreates the past's horrors, empowering them anew, if only temporarily in the attempt to narratively contain or vanquish them. Accordingly, neo-Victorianism is always Gothically double or hybrid in its intentions as well as its effects, explaining what are paradoxically perceived to be its coexistent subversive and reactionary tendencies (see Gutleben, 2001) – much like those often ascribed to Gothic literature. Drawing on metaphors of 'grafting' and 'cross-pollination', Christian Gutleben fittingly describes neo-Victorian writing as partaking of 'oxymoronic hybridity' (Gutleben, 2011: 61). I would argue that this determinative instability extends to neo-Victorian works' (sub-)generic classification,[17] which is rarely straightforward, but seemingly more a matter of generic accretion. Should Kneale's *English Passengers* be regarded as a quest narrative, a work of neo-Victorian Imperial Gothic, a seafaring adventure tale, or a historical 'faction'? Is Carey's *True History of the Kelly Gang* best categorized as a neo-Victorian crime novel, biofiction, or a postcolonial text? Does Waters' *Fingersmith* constitute a multiple text adaptation of Charles Dickens' *Oliver Twist* (1838) and *Great Expectations* (1860–1) and Wilkie Collins' *The Woman in White* (1859–60), a crime fiction, a neo-sensation novel, or a lesbian romance? The answer in each case is arguably 'all of the above – and then some'. For instance *Fingersmith* might also be described as a (part) pornographic fantasy, a Doppelgänger tale, a *Bildungsroman*, a family romance and, particularly in its depictions of Maud Lilly's childhood, as a confessional fiction of child abuse. The only designations that would appear to encompass all possible classifications in each case are 'Gothic' and 'trauma narrative', or perhaps 'trauma Gothic'.

Gutleben notes that the concept of hybridity, for example as regarded race relations, was already 'highly problematic for the Victorians, at the same time a promise of fecundity and a threat of corruption, both a possibility of rejuvenation and a risk of degeneration' (Gutleben, 2011: 61). Adapting Gutleben's comments to explicate contemporary literature's Gothicization of nineteenth-century history, one might say that the neo-Victorian simultaneously constitutes a promise of transcending (or at least reaching an accommodation with) historical traumas and the risk of potential renewed traumatization, not least through the recycling of invidious past ideologies. Hence neo-Victorianism and the historical fictions of writers like Waters and Byatt constantly revive the traumas of the nineteenth-century past within the cultural consciousness of the present, ensuring as much as attesting to their continued afterlife, their power to defy conclusive representation, and thus their eventual Gothic return once more.

Notes

1 As Christian Gutleben and I argue elsewhere, '*neo-Victorianism is by nature quintessentially Gothic*: resurrecting the ghost(s) of the past, searching out its dark secrets and shameful mysteries, insisting obsessively on the lurid details of Victorian life, reliving the period's nightmares and traumas' (Kohlke and Gutleben, 2012: 4, emphasis in original).

2 This 'Gothic culture' is perhaps most obvious in the flourishing cult of vampire fiction and films, but also in the popularity of such exhibitions as Dr Gunther von Hagens' *Body Worlds* (*Körperwelten*) or the revival of contemporary freak-shows, such as in the 2012 'The Royal Family of Strange People' at the Priceless London Wonderground festival at Southbank Centre or 'The Congress of Curious People' held annually at Coney Island, New York.

3 The concept of trauma, of course, predates the advent of institutionalized Trauma Studies. For a detailed genealogy stretching back to the nineteenth century see Luckhurst (2008).

4 Further Gothic tropes worth mention are the disappeared/missing manuscript in a letter never sent (detailing the aforementioned massacre, and the writer's later falsification of his testimony) and the ironic use of the spectral trope in the indigenes' perception of the white men as 'Ghosts' (Kneale, 2001: 54). The latter designates not only the whites' alien appearance to the aborigines, but also their out-of-placeness and un-belonging in a country they conquer but never seek to truly understand, a ghostliness they attempt to overcome by the ruthless extermination of the colonized land's original inhabitants so that they can assume the indigenes' rightful place, in the process turning the aborigines into literal ghosts. By the end of the novel, only a handful of indigenes survive, most of these of mixed-race like Peevay.

5 To this might be added updated Western versions of manifest destiny transposed to the global stage, as well as various constructed hostile Others, such as 'the terrorist' and 'the insurgent'.

6 'Future Pasts' is the subtitle of Part I of Higdon's monograph.

7 In the complex double-crossing conspiracy that enables Maud's flight from Briar and her subsequent marriage to Richard 'Gentleman' Rivers, Sue too finds herself incarcerated in an asylum, namely as 'Mrs Rivers', re-enacting her mother's wrongful incarceration and that of Maud, until the latter was brought to Briar at age eleven once 'orphaned'.

8 Sue encounters a house of locked doors, echoing the women's state of be-ing 'locked in' to a traumatic cycle of permanent reliving and repetition of the past, albeit with minor variations.

9 This bridging technique is not unique to Byatt's novel, of course, having been employed in other twenty-first-century neo-Victorian novels such as Sebastian Faulks' *Human Traces* (2005).

10 All the children have their own fabulations and fictional doubles created for them by Olive.

11 Isobel Armstrong asserts as much in her response to James Wood's re-view of the novel: 'It is a projection of the part of Olive that has never dealt with her own experience of the underground, the tragic coal-mining district where she grew up' (Armstrong, 2009).

12 As Mark Llwellyn notes, like the other Wellwood children's stories, *Tom Underground* is 'a private text between writer and reader, mother and child', producing a quasi incestuous 'shared space where the de-sires between the two parties can be enacted', eroticising the writing act (Llewellyn, 2010: 140).

13 Not coincidentally, the narrative section immediately preceding Philip's re-entry into the story describes a load of 'full-size flat images of soldiers ... with realistic faces, with moustaches and glasses under their tin hats. They were puppets. They had flat strings snaking over the mud, operated by puppeteer soldiers hidden in foxholes and craters ... inviting the Ger-mans to fire on them and reveal their own positions' (Byatt, 2009: 606).

14 Another imagistic link is Humphrey's gift to Olive on the opening night of the puppet drama *Tom Underground*: 'a double row of amber beads', one of which encases a 'lace-winged fly ... which had left traces, in the hard translucent bead, of its struggle to escape the oozing sap' (Byatt, 2009: 525). A further pre- and post-Victorian doubling involves Humphrey and Violet's injured and traumatized son Florian, the only Wellwood boy still living after the war, whose sleepless wanderings recall Pamona's somnam-bulism: 'At night he walked. He could be heard, his limping leg thumping,

his wheezing a steady, sinister sound, on stairs and in corridors' (Byatt, 2009: 593).

15 These may also include wholly imaginary settings, e.g. utopian, dystopian, or alternative geographies/worlds, as employed in some steampunk fiction.

16 A pertinent example would be D. M. Thomas's *Charlotte* (2000), with its appropriative re-writing of both Charlotte Brontë's *Jane Eyre* (1847) and Jean Rhys's *Wide Sargasso Sea* (1966).

17 Note that I differ from Gutleben on this point, who specifically excludes generic considerations from neo-Victorian hybridity: 'The specificity of neo-Victorian fiction's hybridity ... is temporal and historical and not generic' (Gutleben, 2011: 64).

Works Cited

Arias, R. and P. Pulham (eds) (2010) *Haunting and Spectrality in Neo-Victorian Fiction: Possessing the Past*. Basingstoke: Palgrave Macmillan.

Armstrong, I. (2009) [on-line version of untitled response to James Wood's Review of *The Children's Book*], Letters, *London Review of Books* 31(20) (22 October): n.p., accessed May 2012, http://www.lrb.co.uk/v31/n19/james-wood/bristling-with-diligence.

Byatt, A. S. (2009) *The Children's Book*. London: Chatto & Windus.

Davies, H. (2012) *Gender and Ventriloquism in Victorian and Neo-Victorian Fiction: Passionate Puppets*. Basingstoke: Palgrave Macmillan.

Drury, Ian (2012) 'Queen's advisers tell her to drop "empire" from honours as it's "inappropriate" in post-imperial Britain', *Mail Online* (6 May), n.p., accessed May 2010, http://www.dailymail.co.uk/news/article-2140268/Queens-advisers-tell-drop-empire-honours-inapproriate-post-imperial-Britain.html

Faber, M. (2002) *The Crimson Petal and the White*. Edinburgh: Canongate.

Gutleben, C. (2001) *Nostalgic Postmodernism: The Victorian Tradition and the Contemporary British Novel*. Amsterdam and New York: Rodopi.

Gutleben, C. (2011) 'Hybridity as Oxymoron: An Interpretation of the Dual Nature of Neo-Victorian Fiction', in V. Guignery, C. Pesso-Miquel and F. Specq (eds) *Hybridity: Forms and Figures in Literature and the Visual Arts*, pp. 59–70. Newcastle upon Tyne: Cambridge Scholars Publishing.

Higdon, D. L. (1984) *Shadows of the Past in Contemporary British Fiction*. Athens, OH: The University of Georgia Press.

Kaplan, C. (2007) *Victoriana: Histories, Fictions, Criticism*. Edinburgh: Edinburgh University Press.

Kneale, M. (2000/2010) *English Passengers*. London: Penguin.

Kohlke, M.-L. and C. Gutleben (2010a) *Neo-Victorian Tropes of Trauma: The Politics of Bearing After-Witness to Nineteenth-Century Suffering*. Amsterdam and New York: Rodopi.

Kohlke, M.-L. and C. Gutleben (2010b) 'Introduction: Bearing After-Witness to the Nineteenth Century', in M.-L. Kohlke and C. Gutleben (eds) *Neo-Victorian Tropes of Trauma: The Politics of Bearing After-Witness to Nineteenth-Century Suffering*, pp. 1–34. Amsterdam and New York: Rodopi.

Kohlke, M.-L. and C. Gutleben (2012) 'The (Mis)Shapes of Neo-Victorian Gothic: Continuations, Adaptations, Transformations', in M.-L. Kohlke and C. Gutleben (eds) *Neo-Victorian Gothic: Horror, Violence and Degeneration in the Re-Imagined Nineteenth Century*, pp. 1–48. Amsterdam and New York: Rodopi.

Llewellyn, M. (2010) '"Perfectly innocent, natural, *playful*": Incest in Neo-Victorian Women's Writing', in M.-L. Kohlke and C. Gutleben (eds.) *Neo-Victorian Tropes of Trauma: The Politics of Bearing After-Witness to Nineteenth-Century Suffering*, pp. 133–60. Amsterdam and New York: Rodopi.

Luckhurst, R. (2003) 'Traumaculture', *new formations* 50: 28–47.

Luckhurst, R. (2008) *The Trauma Question*. London and New York: Routledge.

Miller, K. A. (2007) 'Sarah Waters' *Fingersmith*: Leaving Women's Fingerprints on Victorian Pornography', *Nineteenth-Century Gender Studies*, 4(1) (Spring): para. 1–17, accessed May 2012, http://ncgsjournal.com/issue41/miller.htm

Mitchell, D. (2004) *Cloud Atlas*. London: Sceptre.

Mitchell, K. (2010) *History and Cultural Memory in Neo-Victorian Fiction: Victorian Afterimages*. Basingstoke: Palgrave Macmillan.

Muller, N. (2009/2010) 'Not My Mother's Daughter: Matrilinealism, Third-wave Feminism & Neo-Victorian Fiction', *Neo-Victorian Studies* 2(2): 109–36, accessed May 2012, http://www.neovictorianstudies.com/

Sage, V. and A. L. Smith (1996) 'Introduction', in V. Sage and A. L. Smith (eds) *Modern Gothic: A Reader*, pp. 1–5. Manchester and New York: Manchester University Press.

Seltzer, M. (1997) 'Wound Culture: Trauma in the Pathological Public Sphere', *October* 80 (Spring): 3–26.

Vickroy, L. (2002) *Trauma and Survival in Contemporary Fiction*. Charlottesville and London: University of Virginia Press.

Wallhead, C. and M.-L. Kohlke. (2010) 'The Neo-Victorian Frame of Mitchell's *Cloud Atlas*: Temporal and Traumatic Reverberations', in M.-L. Kohlke and C. Gutleben (eds) *Neo-Victorian Tropes of Trauma: The Politics of Bearing After-Witness to Nineteenth-Century Suffering*, pp. 217–52. Amsterdam and New York: Rodopi.

Warwick, A. (2007) 'Victorian Gothic', in C. Spooner and E. McEvoy (eds) *The Routledge Companion to Gothic*, pp. 29–37. London and New York: Routledge.

Waters, S. (2002) *Fingersmith*. London: Virago.

Whitehead, A. (2004) *Trauma Fiction*. Edinburgh: Edinburgh University Press.

Wood, J. (2009) 'Bristling with Diligence' [online version of Review of A. S. Byatt's *The Children's Book*], *London Review of Books* 31(19) (8 October): 6–8, accessed May 2010, http://www.lrb.co.uk/v31/n19/james-wood/bristling-with-diligence

Remembering the 1980s in David Mitchell's *Black Swan Green*

Christopher Vardy

Introduction

The 1980s linger in British collective memory. The adult narrator of David Mitchell's short story 'Preface' – also a schoolboy and minor character in the author's 1980s bildungsroman *Black Swan Green*[1] – is deeply nostalgic for the decade of his childhood and highly critical of the atomized twenty-first-century Britain he now inhabits. Yet he is unable to conceptualize the causal relationship between the 1980s and now: between neoliberal past and present. A more astute character remarks that '*Our childhoods […] are our Old Testaments. Our Books of Genesis, our Deuteronomies. It's all written down there. And once writ, it can't be unwrit.*' (Mitchell, 2006a: 16). In this suggestive (if somewhat ironic) formulation, childhood does not simply represent a prior state. These biblical metaphors suggest a mythologized period of birth and emergence that assumes a historical *tabula rasa*, and which establishes the laws and norms – economic, political and moral – that determine subsequent history and society. 'Preface' and *Black Swan Green* both clearly position the 1980s and the emergence of Thatcherite neoliberalism in these decisive terms: as contemporary Britain's collective childhood.

Mitchell is not alone in doing so. Critic Simon Reynolds notes that '[i]nstead of being the threshold to the future, the first ten years of the twenty-first century turned out to be the "Re" decade[: ...] *re*vivals, *re*issues, *re*makes, *re*-enactments. Endless retrospection.' (Reynolds, 2006: xi, emphasis in original). The last decade saw a proliferation of cultural production that explores the recent past: from documentary, TV drama, theatre and film, to visual and performance art.[2] At the same time, there has been a marked resurgence in production of (and critical interest in) historical fiction. These trends intersect in a range of 'neo-1980s' novels (Brooker, 2005: 104), including Alan Hollinghurst's 2004 Booker Prize winning *The Line of Beauty* (2004), David Peace's *GB84* (2004), Will Self's *Dorian – An Imitation* (2002) and Denise Mina's *The Field of Blood* (2005), and Irivine Welsh's *Skagboys* (2012), that remember the 1980s as a cultural and ideological sea change. In these texts, the dominant elements of recent history – hyper-consumption, deindustrialization, widening social inequality, globalization, the homogenization of national and regional cultures, and the digital technological revolution – are presented as products of that decade's neoliberal politics. Arguably, this prevalent focus on the 1980s (a heterogeneous decade that is too often figured as metonymically interchangeable with Thatcherism and the figure of Margaret Thatcher) can obscure other, more wide-ranging historical influences. Yet there is little doubt that the 1980s – which saw the rise of a new, radical and intensely divisive socio-economic paradigm – was a particularly foundational and divisive period for modern Britain, and one that contemporary cultural production increasingly and obsessively returns to.[3]

This essay analyses the ways in which twenty-first-century fiction remembers the 1980s through a reading of David Mitchell's *Black Swan Green* (2006b). This deceptively simple *bildungsroman* is set in 1982 against the backdrop of the Falklands/Malvinas conflict and ambivalently fuses nostalgia with political critique. I argue that *Black Swan Green* simultaneously enacts and problematizes the widespread contemporary understanding of the 1980s as an aesthetic defined by fetishized consumer culture: what I term a 'retro-memory' of the recent past. The novel juxtaposes this selective and seductively nostalgic vision with more troubling memories of the period, particularly the pervasive anxiety over Cold War militarism and potential nuclear conflict, and the increasing brutality of social relations in Thatcher's Britain. *Black Swan Green* reasserts these perspectives on the 1980s through a focus on the ideological and historical contexts that shape its adolescent narrator Jason Taylor and his seemingly 'ordinary' interactions with his everyday material environment. Mitchell's novel offers a perceptive take on the apparently quotidian, and presents a complex and contradictory vision of life in the early 1980s. In counterpointing but not cohering a variety of narratives about that decade, it suggests that our contemporary collective memory of the recent past is similarly fraught and inconsistent.

Collective memory/remembering

Before defining retro-memory and moving on to analyse *Black Swan Green*'s engagement with our collective memory of the 1980s, it is worthwhile briefly outlining the ways in which this essay deploys the crucial concepts of memory and remembering. How meaningful is the concept of cultures collectively *remembering* the past? Indeed, is it possible to have a *collective* memory of anything at all, let alone a diverse 10-year stretch of time? Peter Middleton and Tim Woods argue that in the wake of postmodern historiography, and following the memory 'wars' of the 1990s and the rise of digital mnemo-technologies, memory rather than historical discourse is simultaneously considered to be the 'super-highway to the past' – with that metaphor's resonance of time-space compression – and understood to be highly contingent and subject to constant revision (Middleton and Woods, 2000: 5). They contend that cultural texts like historical fictions help to construct our shared understandings of the past – what we commonly term collective or social memory – while also critically reflecting upon the paradigms of 'memory' and 'history' that govern this process. Similarly, Kate Mitchell argues that rather than focusing on whether a text represents the past accurately or problematizes such historical representation (as with Linda Hutcheon's influential definition of postmodern *historiographic metafiction*),[4] it is productive to consider historical novels as 'memory-texts' that 'emerge from and participate in [other] contemporary memorial practices' and which foreground the 'always unfinished *process* of remembering' (Mitchell, 2009: 29, 32). Historian Dan Stone also theorizes remembering as a cultural process, but focuses more on its political potential to expose, challenge and contest 'how narratives and stories about the past structure societies in the present' (Stone, 2010: 25).

These perspectives are useful in their focus on the historical novel and other cultural production as part of – and reflexively engaging with – the workings of a broader memorial culture. Collective memory is best understood not as a social analogue for individual memory: either as a kind of abstract collective unconscious or an aggregate or median of individual memories. Nor is it necessarily predicated on trauma or deterministic models of traumatic memory and subjectivity. Instead, following Mitchell and Stone, this essay uses a model of collective memory that focuses on *remembering* as a dynamic, politicized process (rather than accessing extant and/or accurate pre-existing *memories*), and which foregrounds the ways in which the meanings of past events are always in flux: continually reconstructed and contested through contemporary culture. *Black Swan Green* is a text that remembers the 1980s in this way: it both enacts and interrogates this historiographic process and other memorial forms. Most overtly of all, the novel is enmeshed in one of the dominant contemporary forms of remembering the recent past: materialistic and often intensely nostalgic *retro-memory*.

Retro-memory

Retro, heritage, vintage: the fetishization of historical objects and styles defines a retrospective culture where the past is primarily a commodified aesthetic. However, retro is not simply a twenty-first-century phenomenon, and fetishistic attitudes to material culture and object-based historiographies are hardly new developments. Raphael Samuel argues that retro culture – a minority taste for aesthetes and collectors in the nineteenth and early twentieth centuries – 'acquired a wider resonance in the prosperity of the 1960s as an alternative version of consumerism, pandering to the nostalgia for a simpler life,' and proliferated exponentially in the decades that followed (Samuel, 1994: 92). Joseph Brooker similarly contends that retro's transformation into a ubiquitous mode of consumer culture can be clearly dated to the 1980s (Brooker, 2010: 210–11). So what is so distinctive about twenty-first-century retro?

Two distinguishing factors are the digital revolution and the globalized neoliberalism that David Harvey argues is inextricable from it (Harvey, 2005: 4), which have both dramatically altered the past's presence in our material world. Reynolds suggests that the Internet and other contemporary memory-technologies offer a new experience of pastness:

> Old stuff either directly permeates the present, or lurks beneath the surface of the current, in the form of on-screen windows to other times. We've become so used to this convenient access that it is a struggle to recall that life wasn't always like this; that until relatively recently, one lived most of the time in a cultural present tense, with the past confined to specific zones, trapped in particular objects and locations. (Reynolds, 2011: 57)

Digital objects replay vast swathes of the accumulated past on demand, at our leisure, wherever we are: an instant and seemingly infinite archive that encompasses everything, from an early Beatles gig to the digitally enhanced Kennedy assassination and looped impacts of 9/11. Reynolds' argument that in the past, people 'lived most of the time in a cultural present tense' is simplistic and misleading – forms of revivalism have a long history – but it is undeniable that the ways in which subjects perceive, experience and consume their history are changing rapidly and in unprecedented ways. And retro represents in part a cultural anxiety at this lack of material boundaries and limits in our twenty-first-century relationship with the past: an indiscriminate and proliferating digital glut of memory. As novelist Gordon Burn notes, a few words tapped into YouTube brings 'so many moments of the past crowding back – a pandemonium of fragments' that leaves contemporary subjects synaesthetically overwhelmed (Burn, 2008: 175). Retro represents a valorized alternative to this chaos: a nostalgic fantasy of a fixed and more authentic window to another time. The fetishized historical object becomes a commodified symbol of obsolescence and rapid change around which other dissatisfactions with modern life can congeal, but it also signifies tangibility in an unreal world where 'the analogue and artisanal ... are equated with a sort of spiritual integrity.' (Burn, 2008: 91). Walter Benjamin's concept of the 'aura' possessed by an original artefact or artwork is now diffused, arguably indiscriminately, throughout pre-digital material culture (Benjamin, 1999: 214). As long as it is in grainy analogue, even the recording or reproduction now signifies authenticity: a material portal to a supposedly simpler time. It is through these sought-after commodities that twenty-first-century culture remembers the recent past.

So, like the obsessive collector described by Burn, we yearn for retro-objects 'to possess a moment which remains pure, unreproduced except in memory, and is not available to be freeze-framed, or focus-shifted or enhanced – *exhausting all the reality stored in its magnetic pores*' (Burn, 2007: 212, emphasis in original). The fantasy to 'possess' an authentic and affective material link to one's personal or collective past – with possession's simultaneous suggestions of ownership and fetishism – is deeply nostalgic. And nostalgia – a painful longing/'algia' for 'nostos'/home – is widely considered the dominant mode of late capitalism, with its homogenizing erosion of local and national cultures. Charged by many critics, notably Fredric Jameson, with being an ahistorical and numbing commercial palliative,[5] contemporary nostalgic desire is more sympathetically defined by Svetlana Boym as a materialistic but 'affective yearning for a community with collective memory, a longing for continuity in a fragmented world.' (Boym, 2001: xv) Their conclusions about nostalgia may differ, but both agree that this politically fraught desire for the past is expressed through – and structured by – fetishized historical objects. As *Black Swan Green's* thirteen-year old narrator Jason Taylor puts it, when one forges a relationship with the past, 'Photos're better than nothing, but things're better than photos 'cause the things themselves were part of what was *there*.' (*BSG*, 368)

As this essay's reading of *Black Swan Green* will suggest, the commercialized retro-memory of a lost and less complicated past often manifests itself through an idealized focus on childhood, as two cultural fantasies of innocence and fixity become imbricated. Indeed, Brooker argues that the valorization of childhood is central to the development of twenty-first-century retro-culture:

> The aspects of the past being revived are primarily those that appealed to the young ... Contemporary retro is also fuelled by affluence, and by the demographic shift in which, for an increasing proportion of the population of developed countries, childrearing takes place later. *Childhood itself can thus become prolonged or fondly replayed.* (Brooker, 2010: 213, emphasis added)

Rather than putting away childish things, we heap undue historical meaning upon them. In *Black Swan Green*'s afterword, Mitchell acknowledges 'debts of detail' (*BSG*, 373) to Andrew Collins' memoir *Where Did It All Go Right?* (2003), a text which exemplifies this fetishistic retro-memory of childhood and the desires it represents. Collins tells the story of a 'normal' upbringing (explicitly contrasted with the late twentieth century boom in 'misery memoirs' of traumatic childhood) through a surfeit of period details and references. The book's website – an interactive archive designed to be 'an oasis of happy uneventful childhood memories' – is prefaced with the suggestive invitation 'that no story is too mundane or "ordinary" to tell! It's the universal truths we're after. So, as much detail as possible (names of aunties, sweets, streets, games, guinea pigs) and don't be shy' (Collins, 2003b). A universalized and Edenic collective memory of childhood is structured by seemingly 'mundane' period details. Toys, games, music, TV programmes and other cultural products imbue this nostalgic version of the recent past with a reality-effect. Collective experience is not defined by community, class, shared labour, or identity politics; rather, these neoliberal collectivities of consumption evoke a shared experience of 'normal' life through a collection of retro-signifiers that seem to authenticate and universalise our personal memories. We too remember (or understand the signification of) the Rubik's Cube or the Raleigh Chopper, *Abbey Road* and Fleetwood Mac: we have this in common; it offers a pleasurable and melancholy shared experience of the idealized past contrasted with the atomized present. Our childhoods – individual and collective – are a troublingly fantastic 'oasis' against which the complex adult world can never compete. As in Benjamin's definition of the collector's fetishistic desire for metonymy and control, our recent past is 'present, and indeed ordered, in each of [these] objects' (Benjamin, 2002: 207). Our collective childhood is defined and *fondly replayed* through its consumer detritus.

There is a particular paradox at the heart of retro-engagements with the 1980s: the desire to escape from a socially fragmented and seemingly immaterial contemporary life to a nostalgic and materialistic vision of the decade that shaped that life more than any other; the irony of memorializing through vintage, retro and heritage modes the very period that consolidated their commodification of the past. Yet, as I have suggested, this retro-memory of the 1980s is a dominant narrative in contemporary culture. Popular series like *I Love the 1980s* (BBC, 2001) are comprised of nostalgic surveys of the decade's consumer culture – toys, fashion and music – often with celebrity talking heads reminiscing about simpler technologies as a metaphor for simpler times. Another notable example is the drama *Ashes to Ashes* (BBC, 2008–10) and its evocation of the 1980s through pop culture truisms and retro-signifiers. The programme's reflexive formal gloss – that its period setting is the trauma-fantasy of a dying woman, remembering her 1980s childhood through the prism of twenty-first-century retro-memory – still facilitates an alarmingly conservative conception of the decade. The commodification of the past – like the interrelated idealization of childhood – often masks more complex and troubling historical narratives. And *Black Swan Green*'s presentation of *retro-memory* is, if not overtly critical, then decidedly ambivalent; in Mitchell's text, retro signifies 'retrograde' and 'retrogressive' as much as 'retrochic.'

'You've obviously forgotten what it's like'

The novel's narrator is thirteen-year-old Jason Taylor, who lives in the eponymous Black Swan Green: a parochial Midlands village that represents middle class middle-England in the early 1980s. Brooker describes *Black Swan Green* as a retro-inflected 'reconstruction of childhood's travails [which] does not primarily aim to be a state of the nation address' (Brooker, 2010: 215). It is certainly not a programmatic 'state of the nation' novel, and its provincial setting – dismissed by Jason as so 'boring' that 'no one ever knows where it is' (*BSG*, 215) – is less obviously ambitious than Mitchell's transnational and temporally complex novels *Ghostwritten* (1999) or *Cloud Atlas* (2004).[6] However, Jason's description of his modest surroundings – viewed at night from the apex of a fairground ride – as a 'galaxy squashed flat' (*BSG*, 319) is indicative of the novel's broader vision. Its thirteen month-by-month chapters set between 1982 and 1983 offer less of a linear narrative and more a succession of linked incidents, represented by the 'series of thirteen dinosaur postcards' Jason buys: '[e]ach one's got a different dinosaur, but if you put them end to end in order, the background landscape joins up and forms a frieze' (*BSG*, 213). This cumulative metaphor suggests that just as *Black Swan Green* presents Jason's identity as mutable and accretive, a multifaceted historical period like the 1980s can only be understood as the simultaneous interaction of many complex events, contexts, desires and ideologies. The novel suggests that 'childhood's travails' (a problematically universal and dehistoricized idea of childhood) are in fact determined by these specific historical circumstances, and that Jason's seemingly ordinary adolescent experiences can illuminate them. Behind its deceptive simplicity lies what Ali Smith terms 'a knowing foray into a contemporary novelistic mode, the late-20th-century coming-of-age novel, the land of Hornby and Coe' (Smith, 2006). The novel reflexively charges contemporary culture and its idealization of both childhood and the 1980s with a form of selective amnesia. If, like Jason's father, we unthinkingly desire our recent past, we've *obviously forgotten what it's like* (*BSG*, 211).

However, from its first page, *Black Swan Green* presents the 1980s through the lens of retro-memory: an excessive accumulation of nostalgic objects and period detail. The narrative abounds with cousins 'busy solving a Rubik's cube at high speed' (*BSG*, 53) and classmates described as 'rows and columns of faces ... like a screen of Space Invaders' (*BSG*, 44–5). Scenes unfold around 'the Asteroids console' (*BSG*, 73) or the 'Sinclair ZX Spectrum 16k' (*BSG*, 291), with a constant backdrop of iconic 80s tracks like '"Don't You Want Me?" by Human League [...] thumping out dead loud' (*BSG*, 1). The specificity is relentless and not confined to pop music: few brand names and elements of early-1980s pop culture escape a name-check. Brooker persuasively links this excessive interest in period detail with an attempt to 'plausibly convey the priorities of a child: the latest challenge that Mitchell, a formidable technician, had set himself' (Brooker, 2010: 214). A two-way association can be gleaned here between childhood and retro-materialism. Childhood is associated with nascent consumerism and a particular awareness of/investment in the material object, while retro-memory – which transposes these fetishisms into historiography – is inherently childlike, or, more pejoratively, childish.[7] Adolescence is certainly presented in *Black Swan Green* as a materialistic and brand-conscious time, an association playfully satirized when Jason learns that his sister Julia has ended her relationship with boyfriend Ewan: '"Oh." But Ewan had a silver MG. "I liked Ewan." "Cheer up. Stian's got a Porsche"' (*BSG*, 341). However, even taking into account the novel's attempt to represent the materialistic priorities of an adolescent (and the emergence of a neoliberal subjectivity increasingly predicated around consumerism) the scale of *Black Swan Green*'s collection of period detail is obsessive. A car is never just a car: it is 'a sky-blue VW Jetta' (*BSG*, 357), a 'Vauxhall Viva' (*BSG*, 86), a 'white Ford Granada Ghia' or a 'Datsun Cherry' (*BSG*, 53). Meals and snacks become a periodising name-check: 'Findus ham'n'cheese Crispy Pancakes, [...] butterscotch Angel Delight for pudding' (*BSG*, 13); 'Mum'd bought Maryland Chocolate Chip Cookies. They're new and totally lush' (*BSG*, 159). These childhood references are occasionally very subtle: a radio alarm is described as 'glowing in numerals of mekon green' (*BSG*, 44), the Mekon being a green alien antagonist in the *Eagle*'s Dan Dare comic strip, which was relaunched in 1982. More often, they're less than subtle: "'Morning,' I said. "What's that magazine?" Julia held up the front cover of *Face*.' (*BSG*, 45). The materiality of pre-digital technologies is particularly lovingly fetishized throughout: from vinyl LPs and Betamax cassettes to Jason's love for his 'Silver Reed Elan 20 Manual Typewriter', particularly 'how it's got no number 1 so you use the letter "l."' (*BSG*, 41).

Mitchell was criticized by many reviewers for this '[overdoing of] the period detail ... striving to situate his story in 1982 in a way that someone actually writing in 1982 would never bother to' (Jones, 2006). However, the scale of this materialistic excess goes beyond historical fiction's need for authentication or even a novelistic pastiche of period detail. As the style of Jason's first-person narration makes clear, *Black Swan Green* always has one eye on his future and our present. Past and present tenses can blur in the course of a single sentence: 'I had one of those odd moments when now isn't now' (*BSG*, 153). The fusion of past and future tenses at the end of the novel further emphasizes its retrospective position: 'How Grant Burch pushed docile Philip Phelps over the edge, I'll never learn. That was the last time I'll ever clap eyes on them' (*BSG*, 367). The novel's narration highlights its status as a twenty-first-century text. *Black Swan Green* reflexively presents readers with a retro-1980s: the materialistic decade as we materialistically remember it now, packed full of the signifiers that are objects of nostalgic desire, popular media reminiscence and desired retro-commodities in contemporary life.

Of course, there is nothing inherently wrong with remembering the past materialistically. However, this retro-fetishism ignores the more changeable (and difficult to capture) ideological and political contexts in which objects circulated and signified in the past. Material things never signify consistently: historical context and perception create them. This is neatly demonstrated in *Black Swan Green* by Jason's changing perception of the same set of objects over time, as unhappiness over bullying at school increasingly erodes his childish optimism: 'A velvet staircase sliced sunlight across the hall. A blue guitar rested on a sort of Turkish chair. A bare lady in a punt drifted on a lake of water lilies in a gold frame.' (*BSG*, 180); 'A knackered blue guitar'd been left on a broken stool. In the gaudy frame a shivery woman sprawled in a punt on a clogged pond.' (*BSG*, 191); 'The guitar's blue paint'd flaked off like a skin disease. In her yellow frame a dying woman in a boat trailed her fingers in the water.' (*BSG*, 208). *Black Swan Green* remembers the 1980s through the materialistic lens of retro-memory, but it also seeks to recapture the historical contexts that determine our perceptions of the other objects and environments that comprise our 'normal' world. In doing so, it undermines the fantasy diagnosed by Bill Brown (and embodied by retro-memory) that material things offer us 'dry ground' above the 'instabilities and uncertainties, the ambiguities and anxieties' of twenty-first-century life (Brown, 2001: 1). While seductively presenting a commodified fantasy of innocent childhood and the recent past, the novel uses things to simultaneously remember other, less palatable visions of growing up in Thatcher's Britain. Like Jason's description of the Tudor warship *Mary Rose* being dragged from the seabed in 1982, with its 'silty, drippy, turdy timbers [that] look nothing like the shining galleon in the paintings' (*BSG*, 278), the text emphasizes that our idealization of the 1980s is an illusion that occludes a much more complex hidden reality. Within the excessively *materialistic* framework of nostalgic 'stuff', a forgotten 1980s can be textually remembered through another engagement with *materiality*: Jason's adolescent perceptions of the material world.

The nuclear 1980s

Despite the fear that if his peers find out 'they'd gouge [him] to death behind the tennis courts with blunt woodwork tools and spray the Sex Pistols logo on [his] gravestone' (*BSG*, 4), Jason is a budding poet, and his first-person narration is defined by inventive attempts to figure his environment. The novel makes clear that this creativity and perceptiveness is shaped and delimited by the ideological and historical contexts that determine Jason in the early 1980s, and uses this process to explore and denaturalize that historical moment. *Black Swan Green* counters retro-memory by drawing parallels between the brutality of adolescent social relations and the period's disturbing militarism. The early 1980s saw a resurgence of Cold War tensions: from Ronald Reagan's bellicose proliferation of the nuclear arms race to the chilling public information programme 'Protect and Survive', which prompted hysterical media coverage in Britain (McSmith, 2010: 45–8). A 'Britain and the Bomb' special issue of the *Daily Mirror* in November 1980 exemplifies this apocalyptic mood with biblically-inflected headlines intoning 'Only the chosen will be saved' alongside arresting photographs of 'the nuclear family' who have survived the atomic blast but are stuck in decontamination suits and 'can't even touch each other' (Anon, 1980: 1, 3, 11). Since 1989 and the end of the Cold War, the fear of nuclear war is often airbrushed from collective memory, or fixed in metonymic moments like Reagan's 1983 'Evil Empire' speech or the Greenham Common protests of 1982. These histories incorporate Cold War tensions into important narratives of global high politics and identity politics, but often obscure their effects on the regular realities of life during the 1980s. However, *Black Swan Green* reasserts the nebulous *everyday* horror of living with the possibility of nuclear annihilation through Jason's interactions with day-to-day 'stuff'.

From the beginning of the novel, references to nuclear threat abound. While illicitly exploring his father's study, Jason fleetingly notes that 'the office phone's red like a nuclear hotline' (*BSG*, 1), before playing a solitary war game:

> Dad's swivelly chair's a lot like the *Millennium* Falcon's laser tower. I blasted away at the skyful of Russian MiGs streaming over the Malverns. Soon tens of thousands of people between here and Cardiff owed me their lives … I'd refuse all medals. 'Thanks, but no thanks,' I'd tell Margaret Thatcher and Ronald Reagan when Mum invited them in, 'I was just doing my job.' (*BSG*, 2)

This childhood fantasy disquietingly blurs the boundaries between the sanitized and heroic conflict of SF action films like *Star Wars* – with its *Millennium Falcon* crewed by virtuous rebels – and the exigencies of a real nuclear conflict. But the Cold War undercurrent transcends pop-culture fantasy. Nuclear imagery inflects Jason's perceptions of a range of everyday experiences: he watches girls spill 'out of [a] photo booth after the fourth nuclear flash' (*BSG*, 214); empty school corridors look 'like a neutron bomb's vaporized human life but left all the buildings standing' (*BSG*, 266); a friend at the fairground is 'laughing like Lord Satan in a mushroom cloud' (*BSG*, 324); an intimidating group of mods prompts Jason to reflect that '[a]fter the nuclear war, kids like them'll rule what's left. It'll be hell.' (*BSG*, 236). These references and material metaphors may seem banal and everyday, but are cumulatively disturbing symptoms of a pervasive nuclear fear in the 1980s that produces subjects haunted by fantasies and nightmares of atomic fallout and radiation sickness:

> I'm with the last bunch of survivors, after an atomic war. We're walking up a motorway. No cars, just weeds. Every time I look behind me, there're fewer of us. One by one, you see, the radiation's getting them … It's not that I'll die that bothers me. It's that I'll be the last one. (*BSG*, 10)

Even Jason's reading material at his speech therapy sessions is implicated: he is set Robert C. O'Brien's *Z for Zachariah* (1974), a dystopian tale of a child attempting to survive in the aftermath of World War III (*BSG*, 37). *Black Swan Green*'s focus on the Cold War is significant in other ways. Just like the weather report of strong winds blowing in from Russia, Jason's narration and its nuclear undertow always subtly reinforce that the seemingly parochial Black Swan Green – and neoliberal Britain – is deeply enmeshed in global currents, political as well as meteorological: 'Strange to think of a Red Army sentry on a barbed-wire watchtower shivering in this very same icy wind. Oxygen he'd breathed out might be oxygen I breathed in.' (*BSG*, 343).

The paranoid effect of the twists and turns of the 1982 Falklands/ Malvinas conflict are also illustrated by the increasingly militaristic similes and metaphors through which Jason figures his material surroundings. Innocently caught up in the patriotic fervour of the war's early days – which he likens to the World Cup with fleet statistics for each side (*BSG*, 121) – everyday things become opportunities for playful fantasies of idealised conflict: 'Pudding was apple sponge. The syrup trail from my spoon was the path of our marines … I bravely led our lads yomping over custard snow to ultimate victory in Port Stanley' (*BSG*, 128). But with the sinking of the HMS *Sheffield*, the death of a local boy on the HMS *Coventry* that 'killed the thrill of the war' (*BSG*, 140) and gossip that the conflict could escalate into a US-Soviet nuclear exchange, Jason's growing awareness of the costs of conflict transforms his everyday environment into something much more threatening and equivocal: 'birdsong strafed and morsed' (*BSG*, 137); 'birds detonated out of the oak without warning and we jumped but didn't laugh about it' (*BSG*, 138); 'Rain began its blitz, tranging bullets off the roof and strafing the puddles round the barn.' (*BSG*, 102). Just as the war unconsciously 'seep[s] in' (184) to Jason's poetry, none of his schoolboy possessions can escape the haunting association with global battles raging 8000 miles away:

> Right now. That's what freaks me. I dip my fountain pen into a pot of ink, and a Wessex helicopter crashes into a glacier on South Georgia. I line up my protractor on an angle in my maths book and a Sidewinder missile locks on to a Mirage III. I draw a circle with my compass and a Welsh guard stands up in a patch of burning gorse and gets a bullet through his eye. How can the world just go on, as if none of this is happening? (*BSG*, 132)

M. J. Harrison criticises *Black Swan Green* for divorcing objects from their cultural context: 'in their own time ... objects carry a cultural charge, which the novelist must surely retrieve and communicate if the past isn't to become a combination of product placement and notebook entry, on the lines of "1982: remember to mention the Datsun Cherry"' (Harrison, 2006). He is partly correct: the novel's frameworks of retro-1980s signifiers are inert. But Harrison ignores the distinction between this materialistic contemporary collective memory of the 1980s and the novel's rich, suggestive, politicised presentation of the more mundane things through which Jason lives and perceives his life. These adolescent interactions are suffused with the shifting ideological currents of the period, and offer marginalized and disturbing memories of the 1980s. *Black Swan Green* reflects Raphael Samuel's belief that a closer attention to the meanings of 'ordinary' material objects can produce a 'whole new family of alternative histories, which take as their starting point the bric-à-brac of material culture, the flotsam and jetsam of everyday life.' (Samuel, 1994: 114). Materialistic retro-memory can be challenged (if not effaced) through the historiographic potential of our seemingly humdrum material environment. After all, as anthropologist Daniel Miller argues, a culture's 'whole system of things, with their internal order, make us the people we are.' (Miller, 2010: 53). And contemporary fiction can use these systems, rather than metonymic or event-driven histories, to figure the subtleties of historical subject-formation: to textually remember who we were then, and how that shaped who we are now.

A brutal childhood

Twenty-first century cultural production remembers the 1980s as a acutely formative period for contemporary Britain: our neoliberal childhood. *Black Swan Green* makes clear that childhood and adolescence are not pre-discursive, innocent states: that these periods of intense subject-formation cannot somehow be separated from ideology, politics and historical events. In doing so, the novel not only challenges retro-memory's nostalgia for the 1980s, but also the interrelated cultural valorization of childhood. Instead, the brutality of childhood and the militarism and social stratification of neoliberal Britain are presented as mutually constitutive.[8] This dynamic is highlighted when Jason, out walking, is shocked by Harrier jump jets zooming over the Malvern Hills, and reflects on their association with the prospect of nuclear conflict:

> When World War III comes, it'll be the MiGs stationed in Warsaw or East Germany screaming under NATO radar. Dropping bombs on people like us. On English cities, towns and villages like Worcester, Malvern and Black Swan Green.
> Dresden, the Blitz and Nagasaki …
> Mrs Thatcher was on TV yesterday talking to a bunch of schoolkids about cruise missiles. 'The only way to stop a playground bully,' she said, as sure of her truth as the blue of her eyes, 'is to show to the bully that if *he* thumps *you*, then *you* can jolly well *thump him back* a lot harder!'

> But the threat of being thumped back never stopped Ross Wilcox
> and Grant Burch scrapping, did it? (*BSG*, 113–14)

The politics of international conflict are presented as inextricable
from the politics of childhood. The Thatcher government's controversial agreement in 1980 that US cruise missiles able to be quickly
launched against the Eastern bloc would be primed and ready on UK
soil escalated global nuclear tensions and catalysed a revival of CND
and the nuclear protest movement. On one level, Thatcher's framing
of a complex and potentially devastating geopolitical issue through
the oversimplified schoolyard logic of deterrence and mutual 'thumping' suggests a crass, patronising and dangerously cavalier – indeed, to
use its negative association, an adolescent – approach to the nuclear
arms race. But this link to the politics of the playground scrap is not
just abstract critique of Thatcherism: the reference to a specific fight
between Jason's schoolmates Grant Burch and Ross Wilcox suggests
that violence structures both adolescent social relations and *Black
Swan Green's* broader (and arguably dystopian) conception of British
society in the 1980s where '[h]ate doesn't need a *why*. *Who* or even
what is ample.' (*BSG*, 250).

Childhood is defined by harshness and alienation from the novel's
opening pages, as a game of British Bulldogs on a frozen pond starts
with team-picking: 'About twenty or twenty-five of us boys, plus
Dawn Madden, stood in a bunch to be picked like slaves in a slave
market' (*BSG*, 6). The game's violence makes Jason conclude that
'[g]ames and sports aren't about taking part or even about winning.
Games and sports're really about humiliating your enemies.' (*BSG*,
7). Childhood – like British society – is brutal and militaristic: 'It's all
ranks, being a boy, like the army' (*BSG*, 4). It is also sharply stratified
according to class: 'These gaps aren't easy to ignore. There are rules.'
(*BSG*, 108). Far from an idyll, childhood is a lonely and paranoid
time: Jason may not understand a peer's joke, but, he realises '[t]here's
no one I can trust to ask what it means.' (*BSG*, 10). As the novel progresses, he becomes the subject of an intensifying campaign of bullying, which he tellingly figures through the same military metaphors
and similes that define his experience of the Falklands campaign: a

link between violence at an individual and societal level. After yet another cruel public barb about his stammer, 'a fresh bomb of laughter blew [him] into tiny bits' (*BSG*, 206); following more mockery '[l]aughter acker-ack-acked after [him], like machine guns.' (*BSG*, 274). It is no coincidence that the book a panicking Jason is forced to read aloud in class, despite his speech impediment, is William Golding's 1954 tale of adolescent savagery *Lord of the Flies* (*BSG*, 264). Jason's headmaster may blithely assert 'that the victimization of the few – or even the one – by the many has no place in our school' (*BSG*, 262) but the novel intimates that all levels of 1980s society are in fact structured by this predatory logic.

Thatcherite rapacity is stereotypically embodied by Jason's boorish Uncle Brian, who condemns globalization but revels in the mass bankruptcies that pay for his holidays to the Italian lakes: 'Tell you, I'm grateful to that woman in Downing Street for this financial – what's the latest fad? – anorexia. Us number-crunchers are making a killing! And as partners' bonuses are profit related, yours truly is sitting rather pretty.' (*BSG*, 57). Even his maxim for child rearing is capitalistic: 'Nothing beats the profit motive, right?' (*BSG*, 59). The brutality of this increasingly unfettered capitalism eventually costs Jason's father his job, as he is unfairly denounced by an ambitious protégée. From harshly competitive economic relations and the Falklands/Malvinas war to Jason's bullying and the Black Swan Green villagers' hysterical reaction to a planned travellers' camp, individuals and groups at all levels of society are presented as brutally intolerant towards perceived weakness or outsiders. Jason concludes that 'perhaps mass gang-ups just have a will of their own that swallows up resistance. Maybe gang-ups're as old as hunters in caves.' (*BSG*, 257).[9] Fear and bigotry always have violent consequences: leaders – be they Mrs Thatcher, General Galtieri or the vicar's wife whose anti-traveller invective leaves her basking in 'a standing ovation like a cold man smiling into a bonfire' (*BSG*, 289) – 'can sense what people're afraid of and turn that fear into bows and arrows and muskets and grenades and nukes to use however they want. That's power.' (*BSG*, 288–9).

Attacking Thatcherism as a corrosive force in British life is a common feature of neo-1980s fiction. However, the tone of *Black Swan*

Green's sustained critique has contradictory political connotations. As has been argued, the novel is keenly concerned with delineating the *specific* social and historical contexts of the 1980s through the minutiae of Jason's adolescent life: undermining retro-memory's idealized version of adolescence through remembering the anxieties and losses of modern Britain's transition from welfare capitalism to Thatcherism. However, the text's condemnations of collective violence and nationalistic/militaristic enactments of power are also framed in *transhistorical* terms: the brutal 1980s are a highpoint in the transhistorical cycle of venality and fear that defines Mitchell's work.[10] Thatcherism, with its divisive and authoritarian brand of neoliberalism, is presented as the logical political outcome of a perennially brutal society, or even more problematically of 'human nature' itself (defined as a timeless 'mass gang up' in which only the scale of the weapons changes) rather than as a specific hegemonic project achieved politically, ideologically and through state violence.[11] Troublingly, this argument echoes that of neoliberalism's proponents, who contend that their project is based on natural human values and is therefore inherently ethical. As Thatcher herself stated: 'I willingly grant the influence of free market economists like Friedrich von Hayek and Milton Friedman. But the root of the approach we pursued in the 1980s lay deep in human nature, and more especially the nature of the British people'.[12] A central element of this Thatcherite narrative is the politically resonant figure of childhood:

> [C]hildhood experience and upbringing, Mrs Thatcher's favourite idiom ... offers the poignant, if illusory, promise, of a return to a security that has in later years been lost. As Mrs Thatcher put it in an early interview: 'I want decent, fair, honest, citizen values, all the principles you were brought up with.' (Samuel, 1998: 329)

Through Jason's experiences and perceptions, *Black Swan Green* forcefully suggests that the principles twenty-first-century Britain was 'brought up with' in the 1980s were anything but decent, fair and honest. Instead, it inverts the idyllic political resonances of childhood to signify insecurity, anxiety, and the constant threat and experience of violence: undermining idyllic retro-memory. However, the para-

dox is that in focalizing its critique of Thacterism, through dehistoricized concepts of timeless human savagery and childhood violence,
the novel risks naturalizing the very target of that critique. As Harvey
suggests, neoliberalism can be understood as 'as a failed utopian rhetoric masking a successful project for the restoration of ruling-class
power' (Harvey, 2005: 203–4); *Black Swan Green* problematically
presents the roots of this ideological programme in a depoliticized
notion of perennial 'human nature', albeit one that is dystopian rather
than utopian.

Conclusion

Like the simultaneous evocation/undermining of an idealized 1980s
through rose-tinted retro-memory, this expression of historical critique in transhistorical terms highlights the contradictions that define
Black Swan Green. The novel's criticisms of the 1980s can seem in-
congruous alongside its lovingly materialistic form; and suggestions
that Thatcherism is the logical product of society, rather than being in
many ways imposed upon it, are highly questionable. However, the
fact that these oppositional memories of the recent past cannot be
reconciled or cohered into a singular vision of 'the 1980s' does not
render the novel's *remembering* somehow unsuccessful or invalid. Instead, these contradictions highlight twenty-first-century culture's in-
conclusive and fraught understanding of this decisive – even revolutionary – period for contemporary Britain. In the twenty-first century,
the 1980s signify many different things, often simultaneously. It is the
brutal period of rampant capitalism and selfishness that dismantled
the post-war consensus and laid the foundations for neoliberal *now*.
It is the root of the global financial crisis that has shattered neoliberal
sureties since 2008. It is an object of nostalgic desire; an alluring, simpler time that offers a retreat from the complexities of contemporary
life. It represents a valorised period of ideological conflict – of tan-
gible political oppositions and options – that vanished in the bland
centrism of the 1990s and seems vibrant by contemporary standards.
And it is a ten-year stretch of time that a majority of the British popu-

lation lived through: it is rooted deeply in our personal memories. *Black Swan Green* cannot resolve these contradictory '1980s'. Instead it uneasily juxtaposes them through a strange, disjunctive blend of nostalgia and revisionist political critique, and in doing so demonstrates the inconsistencies that define our twenty-first-century collective memory of that decade.

Mitchell's novel can be critiqued for drawing occasionally crude analogies between historical events and personal stories, as in the chapter 'Rocks', which counterpoints the Falklands conflict with an allegorical dispute over a rockery that reveals Jason's parents' disintegrating marriage. Given childhood's Romantic associations with truth and authenticity, Jason's age also allows the text to display a trite morality: '*I* want to bloody kick this *moronic bloody* world in the bloody *teeth* over and over till it bloody *understands* that *not hurting people* is ten bloody *thousand* times more bloody important than being *right*.' (*BSG*, 149). These examples suggest the limitations of *Black Swan Green's* adolescent narration: the inability to view complex historical events in anything other than intensely personal terms. However, this criticism should be balanced with the understanding that the novel's localizing of global events is a means – arguably the only means – of figuring the personal effects of complex and seemingly abstract geopolitical issues, particularly in an increasingly globalized world. The novel's presentation of the minutiae of life in middle-England emphasizes that this seemingly humdrum environment is in fact deeply enmeshed in Cold War politics and the global socio-economic shifts of neoliberalism. In this sense, *Black Swan Green* undercuts its own parochialism: the novel may be focalized through a solipsistic adolescent, but his narration collapses the neat opposition between local and global. It does this most effectively through its focus on Jason's historically determined experiences and perceptions of his 'everyday' environment. The seemingly quotidian is revealed to be a politically resonant framework that novels can use to challenge idealized retro-memory and remember the complex and troubling dimensions of the 1980s: contemporary Britain's divisive and determining collective childhood.

Notes

1 All quotations from *Black Swan Green* will be indicated parenthetically within the body of the text, with original emphasis.

2 Even focusing on texts that engage with one decade – in this case the 1980s –the volume and range of this cultural production is clear. Fiction not already mentioned in this essay includes Jake Arnott, *He Kills Coppers* (2001); Nicola Barker, *Five Miles From Outer Hope* (2000); Tim Binding, *Anthem* (2004) and *The Champion* (2011); Anthony Cartwright, *How I Killed Margaret Thatcher* (2012); Helen Cross, *My Summer of Love* (2001); Philip Hensher, *The Northern Clemency* (2008); Edward Hogan, *Blackmoor* (2008); Tim Lott, *Rumours of a Hurricane* (2002); Val McDermid, *A Darker Domain* (2008); Denise Mina, *The Dead Hour* (2006); David Peace, *Nineteen Eighty* (2001), *Nineteen Eighty Three* (2002) and *The Damned United* (2006); Joe Stretch, *The Adult* (2012); Cathi Unsworth, *The Singer* (2008) and *Weirdo* (2012). Perhaps the most successful films exploring the 1980s are *Billy Elliot* (dir. Stephen Daldry, 2000), *This is England* (dir. Shane Meadows, 2006) and *The Iron Lady* (dir. Phyllida Lloyd, 2012). Television drama includes *The Falklands Play* (2002), *Ashes to Ashes* (2008–2010), *The Line of Beauty* (2006), *The Long Walk to Finchley* (2008), *Margaret* (2009), *Money* (2010), *Red Riding Trilogy* (2009), *Royal Wedding* (2010), *The Field of Blood* (2011), *This is England '86* (2010), *This is England '88* (2011), and *Worried About the Boy* (2010). Two high profile pieces of visual/performance art are Jeremy Deller's Turner prize-winning re-enactment of *The Battle of Orgreave* (Artangel, 2001) and Marcus Harvey's *White Riot* (White Cube Hoxton, 2009). Some notable plays include Alan Bennett's *The History Boys* (National Theatre, 2004), David Eldridge's *Market Boy* (National Theatre, 2006), Ron Rose's *The Enemies Within* (originally performed at the Bolton Octagon in 1985; revived there in 2009), Robin Soans' *Talking to Terrorists* (Royal Court, 2005), Moria Buffini's *Handbagged* Jack Thorne's *2nd May 1997* (Bush, 2009), Roy Williams' *Sucker Punch* (Royal Court, 2010), *Billy Elliot the Musical* (Victoria Palace Theatre, 2   005–), *Thatcher – The Musical!* (Foursight Theatre Company, 2006) and *The Death of Margaret Thatcher* (Courtyard Theatre, 2008).

3 Margaret Thatcher died in April 2013, while I was revising this essay. The intense and ongoing debate prompted by her death – which ranged immediately from hagiography to vitriol – clearly demonstrates the divisive resonances of the 1980s in twenty-first-century culture. It also evidences

the widespread understanding of the 1980s (and by association, Thatcherism) as a determining period for contemporary Britain. The complex workings of collective memory – contingent on events, intensely politicized and contested, and always iterated through contemporary contexts and cultural production – are also on display in real time: from newspaper editorials and television specials to social media debate and public protest. It is certainly too soon to understand the lasting effects of Thatcher's death on collective understandings of the period: given the parlous state of the UK economy, it could catalyse further debate about the viability of the neoliberal settlement; or (as occurred following the death of her ideological counterpart Ronald Reagan in 2004) she could be blanched of her divisive associations and absorbed into the national pantheon of 'great' leaders. It is perhaps more likely that both narratives will be propagated simultaneously and clash further; with the meaning of the 1980s continuing to be fought over and refigured in contemporary British culture.

4 For elucidation of the influential but too often over-simplified term 'historiographic metafiction', see Hutcheon (1988, 1989).

5 For an influential analysis of nostalgia, late capitalism and postmodernism, see Jameson (1991). The essay 'Nostalgia for the Present' offers a particularly relevant analysis of period detail and contemporary historicity (Jameson, 1991: 279–96).

6 Many reviews of *Black Swan Green*, and much of the scant academic engagement with the novel, focus on its 'structural dissimilarity [...] to Mitchell's earlier and more experimental fiction.' (Dillon, 2011: 4).

7 There is a long cultural tradition of children being understood to be particularly aware and responsive to their natural and material surroundings. For a notable example, see Benjamin (2006: 99–100, 140–2, 152–8).

8 A useful American intertext is political journalist David Sirotta's polemical survey of 1980s popular culture. He argues that there is a direct link between the promotion of militarism in 1980s cultural production aimed at children and adolescents – much of which he asserts was a form of propaganda – and the increasing acceptance of militarism as a 'natural' element of American life (Sirotta, 2011: 139–70).

9 Jason rapidly comes to realize that 'the villagers *wanted* the gypsies to be gross, so the grossness of what they're not acts as a stencil for what the villagers are.' (*BSG*, 288). As Jones shrewdly notes in 'Outfoxing Hangman', Jason appears to have internalized the argument of Edward Said's *Orientalism*. While this theoretical sophistication certainly stretches credulity

in a thirteen year-old narrator, it is representative of Mitchell's theoretically aware (and overt) fiction.

10 This transhistorical vision of violence exemplifies the cyclical model of history that appears throughout Mitchell's interconnected novels, notably in *Cloud Atlas*, which tracks capitalist predation and exploitation from the eighteenth-century slave trade to a post-apocalyptic future. Typically for a Mitchell text, Jason actually encounters a character from *Cloud Atlas* during the course of *Black Swan Green* – Eva, who teaches him French and plays him the work of Robert Frobisher, a composer from the earlier novel who was obsessed with Nietzsche and reincarnation: 'Recurrence is the heart of his music. We live *exactly* the same life, Robert believed, and die *exactly* the same death, again, again, again, to the *same* demi-semiquaver. To eternity.' (*BSG*, 202).

11 For what is still the most persuasive account of Thatcherism, its complex provenance, and its ideologically contradictory 'authoritarian populism' (see Hall, 1983).

12 The quotation is from Margaret Thatcher's speech at the International Free Enterprise Dinner, 20th April 1999, and is sourced from Cartwright (2012: 241).

Works Cited

Anon, 'Britain and the Bomb' (1980) *Daily Mirror* (6 November): 1–11.

Benjamin, Water (1999) *Illuminations*, trans. Harry Zorn. London: Pimlico.

Benjamin, Water (2002) *The Arcades Project*, trans. Eiland, Howard and Kevin McLaughlin. Cambridge, MA: Harvard University Press.

Benjamin, Walter (2006) *Berlin Childhood Around 1900*, trans. Howard Eiland. Cambridge: Belknap Press.

Boym, Svetlana (2001) *The Future of Nostalgia*. New York: Basic Books.

Brooker, Joseph (2005) 'Neo Lines: Alan Hollinghurst and the Apogee of the Eighties', *The Literary Criterion* 40(3–4): 104–16

Brooker, Joseph (2010) *Literature of the 1980s: After the Watershed*. Edinburgh: Edinburgh University Press.

Brown, Bill (2001) 'Thing Theory', *Critical Theory* 28(1): 1–22.

Burn, Gordon (2007) *Best and Edwards: Football, Fame and Oblivion*. London: Faber and Faber.

Burn, Gordon (2008) *Born Yesterday*. London: Faber and Faber.

Collins, Andrew (2003a) *Where did it all go right? Growing up normal in the 70s*. London: Ebury.

Collins, Andrew (2003b) 'Where did it all go right?', accessed June 2012, http://www.wherediditallgoright.com/memories.html

Cartwright, Anthony (2012) *How I Killed Margaret Thatcher*. Birmingham: Tindal Street Press

Dillon, Sarah (2011) 'Introducing David Mitchell's Universe: A Twenty-First Century House of Fiction' in Sarah Dillon (ed.) *David Mitchell: Critical Essays*, pp. 3–23. Canterbury: Gylphi.

Hall, Stuart (1983) *The Hard Road to Renewal: Thacterism and the Crisis of the Left*. London: Verso.

Harrison, M. John (2006) 'Remember the Datsun Cherry', *Times Literary Supplement* (May 28).

Harvey, David (2005) *A Brief History of Neoliberalism*. Oxford: Oxford University Press.

Jameson, Fredric (1991) *Postmodernism or, The Cultural Logic of Late Capitalism*. London: Verso.

Jones, Thomas (2006) 'Outfoxing Hangman', *London Review of Books* 28.9, accessed December 2011, http://www.lrb.co.uk/v28/n09/thomas-jones/outfoxing-hangman

Hutcheon, Linda (1988) *Poetics of Postmodernism*. London: Routledge.

Hutcheon, Linda (1989) *Politics of Postmodernism*, London: Routledge.

McSmith, Andy (2010) *No Such Thing as Society*. London: Constable.

Middleton, Peter and Tim Woods (2000) *Literatures of Memory: History, time and space in postwar writing*. Manchester: Manchester University Press.

Miller, Daniel (2010) *Stuff*. Cambridge: Polity Press.

Mitchell, David (2006a) 'Preface', *The Telegraph*, 29 April, accessed April 2012, http://www.blackswangreen.co.uk/extra_material.html

Mitchell, David (2006b) *Black Swan Green*. London: Sceptre.

Mitchell, Kate (2010) *History and Cultural Memory in Neo-Victorian Fiction*. Basingstoke: Palgrave Macmillan.

Reynolds, Simon (2011) *Retromania: Pop Culture's Addiction to Its Own Past*. London: Faber and Faber.

Samuel, Raphael (1994) *Theatres of Memory Volume 1: Past and Present in Contemporary Culture*. London: Verso.

Samuel, Raphael (1998) *Island Stories: Unravelling Britain, Theatres of Memory*, Volume 2. London: Verso.

Sirotta, David (2011) *Back to Our Future: How the 1980s explain the world we love in now – our culture, our politics, our everything*. New York: Ballatine Books.

Smith, Ali (2006) 'Neither sweet nor as simple', *The Telegraph,* 14th May, accessed April 2012, http://www.telegraph.co.uk/culture/books/3652162/Neither-sweet-nor-as-simple.html

Stone, Dan (2010) 'Beyond the Mnemosyne Institute: The Future of Memory after the Age of Commemoration', in Richard Crownshaw, Jan Kilby and Anthony Rowland (eds) *The Future of Memory,* pp. 17–36. New York and Oxford: Berhahn Books.

ALL GREAT HOUSES RESEMBLE CRIMES
ISSUES OF HOUSING IN THE TEXTS OF GORDON BURN, DAVID PEACE AND ANDREW O'HAGAN

Rhona Gordon

Rachel Whiteread's *House* (1993), which was in existence between October 1993 and January 1994, was the solid concrete cast of a condemned Victorian terraced house. It was a house that was not a house, a space that could not be entered and that would offer no shelter. *House* reflects the dichotomy present in ideas of late twentieth century housing and displays the paradox of domesticity and danger, the uncanny made real. The work raises issues of home ownership and what can and should be done with the physical premises that become a house. Do houses provide shelter or concealment? Or both? How do issues of class become inscribed in the buildings we call home? These tensions can be seen in the novels and non-fiction texts of Gordon Burn, David Peace and Andrew O'Hagan and in particular Burn's *Happy Like Murderers* (1998) and *Somebody's Husband, Somebody's Son* (1984), Peace's *Red Riding Quartet* (1999–2002) and O'Hagan's *Our Fathers* (1999).

Jamie Bawn, the narrator in O'Hagan's *Our Fathers*, argues that; 'The greatest domestic issue of our poor century. Housing' (*OF*, 156). Indeed the latter half of the twentieth century saw huge changes in housing policy throughout Great Britain. From a post war boom and slum clearances through to the Thatcher government's right to buy

109

policy, the idea that everyone should be home owners gained increasing prominence while, conversely, council houses were sold to their occupants. At the end of the twentieth century the Modernist tower blocks built to house large sections of the working class were largely associated with crime, violence and poverty. Houses, as shall be seen, became contested political spaces and the link between corrupt practices that informed the construction of houses and the subsequent disregard that tower blocks inhabitants show their dwellings will be explored. Furthermore the link between crimes committed by powerful bodies and the crimes committed by home owners will be examined as there is the suggestion that there is something within the idea of modern housing that creates a space for crimes to be committed.

Philip Tew argues that the election of Margaret Thatcher, and the circumstances that allowed her rise to power, signalled a significant change in all aspects of modern life:

> In terms of culture, politics, world affairs, identity politics, and creativity the 1970s represent both a watershed and a period of fundamental change for Britain, one that in retrospect, can be seen to rival and not be simply an extension of changes brought about by the end of the Second World War. (Tew, 2007)

It is this period in history that Burn, Peace and O'Hagan seek to re-examine in the closing decades of the twentieth and early twenty first century and all explore the ways in which the idea of what constituted a home radically altered under Thatcher's leadership.

The state of the housing market at the end of the twentieth century can be traced back to the 1960s. The Conservative Party's Housing policies after 1964 were created to avoid, as much as possible, subsidizing those who were not in need and to begin to sell council houses at market value. When the Conservatives returned to Government in 1970 they removed the restrictions that has been placed on the sale of council houses in 1968 and also deregulated rent levels so that, in their thinking, market forces would make better use of the housing stock with supply and demand being met. Yet what actually happened was a rise in unscrupulous landlords who were able to charge whatever they liked in terms of rent and which, in turn, led to a decrease in new built houses:

> Rather than freeing the market and releasing the natural forces of demand and supply an increase in house prices and rise in interest rates had led to a slump in private building. Not only were fewer tenants coming forward to buy their existing houses but fewer households of all types were willing and able to buy. The effective demand for house purchase had declined and local authority housing waiting lists had lengthened alarmingly. In 1974 it was reported that 30,000 newly built houses remained unsold compared with a norm of some 10,000. The number of house completions in 1973 was 294,000 – the lowest figure since 1959. (Forrest and Murie, 1998)

The 1970s saw significant changes in housing policies, by both major political parties, that eventually paved the way for the Conservative government's Right to Buy policies in the 1980s. After the slum clearance of the 1950s and tower block building of the 1960s, successive Housing Acts of the 1970s centralized housing policy leading to a loss of local autonomy. The Housing Act 1972 began to remove restrictions on selling houses. In 1974 Margaret Thatcher, then spokesperson on the Environment promised nine and a half per cent mortgage interest rates, the abolition of rates and a Bill to enforce the sale of council houses. New polices were developed to increase the number of houses that were owner occupied including mortgages becoming more easily available as well as loan schemes, and equity sharing making it easier than ever before to own your own home. Alongside the increased drive to have people buy their own home, the image of council housing was becoming increasingly negative. This was in part due to the drab nature of relatively new tower blocks combined with subsequent Conservative propaganda and it ceased to matter that the majority of council properties were houses with gardens. These policies can be traced back to the post-war Conservative government who sought to create a property-owning democracy.

In 1979, the newly elected Conservative government radically changed its approach to council houses from one of lack of interest to complete restructuring. The Government's success was widely put down to their housing policies, which included the right for council tenants to buy their homes. Indeed their election campaign was dominated by housing issues:

> The Conservative manifesto of 1979 referred to housing under the heading 'Helping the Family' and devoted one and a half pages to it – more than to social security or education or health or welfare or the elderly or the disabled. The issues referred to under housing were principally about ownership and the sale of council houses and no reference at all was made to the investment in new building or improvement or to homelessness or housing need. (Forrest and Murie, 1998)

The point of all this, argued Prime Minister Thatcher was to advance towards:

> Making a reality of Anthony Eden's dream of a property-owning democracy. It will do something else – it will give to more of our people the prospect of handing something on to their children and grandchildren which owner occupation provides. (Forrest and Murie, 1998)

Property ownership is re-configured as a marker of success, a visible legacy to be passed on to future generations. A clear divide was engineered between those with success and ambition, the middle classes, and those people who cannot join this 'democracy' – the lower working classes. As a result of these polices ideas of types of dwellers have proliferated. Home owners tend to be middle-class professionals, renters are young, possibly unemployed while those in council housing are often in the worst of social conditions.

Tenants who refused to buy their own homes faced increasing rents that in some cases rose above their potential mortgage payments. This had a huge impact on Britain's economy as by 1986 discounts on council houses came to £5.6bn, vastly below market value (Forrest and Murie, 1998). The sale of council houses mirrored what was happening throughout society in the 1980s with the sale of British Telecom, British Gas and Jaguar, among other companies, signalling the way industry was increasingly being privatized in the name of a creating a more productive and profitable business sector and society as a whole.

While Burn, Peace and O'Hagan examine issues of housing over the last quarter of the twentieth century strikingly similar issues are still prevalent in the early twenty-first century with housing remaining a hot political issue. Due to the widespread sale of council houses, and the lack of replacement buildings, the opening decades of the twenty-first century experienced a housing shortage which has lead to a market that is generationally skewed in favour of older generations. In 2010, the *Observer* noted that:

> Since 1997, under a Labour government, 481,530 council homes have been sold off. By contrast, in the region with the greatest social housing need, Yorkshire and the Humber, just 24 council homes have been built in the same period. (MacShane, 2010)

Young people and first time buyers found it increasingly difficult to get onto the housing market. The Conservative-Liberal Democrat coalition government, under Prime Minister David Cameron, sought to manage the housing crisis by numerous contentious plans that typified their political bias including potentially stopping immigrants from gaining immediate access to social housing (Tapsfield, 2013) and proposing scrapping housing benefits for under-25s, though this was eventually dropped (Helm and Stewart, 2012). As shall be discussed houses provide the impetus and locale for criminal acts, criminal acts that find parallels decades later in the cases of Shannon Matthews, Natascha Kampusch and Josef Fritzl.

Issues of home ownership, and crimes that are committed within a house, are the central themes in Gordon Burn's 1998 non-fiction literary account *Happy Like Murderers* which details the home life and eventual arrest of serial killers Fred and Rosemary West. Over a period of twenty years, from 1967–87, Fred and Rose murdered at least twelve young women as well as assaulting numerous other victims. The central character of the text is 25 Cromwell Street the final home of the Wests and the place where they carried out the majority of their murders. Andrew O'Hagan in *The Missing* (1995), a source of *Happy Like Murderers*, notes of the Wests' victims who lodged at Cromwell

Street, 'Most of them just wanted a nice home' (*TM*, 239). As Burn demonstrates this could also be equally true of Fred and Rose West. Fred, and to a lesser extent Rose, is shown by Burn to be obsessed with owning the three storey building on Cromwell Street. The house was inspiration for their crimes, and is both blamed and offered as explanation by Fred when questioned by the police. When asked by he and Rose assaulted Carol Raine, then working as his nanny, he answers: 'All I want is to buy the house and settle down' (*HLM*, 69).

Burn repeats the phrase 'Real owners of a real house' (*HLM*, 196) throughout his narrative and indeed the text mimics Fred's obsession with 25 Cromwell Street and just as Fred gave impromptu tours to unsuspecting visitors, Burn gives his reader multiple tours around Cromwell Street and offers continual updates on the state of the property as Fred makes constant home improvements. We are also given a history of the house going back several generations and Rose's thoughts on the interior decor. Indeed to understand Fred, Burn argues that you must understand 25 Cromwell Street. The perverted and murderous goings on in the house were an expression of Fred's mind, his fantasies acted out. In loving the house he loves himself and gains affirmation of his self and his place in the world as Burn argues the house was his all consuming focus, 'He invested everything he was and had in it. He had an impoverished, perverted and murkily complex interior life' (*HLM*, 185). This is a dark take on Gaston Bachelard's argument that 'the house shelters daydreaming, the house allows one to dream in peace' as 'the house is one of the greatest powers of integration for the thoughts, memories and dreams of mankind' (Bachelard, 1994). Twenty-five Cromwell Street allows a space for murderous dreams to become reality.

But why should this house mean so much to the Wests? Or indeed to their victims? During the 1950s and 1960s the idea of class was changing in Britain as was the idea that you were tied to the class you were born into. In post-war Britain social boundaries were loosening as employment and education allowed increasing social mobility. For a working class family, like the Wests, a lower working class family at that, the three-storey house in Cromwell Street was a way to transcend their social class. Working class families were able to purchase their own homes, in part due to increased personal earning and the Governmental polices put in place to encourage home ownership. Post war Britain saw a huge rise in personal consumption that would extend to the buying of property:

> During these years, total production (measured at constant prices) increased by 40 per cent, average earnings (allowing for inflation) by 30 per cent, while personal consumption, measured in terms of ownership of cars and televisions, rose from 2 ¼ million to 8 million and 1 million to 13 million respectively. (Hill, 1995)

What can be seen here are the beginnings of conspicuous consumerism marking success and homes as huge visual signifiers of accomplishment. The image projected to the outside world was key. What Burn makes clear is how the Wests were obsessed with outside respectability but could neither voluntarily nor involuntarily take this respectability in their private life. They were interested in materially advancing themselves but not socially and intellectually. By owning their own home the Wests were able to exploit the respectability of a seemingly middle-class life. Carol Raine, while living with the Wests notes that the image they projected bore no relation to their inner lives; 'It was just a rather lived-in house. It was quite tatty; nothing has been done. A little man trying to be a big man. That was Carol's verdict on the husband' (*HLM*, 45).

Yet it is this veneer of middle-class respectability that allowed the Wests to carry out their crimes for so long as it is implicit that homeowners would not be involved in the disappearance or murder of young women. It is this cloak of respectability the Wests hide behind and exploit. Twenty-five Cromwell Street afforded Fred West a privacy he relished, a space hidden from the public in which he could act as he pleased and which allowed him to drawn in and exploit an ever-moving population. On the discovery of the multiple missing girls below the Wests' floorboards O'Hagan argued that Britain seemed to be broken, 'Gloucester, and Britain beyond, seemed suddenly like a kingdom of broken nets, lost connections, social incohesion, and traps' (*TM*, 198). It was this 'broken net' that Burn argues Fred exploited: 'Community strangles ... He had a strong inclination to be private and unobserved. Community throttles' (*HLM*, 115). Home ownership allowed the Wests to be part of the community but operate unnoticed.

As well as providing a front to the outside world the house itself is a dangerous agent in the continual acts of abuse that Rose inflicted upon her children: 'She would use anything; knives, belts. The house itself – walls, ceilings, windows, doors – could be a weapon' (*HLM*, 240). This is one of the numerous occasions of the uncanny, of the familiar made unfamiliar, the homely made unhomely, which can be seen throughout Burn's text and indeed in all three writers' works. The Wests' story is one that is highly uncanny as all their actions are seemingly normal from an outsider's point of view – married with children, homeowners and members of the community. Yet their secrets continually threaten to spill into public view. One definition of the uncanny is that which 'applies to everything that was intended to remain secret, hidden away, and has come into the open' (Freud, 2003). The Wests' lives are full of secrets that would eventually be exposed and Burn depicts the horrible juxtaposition between the banality of everyday and the consequences of murder as Fred would: 'sit on the edge of the bath and talk to him across the space of a dead girl's body' (*HLM*, 210). Fred himself is an uncanny individual. Freud explains how people can be uncanny:

> We can also call a living person uncanny, that is to say, when we credit him with evil intent. But this alone is not enough: it must be added that this intent to harm us is realized with the help of special powers …. The uncanny effect of epilepsy or madness has the same origin. Here the layman sees a manifestation of forces that he did not suspect in a fellow human being, but whose stirrings he can dimly perceive in remote corners of his own personality. (Freud, 2003)

Evil alongside intent and madness combine to create the uncanny personality and it is notable that Fred was obsessed with rendering his home, the scene of many crimes, as the locale of safety for his family and making the strange and unfamiliar, in a reversal of the uncanny, familiar. The Wests' children were conditioned to believe that danger was outside, further trapping them inside with the real danger of their parents: 'Inside was safe and outside was full of dangers' (*HLM*, 184).

The origin of the uncanny links back to the male fear of the female body, Freud argued that female reproductive organs are uncanny, both familiar and unfamiliar, for men: 'what they find uncanny is actually the entrance to man's old "home", the place where everyone once lived ... Here too, the uncanny is what was once familiar' (Freud, 2003). Fred's interrogation of the female body is located within an age-old male fear of the uterus. Hélène Cixous has described the female body as the 'uncanny stranger on display' (Cixous, 1985) and Sawday explains this fear as:

> The focus of this fear was the uterus, an organ held to possess a will of its own, 'a separate animal creature housed inside a woman.' ... Like disease, the uterus operated according to its own laws, travelled at its own pace, hid itself from the searching gaze of natural scientists, and demonstrated its presence by a token: blood (Sawday, 1995).

The case of the Wests is a conflation of the uncanny in both senses of the word – of the homely made unhomely and of the male fear of the female reproductive organs.

It is within his home that Fred and Rose carry out the majority of their violent attacks on women as the site of the uncanny becomes a place to investigate and expel the uncanny body. Fred's constant house renovations took place at the same time as he was murdering women and both the house and women take the brunt of his controlling obsessions. In describing Fred exploring Rose's vagina, Burn references Freud:

> The opening to a strange and secret place. This *unheimlich* place which is the entrance to the former home of all human beings. The place where Fred lived once upon a time and in the beginning. A place of unaccounted secrets and horrors. (*HLM*, 212)

Fred seeks to explore spaces that are not his and expose the secrets and horrors, as he sees it, within. The domestic space was traditionally a woman's place and in remodelling the house he is demonstrating his control over the female body.

So, it was more than a house for Fred, it was his whole world, his life's work, and in destroying the house the police had tried to destroy him and his whole internal world. When the police finally arrest Fred and Rose, and search for bodies, they dig up the back garden and the cellar. Fred acts like he has been physically wounded when he sees the destruction carried out by the police: 'He kept falling off the duckboards that had been laid across the garden. Sliding in the mud. It didn't look like his house' (*HLM*, 373).

Burns' text ends with 25 Cromwell Street being demolished and turned into a pathway. It was decided not to fill the space so it appears as a negative gap – a space where a house should stand. An uncanny pathway that is not a pathway. *Happy Like Murderers* ends where it began with the consideration of the house. Twenty-five Cromwell Street now demolished, Burn details the building work that took place to turn the wreckage into a public walkway: 'They installed "Urbis" – model lamp columns painted gloss black and "Son-T" lanterns on five-metre steel columns' (*HLM*, 388). The attention to detail is reminiscent of Fred's obsessive re-building and it is as if his presence still occupies some temporal space. Even without the house the memory of him lingers on as Burn makes the point, in the closing lines of the novel, the empty space is a continual reminder of what is missing: 'A country lane introduced to the city … Underneath is the cellar void. And under the cellar five cores of concrete buried in Severn clay. The fact of something behind. It imposes itself and won't go away (*HLM*, 388). A house-shaped space, where the house is missing, which recalls, inversely, Rachel Whiteread's *House*. While *House* made concrete what was missing, the walkway acts as a negative, a potential space that seeks to hide what was originally there. In solidifying a negative space, a house that does not exist, *House* signifies that a negative space is just as effective in memorializing what is not there and acts as a visible reminder of previous lives. Similarly the walkway, which contains nothing, has the power of memory in its ordinary nothingness as the imprint on the house lingers long after the physical premises has been destroyed.

This link between houses and crimes can be seen throughout David Peace's *Red Riding Quartet*. In the *Quartet* there is no escape, no safe spaces, from the terrors outside and homes offer no shelter from the outside world. The collected title of the *Quartet* hints at the wolf that lurks within the home and threatens to consume those who knock at the door. In *Nineteen Seventy Four* journalist Eddie Dunford remembers, 'Barry Gannon had one said something like, "All great buildings resemble crimes"' (*1974*, 82). This recalls the idea that 'All property is theft' and foreshadows the link between social crimes against sections of society and violent crimes against individuals that recur throughout the *Quartet*.

As with *Happy Like Murderers* danger lurks indoors and offers no protection to the horrors of the outside world. The idea that danger lurks in houses has a long history from Gothic literature of Edgar Allan Poe to Agatha Christie mysteries. Sherlock Holmes, travelling to the Hampshire countryside, in 'The Adventure of the Copper Beeches', explains to Watson:

> You look at these scattered houses, and you are impressed by their beauty. I look at them, and the only thought which comes to me is a feeling of their isolation and of the impunity with which crime may be committed there. .. It is my belief Watson, founded upon my experience, that the lowest and vilest alleys in London do not present a more dreadful record of sin than does the smiling and beautiful countryside (Conan Doyle, 1981).

Peace carries on this idea that houses hide crimes as corrupt house construction that is at the heart of the *Red Riding Quartet* with illicit deals between the police, councillor William Shaw, construction owner Bob Foster and architect John Dawson: 'Dawsongate: Local Government money for private housing; substandard materials for council housing; back-handers all round' (*1974*, 37). Councillor T. Dan Smith and architect John Poulson haunt the *Red Riding Quartet*. As the *Quartet* begins Poulson was sentenced to five years in jail in 1974 for fraud, in particular relating to the bribery of T. Dan Smith, and other government officials as it was discovered that that building contracts were awarded illegally. *Nineteen Seventy Seven* mentions Poulson's release and suggests there is one rule for those with power and influence and one rule for everyone else. These corrupt practices take place against a backdrop of changing housing policies as we see local councils selling off houses to private companies. The *Red Riding Quartet* maps the changing landscape of British housing. Mrs Ridyard describes the view from her window: '"There was a lovely view before they put them new houses up." I looked out of the window, across the road, at the new houses that had spoilt the view and no longer looked so new' (*1974*, 30) and 'Brunt Street, Castleford. One side pre-war terrace, the other more recent semi-deatched' (*1974*, 55).

Alongside housing, the focal point of the corrupt scheme was a shopping centre: 'It was all for a shopping centre, The Swan Centre' (*1974*, 288). In order to create a space for the proposed shopping centre, police burned a local gypsy camp down. The disregard for a vulnerable, arguably poor, section of society is symbolic of changes that were happening at political policy-making level. As a result, argues Peace, these unregulated spaces are able to shelter crimes, 'Under those beautiful new carpets, between the cracks and the stones' (*1974*, 276). These spaces allow for murder to be hidden, both in terms of hiding bodies and concealing the perpetrators. Watching over the skeletons of the houses, Dawson and his colleagues also watch over the bones of the missing girls. This motif is repeated in *Nineteen Eighty* when Mrs Ridyard shouts that she sees her daughter under the new carpets, 'She is pointing at the new and detached houses across the road' (*1980*, 251).

The idea of houses as uncanny structures is signified by the swan motif, which is present throughout all architect John Dawson's work. His home, Shangrila, is an ostentatious bungalow rumoured to have cost half a million pounds and it looks like a sleeping swan, while his brother lives in 'Little Cygnet'. This swan imagery extends to the mental institution that journalist Jack Whitehead enters into; it is a 'huge old house squatting back from the road amongst the bare trees and empty nests, its modern wings extending out into the shadows' (*1980*, 111). In Celtic and Greek mythology Swans have been long been associated with death and Dawson's houses are the visual representations of the corruption and death they are built on. Yet what was it that captured the public's imagination? Was it the ambition, the artistry or the fact that someone could own this symbol of middle class aspiration?

It is against this backdrop of corruption that the Yorkshire Ripper is operating. Burn explores the link between the Ripper and housing, in *Somebody's Husband, Somebody's Son*, foreshadowing concerns that would appear in his study of the Wests. *Somebody's Husband* is divided into parts that relate to houses – Part One – House, Part Two – Room, Part Three – Other Rooms. Burn's text provides a history of twentieth-century housing and details the Sutcliffe family's various houses from slum to terrace to owner–occupier in the suburbs.

Nicole Ward Jouve in her study of the Yorkshire Ripper makes the connection that Sutcliffe's attacks against women increased when he and Sonia were in the process of buying their first home at 6 Garden Lane, Bradford: 'Seven murders or attempted murders in 11 months', the period corresponding to the purchase of the 'dream house. Nine in just over a year, the best year they've ever had in terms of their career prospects and social ascent' (Ward Jouve, 1986).

The house at Garden Lane becomes emblematic of a new founded domesticity and, arguably femininity, which Sutcliffe was driven to destroy. With the rise of capitalism, the idea of the home becomes linked with domesticity, and by extension, women as, 'with the rise of industry, material production was "split" between its socialized forms (commodity production) and the private (unpaid) labour of wives in the home' (Ward Jouve, 1986). Homes as symbols of female domesticity were being eroded by women working. Yet for Sutcliffe's generation it was no longer necessary for women to become housewives, indeed Sonia had a career as a teacher. With the home space becoming less recognizably female and political ideologies increasing the focus on home ownership and ideas of social climbing this in turn meant homes became increasingly loaded symbols of desire and uncertainty.

On moving into 6 Garden Lane the neighbours' reactions to the new couple typify the emerging connection between middle class respectability and home ownership. Sutcliffe inadvertently causes offence when parking his 32-ton truck outside his new home. The neighbours complain: 'This is residential. It's not one of these new estates' (*SHSS*, 177). Sutcliffe is put in his social place and this exchange demonstrates how closely ideas of class are transcribed on homes.

When Sutcliffe was eventually caught, both Sutcliffe's friends and family express their shock in relation to home ownership: 'When they heard, Laurie Ashton and his wife, Cath … couldn't believe it was the same Peter Sutcliffe they knew, now living in a £35,000 house in Heaton' (*SHSS*, 288). For Sutcliffe's brother:

> 'He had everything going for him,' Carl found himself thinking obsessively, and then repeating aloud. 'Nice house, steady job, enough money, good looking [….] He was totally different to what I imagined this murderer to be'. (*SHSS*, 289)

Again there is the idea that crime happens elsewhere, it does not happen to or is carried out by middle-class homeowners in respectable areas of the city.

Sonia Sutcliffe denied there was a connection between her home and her husband's crimes and was emphatic that her home life was unblemished: 'It's my home and I have worked to make it beautiful. Nothing bad has ever happened to me here. No grisly murders were committed here and no bodies buried. It is not a house of horrors but a very nice home' (*SSSH*, 350). One of the few opinions that Burn offers in the texts strenuously denies this and argues that the house was key to the crimes and to say otherwise was to ignore the facts:

> the knife which had been used to murder Helen Rytka and then returned to the kitchen drawer where her husband had found it; the blood splattered clothes he washed in the kitchen sink … and the trousers Sutcliffe was wearing when he attempted to decapitate Jean Jordan on the night of the house-warming party at the Garden Lane, which he later buried in the garden. (*SSSH*, 350)

As with the Wests, Sutcliffe's home, therefore, was central in concealing his crimes literally and also in providing him with a facade of middle class respectability.

That houses can be used in this way is a result of the changes in twentieth-century housing that run from policy making to construction. Peace makes reference to T. Dan Smith and John Poulson and the mechanisms of power that have informed the creation of mass housing, and Andrew O'Hagan in his first novel *Our Fathers* fully explores the powers that created social housing and the resulting consequences, in his novel which can be read as a eulogy for modernist building projects.

The novel charts the reforms of fictional Glasgow City Councillor Hugh Bawn, housing supremo, known as Mr Housing. Taking up the mantle from his mother's post-war housing campaigns, Bawn became famous for constructing tower block as quickly and cheaply as possible. O'Hagan fictionalizes the creation of mass housing that was constructed in the Gorbals area of Glasgow and throughout the West coast of Scotland. In a telling statement, Bawn 'invented a motto for the City Housing Department: "The maximum number of houses in the shortest possible time"' (*OF*, 117). For him 'Le Corbusier was an honorary Scot' (*OF*, 145). The number of people living in high-rise tower blocks rose significantly in the 1960s and 1970s. Indeed between 1955 and 1975 an estimated 440, 000 flats were built in the UK, the vast majority in response to slum clearances and 90 per cent constructed in urban areas (Shapely, 2008). In terms of proportions of population movement:

> While the proportion of approved tenders which were in blocks of flats of five storeys or more averaged 6.9% annually from 1953 to 1959, it rose to 25.7% in 1966 and fell to 9.8%, dwelling in blocks of flats of less than five storeys rose from 27% in 1967 to 38% in 1970. (Forrest and Murie, 1998)

The West of Scotland saw numerous high-rise estates built from the 1960s onwards in cities and also in the New Towns that lay outside Glasgow. Some of the most notorious were built in the Gorbals, Glasgow such as the Queen Elizabeth flats, designed by Basil Spence, which began construction in 1961 and after found to be poorly built and asbestos ridden, were eventually destroyed in 1993. As will be explored, O'Hagan's text is a eulogy to Modernist housing that examines the social crimes that were inflicted on a generation by corrupt officials who thought they knew what was best for the working class communities they sought to re-order.

The fate of these substandard flats is detailed by O'Hagan. Less than forty years after they are constructed they are condemned as unfit for human habitation and Hugh's grandson Jamie is in charge of knocking down the flats his grandfather built. Modernist housing was meant to provide a place for working class communities to thrive and a place that signalled equality. Yet the striking appearance of the tower block, different from all other houses meant that their appearance signalled the difference of the inhabitants:

> It could be argued that Modern housing has from its inception run counter to the growth of individualism which has resulted from the differentiation of labour in modern society. Modern architects tried to apply the criteria of mass production to housing in the form of standardisation, uniformity and economies of scale. However, in the sphere of consumption commodities ... exactly the opposite of the principles applied to Modern housing. (Brindley, 1999)

O'Hagan describes how modern housing increasingly did not meet the needs of the occupants, as the idea of what a home should comprise of was changing as there was a shift from a home being merely a safe, clean living space to being a place of leisure with a garden, room to socialize and decorated in a way to reflect the inner life of the inhabitants. Original occupants of the high-rise buildings praise their design: 'Demolish all the prefabs and get on with the high flats. To hell with the gardens. Homes are all that matter here' (*OF*, 121). And here is one of the crux's of modern housing – the quick fixes of the 1960s were conceived with no real thought for the potential inhabitants, many of them working class. The planners envisioned none of the ways of living that are now taken as standard and did not appreciate the massive changes that were occurring in technology. They thought: 'Nothing of satellite telly and dining rooms. People wanted to be like other people. And now they want to be themselves. They want garages and trips abroad and a different-coloured door' (*OF*, 192). What the planners failed to see was the political manoeuvrings that would allow houses, and not high-rise flats, to be become the symbols of better living. They failed to see how issues of class would be inscribed so deeply in our homes.

By the time the narrative of *Our Fathers* reaches the 1990s there are allegations, not just of substandard building practices, but of corruption; 'You know his picture's been in the paper. There's a court-thing in Glasgow. They're trying to say he ... misappropriated money. It's a load of rubbish' (*OF*, 135). Recalling the case of T. Dan Smith and John Poulson, it seems as if there is something about the nature of mass house building that attracts corruption at a higher level and suggests the question, if the housing was not for the working class would the powerful agencies involved be as corruptible? The possibility of Hugh's illegal dealings, and the question of how far do corrupt acts impede into everyday life, is raised when Jamie finds that his grandparents' electricity meter has been rigged: 'The electricity meter caught my eye as I came up. The wheel wasn't moving. A length of twisted coat-hanger was threaded through the box, holding the wheel at a stop' (*OF*, 174).

Yet Hugh's illegal practices, actual and suspected, are problematized as throughout the narrative Hugh is continually shown to believe in his housing revolutions and did genuinely believe he was doing good for the working class communities he served. Hugh ends up living in a flat in one of his high tower creations until he dies, faithful to his ideas until the end. This mirrors T. Dan Smith's post-prison life as Smith moved into the poorly constructed high-rise blocks Cruddas Towers in Newcastle, which he helped to commission and create.

A question that runs throughout the narrative is how can people be expected to take care of their dwellings when no care has been invested in the initial planning or construction. O'Hagan argues that, 'We shape our buildings, afterwards they shape us. The sliding door of the 'Evens' lift was trapped in a mangled pram' (*OF*, 69). Here the working classes' lack of power is seen as their needs are ascribed to them and they themselves are not consulted. It is this examination of the prizing of middle-class needs at the expense of the working classes that unites the texts of Burn, Peace and O'Hagan.

The complex relationship between houses and the people that dwell within them is exposed. In the last half of the twentieth century, issues of housing have been bound closely with issue of class. Huge ideological changes meant ownership equalled success however in the case of Fred and Rosemary West and the Yorkshire Ripper Stuart Sutcliffe home ownership was able to inspire and hide crimes. Aswell as sheltering criminals, political and powerful agencies were able to exploit housing that was largely designed for the working class. As can be seen in all three writers works, political agencies create our housing and as a result our behaviour and sense of place in the world is moulded, sometimes with extreme consequences.

Works Cited

Bachelard, Gaston (1994) *The Poetics of Space*. Boston, MA: Beacon Press.

Brindley,Tim (1999) 'The Modern House in England An Architecture of Exclusion', in Tony Chapman and Jenny Hockey (eds) *Ideal Homes? Social change and domestic*, pp. 30–43. London and New York: Routledge.

Burn, Gordon (1998) *Happy Like Murderers*. London: Faber and Faber.

Cixous, Hélène (1985) The Laugh of the Medusa', in Elaine Marks and Isabelle de Courtivron (eds) *New French Feminisms*, pp. 245–70. Brighton: The Harvester Press.

Conan Doyle, Arthur (1981) 'The Adventure of the Copper Breeches', in *The Penguin Sherlock Holmes*, pp. 316–34. London: Penguin Books.

Forrest, Ray and Alan Murie (1998) *Selling the Welfare State: The Privatisation of Public Housing*. London: Routledge.

Freud, Sigmund (2003) *The Uncanny*. London: Penguin Books.

Helm, Toby and Heather Stewart (2012) 'George Osborne set to drop plan to end housing benefit for under-25s', *Observer*, 2 December, accessed April 2013, http://www.guardian.co.uk/politics/2012/dec/02/george-osborne-housing-benefit-under-25s

Hill, John (1995) *Sex, Class and Realism: British Cinema 1956–1963*. London: British Film Institute.

MacShane, Denis (2010) 'Can David Cameron match Harold Macmillan's achievement in house-building?', *Observer*, 15 August, accessed April 2013, http://www.guardian.co.uk/uk/2010/aug/15/social-housing-shortage-cameron

O'Hagan, Andrew (1995) *The Missing*. London: Faber and Faber.

O'Hagan, Andrew (1999) *Our Fathers*. London: Faber and Faber.

Peace, David (1999) *Nineteen Seventy Four*. London: Serpent's Tail.

Peace, David (2000) *Nineteen Seventy Seven*. London: Serpent's Tail.

Peace, David (2001) *Nineteen Eighty*. London: Serpent's Tail.

Peace, David (2002) *Nineteen Eighty Three*. London: Serpent's Tail.

Sawday, Jonathan (1995) *The Body Emblazoned*. London and New York: Routledge.

Shapely, Peter (2008) 'Social Housing and Tenant Participation', *History and Policy*, accessed 27 May 2009, http://www.historyandpolicy.org/papers/policy-paper-71.html

Tapsfield, James (2013) 'David Cameron to announce tougher test for social housing, including keeping immigrant families off council house waiting lists for five years', *Independent*, 24 March, accessed April 2013, http://www.independent.co.uk/news/uk/politics/david-cameron-to-announce-tougher-tests-for-social-housing-including-keeping-immigrant-families-off-council-house-waiting-lists-for-five-years-8547330.html

Tew, Philip (2007) *The Contemporary British Novel*. London and New York: Continuum.

Ward Jouve, Nicole (1986) *The Streetcleaner: The Yorkshire Ripper on Trial*. London and New York: Marion Boyars Publishers.

Hilary Mantel and the Historical Novel

Sara Knox

Three years before Hilary Mantel's coup with *Wolf Hall*, scholar Suzanne Keen identified the cultural and economic preconditions in the United Kingdom for a comeback of literary historical fiction: changes to the National Curriculum that had lead to greater emphasis on the teaching of history using methods peripheral to the discipline (the popularity, for instance, of novels as content vehicles for engendering student interest) and, more importantly, 'a booming heritage industry's focus on a positive, marketable past capable of inspiring patriotism and attracting tourists' (Keen, 2005: 167). While hardly seeing the Tudor world as a 'positive' past,[1] Mantel seems to have been conscious of the marketability of a Tudor story. The quincentenary of Henry VIII's coronation was looming, and it 'would be a very big deal in England'. So much so, that it might 'be difficult to sell a book about Henry after that, when everyone was sick of him' (Mantel cited in MacFarquhar, 2012: 55). The public already had Philippa Gregory's bestselling *The Other Boleyn Girl* and the Showtime television production *The Tudors* to contend with – how much more of that great, and great-girthed monarch, could it stand? At the point that Hilary Mantel was contemplating her Tudor story, she was already a well-respected novelist. Her weighing of the wisdom of timing for the new project reveals something of the rigours of writing historical fiction: the demands the genre makes even before word is put to page. It is an

activity that taxes scholarship as well as craft, for the facts of the matter *matter*. Mantel's caution – her weighing of the moment – suggests
a sense for the riskiness inherent in all new projects, but more specifically the risks of embarking upon a literary historical novel when the
lights of that genre had been waning for a century: the pre-eminence
that had once defined the possibilities of the novel long since past.
But within a few years the critical and popular success of *Wolf Hall*
and *Bring Up the Bodies* had returned to the literary historical novel
at least part of its earlier cachet: a situation that makes the case for a
closer look at Hilary Mantel as a writer of historical fiction, and for a
consideration of the state of the genre today.[2]

What the literary historical novel is, and what it should or shouldn't
do, are questions that have exercised critics, readers and authors from
the period of the genre's triumph to that of its decline. Canvassing
the attitude of his contemporaries in the interwar period, Ernest Bernbaum found that empiricism and literary naturalism had done for
the historical novel and for its criticism alike (1926). Not since Ha-
zlitt had anyone made 'an explicit statement of its nature, a defense
of its being' so that the genre 'lay exposed, like any nation, person,
institution, or type, that does not know its deepest self, to this devastating question: what rational right have you to exist?' (Bernbaum,
1926: 428). Tarred by the brush of melodrama, then by the failure to
address the momentous 'now' (and the 'here', as exemplified by the
modernist exercise of 'stream of consciousness' narrative point view,
à *la* Joyce), the historical novel was further insulted by a line of materialist criticism – most recently articulated by Perry Anderson – that
sees it as a product of romantic nationalism. In this way the preemi-
nent novel of the genre at its height, *War and Peace*, fails as an exem-
plar because Tolstoy stages a 'conflict ... that lacks any truly imagined adversary' so that 'the enemy remains essentially abstract. Not
a concrete figuration of two contending historical forces' (Anderson,
2011). In other words, the novel does not do the judicious work that
defines the historical imagination. Neither could the 'rational right'
of the genre to exist be established by 'mere' popularity, nor by the
pragmatic needs of the novelist (Harriet Martineau: why not 'derive
the plot ... from actual life, where the work is achieved for us' [cited

in Berger, 1977: 166]).[3] The crux of such challenges to the genre's 'rational right to exist' is the insufficiency of the novelist's imagination at authorising historical interpretation. In a frequently quoted letter dated 5 October 1901, Henry James warns Sarah Orne Jewett of the almost impossible requirements for a true representation of an era, and its habits of mind. 'You may multiply the little facts to be got from pictures and documents, relics and prints, as much as you like', writes James, but '*the* real thing is almost impossible to do, and in its absence the whole effect is nought; I mean the invention, the representation of the old consciousness' (emphasis in original). His last word to Jewett was about the cheek of it all: 'you have to simplify back by an amazing tour de force – and even then it's all humbug' (cited in Horne, 1999: 360). James' letter is itself too frequently 'simplified back' to those final three words: 'it's all humbug', forgetting what a perfectionist James was; how high set was his bar. Literary naturalism's critique of the historical novel is that some feats of imagination are hubris: efforts beyond the artist and therefore beneath the art. But this is to miss James' qualifier. 'The real thing is almost impossible to do', which means: it can be – might be – done. Which is surely reason enough to make the attempt.

The question of what the literary historical novel is, and what it should and should not do, seemed to have found its moment in 2012, the year in which Hilary Mantel won her second Man Booker prize for *Bring Up the Bodies* – seventeen years after the publication of her first historical novel, *A Place of Greater Safety*. *Bring up the Bodies* is the second instalment of three novels on the rise and fall of Thomas Cromwell. The first, *Wolf Hall*, had won Mantel the Man Booker in 2009. Peter Carey, J. G. Farrell, Peter Carey and J. M. Coetzee are the only other authors to share the honour of having won two Booker prizes, but Mantel is the only person in the history of the prize to win twice in quick succession, and to win for historical novels *in series*. Mantel's Man Bookers (should we call these Man-tel Bookers?) are also distinctive in that her novels represent an era more remote than any other winning 'historical': 250 years earlier than those treated, say, by Barry Unsworth's *Sacred Hunger*. What is notable, then, about Mantel's double-win is not only how pre-eminently 'historical' the novels are, but also the complexity and breadth of the history they offer, intra- and extra-textually. They play out along the same line of historical events – what *Wolf Hall* begins, *Bring Up the Bodies* continues – but differ in technique and strategy, as the author learns her subject (Tudor history and the political and intellectual progress of the Protestant reformation) and her Subject (Thomas Cromwell, from whose point of view the events are narrated). In *Wolf Hall* we have the Cromwell with a 'very large ledger. A huge filing system, in which are recorded (under their name, and also under their offence) the details of people who have cut across' him (*WH*, 481). Here is a point of view character with considerable reach, power and partiality. In *Bring Up the Bodies* the relationship of the reader to that subtle, overarching intelligence at the centre of the books has been clarified. It is Cromwell who happens to the world evoked (the Court and Privy Chamber, his Putney household, etc.), and to the reader encountering it. While the first line of *Wolf Hall* is a line of dialogue, a challenge spoken to the boy Cromwell, ('So now get up' [*WH*, 3]), the first line – and word – of *Bring Up the Bodies* places him more squarely at the nub of the world: 'His children are falling from the sky' (*WH*, 3). This is not Cromwell on his back at another man's feet, but Cromwell with an arm upstretched, the falconer as remote agent of the falcon's violence, 'silent as she takes her prey' (*BUTB*, 3). There are echoes of Yeats' 'The Second Coming' here: the falcon 'turning and turning in the widening gyre', the 'blood-dimmed tide ... loosed' and the 'ceremony of innocence' drowned (Yeats, 1958: 210–11). All that 'He, Thomas Cromwell' has gained, he stands to lose.

In *Bring Up the Bodies* we are closely schooled about narrative partiality – the second novel builds on the first book by strengthening Cromwell as a pivot of its action. He is agent and doer, an author of change. This is not only a matter of our orientation to Cromwell as the central character (who is speaking? 'He, Thomas Cromwell' is speaking) it is an argument in the making *about* Thomas Cromwell (Mantel: 'look to my book for accuracy where I can contrive it, but don't look to it for impartiality' [Mares, 2009]). Taken together, the series proposes a history. That they do so troubles some people – particularly (and predictably) Tudor historians. Susan Bordo takes issue with the author's partiality in *Bring Up the Bodies,* arguing that what gets storied (or omitted from the story) *tells* on Cromwell, with whom both author and reader are closely tied. Mantel 'excludes some key historical material' that 'might cause readers to question (her) Cromwell's view of Anne [Boleyn] as an unfeeling strategist', and show Cromwell to be 'more like a thug' than the author would have us take him (Bordo, 2012). Or rather a different kind of thug – Mantel's Cromwell is not at all averse to cowing people, though he does so less with violence than by play upon other people's expectations about what kind of man he was, a man from a 'dishonourable estate' (*WH*, 70), with a past career as a soldier in Italy. Bordo's (2012) concluding judgment vindicates Mantel the novelist but condemns her as a writer of history: 'the imaginative fiction of "Cromwell's point of view" is both the novel's greatest achievement and a handy rationale for playing very loose with the facts'. But the judgement sits beneath an equivocation (the subtitle of the piece):[4] 'whether we approve of the liberties taken with history depends on who is taking them – Hilary Mantel or Showtime' (Bordo, 2012). Mantel's current pre-eminence as a novelist, and the referred glamour of that eminence on literary historical fiction more generally, secures the ground for the return of a long embattled genre to respectability.

I would here like to assess the contribution of Hilary Mantel to the historical novel – and the question of its existence, its reason for being – by taking up a thread left dangling by A. S. Byatt in her essay 'Forefathers' where she discusses the relationship of the historical novel to secrecy, revelation, and the power of interrogation. Byatt first observes the tenacity of writers working in the genre to imagine an 'extraordinary variety of distant pasts' (Byatt, 2000: 36) despite the dictum that 'we cannot know the past ... and therefore should not write about it' (Byatt, 2000: 38). Whether a technique of 'historical ventriloquism' like that practiced by Peter Ackroyd in *The Last Testament of Oscar Wilde* (1983), or 'novels which play serious games with the idea of narrative itself' like Graham Swift's *Waterland* (Byatt, 2000: 48), or the 'apparently straightforward, realist narrative' of Hilary Mantel's *A Place of Greater Safety* (Byatt, 2000: 54), she finds the contemporary English historical novel effectively engaged in telling us what we cannot know (Byatt, 2000: 56). Discussing Mantel's 'experimental third person narrators' in *A Place of Greater Safety* as inheritors of the 'knowledgeable narrators' of George Eliot (Byatt, 2000: 54), Byatt suggests that narrators do not have the 'omniscience of a god' mistakenly taken to characterize the nineteenth-century narrator, but are fictive narrators of small compass and considerable acuity, who 'can creep closer to the feelings and the inner life of characters ... than any first-person mimicry' (Byatt, 2000: 55). Her sense of Mantel's ability to 'tell us what we can't know' hinges partly on the novelist making history accessible (viz. the past we cannot know) and partly in her success at bringing the *made* world near to the reader where the historical record – Henry James' 'little facts' – might leave the reader hanging.[5] But the question of *what we cannot know* shades into that of *what we should not know* when Byatt observes in passing that there is an 'interesting path to be explored along the connections between modern historical novels and the popular genres that tell stories about secrecy' (Byatt, 2000: 57). She quotes historian Richard Cobb on the compulsions of the historian to get the 'foot in the door, to get behind the façade, to get inside'. For that 'is what being, or becoming, an historian is all about – the desire to read other people's letters, to breach privacy, to penetrate into the inner room' (cited in Byatt, 2000: 56). The idea of trespass presumes a realm of privacy, but is imagination the realm of privacy against which all trespasses must be defended? Or is imagination the culprit, the trespasser on fact and the real of a vanished past?

In Hilary Mantel's historical novels the question of knowledge – its standpoint, its limitations, its rights – looms large. So too does that question loom large in the criticism of her work, and of the genre more broadly: in regard to the construction of the historical novel (narrative technique and plotting); in terms of the *weltanschauung* – what James' terms the 'old consciousness' – that the novel must evoke; and in the way historical novels are weighed as historiographical representations, as propositions for imagining a specific past and historical persons.

As it is distinctive among Mantel's historical novels, *The Giant, O'Brien* is worth treating briefly at the outset of this discussion. It is

Mantel's only historical novel where she departs markedly from historical evidence. But it is at the points that Mantel departs from the history that she is able to engage History. Her giant, O'Brien, is a bard and a scholar (the real one was probably mentally impaired), but his entourage is composed of men very like 'the fiends' that haunt the medium Alison in *Beyond Black*. The giant entertains his crew with stories – stories they come to know so well that when he is not quick enough to oblige, they stutter out a bastard version themselves. The stories are scenes within the scenes out of which the novel proper is constructed, and the giant's embellishment on the furnishings of rooms or the food on the table points up the poverty of the situation he and his crew are condemned to. When O'Brien's entourage tells one of his stories, taking turns to remember it, the half-wit Pybus does not need to elaborate comforts. His is a modest ideal. 'So she comes in and she sees it's a snug little place, a fire blazing and an iron pot over it, and a rabbit cooking in the pot' (*GO*, 146). But when the Giant tells a story he holds a larger version of the storied world behind the words he chooses: 'he saw Tannikin, a big-boned, likely lass of fifteen or sixteen, her snout pressed to a window pane, the shutter clipped back one fold; beneath her, far below, the little golden ships passing silently down the Rhine' (*GO*, 154). The freak and his entourage have come out of Ireland, chased by famine and poverty; they are dispossessed of house and history. Stories are the only claim they have left on either. But it's flesh – not even flesh, but the bones brought out of the anatomist's broiling vat – that the stories come down to. The Surgeon John Hunter has no interest in stories. They cannot be anatomized. The only stories of use to him are the ones he teaches to his grave robbers, little melodramas to prompt the staff of poor house or hospital to release a pretty corpse.

The *Giant O'Brien* shares with the other three novels a narrow compass to the stage of action: it is largely set in the claustrophobic cellars where they are lodged for the duration of the giant's London showing as a freak. The use of free indirect point of view moves swiftly across differently cramped stages of action so that the reader gets a sense for the short work that time, history, and circumstance will make of the characters.

The Giant says, 'Joe, whenever I pass a stairhead, I feel an attraction to fall down it.'

Bitch Mary comes home with her face beaten in.

Joe says, These are not the days we have known.

John Hunter keeps to his routine. He rises in the dark, and rinses his mouth in water that has stood since the night before. (*GO*, p. 167)

As he is nearing his death, and knowing that his own men intend to deliver his corpse to Hunter, the giant broods upon his estate. While the poet has 'his memorial in repetition, and the statesman his in stone and bronze', for the Giant, O'Brien and others brought as low 'there is the scrubbed wooden slab and the slop bucket, there is the cauldron and the boiling pot' and then, not even that. No trace remains, corporeal or otherwise: 'he is a stench in the nose for a day or a week, so he is a no-name, so he is oblivion. Stories cannot save him' (*GO*, 205).

As the passage continues, it lifts free of the brooding Giant to a wider, more authorial, meditation on the core of things. The stuff of the world seems, at first, stubborn ('when human memory runs out, there is the memory of animals; behind that, the memory of the plants, and behind that the memory of the rocks') but it cannot withstand a blankly indifferent time: 'the wind and the sea wear the rocks away; and the cell-line runs to its limit, where meaning falls away from it, and it loses knowledge of its own nature' [*GO*, 205]). The last line of the passage turns back from what is lost – from the losing – to those who stand its cost: 'Unless we plead on our knees with history, we are done for, we are lost. We must step sideways, into that country where space plaits and knots, where time folds and twists: where the years pass in a day' (*GO*, 205). That country is the land of the *Sidhe* – 'those that can outlive the moon' (Yeats, 1958: 481) – but it is also History: a History too old, and vast, for stories. The record has its limit.

The use and abuse of the record, and the question of knowledge – facts promulgated or withheld, ideas traded upon or proscribed, associations owned or denied – is at the heart of Mantel's other three historical novels. In her evocation of the Royal Court, of Cromwell's Putney, and of county and country in *Wolf Hall* and *Bring Up the Bod-*

ies the covert is dangerous, although a danger Cromwell recognizes as 'the way of the world' – and like the world – a danger that even-handedly presages a bad end: 'a knife in the dark, a movement on the edge of vision, a series of warnings that have worked themselves into flesh' (*WH*, 76). These threats are general, even democratic, but they loom large for Cromwell since he's made himself so much the centre of things, agent – even – of actions accounted to others. 'He used to say, "the king will do such and such." Then he began to say, "We will do such and such." Now he says, "This is what I will do."' (*WH*, 28). And the spectre of knowledge haunts Mantel's earlier historical novel, *A Place of Greater Safety*, where questions posed by Enlightenment social thought are answered by ever more bloody inquiries into the workings of order as Danton, Robespierre and Desmoulins work to imagine and bring into being a revolution that is something more than the one events have served them.

The question of what-is-knowable but also of who-knows-what leads us to narrative authority and to techniques of narration, but also brings into view the historiographical nature of literary histori-cal fiction in its constructed-ness and subjectivity (see Collingwood, 1946; Young, 2011), as well as its intrusiveness: its tendency toward trespass. That impulse would not be foreign to Mantel, the author, or to her characters. It is hard to imagine Thomas Cromwell or Ca-mille Desmoulins scrupling much at reading another's letters, or even from writing them: as Cromwell does for the King (*BUTB*, 210). And Mantel could not have served the history, or drawn her character, without having read letters – Cromwell's letters – as they are 'virtu-ally our only source' (Mares, 2009) in the documentary record where Cromwell speaks directly, for himself and as himself. To read a histori-cal resource is not to trespass, where the past – and the dead – have by rights given up their ground, but nevertheless the spectre of trespass, and questions about the propriety of knowledge, haunt Mantel's his-torical novels.

Mantel's protagonists are animated by tensions between the im-pulse to know and the countervailing pressure to repress *some* knowl-edge – to obscure a fact, keep a story from the gossips, or suppress a thought. *Wolf Hall* and *Bring Up the Bodies* treat a period in which the concept of privacy as we recognize it did not exist, while the concept of rights upon which privacy discursively rests is only coming into view in the period of revolutionary upheaval in Europe, the larger world enclosed by the 'inner rooms' – the domestic interiors – within which the action of *A Place of Greater Safety* is staged. It narrates the revolution from a near, even an intimate, proximity to Desmoulins, Danton and Robespierre (and to a lesser extent, the wives of Desmoulins and Danton) in a 'blurring of the boundaries between the political and the domestic' (Hidalgo, 2002: 205). Seldom do we glimpse the *public* revolutionary about his work, unless it is in the moment just prior to a significant political act or utterance, at its formation but not its completion. Someone says something to someone else; a joke is made at another's expense while the real cost – a career, a corpse – is still to be counted; the seed of a plan is sown, a rumour set about, an accusation made; something is committed to writing, for private record or publication. In *A Place of Greater Safety* it is not the concept of privacy *per se* that is canvassed but the disappearance of the 'private' (private life sacrificed to public *vertu*; private rooms become meeting houses). That the 'private' is so swiftly disappearing is fateful for everyone caught up in the revolutionary events in Paris, but particularly so for Danton and Desmoulins. A newly minted man of the people for his part in the street riots leading to the storming of the Bastille, Camille finds his likeness turned out on crockery: '[t]his is what happens when you become a public figure, people eat their dinners off you' (*APOGS*, 249), while Gabrielle Danton discovers that she and her husband are to have little space to themselves in their new apartment: '[a] curtained alcove sheltered twin beds, marked off their private territory from the patriotic circus it had become' (*APOGS*, 346). The private is a preserve of privilege and privilege is quickly becoming a liability, as Mirabeau lugubriously observes: 'I can remember the days…when we didn't have public opinion. No one had ever heard of such a thing' (*APOGS*, 325). This is a response to Danton's fondly barbed characterization of Camille, who 'has to be running ahead of public opinion all the time' (*APOGS*, p. 324). Camille leads opinion, but there is also something fugitive and vulnerable in all this 'running ahead'.

A Place of Greater Safety is in many ways a domestic novel. Marking the 30th anniversary of the Virago Imprint, Mantel wrote to recuperate the novel of the domestic from charges that it concerns were 'narrow'. On the contrary, the domestic novel 'need not be small, or tame' (Mantel, 2008a) – it is anything but. 'Homes are very unsafe places to linger', she writes. 'The crime statistics will tell you the streets are safer. *Everything, even warfare, happens first in the kitchen, in the nursery, in the cradle*' (Mantel, 2008a, emphasis added).[6] 'Everything, even warfare': everything, even religious upheaval, dynastic struggle, and revolution. Private life is the life of *A Place of Greater Safety*, even as those lives are thrust onto the public stage. The drama of the work derives from the relationships between the major characters: affections and allegiances compromised, then betrayed, in struggles more intimate than the breaking down of political and ideological alliance. The characters are at odds with themselves, and the Robespierre that Mantel evokes is very much the man she had characterized twenty years later (in a review of Ruth Scurr's biography of Robespierre) as a 'fissiparous bundle of contradictions' (Mantel, 2008b).[7] Robespierre is creating his republic of *vertu* with every speech he gives and article he writes, but still declares his unwillingness to disapprove of Camille, even as Danton draws his attention to his friend's unsavoury sexual habits. Robespierre refuses to hear, calling it a 'private concern' (*APOGS*, 420). It is over this distinction between the public and the private that the crisis ensues. Danton falls after being implicated in a conspiracy of profiteering (the revolutionary nation is at war), a 'stock market scandal' characterized – tellingly – by 'insider trading' (Mantel, 2009b). And what condemns Desmoulins, finally, is his commitment to private life – not his own so much as that of an increasingly wide-array of citizens condemned by the Committee for Public Safety, with its private proceedings and its process bearing down on evidence that is, as likely as not, public rumour.[8] Camille remonstrates with Robespierre as the Terror deepens, first doing so in public, and then face-to-face. His article about the tyranny of the reign of Emperor Tiberius makes its accusation by analogy, his revolution having become the thing it derides: 'the corruption of all human feeling, the degradation of pity to a crime' (*APOGS*, 770).

Desmoulins means the reader to see Robespierre's agent, Antoine de Saint-Just, as the instrument of tyranny, but when Robespierre reads the article he recognizes himself. When they meet to discuss this last instance of Camille's fervor for liberty, it is on a bridge over the Seine, for 'inside' – as Robespierre puts it – 'you can't keep secrets' (*APOGS*, 771). To which Camille replies, 'you see – you admit it. You're eaten away with the thought of conspiracy. Will you guillotine brick walls and doorposts?' (*APOGS*, 771). Those 'brick walls and door posts' are what sets home off from the world – border to the last preserve of the private. But for Robespierre there is only one inside that counts, one sanctified preserve. After he has agreed to Saint-Just arraigning Camille before the Tribunal, Robespierre tells him: '[w]hen this business is over, and Camille is dead, I shall not want to hear your epitaph for him. No one is ever to speak of him again, I absolutely forbid it. When he is dead, I shall want to think of him myself, alone' (*APOGS*, 862). This inside is the *place of greater safety*. Not that arch public face of memory, posterity ('your epitaph'), nor even the grave itself: it is thought, and that fragile vessel, memory.

For the Thomas Cromwell of *Wolf Hall* and *Bring Up the Bodies*, the place of greater safety is even more remote, beyond his power to conjure or keep. It is not memory, for the dead do not dwell only there: after his wife, then his daughters, die they can be glimpsed on the stair, they put their small hands beside his on the page as he stands reading by the window. Despite his faith, Cromwell finds little practical comfort in his own inviolate soul: it is not a ground to stand upon; it does not even belong to him. When he imagines the dead in their afterlife, it is in Augustinian terms, resurrection in the shadow of mourning (Augustine: 'the flesh resurrects in order not to possess but to be possessed, not to have but to be had' [cited in Segal, 2004: 279]). When his eldest daughter dies of the sweating sickness Cromwell thinks of her, suddenly complete, not the girl still learning Greek, but the girl 'who knows it now'. He wonders if that is how it is, 'in a moment, in a simple twist of unbecoming,' the dead suddenly knowing 'everything they need to know' (*WH*, 152). For the Cromwell we meet at the height of his power, there is only one place of respite from its burdens, only one way to shake off the constant nagging fact of what needs to be done (what he must do). After he has terrified Mark Smeaton, breaking him for the confession that will condemn Anne Boleyn, Cromwell retires to bed. He cannot sleep, and 'it is only in his dreams that he is private'. Cromwell nurses his wakefulness, remembering the ascetic Thomas More, who 'used to say you should build yourself a retreat, a hermitage, within your own house. But that was More: able to slam the door in everyone's face. In truth you cannot separate them, your public being and your private self...' (*BUTB*, 281). Cromwell would not follow More's thinking, being Wolsey's man. When Cromwell first marked down Mark Smeaton it was with the thought 'the cardinal always says, there are no safe places, there are no sealed rooms' (*WH*, 199): meaning, *nowhere we won't have an eye and an ear on you, Mark Smeaton*. But in the context of his later interrogation of Smeaton, 'no safe places' and 'no sealed rooms' has a meaning more pointed. It is Cromwell who is without a place of greater safety.

Early in the novel of that name, we find Robespierre crafting his public position on the matter of private interests: '...private interests and all personal relationships must give way to the general good'. The young lawyer from Arras then puts down his pen and remonstrates with himself: 'this is all very well, it is easy for me to say that, I have no dearest friend. Then he thought, of course I have, I have Camille' (*APOGS*, p. 109). Put in mind of his friend, he searches for his last letter from him, which is 'rather muddled, written in Greek'. It seems to Robespierre that by 'applying himself to the dead language, Camille was concealing from himself his misery, confusion and pain; by forcing the recipient to translate, he was saying, believe that my life to me is an elitist entertainment, something that only exists when it is written down and sent by the posts' (*APOGS*, 109–110). The passage draws for the reader the whimsical Camille and shows us the central tension – and tragedy – for Robespierre, the seed of his betrayal of his friend to the guillotine. But so too is there something of the reflexive here, a take on historical narrative, the novel, and the historiographical all at once: 'elitist entertainment', 'something that only exists when it is written down' and transmitted; something that obliges a work of interpretation, and something that obfuscates as much as it reveals.

While it would be too much to suggest that Mantel's historical novels are 'historiographic metafictions' in Linda Hutcheon's (1996: 474) terms they nevertheless do 'problematize the question of historical knowledge' without either the play of the mendacious or the self-referential knowingness of the postmodern historical novel. Respect for fact and the historical record grounds the fiction for the author must keep the 'conjecture... plausible and grounded in the best facts one can get' (Mantel, 2009a). This commitment to the history in the fiction does not forestall the scholar/story-teller's healthy respect for the labour of interpretation, whatever the degree of its imaginative working of the facts. 'The past is not dead ground', writes Mantel, 'and to traverse it is not a sterile exercise. History is always changing behind us, and the past changes a little every time we retell it.' Then, implicating herself in the comment, she adds: 'the most scrupulous historian is an unreliable narrator' (2009a). In *Bring Up The Bodies*, Thomas Cromwell meditates on the slippery Thomas Wyatt, 'the cleverest man in England' (*BUTB*, 347). He explains to the doubtful Risley (who is of the opinion that Cromwell is the cleverest man in England) Wyatt's capacity to 'write' and then as quickly 'disclaim' himself: 'He jots a verse on some scrap of paper, and slips it to you, when you are at supper or praying in the chapel. Then he slides a paper to some other person, and it is the same verse, but a word is different. Then that person says to you, did you see what Wyatt wrote? You say yes, but you are talking of different things' (*BUTB*, 347). The slipperiness Cromwell identifies is a characteristic of Wyatt, and of the word that 'some other person' reads and makes quite something else of. But the slipperiness of the author resides in his craft, and it is behind this shield that Cromwell's Wyatt stands when pressed about his work:

> ... you trap him and say, Wyatt, did you really do what you describe in this verse? He smiles and tells you, it is the story of some imaginary gentleman, no one we know; or he will say, this is not my story I write, it is yours, though you do not know it. He will say, this woman I describe here, the brunette, she is really a woman with fair hair, in disguise. He will declare, you must believe everything and nothing of what you read. (*BUTB*, 348)

The substance of the art is indivisible: it can't be 'taxed'. Cromwell is admiring the infuriating Wyatt, how self-contained he is; that collected *hauteur* under interrogation. But from whence comes that strength? 'You point to the page, you tax him: what about this line, is this true? He says, it is poet's truth. Besides, he claims, I am not free to write as I like. It is not the king, but metre that constrains me. And I would be plainer, he says, if I could: but I must keep to the rhyme' (*BUTB*, 348).

The whole passage can be read as at once a justification for, and a critique of, the imaginative work of the historical novel and the 'trespasses' of the novelist. Consider the context for the passage: Cromwell is characterizing Wyatt – the Wyatt who is lucky, protected. There is evidence that could have damned him along with the other 'conspirators' in Anne's sexual betrayal of the King but when Mark Smeaton is naming names, and blurts Wyatt's, Cromwell is definite: 'No, not Wyatt' (*BUTB*, 283). Partiality and evidence contest here, and partiality wins. It is necessary for Cromwell to preserve Wyatt, for Wyatt is a principal embodied – albeit a troubled principal. The passage tellingly turns from its mediation on art ('A Statute is written to entrap meaning, a poem to escape it' [*BUTB*, 348]) to the messages of Angels, and the elusiveness of their nature. Cromwell has no doubt that Angels exist, but knows not whether they have the 'plumage of falcons, crows, peacocks' (*BUTB*, 348). And the only evidence he has from someone ('a turnspit in the papal kitchens') who has seen one provides little comfort, for 'the Angel's substance was heavy and smooth as marble, its expression distant and pitiless; its wings were carved from glass' (*BUTB*, 349). These are terrifying emissaries of the only truth that counts, the truth toward which a 'poet's truth' is aimed, but can never reach.

In this passage – from Cromwell explaining Wyatt to Risley, to the meditation on art and the nature of angels – it is difficult not to hear the author remonstrating with critics like Bordo: 'You point to the page, you tax him: what about this line, is this true?' Mantel's defence is 'poet's truth': 'I would be plainer, but I must keep to the rhyme'. For the literary historical novelist, history is 'the king' that does not constrain, and form 'the metre' that must. But if this is a defence, it is a qualified one: recognizing the privilege of the interpretation, and its trespass (Wyatt is favoured, Wyatt is protected; Wyatt's 'lines fledge feathers' – so just leave him to his work). For there are Angels, they hover at a farther horizon. They are History – which is the blind passing of human time on this earth, not the 'history' that remembers us.

Notes

1 In writing historical fiction 'the danger you have to negotiate is not the dimpled coyness of the past – it is its obscenity' (Mantel, 2009a).

2 The relative liveliness of the genre of literary historical fiction is pointed given the woes of literary publishing, and the book trade in the United Kingdom particularly.

3 Hilary Mantel has frequently referred the need to serve the history, as well as the demands of fiction. Fidelity to the history – to knowing what one is writing about – is the first necessary step: 'if you understand what you're talking about, you should be drawing the drama out of real life, not putting it there, like icing on a cake' (cited in MacFarquhar, 2012: 55).

4 It is difficult to establish whether this is Bordo's words, or that of the Chronicle editors, summarizing the piece. The text does not appear in the version of the article produced by the print command, but does appear as the text preceding the tiny URL or URL produced on using the 'share' function (for twitter, the web, and Facebook etc.). The qualification is, therefore, the public face of the article.

5 Byatt reasons from the evidence of her own use of such narrators in *Possession*, where they are employed to 'tell what *the historians and biographers of my fiction* never discovered' (Byatt, 2000: 56, emphasis added), that I – to flesh out the history *in* the novel, not the history outside of it (against which it may be held accountable). Having evoked history, Byatt can discount its claims on the novel.

6 See also Knox (2010) for a discussion of the domestic in Mantel's work more generally.

7 In evaluating the contribution of Hilary Mantel to contemporary literature it's important to bear in mind her extensive work as a critic. In respect to her status as an historical novelist, it is also more than worthy of note how often she is called upon as an historian, even if in the *de facto* terms of a literary reviewer of non-fiction. In the *London Review of Books* she has regularly reviewed non-fiction dealing with revolutionary France

and the principal figures in the revolution. See, for example, two of her lengthy and scholarly meticulous reviews, one of a collection of essays about Robespierre (Mantel, 2000) and the second, a review of a recent biography of Danton (Mantel, 2009b). She is now being increasingly called upon to review works dealing with Tudor history. For a discussion of the relationship between Mantels criticism and autobiographical writing, and historical fiction as 'research fiction', see Knox (2008).

8 There is an exchange between Fouquier-Tinville and Danton's co-conspirator, Lacroix, toward the end of the novel: 'You will be judged solely on the documentary evidence'. Lacroix: 'What the hell does that mean? ...What documents? Where are they?' (*APOGS*, 866). Compare this to the tired cynicism of Anne Boleyn as Cromwell puts the charges of infidelity and incest to her. He advises that she show penitence and that she 'patiently...bear with the process', to which Anne replies, 'Ah, the process....And what is this process to be?' (*BUTB*, 344)

Works cited

Anderson, Perry (2011) 'From Progress to Catastrophe: Perry Anderson on the Historical Novel', *London Review of Books* (28 July) accessed April 2013, http://www.lrb.co.uk/v33/n15/perry-anderson/from-progress-to-catastrophe

Berger, Morroe (1977) *Real and Imagined Worlds: The Novel and Social Science*. Cambridge, MA: Harvard University Press.

Bernbaum, Ernest (1926) 'The Views of the Great Critics on the Historical Novel', *PMLA* 41(2): 421–41.

Bordo, Susan (2012) 'When Fictionalized Facts Matter: From "Anne of a Thousand Days" to Hilary Mantel's New *Bring Up the Bodies*', *Chronicle of Higher Education* (6 May) accessed December 2012, http://chronicle.com/article/When-Fictionalized-Facts/131759/

Byatt, A. S. (2000) *On Histories and Stories: Selected Essays*. London: Chatto and Windus.

Collingwood, Robin (1946) *The Idea of History*. London: Oxford University Press.

Hidalgo, Pilar (2002) 'Of Tides and Men: History and Agency in Hilary Mantel's *A Place of Greater Safety*', *Estudios Ingleses de la Universidad Complutense* 10: 201–16.

Horne, Philip (1999) *Henry James: a Life in Letters*. New York: Viking.

Hutcheon, Linda (1996) 'The Pastime of Past Time: Fiction, History, Historiographic Metafiction', in Michael J. Hoffman and Patrick D. Murphy (eds) *Essentials of the Theory of Fiction*. London: Leicester University Press.

Keen, Suzanne (2005) 'The Historical Turn in British Fiction', in James English (ed.) *A Concise Companion to Contemporary British Fiction*. London: Blackwell-Wiley.

Knox, Sara (2010) '"Giving Flesh to the Wraiths of Violence": Super-Realism in the Fiction of Hilary Mantel', *Australian Feminist Studies* 25(65): 313–23.

Knox, Sara (2008) 'On the Nearness of Distant Things: Researching the Historical Novel', *Heat* 16: 165–82.

MacFarquhar, Larissa (2012) 'The Dead are Real', *The New Yorker* (15 October): 46–57.

Mantel, Hilary (2008a) 'Author, Author', *Guardian* (24 May), accessed December 2012, http://books.guardian.co.uk/print/0,,334340458–110738,00. htm

Mantel, Hilary (2009a) 'Booker Winner Hilary Mantel on Dealing with History in Fiction', *Guardian* (17 Oct), accessed December 2012, http:// www.guardian.co.uk/books/2009/oct/17/hilary-mantel-author-booker

Mantel, Hilary (2009b) 'He Roared', *London Review of Books* 31(15), accessed December 2012, www.lrb.co.uk/v31/n15/hilary-mantel/he-roared

Mantel, Hilary (2009c) *Wolf Hall*. London: Harper Collins.

Mantel, Hilary (1998) *The Giant, O'Brien*. London: Fourth Estate.

Mantel, Hilary (2006) 'If You'd Seen His Green Eyes', *London Review of Books* 28(8), accessed December 2012, http://www.lrb.co.uk/v28/n08/ mant01_.html

Mantel, Hilary (1992) *A Place of Greater Safety*. London: Viking.

Mantel, Hilary (2012) *Bring Up the Bodies*. New York: Henry Holt and Company.

Mares, Peter (2009, 18 June) 'Hilary Mantel's *Wolf Hall*' [Radio Interview], The Book Show. ABC Radio, accessed December 2012, http://www. abc.net.au/radionational/programs/bookshow/hilary-mantels-wolf-hall/3131120

Segal, Alan (2004) *Life After Death: a History of the Afterlife in Western Religion*. New York: Doubleday.

Yeats, William Butler (1958) *The Collected Poems of W.B. Yeats*. London: Macmillan and Co Ltd.

Young, Samantha (2011) 'Based on a True Story: Contemporary Histori-cal Fiction and Historiographical Theory', *Otherness: Essays and Studies* 2(1), accessed December 2012, http://www.otherness.dk/fileadmin/ www.othernessandthearts.org/Publications/Journal_Otherness/Other-ness__Essays_and_Studies_2.1/1._Samantha_Young.pdf

PART III

SPACES

Contemporary British Fiction, Environmental Crisis and the Pastoral

Deborah Lilley

> This wholly new conception of the precariousness of our relations with nature is bound to bring forth new versions of pastoral. (Leo Marx, 'Does Pastoralism Have a Future?', p. 222)

The appearance of the pastoral mode in twenty-first-century writing in Britain is intertwined with the treatment of environmental concerns, where elements of the mode are tested and transformed in writing about the relationship between humans and nature. This essay considers the manifestation of the pastoral in contemporary British fiction in conjunction with and in addition to a number of recent theorizations of the mode. Exploring some of the ways in which the pastoral is being written and read, this essay examines the emergence of versions of pastoral shaped by their intersection with environmental crisis.

The representation and interpretation of environmental crisis calls up new circumstances for the pastoral to operate within, posing both an opportunity for the application of the conventions of the mode, and a threat to the principles upon which they are based. Though offering a means of depicting and reflecting upon the relationship between the human and the non-human, the acknowledgement of environmental crisis and its representation can be readily understood as a challenge to the pastoral. Both the cultural criticism and the connections between humans and nature made possible through pastoral necessarily avoid ecological concerns due to the idealized version of nature and the romanticized reciprocal relationship between nature and humans that it depends upon. These conventions are impeded by recognition of the causes and the effects of ecological crisis. However, their inverse form, the anti- or counter-pastoral, is equally stalled. Environmental uncertainty threatens the stability of nature, or rather, the stability of the interrelationship between humans and nature upon which the pastoral contrasts between the country and the city, the human and the non-human, are based. The correlation between the human and the natural established in Theocritus' first Idyll, through the story of the effects of the death of Daphnis upon the natural world, is both disrupted and instated in new, and newly verifiable, contexts.[1] Disturbed by the premise of environmental crisis, both pastoral and anti-pastoral responses appear out of kilter.

Yet pastoral topics and techniques are being used in contemporary British writing that approaches environmental concerns. As Marx anticipated, alternative ways of composing the pastoral and negotiating the obstructions to its conventional expectations can be seen to emerge. The introduction of ecological considerations destabilizes the anthropocentric orientation of pastoral nature and in so doing, provokes questioning of the interconnectivity that is seen to underpin the pastoral relationship between humans and nature. This essay identifies the features of contemporary pastoral found in the writing of environmental crisis, demonstrating that the mode is being adapted to account for the 'precariousness' that at once predicates and comes to define it in this context. First outlining the critical intersection of pastoral and environmental crisis, I then examine in detail how innovative engagements with the tradition can be found in Liz Jensen's *The Rapture* (2009) and Ali Smith's *The Accidental* (2005). Analysing Terry Gifford's and Martin Ryle's readings of these novels as 'post-pastoral' and 'neo-pastoral' respectively, I argue that these examples show that further understanding is demanded of the mode to account for its contemporary scope and function. Using John Burnside's *Glister* (2008), I argue that the form is both oriented towards and re-oriented by environmental crisis.

Ecocriticism and the pastoral

Marx's plural prediction of 'new versions' of pastoral gestures not only towards the multiple possibilities generated by the uncertain conditions of environmental crisis, but also towards the heterogeneity associated with pastoral writing. The complex and often contradictory social, economic, political and ecological perspectives to which the conventions of pastoral have been attributed and from which they have been understood contribute towards its interpretation as a generally 'contested term' (Loughrey, 1984: 8).[2] Accordingly, the development of 'the ecocentric repossession of pastoral' anticipated by Lawrence Buell has been tempered by what Greg Garrard has described as the 'problematic' character of the tradition (Buell, 1995: 52; Garrard, 1996: 459). Despite this, the continued interest in writing and reading the mode alongside the emergence of environmental criticism also indicates the potential that Garrard attributed to the pastoral 'as a questioning, as itself a question' (Garrard, 1996: 464).

In *The Penguin Book of English Pastoral Verse*, John Barrell and John Bull predicted a 'revival of interest in the Pastoral' alongside 'the current concern with ecology' (Barrell and Bull, 1974: 432). Their expectation is based upon a reiteration of the idealized conditions of the contrasts of pastoral, envisaging 'Industrial Man looking away from his technological wasteland to an older and better world' that would serve a palliative function in the context of environmental damage (Barrell and Bull, 1974: 432). In a similar tone, Joseph Meeker succinctly dispensed with the possibility of productive pastoral writing in response to ecological crisis, stating that 'escape into fantasies is not a workable solution to urban and existential ills' (Meeker, 1997: 73). Highlighting the 'enamelled' world of pastoral, based on the artificially orchestrated relationship between the country and the city, Raymond Williams suggested that 'we must not limit ourselves to their contrast but go on to see their interrelations and through these the real shape of the underlying crisis' (Williams, 1973: 18, 297).

However, these kinds of approaches to pastoral are difficult to locate in a straightforward form in contemporary writing. Yet other, more complex engagements with the mode in relation to environmental crisis can be found which develop, contest and question the readings set out above. The 'interrelations' that Williams pointed to are supplemented by the signs of environmental crisis, illustrating the connections that exist in relation and in addition to the social and political connections upon which his criticism of the pastoral was based. As this essay demonstrates, examples such as *The Rapture*, *The Accidental* and *Glister* provoke fresh consideration of the possibilities, as well as the limitations, of pastoral writing.

Critically and creatively, the pastoral continues to be re-imagined and re-evaluated, suggesting that Glen Love's proposition that 'we need to redefine pastoral in terms of the new and more complex understanding of nature' is still underway (Love, 1996: 231). Acknowledging that '[t]he pastoral has long been deemed unsuitable and escapist', Astrid Bracke posits questioning 'what such problematic texts reveal about our experience and perceptions of the (natural) environment' within 'a mature ecocritical practice' (Bracke, 2010: 766). Paraphrasing Buell's call for pastoral to form the basis for a 'mature environmental aesthetics' in *The Environmental Imagination* (Buell, 1995: 32), Bracke here points towards the increasingly self-reflexive formulation of contemporary versions of pastoral. Pastoral provides not only the opportunity to temporarily escape from instances of crisis but also the possibility to reflect upon and address those issues.

In this way, Marx's influential definition of 'complex pastoral'[3] can be understood to underpin numerous contemporary readings of the pastoral:

> Most literary works called pastorals ... do not finally permit us to come away with anything like the simple, affirmative attitude we adopt toward pleasing rural scenery. In one way or another ... these works manage to qualify, or call into question, or bring irony to bear

against the illusion of peace and harmony in a green pasture. (Marx, 1964: 25)

Building upon Marx's assertion, the critical potential of a pastoral that acknowledges and develops the challenge brought by environmental crisis to the contrasts upon which it is based signifies new opportunities for its use. For example, Dana Philips reads a 'blocked pastoral' in Don DeLillo's *White Noise* (1984), in which the pastoral desire to retreat into a restorative nature that exists in contrast to the human world is 'expressed as a perpetually frustrated impulse' (Philips, 1998: 236). The collision between pastoral expectations and environmental crisis is read here as illustrative of a breaking point, wherein the patterns of pastoral or anti-pastoral are interrupted and can no longer be completed. This impediment is itself environmentally illuminative. In a similar vein, Nick Selby identifies a 'choked pastoral' in which the pastoral impulse is both deployed and questioned within the same work (Selby, 2011: 897).

Developing these ideas further, Terry Gifford and Martin Ryle in particular are reading new discursive shapes of pastoral which envisage adapted versions of the mode as critical spaces in which to approach environmental crisis. Gifford has described what he has called the 'post-pastoral' as 'a term that characterises writing which avoids the traps of the closed circuit of both pastoral and counter-pastoral constructions of nature', and 'finds a language to outflank both with a vision of accommodated humans that acknowledges the problematics involved in achieving this' (Gifford, 1999: 148, 149).[4] This conception of 'post-pastoral' captures the interconnectivity between the human and the natural and conveys a sense of responsibility towards and respect for this knowledge. In another way, Ryle has defined an alternative 'neo-pastoral' that adds a similar awareness of the interconnectivity between the contrasts of the pastoral to the critical perspective that they may offer, along with a self-conscious approach to the representation of that perspective. Ryle has described the 'eco-didactic' value of 'neo-pastoral', understood as 'a self-reflexive mode of writing that is aware, and makes its readers aware, of its indebtedness to pastoral, and has adopted elements of that convention to intervene in current culture and politics' (Ryle, 2009: 16).

These readings take on Love's speculation that 'a pastoral for the present and the future calls for a better science of nature, a greater understanding of its complexity ... and a more acute questioning of the values of the supposedly sophisticated society to which we are bound' (Love, 1996: 235). In different ways, both Gifford and Ryle describe the conventions of pastoral re-configured around imperatives of environmental consciousness and accountability. Attention towards the representation of nature and the pastoral relationship between the human and the natural, and the effects of such representation, are central to these versions of contemporary pastoral.

The Rapture and 'post-pastoral'

In an essay published in 2010, Gifford examines the ways in which Liz Jensen's eco-thriller *The Rapture* could be considered to be an example of contemporary environmentally-oriented 'post-pastoral' writing. *The Rapture* traces the discovery of and the failure to prevent a deep-sea drilling project for frozen methane, which results in a climatic disaster that has been predicted by a teenager named Bethany, who appears to possess a connection to nature that exceeds reason and conventional understanding. Gifford's analysis focuses in particular upon Bethany's unique connection to the changes underway in the natural world that lead to a succession of international crises of escalating magnitude, and the interconnected sense of the global that emerges in their wake. The essay traces the ways in which the novel moves beyond the 'closed circuit of pastoral and anti-pastoral' in the context of environmental crisis, exploring the ways that the novel intersects with theories of biosemiotics and globalization, highlighted as 'post-pastoral' means of interpretation.[5]

Gifford imagines 'post-pastoral' as a mode of writing for responsibility, with an active environmentalist function. The mode seeks to acknowledge, in positive and negative instances, and to renew, in environmentally effective ways, our understanding of the connectivity between humans and nature. Defined by a 'humbling' and non-idealized sense of 'awe in attention to the natural world', through the process of 'consciousness' becoming 'conscience' (Gifford, 1999: 15, 151, 163) such writing would engender 'a reciprocal responsibility for future manipulations of the circumstances of engagements with environments ... transformed into pastorals of responsibility for the global environment' (Gifford, 2009: 247).

Gifford suggests that the novel lacks a truly post-pastoral 'unidealised sense of "awe"' (Gifford, 2010: 725) and an adequate sense of responsibility for the understanding of the interrelations between human and non-human that the narrative sets out. He explains that '[i]t would be difficult to argue that Jensen's novel attempts to raise any of the questions expected of a post-pastoral text' (Gifford, 2010: 725). Despite the understanding of interconnectivity that the threat of catastrophic anthropogenic climate change discloses, the protagonists lack a direct and localized sense of place founded on knowledge and experience. As such, the characters fail to cultivate a connection to nature that would drive the kind of 'post-pastoral' outcome that Gifford anticipates: '*The Rapture* merely exploits current anxieties without a sense of the values by which we might act to avoid its narrative outcome ... The planet certainly has a future at the end ... but there are no signs that anyone at any point in the novel is willing to take responsibility for it' (Gifford, 2010: 726).

From this viewpoint, the text fails to evoke a version of nature, or of the relationship between the human and the natural, that is sufficiently convincing in value to call back from the brink. Though the final sections of the novel relate the gradual acceptance of Bethany's predictions of global catastrophe, this process is contrasted with the rapid escalation of the situation, and the failure of the protagonists to convince the world of their knowledge in time to prevent the disaster. The novel both acknowledges and demonstrates resistance to Gifford's 'post-pastoral' criterion that 'consciousness becomes conscience' (Gifford, 1999: 165). Though the interconnectedness of nature and culture is undeniably present in the novel, responsibility for this knowledge does not really occur within its pages. The novel breaks out of the 'closed circuit of both pastoral and counter-pastoral'

(Gifford, 1999: 148) through global environmental catastrophe, rather than via Gifford's 'post-pastoral' means.

However, the version of pastoral that the novel comes to represent is certainly transformed through its intersection with environmental concerns. Despite this, neither the cultural nor ecological landscape within the novel are productively altered, at least not within the scope of the text or within the boundaries of the recognizably human society that appears to have ended at the closure of the novel. Instead, the novel uses pastoral as a means to convey a wake-up call, or to relate a kind of cautionary tale, describing an environment in which the influence of human action and its effects upon the natural world are unmistakable and seemingly inextricable. Although misaligned with the criteria for environmentally oriented pastoral set out by Gifford, it can be understood to raise several questions about pastoral, environmental crisis, and the parameters of 'post-pastoral' itself. Jensen sets the 'post-pastoral' knowledge developed by the characters throughout the novel alongside typically pastoral traits of nostalgia and idealization and anti-pastoral hardships, capturing a sense of the difficulty of dealing with and acting upon such knowledge. Another look at the novel can illustrate the ways that such tensions are exploited.

Set in the indeterminate near-future and culminating at the former 2012 Olympic stadium in East London, the narrative follows Bethany's therapist, Gabrielle, and relates an unfamiliar account of familiar cultural and geographical landscapes. The novel presents an aesthetic and ecological landscape that is anything but pastoral. Neither a pristine nor benevolent version of nature is accessible. Dangerous and unpredictable, the natural world appears unsympathetic to the needs of its human inhabitants: the weather is 'ferocious' (*TR*, 124) and is becoming resistant to familiar means of interpretation: 'it's effectively the second autumn of the year. The first shrivelled the leaves on the branches and sun-blasted the fruit to ripeness back in May' (*TR*, 160); 'five years ago, the British seasons made some kind of sense. Not any more' (*TR*, 54). We are told that 'that summer ... the rules began to change' (*TR*, 1).

Through the connection of conditions of the environment to human action, the novel appears to be anti-pastoral. To describe the conditions of unfamiliar weather, Jensen frequently appropriates industrial and mechanical terms. The 'sky pressed down like a furnace lid' (TR, 3), and 'charcoal clouds erupted on the horizon and massed into precarious metropolises of air' (TR, 4); the heat conveyed by the wind is likened to 'a hairdryer with no off switch' (TR, 35). Here, the novel reconfigures the understanding of pastoral nature as a celebration of the productive interaction of human and natural forces.

Further, it is through the destruction of pastoral landscapes that the effects of unpredictable weather is registered, where storms are 'flattening corn, uprooting trees, smashing hop silos and storage barns, whisking up torn rubbish sacks that pirouetted in the sky like the ghostly spirits of retail folly' (TR, 4). The description aligns the pastoral images of agricultural activity with the accumulation of waste and consumer culture, blending together pastoral and anti-pastoral signs of the impact of human action.

Through vivid descriptions of the degraded landscape accompanied by ominous signs of impending catastrophe we see a landscape in which the interconnectivity between human and non-human elements is irrefutable. The environment bears traces of the evidence of human action, from the 'Starbucks beakers, gossip magazines, buckled beer-cans, burger cartons gaping open like polystyrene clams' that clutter the pavements of the seaside town of Hadport to the pollution that litters the atmosphere visible from its shore, where 'a spritz of bright air meeting water, of delicate chemical auras dancing around one another before mingling and ascending to the stratosphere' (TR, 5). In its 'vision of an integrated natural world that includes the human', the novel demonstrates a level of correspondence to Gifford's description of 'post-pastoral' (Gifford, 1999: 148).

However, this knowledge fails to lead to the emergence of new responsibility towards or reparation of that situation. The degraded landscape is relayed along with a sense of human culpability that is accompanied by acceptance or even resignation. The characters' eyes are open to the state of the environment, the threat that it is coming to pose to their own futures, and to the collective human role in the development of the situation. Despite this, the understanding of the interconnected environment is described without the possibility of aversion or repair: 'Cause and effect. Get used to the way A leads to B. Get used to living in interesting times. Learn that nothing is random. Watch out for the tipping point. Look behind you: perhaps it's been and gone' (*TR*, 4). The characters' resignation depicts a negative version of Gifford's 'vision of accommodated humans' (Gifford, 1999: 149) cognisant of their interconnected place in the world yet lacking the sense of responsibility and the necessity for galvanising change that Gifford couples to it.

Faced with almost unimaginable disaster, Gabrielle momentarily re-evaluates the landscape with pastoral eyes. Revelling in 'the sound of birdsong and the rustle of wind in the reeds', she imagines a landscape of 'patchworked farmland, its hills and cliffs and valleys and gorges, its woodlands of oak and birch and beech and pine, its rivers and cattle pastures and bright swathes of hemp and rape' (*TR*, 266). Instating the selectivity of pastoral vision that the previously unromantic descriptions of the environment had avoided, Gabrielle is right to conclude that 'there is no room for catastrophes' here, because the perspective from which the landscape is described omits from view the traces that could presage such outcomes (*TR*, 266). However, the elements of the environment described at this point exist in combination with those that Gabrielle was prepared to acknowledge earlier on in the novel, before catastrophe became a certainty. The litter, the pollution, and the broken remnants of industry, are the traces through which catastrophe can 'gain entry', and suggest that perhaps it already has (*TR*, 266).

As the signs of disaster begin to become apparent, Gabrielle pits her pastoral fantasy against another understanding of nature, 'I realise the extent of my mistake in accepting the grandiose notion that Earth's plight is man's punishment' (*TR*, 308). Considering that '[n]ature is neither good nor motherly nor punitive nor vengeful. It neither blesses nor cherishes. It is indifferent', she comes to question both pastoral and anti-pastoral interpretations of the situation between the human and the non-human, adopting a perspective outside of these interlinked poles and reflecting upon what can be understood outside of them, '[w]hich makes us as expendable as the dodo or the polar bear' (*TR*, 308). Her conclusions could be read to be unpastoral, or even another kind of escapism that relies on nature as an inert system of cause and effect, but the events of the novel surely demonstrate that human action is part of and subject to the same system, suggesting that Gabrielle's understanding demonstrates a reckoning of nature that looks beyond the scope of the human.

In its self-consciousness towards pastoral and anti-pastoral perspectives, the text conveys a sense of their limitations and in so doing, presents an interaction with pastoral than moves beyond those perspectives. Resisting 'post-pastoral' too, though, the ending of the novel is unquestionably problematic, as Gabrielle surveys the devastated landscape and describes it as 'a world I want no part of' (*TR*, 341). As such, in *The Rapture*, the pastoral is used as a provocation, rather than to effect the kind of 'healing work' that Gifford assigns to it (Gifford, 2006a: 24). Gifford explains that 'post-pastoral's ... ultimate purpose is as a tool for making better choices', a possibility not realized within Jensen's novel (Gifford, 2006c: 176). However, the representation of nature and human–nature interrelations conveyed via the manipulation of the conventions of pastoral and anti-pastoral in the novel raises questions of environmental accountability outside of the prescription of 'post-pastoral'. Beyond the novel, and with consideration of the issues that it explores, the possibility of 'making better choices' remains open.

The Accidental and 'neo-pastoral'

Ryle also envisages a writing of responsibility in contemporary pastoral. His proposition of 'neo-pastoral' writing centres on the critical responsibility of pastoral and its interventionist potential to contribute towards social and political dialogues concerning human-nature relations. Distinguishing his version of pastoral from Gifford's based on the emphasis upon nature and the cultivation of 'awe' in 'post-pastoral', Ryle questions the need for environmentally oriented pastoral writing to define or represent nature as such (Ryle, 2009: 16). Reading Ali Smith's *The Accidental* in 2009, Ryle is interested in the ways that the novel resists and re-imagines pastoral for the twenty-first century. As the use of the term 'eco-didactic' suggests, Ryle emphasizes the use of pastoral to approach, understand and inform contemporary conceptions of environmental concern: he explains that the novel 'represents how we know and deny that we are facing an ecological crisis, of perhaps disastrous proportions' (Ryle, 2009: 9).

Ryle describes the 'eco-didacticism' in the novel as facilitated by its method of 'educative pastoral simplification' (Ryle, 2009: 9), a process that extends from Smith's use of the pastoral technique of a period of sequestered reflection leading to revelatory cognition to what Ryle sees as the stripped-down construction of the novel's pastoral world. Ryle identifies an ambivalent treatment of pastoral nature within the novel, which he suggests is integral to its critical potential, and indeed helps to facilitate such potential. Ryle argues that the novel's focus lies in what the characters' brief time in the countryside can teach them, rather than in the evocation of celebratory nature in the context of environmental crisis. In the novel, there is 'a liminal sense that worlds are being made and unmade', and for Ryle, the novel's 'eco-political theme develops not so much through representations of landscape and nature (of which there are few) as through this urgent temporality' (Ryle, 2009: 11).

Drawing out Smith's depictions of nature as illustrative of her innovative take on pastoral, Ryle advocates Smith's sparing approach to the representation of nature and her astringent treatment of typically pastoral idyllicism and romanticization. Highlighting in particular the passage describing the worker bees' disposal of the drones, Ryle suggests that '[h]ere, "nature" offers no pre-lapsarian harmony counterposed to the fallen world of violence and destruction. Smith refuses the binary opposition between culture and nature ... and this is one reason why *The Accidental* has a sense of inescapable contemporaneity' (Ryle, 2009: 11). Written with environmental crisis in mind, the version of pastoral here is intended to galvanize critical thought and action, and the representation of nature reflects rather than relieves the situation.

Suggesting that 'good eco-politically savvy fiction can dispense altogether with "nature writing"' (Ryle, 2009: 16), Ryle points to a version of pastoral that sidesteps the difficulty of negotiating the distance between the experience and representation of nature emphasized by environmental critics such as Timothy Morton.[6] However, though critical of the way that Gifford 'implies that post-pastoral texts must include memorable descriptions and evocations of nature' (Ryle, 2009: 16), Smith's depiction of nature is memorable for it distinction from and resistance towards pastoral or anti-pastoral representations. Further, it is through the understanding of nature both outside of and in relation to human experience that Astrid in particular comes to gain her environmentally oriented perspective through understanding the interconnected or enmeshed ways of seeing and experiencing. The evocation of nature is integral to this contemporary version of pastoral, and the critical potential that it represents. The distinction of 'neo-pastoral' from 'nature writing' misses the opportunity to account for the ways that the novel's depiction of the processes of interpreting and relating conceptions of nature is central to its innovative treatment of the conventions of pastoral writing.

In Smith's novel, techniques of the pastoral are deployed relatively conventionally in order to unfold this sense of crisis, and to explore our understanding of and responses towards it. Documenting the Smart family's transformative summer holiday in a Norfolk village, *The Accidental* is recognizably pastoral in both structure and outcome: the characters retreat from the city to the country, during which time their conceptions of these locations and of themselves are subject to contemplation and revelation. The characters experience a pastoral interlude or inset in which their eyes are opened to looking differently.[7] Pastoral here is constructed as a process of transition to another place, another perspective, another way of seeing, and both the representation and interpretation of nature and human-nature relations are under scrutiny. Retreat into the countryside takes the family outside of their everyday surroundings and as the familiar elements of the Smart's lives are stripped away, for example, when Astrid's camera is destroyed by Amber, their subsequent experiences challenge their preconceptions of the place and of themselves. Re-focusing their perceptions and interpretations, the Smarts are provoked to question and to refresh their viewpoints through their experiences of the countryside and of each other during their time away.

The ways that the pastoral is used and the means by which its transformative effects are enacted resist typical understanding of pastoral or anti-pastoral approaches. A pastoral contrast between the country and the city foregrounds the evaluation of the village provided from Astrid's point of view at the beginning of the novel. Smith troubles both the contrast between the urban and the rural and the intended or supposed outcome of pastoral retreat. The relieving effect of the countryside does not register. The country is both 'substandard' (*TA*, 7), and indecipherable according to Astrid: 'it is completely light outside now; you can see for miles. Except there is nothing to see here; trees and fields and that kind of thing' (*TA*, 10). The countryside falls outside of her frames of reference and her expectations of its appearance.

At this point, Smith draws attention to the way in which external impressions are applied to pastoral places and dictate their interpretation, destabilizing to some extent the pastoral expectation of the restorative experience of an illuminative perspective uniquely provided by its location. Astrid compares her assessment of the village to her mother's, and questions her repeated enthusiasm for its apparently defining character: 'this is a quintessential place. Her mother keeps saying so, she says it every evening.' (*TA*, 11). As Smith makes plain, Astrid sees a particular version of the countryside and her mother Eve sees a contrasting one, yet both are more closely connected to the places and the perspectives from which they have arrived there, than to the environment visible from their holiday house. The novel questions external and ideological appropriations of place, a quality often attributed to the urban character of pastoral writing, distanced from its rural object. This comparative construction of the urban and the rural comes to be questioned or undermined as the narrative progresses, and their intersection becomes apparent as the local area is mapped out through the narrative. Concerned with the multiplicity of ways of seeing, the novel highlights and challenges the selectivity of pastoral vision. Forms of knowledge and identification are open and subject to question.

As Ryle suggests, Smith demonstrates how the characters each 'enact an attempt to superimpose "pastoral" habits of seeing on a contemporary rural scene' (Ryle, 2009: 16). Describing the depiction of the landscape in the novel, and using in particular the example of Amber and Astrid's picnic in the supermarket car park beside the recycling bins, Ryle explains that the novel 'evokes and subverts pastoral idyll' (Ryle, 2009: 10) through the contrast between the characters' respective evaluation of the location, as 'lovely' and 'horrible' (*TA*, 116). At the same time, the episode draws attention to the broader contrast between the presence of recycling bins proclaiming 'Success. Environment' in a car park (*TA*, 116). Highlighting the juxtaposition of the celebration of environmental consciousness signified by recycling facilities alongside the provision for parking cars, Smith provides an image of selective pastoral vision in practice. Through the conscious depiction of the blinkered character of pastoral ways of seeing, for Ryle, 'Smith's writing activates the potential, and also suggests the screening process' of the disparity that it signifies (Ryle, 2009: 16). The treatment of the distance between pastoral appropriation and experience can be used both to highlight and to distort that disparity. Here, the novel can be seen to be paralleling the selective vision of pastoral discussed above with the selective 'care' of an incomplete environmentalism. As Rupert Hildyard explains, Ryle draws out the ways in which Smith's novel pits "neo-pastoral' reflexivity against ... the transient self-deceptions of pastoral' (Hildyard, 2009).

Through the use of such reflexivity, the illuminative potential of pastoral retreat comes to be reinstated in ways that challenge previous expectations and question, rather than reinforce, previous experiences. As Astrid explores the area with Amber, the novel continues to test the differences between expectation and experience. Approaching a field, Astrid observes that 'it is all golden' (*TA*, 110) before 'walking straight through all the stuff growing in it' to find that it is 'jabby ... dry and very uneven, and the field is huge, much bigger than it seemed from the edge of the motorway where it looked like it would be really easy to walk across' (*TA*, 111). Imagining beforehand that 'she and Amber are giants in a different world' (*TA*, 111), Astrid finds that her experience runs counter to her estimation.

Astrid comes to see the limitations of her initial perspective, and to acknowledge others that exist outside of it. Developing an understanding of the simultaneity, the contrasts and the intersection of different perspectives, she describes her perception of the passing of a minute in time. The complaint of 'nothing to see here' that Astrid makes earlier in the novel is contrasted with a new sensitivity towards the non-human activity within her gaze, '[i]t is actually not true that not a single thing happened in that minute she counted just now. There were birds and things like insects flying. Crows or something probably cawed in the heat above her' (*TA*, 127). Further, she becomes aware of the presence of events beyond the scope of her vision: '[t]here is a tall white plant over behind the wall, cow something ... it must even have grown but in a way that can't be seen by the human eye' (*TA*, 127). Astrid's acknowledgement of the visible and invisible layers of activity in front of her concludes with an incipient awareness of that which is yet to be discerned, though is surely 'all happening in its own world which exists on its own terms in this one even if someone like Astrid doesn't know about it or hasn't found out about it yet' (*TA*, 127). Becoming aware of the non-human, Astrid extends her perception of her environment to encompass levels of life that had previously gone unnoticed. Implicit within her new awareness are the connections between the different 'worlds' that exist within 'this one', and the obligation for responsibility towards those connections.

As such, Astrid's developing environmental consciousness gives new context to her experiences, linking her experiences in the country to her life in the city. She recalls that '[a]t school teachers are always going on about the environment and all the species that are dying out etc. It is all everywhere all the time, it is serious' (*TA*, 128). Reflecting upon her sensitivity towards ways of looking at her environment, Astrid questions how to channel her changing awareness: 'it is hard to know how to make it actually matter inside your head, how to make it any more important than thinking about the colour green' (*TA*, 128).

Accessing a mode of environmental sensitivity and ecological consciousness, Astrid begins to apply the abstraction of environmental crisis to familiar situations, opening up the potential to see those situations afresh. Ryle goes on to suggest that the 'neo-pastoral' structure builds upon and exceeds that of pastoral; the pattern of retreat and return is appended by the haunting quality of its self-reflective revelations: 'on the cusp of ecological disaster, the forms of knowledge and self-criticism will come back, they will continue to haunt us, because they express ... repressed better knowledge' (Ryle, 2009: 17). The ecological significance of the experiences imagined by the pastoral in contemporary writing have an irrepressible resonance that must transcend 'the transience of the pastoral moment' (Ryle, 2009: 16). As in *The Rapture*, the illuminative potential of pastoral in the context of environmental crisis is apparent in *The Accidental*. Further, though Ryle discounts the significance of the evocation of nature in this version of contemporary pastoral, Smith's innovative use of the tradition suggests that consideration of the representation of nature and of the effects of such representation remain central to the imperatives of environmental consciousness, critique and accountability to which its conventions are being put.

Contemporary versions of pastoral

Both *The Rapture* and *The Accidental* deal with evocations and conceptions of nature and the interrelations between the human and non-human in ways that exceed pastoral or anti-pastoral understandings. Through the transposition of such examples of contemporary pastoral into 'post-pastoral' or 'neo-pastoral' frameworks, Gifford and Ryle suggest that the reflexivity of the pastoral movement of retreat, restoration and return when coupled with ecological awareness can inspire a sense of responsibility. However, beyond these appropriations of contemporary pastoral there are many more lines of enquiry to be explored within the experimentation with the mode present in contemporary British fiction.

For example, John Burnside's 2008 novel *Glister* evokes the enmeshing of reverence and responsibility that characterizes Gifford's 'post-pastoral', and poses some of the questions of ethics and self-reflexivity that underpin the didactic potential of Ryle's 'neo-pastoral', and places them within what I see to be a complex framework of contemporary pastoral that supports and contributes to an ongoing conversation about how to represent and respond to ecological crisis.

Burnside's novel engages with the pastoral tradition in order to address themes of environmental crisis, culpability and responsibility. Coming into alignment with Ryle's 'eco-didacticism', Burnside has said of the novel that: 'I did want to write something about the way we have damaged our environment, and continue to do so in all kinds of inventive and subtle ways' (Burnside, 2011). Burnside uses the pastoral in comparably 'inventive and subtle' ways in order to do this; in particular, pastoral tropes are used in the novel to both depict and reflect upon the tensions inherent in representing the causes and the effects of environmental crisis and the ways in which they may be negotiated.

Through the depiction of pollution in the bleak, post-industrial community of Innertown, dominated by the decaying presence of the disused chemical plant that was once its 'best hope' (*Glister*, 12) and now the source of the toxic legacy that has led to its decline, many of the conventions of pastoral are unsettled or even defamiliarized in *Glister*. The topic brings the novel into contact with other instances of pastoral used to reflect upon human action leading to negative environmental effects, understood through the contrast between then-and-now. As Garrard has observed, Rachel Carson's *Silent Spring* (1962) employs this pastoral model to environmental effect (Garrard, 2004: 1). Buell labels such examples of pastoral as 'toxic discourse', tracing its origins back to George Perkins Marsh's *Man and Nature* (1864), though Ken Hilter has more recently identified a similar usage in John Evelyn's 1661 pamphlet *Fumifugium* concerning air pollution in London (Buell, 1995: 39; Hiltner, 2012: 14). However, Burnside complicates such a contrast, muddying the distinction between past and present by locating a blinkered perspective upon the effects of the chemical plant in the town prior to the acknowledgement of its pollution. In so doing, Burnside parallels the selective gaze of an unquestioning pastoral representation with environmentally irresponsible behaviour.

Furthermore, the anti-pastoral premise of the polluted landscape is itself contrasted with the pleasure and beauty that protagonist Leonard finds in the 'the clumps of wild flowers and grasses that grow amid the broken glass and rubble' and 'the hedges dotted with pale, brave-looking flowers' (*Glister*, 66, 62). His pastoral experiences encompass not just the celebration of the seeming tenacity of nature in the unlikely location of the poisoned ruins, but also a backward-looking elegiac consideration of the previous condition of the place that precedes the plant altogether, called towards by the persistence of the flowers.

Echoing Gifford, Burnside has suggested that 'awe is central, is vitally necessary, to any description of the world', as David James also notes in a recent essay on Burnside's fiction (Burnside, 2006: 95; James, 2013: 605). However, Leonard's pastoral experiences at the chemical plant are also staunchly self-reflexive. He is well aware of the allure of making idealising contrasts: 'the world looked more than usually beautiful to me, but I knew it was partly because of the contrast with how ugly things were back in the town' (*Glister*, 213). In another way, Leonard reflects further on the limitations of this contrast, questioning the idealization of nature traditionally associated with pastoral restoration, and reconsidering the means and the effects of pastoral experience: 'they say every place has its own spirit, but when they talk about it in books and poems and stuff, they always mean places like bosky groves ... but why not an old warehouse, or a cooled furnace? Why not a landfill?' (*Glister*, 211).

In his experimentation with the format and conventions of the pastoral, Burnside draws attention towards ways of looking, suggesting a way of seeing that is mindful of the interrelation of the human and the non-human and the multiple and contradictory ways that this interrelation may be perceived. At the end of the novel, the real crisis in Innertown is explained as the town's collective action of turning away from the difficulties that they face, and looking aslant at the causes and the effects of those difficulties, described as 'the sin of omission: the sin of averting our gaze and not seeing what was going on in front of our eyes. The sin of not wanting to know; the sin of knowing everything and not doing anything about it' (*Glister*, 250).

In *Glister*, the pastoral allure of an idealized version of nature in the past or in a distant location is depicted alongside an anti- or counter-pastoral awareness of the interconnectivity between the human and the natural and its effects that can be traced across different times and locations. These perspectives are offset by an ecologically aware self-reflexivity that frustrates and questions the adoption of straight-forward pastoral or counter-pastoral viewpoints. The treatment of pastoral in the novel can be read to illustrate how it can both draw out and add to the pressures that complicate the relationship between pastoral and ecological responsibility.

Burnside's novel can be read as an example of a contemporary version of pastoral that works together the tensions between idealization and experience, highlights awareness of the interconnectivity between the human and the natural, or the urban and the rural domains of the pastoral contrast, and tests the balance between celebration of and responsibility towards this awareness. The version of pastoral that the novel presents shifts throughout the narrative and defies clear or conclusive interpretation. It encounters the uneasy relationship between pastoral, ecology and criticism, and reflects the precarious character of both environmental crisis and of the possibility of a mode of pastoral writing that attempts to respond to it. Burnside takes advantage of the proximity of productive environmental awareness to familiar means of interpretation, and suggests the possibility of their convergence when

> You realise how much of the world is invisible, or just on the point of being seen, if you could only find the right kind of attention to pay it, like turning the dial on a radio to the right channel, the one where everything is clearer and someone is talking in a language you understand right away, even though you know it's not the language you thought you knew. (*Glister*, 64)

The contemporary texts discussed in this essay open up the possibilities contained within an ecologically aware dimension of the mode. Through experimentation with the conventions of the pastoral, contemporary writers are able to adapt the tradition to different purposes: by questioning its conventions and turning its critical viewpoint in upon itself, the pastoral is given further potential. In Virgil's First Eclogue, the country provides a relieving contrast for the 'hapless folk' adversely affected by the 'civil dissension' of the distant city and the consequences of political and military action (Virgil, p. 6).

Several centuries later, in *The Village* George Crabbe rejects Virgil's idyllic model in his suggestion that 'From Truth and Nature shall we widely stray / Where Virgil, not where fancy, leads the way' (Crabbe, p. 2868). In contemporary versions of pastoral, the relationship between the country and the city is challenged differently. The distinctions between the country and the city are unclear and the negative environmental effects of human action transgress such boundaries. It is harder to abstract contemporary incarnations of Virgil's 'hapless folk' from the external discord to which they are subjected. Written in the context of environmental crisis, the connections between pastoral, 'truth' and 'nature' have become reflexive. The 'new versions of pastoral' anticipated by Marx are written with these difficulties in mind.

Notes

1 In Theocritus' First Idyll, 'Thrysis' Lament for Daphnis', the death of Daphnis demonstrates a reciprocity between the herdsman and the landscape, and his death is described as a disturbance to the processes of nature: 'Now, you thorns and brambles, bring forth violets, and/ Let the lovely narcissus flower on the juniper. Let / All things run contrary, since Daphnis is near to death. / Let the pine tree sprout pears, let hounds be torn by stags, / Let nightingales cry out to owls at the day's dawn.' Idyll 1, lines 131–5 (Theocritus, p. 6).

2 Loughrey describes the pastoral as a 'contested term' in response to its application to 'an almost bewildering variety of works' (Loughrey, 1984: 8). This description has often been quoted since, notably by Gifford who argues in *Pastoral* (1999) 'that the pastoral has become not only a 'contested term', but a deeply suspect one, is the cultural position in which we find ourselves' (Gifford, 1999: 147).

3 In *The Machine in the Garden*, Marx distinguishes between 'two kinds of pastoralism – one that is popular and sentimental, the other imaginative and complex' (Marx, 1964). Marx's definition echoes William Empson's definition of pastoral as 'putting the complex into the simple' (Empson, 1935/1995: 17), and is acknowledged as an influence upon Gifford's 'post-pastoral' in *Pastoral* (1999).

4 Gifford most clearly outlines 'post-pastoral' in *Pastoral* (1999), though he has developed and refined the model in numerous subsequent publications (see Gifford, 1995, 2006a, 2006b, 2006c, 2008, 2009, 2010).

5 Gifford refers here to the theory of biosemiotics, in particular that put forward by Wendy Wheeler (2006), and globalization with reference to Ursula Heise's (2008) *Sense of Place and Sense of Planet*.

6 In *Ecology Without Nature*, Timothy Morton (2007) questions the value to environmental discourse in describing nature due to its necessary distance from experience and the multifarious character of the term, 'nature writers fashion compelling *images* of nature ... nature ironically impedes a proper relationship with the earth and its life forms' (Morton, 2007: 2).

7 The term 'inset' is used by Andrew V. Ettin (1984) to describe instances when 'the pastoral is shown to exist within a nonpastoral universe, as an inset within a larger frame of reference'.

References

Barrell, John and John Bull (eds) (1974) *The Penguin Book of English Pastoral Verse*. London: Penguin.

Bracke, Astrid (2010) 'Redrawing the Boundaries of Ecocritical Practice', *ISLE Interdisciplinary Studies in Literature and Environment* 17(4): 765–7.

Buell, Lawrence (1995) *The Environmental Imagination: Thoreau, Nature Writing & The Formation of American Culture*. Cambridge, MA: Harvard University Press.

Buell, Lawrence, (2001) *Writing for an Endangered World: Literature, Culture, and Environment in the U.S. and Beyond*. Cambridge, MA: Harvard University Press.

Burnside, John (2006), 'A Science of Belonging: Poetry as Ecology', in Robert Crawford (ed.) *Contemporary Poetry and Contemporary Science*. Oxford: Oxford University Press.

Burnside, John (2008) *Glister*. London: Vintage.

Burnside, John (2011) *Interview: John Burnside on Glister*. Scottish Book Trust, accessed January 2012, http://www.scottishbooktrust.com/booktalk/john-burnside-glister-interview

Crabbe, George (1783/2000) 'The Village', in Stephen Greenblatt et al. (eds) *The Norton Anthology of English Literature*, Volume 1, pp. 2867–74. London: Norton.

Empson, William, (1935/1995) *Some Versions of Pastoral*. London: Penguin.

Ettin, Andrew V. (1984) *Literature and the Pastoral*. New Haven, CT and London: Yale University Press.

Garrard, Greg (1996) 'Radical Pastoral', *Studies in Romanticism* 35(3): 449–65.

Garrard, Greg (2004) *Ecocriticism*, London: Routledge.

Gifford, Terry (1995) *Green Voices: Understanding Contemporary Nature Poetry*. Manchester: Manchester University Press.

Gifford, Terry (1999) *The New Critical Idiom: Pastoral*. London: Routledge.

Gifford, Terry (2006a) 'Post-pastoral as a tool for Ecocriticism', in Mathilde Skoie and Sonia Bjørnstad Velázquez (eds) *Pastoral and the Humanities: Arcadia Re-Inscribed*. Bristol: Bristol Phoenix Press.

Gifford, Terry (2006b) 'What is Ecocriticism For? Some Personal Reflections on Two Recent Critiques', *Green Letters* 7: 6–14.

Gifford, Terry (2006c) *Reconnecting with John Muir: Essays in Post-Pastoral Practice*. Athens, GA: University of Georgia Press.

Gifford, Terry (2008) 'Recent Critiques of Ecocriticism', *New Formations* 64: 15–26.

Gifford, Terry (2009) 'Afterword: New Senses of "Environment," New Versions of Pastoral', in Philip Tew and David James (eds) (2009) *New Versions of Pastoral: Post-Romantic, Modern, and Contemporary Responses to the Tradition*, pp. 245–57. Madison, WI: Fairleigh Dickinson University Press.

Gifford, Terry (2010) 'Biosemiology and Globalism in *The Rapture* by Liz Jensen', *English Studies* 91(7): 713–27.

Heise, Ursula (2008) *Sense of Place and Sense of Planet: The Environmental Imagination of the Global*. London: Oxford University Press.

Hess, Scott (2004) 'Postmodern Pastoral, Advertising and the Masque of Technology', *ISLE Interdisciplinary Studies in Literature and Environment* 11(1): 71–100.

Hildyard, Rupert (2009) 'Editorial', *Green Letters* 10: 4–7.

Hiltner, Ken (2011) *What Else is Pastoral? Renaissance Literature and the Environment*. Ithaca and London: Cornell University Press.

James, David (2012), 'John Burnside's Ecologies of Solace: Regional Environmentalism and the Consolation of Description', *MFS Modern Fiction Studies* 58(3): 600–15.

Jensen, Liz (2009) *The Rapture*. London: Bloomsbury.

Loughrey, Bryan, (ed.) (1984) *The Pastoral Mode: A Casebook*. London: Macmillan.

Love, Glen A. (1996) 'Revaluing Nature: Towards an Ecological Criticism', in Cheryll Glotfelty and Harold Fromm (eds) *The Ecocriticism Reader:*

Landmarks in Literary Ecology, pp. 225–40. Athens, GA: The University of Georgia Press.

Marx, Leo (1964) *The Machine in the Garden: Technology and the Pastoral Ideal in America*. New York: Oxford University Press.

Marx, Leo (1992) 'Does Pastoralism Have a Future?', in John Dixon Hunt (ed.) *The Pastoral Landscape*, pp. 109–225. Washington, DC: National Gallery of Art.

Meeker, Joseph W (1997) *The Comedy of Survival: Literary Ecology and a Play Ethic*, 3rd edn. Tucson: University of Arizona Press (1974, revised 1980).

Morton, Timothy (2007) *Ecology without Nature: Rethinking Environmental Aesthetics*. Cambridge, MA: Harvard University Press.

Morton, Timothy (2010) *The Ecological Thought*. Cambridge, MA: Harvard University Press.

Phillips, Dana (1998) 'Don DeLillo's Postmodern Pastoral', in Michael Branch (ed.) *Reading the Earth: New Directions in the Study of Literature and Environment*, pp. 235–46. Moscow, ID: University of Idaho Press.

Ryle, Martin (2002) 'After Organic Community: Ecocriticism, Nature and Human Nature', in John Parham (ed.) *The Environmental Tradition in English Literature*. Aldershot: Ashgate.

Ryle, Martin (2009) 'Neo-Pastoral and Eco-Didactics: Ali Smith's *The Accidental*', *Green Letters* 10: 8–19.

Ryle, Martin (2011) 'The Past, the Future and the Golden Age: Some Contemporary Versions of Pastoral', in Kate Soper, Martin Ryle and Lyn Thomas (eds) *The Politics and Pleasures of Consuming Differently*. Basingstoke: Palgrave Macmillan.

Selby, Nick (2011) 'Reading England: Pastoral, Elegy and the Politics of Place in Richard Caddel and Harriet Tarlo', *Textual Practice*, 25(5): 893–911.

Smith, Ali (2005) *The Accidental*. London: Penguin.

Theocritus, Idylls (2002), trans. Anthony Verity, ed. Richard Hunter. Oxford: Oxford University Press.

Tew, Philip and David James (eds) (2009) *New Versions of Pastoral: Post-Romantic, Modern, and Contemporary Responses to the Tradition*, Madison: Fairleigh Dickinson University Press.

Virgil, (1999) *The Eclogues, The Georgics*, trans. C. Day Lewis, ed. R. O. A. M. Lyne, Oxford: Oxford University Press.

Wheeler, Wendy (2006) *The Whole Creature: Complexity, Biosemiotics and the Evolution of Culture*. London: Lawrence and Wishart.

Williams, Raymond (1973) *The Country & The City*. London: Chatto & Windus.

Observing London
From Performer to Spectator

Emma Hayward

In a recent radio interview with Kit Caless (2012), Lee Rourke recalled what it was like to grow up in Manchester next to a disused
canal, describing it as a place 'to go and not be seen' (Caless, 2012).
As a child, the canal was a space of escape for Rourke, a refuge from
the rest of the city and, of course, a retreat from the watchful gaze of
adults, a curious nowhere with the potential to conceal and disguise
those who happen to stumble across it. It is the post-industrial geography of Rourke's childhood landscape that informs the author's debut
novel *The Canal* (2010), in which the protagonist – an anonymous
first person male narrator – observes and negotiates the peculiarities
of a short stretch of London's Regent's Canal. Much like Rourke's account of his childhood, the narrator comes to the canal to escape the
city and, in particular, to elude the endless familiarity and meaningless routine that has come to govern his everyday existence.

The novel begins with the narrator's recollection of his discovery
of a bench on the towpath 'halfway between Hackney and Islington'
(*TC*, 3), that was 'nestled between two large hedges that had long
since over grown' (*TC*, 3). As the repetition of 'between' implies, the
narrator is eager to suggest the liminality of the canal: he is in a place
neither in Hackney nor Islington but on the threshold dividing the
two boroughs, and the neglected hedge life creates a type of retreat

175

from the towpath, which, as the narrator states, made it 'hard for pass-ers-by to see me until they were almost in front of me' (*TC*, 3). The narrator's self-conscious act of concealment in this passage is an im-plicit reworking of the opening to *The Divine Comedy*, in which a spiri-tually lost Dante finds himself astray in a dark forest on the threshold of hell. Throughout the first canto of the 'Inferno', Dante's spiritual confusion is manifested in geographical terms through the liminal landscape within which he finds himself lost: 'obscured' by the dark wilderness of a 'rough' and 'overpowering' forest he is caught between a narrow gorge leading to hell and a hill that ascends to heaven (Sis-son, 1998: 47). The opening stanzas in the first canto are punctuated with images of marginality that accentuate the psychological strain and tension created by Dante's reflections on his wavering spiritual morality. The juxtaposition of the darkness of the forest and the 'glow-ing' mountain, the close proximity between Dante – a living person – and the gorge where 'No living person had ever passed before', and the reference to 'the beach' – an equivocal space between land and sea – all allude to the poet's confused spiritual state (Sisson, 1998: 47). He does not occupy a distinct or clearly defined space but '[s]taggers' (Sisson, 1998: 47) instead through an ambiguous geography.

Being lost in this undefined landscape is by no means presented as a negative or wholly undesirable experience: in a state of trepidation Dante stands at the foot of a hill and 'look[s] up' (Sisson, 1998: 47) to seek comfort from the darkness of the forest but, prompted by curios-ity, he '[t]urn[s] back' (Sisson, 1998: 47) to glance at the defile that leads downwards into hell. The gesture itself is significant because it suggests the poet's romantic desire to confront the unknown. The for-est may well express his spiritual failings but its marginality also signi-fies a potential for Dante to engage with the 'Other'.

The liminality suggested by Rourke's narrator is a bathetic appro-priation of that which is experienced by Dante in *The Divine Comedy*. Whereas Dante had 'lost [his] way' (Sisson, 1998: 47) in a previously uncharted landscape, the prepositions used by Rourke's narrator, rather than creating any sense of uncertainty, suggest an acute geo-graphical knowledge of the area. In much the same way as Rourke, who as a child was afforded a certain level of invisibility by the canal,

Dante is also rendered invisible by his environs, albeit that the narrator of Rourke's novel is merely nestled amidst some unkempt hedges along a towpath that is 'busy with people walking and cycling' (*TC*, 3).

Despite believing that he will remain 'undisturbed', it is only 'three or four hours' (*TC*, 6) into his reverie before the narrator is interrupted by a peculiar old lady who 'reeked of urine and was [dressed] in layers of clothing [...] She had no teeth, only a black hole for a mouth' (*TC*, 6) and who repeatedly asks if he likes the canal.[1] The narrator's exaggerated description of this presumably homeless figure stresses her peculiarity, but in spite of her apparent otherness the narrator is largely unmoved by his encounter: 'I got up from the bench and left her without saying a word. I headed back towards Hackney [...] I was hungry' (*TC*, 6–7). The narrator leaves the liminal space of the bench with ease and informs the reader where he is going, again demonstrating his familiarity with the geography of the canal. The simple statement that concludes this section demonstrates just how quickly the narrator can forget the canal and, in particular, the strangers (and strangeness) he encounters there.

The juxtaposition of his graphic description of the homeless woman and his callous indifference towards her suggests a tension between a desire for a romantic engagement with the unfamiliar and the familiarity of the everyday. This is first brought to the reader's attention in the prologue when the narrator describes what first attracted him to the canal: 'It was something about the light. I'd say it was almost crepuscular, even though it was some time between 8:30 and 9:00 in the morning and light can't be described as *crepuscular* at that time of the day' (*TC*, 1). The narrator immediately diminishes the atmosphere of peculiarity he attempts to evoke by drawing the reader's attention to the implausibility of his own narrative description.

Disillusioned with his life, which he describes as a relentless pattern of 'drinking in the same pub, with the same people, the same faces; drinking the same drinks, saying the same things' (*TC*, 13), the narrator informs the reader that his reason for coming to the canal is to embrace the boredom that other people try to resist by engaging in 'superfluous activity: fashion, lifestyle, TV, drink, drugs, technology, et cetera – the usual things we do to pass the time' (*TC*, 13). Because of this focus on boredom, as well as the self-absorption of the narrator and the philosophical contemplation on the vacuity of life, initial reviews of the novel aligned *The Canal* with the existentialist tradition, comparing Rourke to the likes of Camus and Sartre.[2] However, the boredom and inertia that pervades *The Canal* is also evocative of a different, specifically urban, literary tradition – flânerie. In *The Arcades Project*, Walter Benjamin declared that 'boredom is the threshold to great deeds' (Benjamin, 2002: 105). For Benjamin boredom is a gateway to the extraordinary and a break from the familiar because it precipitates opportunities to experience and notice things one would not normally experience or notice owing to the distractions of routine and 'superfluous activity' (*TC*, 13). For the flâneur, the 'fruits of idleness are more precious than the fruits of labour' (Benjamin, 2002: 453). Like Benjamin's flâneur, Rourke's narrator attempts to remove himself from the familiar rhythms and routines of the city by embracing a form of idleness. In doing so, the city can reveal itself in new ways, enabling the narrator to achieve an experience that is somehow different to the endless acts of consumption and routine that govern his life.[3] However, he proves largely unsuccessful in his pursuit, for what he finds at the canal is not alterity but familiarity, a confirmation of the repetitive existence he is trying to escape.

Walter Benjamin's extensive collection of writing on cities draws attention to a specific set of urban conditions required to alienate oneself from the modern metropolis in order to successfully practice flânerie. Between April and June of 1930, the German periodical *Die Literarische Welt* published Benjamin's 'Paris Diary' – a short series of diary style essays based on his travels in Paris and interviews with literary celebrities. Describing his initial response to the French metropolis, Benjamin makes a distinction between Paris and his native city Berlin. For Benjamin, Berlin is a city that is fully exposed to the eye; it is transparent and precipitates feelings of recognition and familiarity. Every aspect of the city can be easily noticed and assimilated by all: 'what an easy matter it is to overlook this city! ... You can't imagine how uninsistent it is. There are perhaps few cities in which so little is – or can be – overlooked as in Berlin. This may be the effect of the organizational and technical spirit that prevails there, for good or ill' (Benjamin, 2005: 337).[4] Paris, by contrast, is described as 'uninsistent'; it is subtle and understated where even the most familiar details can defy recognition: 'Just think how the streets here seem to be inhabited interiors, how much you fail to see day after day, even in the most familiar parts' (Benjamin, 2005: 337). It is, to borrow from the title of Italo Calvino's (1997) philosophical meditation on Venice, an invisible city, that is to say a city that perpetually folds inwards on itself therefore concealing itself and preventing the individual from viewing it in its entirety all at once. Moreover, those who do not simply use the streets but 'inhabit' them flout the traditional spatial dichotomy between interior and exterior. In this sense, Paris is a liminal city; it can be one thing but something else entirely because it has not been rendered wholly visible and fixed.

In *The Arcades Project*, Benjamin elaborates upon the invisibility that characterizes Paris when he considers the relationship between its streets and the flâneur: 'The street conducts the flâneur into vanished time. For him, every street is precipitous. It leads downward' (Benjamin, 2002: 416). The streets are invested with a certain quality of depth: they are described as 'precipitous' with a trajectory that 'leads downward' into the past ('vanished time'). In this respect, the flâneur's wanderings recall Dante's journey through the nine circles of hell. As well as traversing the horizontal plane of the city's surface the streets also have the potential to carry the walker along a vertical plane that delves beyond the reified sphere of commodification: 'An intoxication comes over the man who walks long and aimlessly through the streets. With each step the walk takes on greater momentum; ever weaker grow the temptations of shops, of bistros, of smiling women' (Benjamin, 2002: 416–7).

The narrator's retreat to the canal in Rourke's novel is a rather trivial interpretation of the descent trope. Whereas Benjamin's flâneur resists the lures of exploitative commodified exchange through a sort of transcendental intoxication, which in turn leads to his Dante-like descent into the unknown regions of the metropolis, Rourke's narrator attempts to flee the superfluous commodified conditions of his existence by literally passing from the surface of the city to the canal that runs slightly beneath it. This proves to be a largely futile effort because, as the narrator quickly discovers, canals are no longer the abandoned, ambiguous nowhere spaces that feature in Rourke's account of his childhood, but instead areas of intensive redevelopment that are being transformed into commodified spaces for leisure and tourism.

In the final part of the novel, the narrator arrives at the canal only to discover that the bench from which he observes has disappeared behind a wooden wall that was erected by construction workers overnight. Not only a powerful symbol for the ways in which urban regeneration operates as an act of exclusion, the wall also signifies the canal's ongoing denaturalization and violent separation from its historical origins as a site of work: rather than enabling the labour and progress taking place along its banks the canal is actively isolated from it. Realizing that he can no longer gain access to the bench, the narrator grows nervous, agitated and self-conscious: 'I stood by the wall. I felt stupid. I was highly visible against it' (*TC*, 130). The canal is fast becoming a privatized space that is too exclusive to permit the narrator's desire for idleness and seemingly pointless observations. The bench may not have distanced the narrator from the canal in the way he hoped it would at the start of the novel, for he was always visible to those passing by, but it did legitimize his idle observations by providing him with a reason for being there and doing nothing. In other words, the narrator avoided attracting any superfluous attention because his actions (or lack of them) corresponded with the bench's function and, in this sense, he was at least able to achieve a partial obscuration. However, now that the bench has been subsumed by a building site, there is no obvious reason for the narrator's sedentariness hence the wall renders him 'highly visible' (*TC*, 130): 'I noticed the workman who was painting it down the far end, towards Islington, looking at me for a short while [...] He must have momentarily wondered what I was doing there' (*TC*, 130–1). In this exchange of glances the distinction between the subject and object of observation has collapsed. Both men watch and are watched in return, both wonder and attempt to anticipate what the other is thinking.

Like the 'Victorian warehouses and Georgian rooftops' that characterize the 'trendy developments' (*TC*, 131) of Wenlock Basin, the canal is also defunct – it was once a base for work but is now a site of leisure and tourism. No longer integral to the industrial workings of the city it has since been superseded by rail and motorway systems. As a space, the canal is in the process of being opened up and illuminated by developers:

> The murky water was shimmering in the odd light, with dark patches of black cut and sliced into geometric patterns that moved forwards with purpose, mirroring the progress that was being developed on either side [...] its bridges and towpaths would soon be widened and extended [...] the bridge [made] into a resting point, a platform to view the new life styles on show. (*TC*, 131)

Any references to the oblique ('murky water', 'dark patches of black') are quickly challenged and opposed by the verbs 'shimmering' 'widened', 'extended', 'view', 'mirroring', suggesting that the canal is no longer a multilayered space that contributes to the working development of the city, but a designated, two-dimensional space from which to view a set of standardized, virtual images. Instead of actively aiding industrial progress the canal now passively mirrors the development taking place alongside its banks. It is no longer the barges that move 'forwards with purpose' on the canal's waters, but a series of intangible 'geometric patterns', that is to say the reflections of the commercial and housing developments that are being erected alongside the canal. This sense of passivity is reiterated by the fact that the bridge's primary function as an architectural structure purposely designed for crossing the water has now been reinterpreted as a 'resting point'. It is interesting that the narrator refers to the bridge as a place from which to 'view' and not from which to watch or observe for the latter would suggest a sustained and detailed engagement with the canal whereas the former suggests a fleeting and cursory glance at what is already obvious and visible. The bridge, then, is no potential replacement for the bench but a gallery from which to consume the developer's image of the canal.

The narrator's description of the canal calls to mind Fredric Jameson's claim that 'the emergence of a new kind of flatness or depthlessness, a new kind of superficiality in the most literal sense, [is] perhaps the supreme formal feature of all the postmodernisms' (Jameson, 1996: 9). Jameson argues that depth models – systems of binary oppositions that previously governed interpretation and analysis, such as the linguistic opposition between signifier and signified or the dialectical one between essence and appearance – have been replaced by 'surface, or by multiple surfaces' (Jameson, 1996: 12). In other words, the surface no longer veils a strange unknown and it no longer gestures towards anything external to itself. In a culture that privileges the simulacral image above all else the concept of depth is lost.[5]

As Rourke's novel suggests, the depthlessness that characterized postmodernism is also a defining feature of the urban landscape of postmodernity, which is precisely what the narrator spends much of his time trying to refute. After witnessing a gang of male youths dump a scooter in the canal the narrator implores his companion (a woman who also spends much of her time sitting on the same bench) to look into the water and confirm that she can see the stolen and abandoned vehicle: "'Look! See it? ... *There!* ... Do you see what they've done?...'" (*TC*, 102). The exclamatory sentences are indicative of the narrator's extremely excitable state, but this excitement is not solely provoked by the antisocial behaviour of the gang but more by the fact that there is now definitely something hidden in the canal. The handlebars that he can see 'breaking through the surface' (*TC*, 102) seem to be the primary trigger for his excitement; they act as a bridge between the visible surface and the invisible realm beneath thereby demonstrating the canal's depth and its potential to host innumerable oddities and relics from another life. Unfortunately, the narrator's companion does not share his excitement and instead confirms that there is simply nothing: "'I can't see anything... *there* ... in the canal. I can't see anything'" (*TC*, 102).

Throughout much of the novel, the narrator expresses a curious interest in the dredgers: 'I wanted to see them, the dredgers, I wanted to see them in action. I wanted see what they might find in the thick sludge' (*TC*, 9). Symbolically they are significant because they have the potential to mobilize the canal, to stir its waters and unearth the hidden detritus of an unfamiliar past. His desire to see the dredgers 'in action' can be interpreted as a desire to transcend the perimeters of his known experience because to confront the historical debris drowned in the murky waters of the canal would grant the narrator an opportunity to engage with the area's exotically unfamiliar past.

However, the dredgers remain absent until much later in the novel, and when they do appear they fail to materialize the other reality that the narrator was hoping for: 'even though the dredger had finally appeared I still didn't feel that everything I wanted – the cleaning of the muck and slutch and filth around me – would ever happen. Nothing appeared. All this waiting. Nothing but here. Endless here' (*TC*, 135). The narrator's wish to see the canal cleaned is ironic as it actually reiterates the effects of late capitalist development: the rendering visible of all that which was previously understated or concealed. As the narrator suggested in his earlier description of the newly regenerated canal, development has diminished any sense of depth and obscurity and has instead transformed it into a simulacral image of itself. Nevertheless, like the flâneur the narrator does, after much idle waiting, have a moment of epiphany, but where the flâneur's engagement with the urban environment proves 'spellbinding' and 'surprising' (Benjamin, 2002: 416), the narrator's epiphany regarding the canal (and life in general) is an anti-climactic realization that there is nothing beyond the immediate present: no spellbinding past, or peculiar other, just a frighteningly relentless and familiar here.

In contrast to the solitary endeavours of the traditional flâneur, the narrator's engagement with the canal revolves largely around his conversations with an anonymous female interlocutor, which further articulates his struggle to disengage from the familiar. During their first conversation, the woman informs the narrator that the dredgers have failed to show up and clean the canal, precisely the observation that was preoccupying the narrator just a few pages earlier. However, when he informs her of this coincidence she simply responds with a 'long, drawn-out yawn' that 'seemed to last aeons' (*TC*, 15). Rather than being appreciated by the characters as common ground with which the two strangers can use to form a connection, the similarity in thought is, if anything, a disappointment, an unwanted confirmation that they are not strangers at all. The narrator's interaction with

the area does not incite bewilderment or alienation, but further comprehension.

In his penetrating examination on the concept of reality in the late
twentieth century – *The Perfect Crime* – Jean Baudrillard contemplates the impact that the rapid accumulation of knowledge and information has had upon the cultural, social and political life of advanced
capitalist societies. He argues that an excess of the real has precipitat-
ed the 'total illumination' (Baudrillard, 2008: 54) of the world. That
is to say, a transparent world in which everything can be immediately
understood, experienced, anticipated and consumed. According to
Baudrillard (2008: 29), 'virtual perfection' leaves no room 'for a critical consciousness and demystification'. That is, a process of demystification is redundant in a world in which we are already 'in possession
of all the information' (Baudrillard, 2008: 29) for there is nothing left
to demystify and therefore no need for critical consciousness or distance. As a result, Baudrillard claims that '[w]e are no longer specta-
tors, but actors in the performance, and actors increasingly integrated
into the course of that performance [...] we are defenseless before the
extreme reality of this world, before the virtual perfection' (Baudrillard, 2008: 29). The distance that once clearly distinguished the observing subject (the 'spectator') from the object of observation ('the
performance') has evaporated, and the former is no longer capable of
alienating themselves from that which they observe.

It is this condition of postmodernity – the transparency caused
by knowing everything and having anything – that Rourke suggests
now governs the individual's geographical experience of London. The
transparency created by late capitalism as identified by Baudrillard is
embedded within *The Canal* and underpins much of the narrator's experience throughout the novel. In particular, it is enacted through the
dual relationship between the narrator and his female counterpart.
The following conversation is centered around the woman's confession to the narrator that she has killed a man in a hit and run:

> I hit someone...
> You hit someone?
> Yes.

Yeah?
In my car...
   In your car?
   [...]
Was it an accident?

...

Was it an accident? Did you...?

...

(*TC*, 55)

Upon hearing this revelation the narrator responds, understandably, with shock and disbelief as the excessive repetition of rhetorical questions implies. However, they are not solely designed to signify the narrator's struggle to comprehend what he has just discovered about his interlocutor. The unrestrained repetition of rhetorical questions self-consciously exposes their own redundancy as the narrator asks his questions after he already has the answer. He does not need to participate in a strenuous dialectical exchange in order to retrieve information for it is already readily available. When he does ask a question first ('Was it an accident?'), he is met by his interlocutor with silence, which not only gives rise to the sinister possibility that it was deliberate but also suggests that the conversation has already been actualized and will be delivered as such without the messy, unplanned for interjections of a listener. In other words, the narrator struggles to influence the direction of the conversation and, in turn, the narrator's interlocutor is incapable of responding to external input from her dialogical partner.

Later on during the same conversation, the narrator presses his companion for more information:

Was it...?
What?
Was it a...?
Hit and run?
Yes
Yes... it was.
Did he...?
What?

Did you ... ?
Kill him?
Yes ...
[...]
Yes, I killed him.
(*TC*, 58)

Here, the narrator performs the role of questioner or interrogator but is again redundant because his interlocutor has assumed the part of both interviewer and interviewee by asking the questions as well as answering them. Moreover, this exchange suggests that the narrator himself is already familiar with his counterpart's narrative because his responses mirror her answers to his half articulated questions. Thus, when the woman anticipates the narrator's question '"Hit and run?"', the narrator replies '"Yes"', to which she then also answers '"Yes"'. This pattern is repeated leaving the reader with the impression that the narrator is, on some level, already aware of his interlocutor's story and is therefore able to anticipate her answers. The sense of familiarity that pervades these dialogical exchanges and the absence of a dialectical force are further heightened by the free direct presentation of speech which makes it difficult for the reader to distinguish between the narrator and his female counterpart, whose identities consequently appear interchangeable. Furthermore, the narrator's inability to establish himself as a lone critical observer in the fashion of Benjamin's flâneur suggests his failure to remove himself from the 'performance' (Baudrillard, 2008: 29), or the scene that he observes. Despite being desperate to escape from the pattern of 'saying the same things' (*TC*, 13) as he indicated at the start of the novel, the narrator is still very much occupying familiar territory, unable to alienate himself from those individuals who occupy the same space as himself.

In *Cityscapes of Modernity*, David Frisby claims that 'Benjamin's flânerie consisted of 'a form of reading the city and its population (its spatial images, its architecture, its human configurations); and a form of reading written texts (in Benjamin's case both of the city and the nineteenth century – as texts and of texts on the city, even texts as urban labyrinths)' (Frisby, 2001: 29). According to Frisby, engaging with the city's rich textuality – understanding the city as a text and wandering through labyrinthine texts on the city – is central to Benjamin's conception of flânerie. Franz Hessel also stresses the significance of the textualization of flânerie in his own definition of the peripatetic art form which he described as 'a kind of reading of the street, in which human faces, shop fronts, shop windows, café terraces, street cars, automobiles and trees become a wealth of equally valid letters of the alphabet that together result in words, sentences and pages of an ever-new book' (Frisby, 2001: 27). Hessel's description of flânerie neatly encapsulates the dual activity of the flâneur by drawing attention to the way in which he semiotically deciphers the city before reconstructing it into textual form.

The flâneur, then, is both a reader and a writer of the metropolis, not only interpreting its myriad of unruly signifiers but also assembling each sign into an image or a narrative on the city, a narrative to be sold in the literary marketplace. This is rather ironic considering one of the primary purposes of flânerie is to establish a critical distance between the observer and that which he observes but by producing literary images of the city the flâneur immediately relinquishes that distance and becomes inextricably associated with commercial exchange. Rather than contradict the flâneur's status as alienated observer, this paradox is suggestive of his perspectival mobility, that is, his ability to move freely between the roles of critical spectator and participant.

Through reading the textual fabric of the canal Rourke's narrator also conforms to this urban tradition. In a moment of *mise en abyme*, the narrator notices two signs printed on the wall that now separates him from the bench: 'I could see that both signs were repeated further along the wall at exactly the same height, maybe four or five times in total' (*TC*, 131). The precisely replicated signs contradict Hessel's suggestion that the city's versatility and malleability allow it to be perpetually rendered into an 'ever-new book' (Frisby, 2001: 27). The fact that the signs appear in the same position over and over again along the wall alludes to the homogenization of the canal, which is further suggested when the narrator contemplates the typographical features of a sign that reads 'creatingthrivingcommunities': 'It was written in everyday font like Helvetica or Impact, all the letters lower case and set as if it was one continuous word' (*TC*, 132). The narrator's description diminishes the potential richness of the canal's textuality: the reference to the 'everyday' font styles creates an awareness of its mode of production – graphically designed on computer before being mechanically reproduced *en mass* – and the aesthetic continuity of the sign, rather than signifying a plurality of thriving communities, actually calls to mind stifling uniformity. Moreover, the narrator goes on to suggest that the sign has, in some respects, already been read and interpreted for him: 'But in case anyone thought it *was* one word, the designers of the sign had coloured the word *creating* in green and the word *thriving* in red; the word *communities* was left black' (*TC*, 132). There is something quite sinister about this observation as it implies that the designers have made a deliberate effort to limit potential alternative interpretations of the sign.

Towards the end of the novel the narrator notices a newly erected barrier across the bridge to block traffic, and accompanying it is the sign: 'Emergency access DO NOT OBSTRUCT' (*TC*, 197). Despite studying the text for some time, the sign only inspires a further feeling of disappointment in the narrator: 'I don't know why but I began to read the sign over and over again, maybe six or seven times, as if I was hoping it would change and say something else to me' (*TC*, 197). The narrator's reading of the canal lacks the polysemy that was present in both Benjamin and Hessel's textual engagement with urban space. In fact, his reading evokes Benjamin's description of Berlin in the sense that the sign holds no signification beyond its literal or intended meaning; regardless of how hard the narrator tries to read past the surface of the canal's text it fails to yield 'something else', there is no alternative narrative hidden beneath.

This is recapitulated shortly after when the narrator notices a large sign erected on the development site alongside the canal that simply reads 'REAL' (*TC*, 198). Presumably, the sign was meant to read 'REAL ESTATE', but it has either been defaced or has been left incomplete, either way it serves as a rather bleak symbolic reminder for the narrator that there is no escaping the endless present and underscores Baudrillard's claim that 'we are defenseless before the extreme reality of this world' (Baudrillard, 2008: 29). The narrator's confinement to the real is once more reiterated by the location of the sign itself, which has been 'thoughtfully positioned, so that it could be viewed from every conceivable angle' (*TC*, 198). It is obvious at this point that the narrator is struggling to discover an alternative to the canal's epidermal narrative and the reader is once more reminded nothing remains hidden from view.

As Frisby (2001: 29) also points out, flânerie, in Benjamin's work, is associated with the act of writing, with the production of 'distinctive kinds of texts' on the city. It is the adherence to the principles of montage in works such as *The Arcades Project* (2002) and 'One-way Street' (Benjamin, 2009) that mark Benjamin's texts as distinctive. The form allows Benjamin to collapse the boundaries between the page and the street, and the distinction between the flâneur and the reader thereby manifesting the experience of the flâneur in the experience of the reader. Theorizing his approach to constructing *The Arcades Project*, Benjamin wrote: 'Method of this project: literary montage. I needn't say anything. Merely show' (Benjamin, 2002: 460). The montage form generates a pseudo-scientific voice, which reiterates the author/flâneur's distance from both the text and the metropolis he observes. As a result, the reader is left to approach the text in much the same way as the flâneur approaches the street: without a predetermined origin or destination. He creates an equivocal textual ground for the reader to traverse, which consequently generates feelings of unfamiliarity.

The regular narrative breaks that permeate *The Canal* formally evoke Benjamin's montage technique, suggesting a discontinuous, fragmented text imbued with regular interruptions and changes. However, the form belies the content of the novel, and instead the structure reiterates the feeling of familiarity and repetition that pervades the narrator's experience of the canal. Despite the typographical promise of contradictions and tensions the narrative is, at times, obstinately uniform. In part four, for example, sections two, three, four and five are all relatively short, varying in length between two paragraphs and two pages, but the breaks seem unnecessary for they do not mark a temporal or spatial shift, neither do they signify a change in tone or perspective. Section two is centered on the narrator's response to the appearance of the developer's wall and the disappearance of the bench, and ends with his rather sombre realization that '[e]verything should be left alone. Nothing should be touched. Because even the dredgers were powerless to halt such unremitting decay' (*TC*, 133). Section three continues this bleak sentiment by beginning exactly where the previous section ended – with the narrator standing by the wall: 'It began to rain. A light, greasy drizzle. It didn't bother me. I was waiting for her. Suddenly, I heard a strange noise: shouting, instructions, and machinery. It came from the direction of the lock at Wenlock Basin' (*TC*, 133). The spatial and temporal coordinates remain the same, and in an act of pathetic fallacy the weather is used to reiterate the dreariness of the narrator's previous statement. The use of 'suddenly' is deceptive; it suggests that something has changed, but this is not the case as the 'strange noise' is merely the sound of the dredgers approaching and, since the image of the dredgers has been cultivated in the reader's imagination since page one, their appearance in the final quarter of the novel is not at all sudden or unexpected. Their arrival holds even less significance when one remembers that only a few lines earlier, at the end of the previous section, the narrator nullified their importance by suggesting that they were powerless to protect the canal from the process of redevelopment and inevitable decline into a simulacral space. The dredgers have lost their symbolic authority – no longer archeological tools with the potential to unearth the unfamiliar narratives of the past but impotent machines incapable of reviving the canal.

This sense of stagnation, which is created by a lack of narrative progression and structural tension, is, however, challenged by the narrator's discursive observations. Take the opening pages of the novel, for example, in which the narrator moves rapidly through a series of memories and observations:

> I turned to the murky water. I watched the Canada Geese. Two of them. Mates. I liked them. I always have done. [...] I began to think about my childhood – I couldn't believe I used to swim in this very

canal [...] On the other side of the bank stood a large white washed building. (*TC*, 4).

The succession of simple and minor sentences conveys a sense of urgency and rapidity; they suggest the narrator's eagerness to observe, to notice the details that constitute the canal. The temporal shift between the present and the narrator's past again implies a sense of movement, as does the random shift in focus from the geese, to the childhood memory and then to the white washed building. The repetition of the personal pronoun is also significant because, in contradistinction to Benjamin's pseudo-scientific voice, it stresses that the narrator is active, that he is the one observing.

This contradiction between inertia and movement conveys the narrator's complicated and contradictory relationship with the canal. As the narrative develops a further tension emerges between the depthless terrain of postmodernity and, in particular, late capitalist development, and the narrator's romantic engagement with the canal. Throughout the novel, one of the narrator's primary objects of observation is a group of office workers in a building located on the opposite side of the water. After he has been mugged by a local gang, the narrator regains consciousness and looks up to notice that the office workers he has attentively observed are now 'staring over at [him]: groups gathered at each looming window' (*TC*, 47). Like the workman painting the fence, whose observational stare collapsed the distinction between subject and object, the office workers who now loom over the narrator undermine any sense of critical distance that the narrator formed through his own observations. By coming to the canal, by removing himself from the city and 'doing nothing' (*TC*, 5) the narrator is self-consciously attempting to establish himself as a critical observer or spectator, but, as this scene demonstrates, this proves to be problematic: the 'looming' windows that frame the workers' view suggest that the narrator is just as much a part of the performance as the office workers themselves. Despite his efforts to instigate a critical distance between himself and that which he observes – the canal – the narrator is still very much part of the performance.

Shortly after this incident, however, the narrator notices a swan on the water which was, as he claims, 'looking directly at me. Right at me. Into me.' (*TC*, 47). A curious moment in the novel, the confrontation with the swan is a sharp contradiction to the narrator's experience in the previous scene. Evoking the Greek myth 'Leda and The Swan', this image elicits thoughts of transformation. As well as being read as a potential symbol for the canal's ongoing metamorphosis into a late capitalist space of leisure and consumption, the swan also symbolizes the narrator's own metamorphosis from performer to spectator. The narrator is now an object of the swan's observation, but unlike the office workers who looked 'over' him, the swan looks 'at' the narrator and 'into' him. The difference in prepositions is significant: the former creates a feeling of depthlessness and is reminiscent of Benjamin's description of Berlin – a city in which it is impossible to 'overlook' (Benjamin, 2005: 337) anything, suggesting that the narrator himself cannot avoid the gaze of others. The use of the preposition in the latter example, by contrast, evokes a feeling of depth and uncertainty: prompted by the swan's penetrative gaze the narrator begins to question his own knowledge and understanding of the world when he realizes it looked '[l]ike it knew something I didn't' (*TC*, 47). Unlike his dialogic interaction with his female counterpart, his interaction with the swan appears to create a feeling of doubt within the narrator. The fact that the canal is becoming a place of unfamiliarity for the narrator is further implied when he reveals, in a tone of bewilderment, that he had '[n]ever [...] seen such a thing before' and 'certainly hadn't had such a thing happen to [him] before' (*TC*, 48). The narrator emphasizes that this experience is unprecedented, not a mere repetition but a wholly unrecognizable moment in his life.

The tension between the restricting conditions of postmodernity and the narrator's desire for a form of romantic engagement with the canal is played out again in the concluding pages of the novel when the narrator changes his point of observation by moving from the towpath to the bridge: 'I looked down at the water: I could see all the way to the bottom, my new height giving me a clearer view of its depths. There were things down there on the bed [...] but not as much as I thought there would be' (*TC*, 199). On one hand, the shift in perspective invests the canal with a new sense of depth but on the other, the narrator's 'clearer view' is also suggestive of the canal's transparent, two-dimensional composition. The narrator's ability to see clearly all the way to the bottom of the canal reiterates his earlier condemnation of the bridge as a viewing platform, and the fact that there is not very much to see further diminishes the canal's romantic allure by suggesting that it does not conceal anything historically or personally meaningful for the narrator.

The narrator's disillusionment with the canal is further accentuated when the narrator looks down and notices something 'in the water, floating, or just beneath the surface, sitting there, stationary, flickering [...] I noticed that what I was looking at was, in fact, me: my own reflection wavering in the water, floating on the canal's surface like some passing, unwanted and discarded product' (*TC*, 199). The prepositions 'in' and 'beneath' create a sense of depth, but after realizing that what he can see in the water is merely his own familiar reflection the narrator uses the preposition 'on' to create, once more, a feeling of depthlessness. Despite his efforts to transcend the limits of his known experience he is seemingly unable to penetrate the surface of the canal and move beyond the recognized self.

The change in the narrator's perspective brings with it an alternative view of the city and he can now see past 'the myriad office blocks, tower blocks, and cranes' to the Gherkin in the distance; to his left he can 'see all the way up to Gainsborough Studios' and '[b]eyond that [he can] see the tower blocks of Hackney'; turning to his right, he claims to 'see past Wenlock Basin, towards Islington and the tunnel' (*TC*, 197). Unlike Benjamin's flâneur and Dante in 'The Inferno', who both descend beyond the surface of the familiar, Rourke's narrator ascends above the surface of the canal and procures a bird's-eye view of London. The narrator suggests that the city is unfolding before him, exposing itself in its entirety. London is not the invisible city of Benjamin's Paris or Calvino's Venice, but is afflicted (as Benjamin would perhaps understand it) with a visibility similar to that of Berlin. Standing on the bridge, or viewing platform, the narrator can see much of the city, but this is not another disappointment, further confirmation that the canal (and the metropolis) is a surface without depth and a perpetual site of familiarity. The passage is evocative of Wordsworth's 'Westminster Bridge' in which the narrator describes how the 'Ships, towers, domes, theatres, and temples lie/Open unto the fields, and to the sky' (Stephen Gill and Duncan Wu, 1997: 136).

The majestic typography of Westminster and the Thames may have been replaced by Hackney's tower blocks and the Gherkin, but, nevertheless, viewing the city all at once appears to instigate a sense of awe within the narrator whose physical relocation from the towpath to the bridge is accompanied by a kind of transcendental experience: 'I felt like I was floating too, or weightless, hovering above the canal, looking down on things. For that fleeting moment, not knowing what was going to happen next, gravity was nothing to me' (*TC*, 199). The narrator is uncertain; he cannot recognize his immediate present and therefore cannot anticipate what will happen in the future. The fact that he feels as though he is 'floating', 'weightless' and 'hovering' suggests that he has achieved some sense of critical distance and that he is no longer confined to the surface.

Prior to this conclusion, the narrator's descriptions of his corporeality have been inextricably associated with inertia and paralysis: he states twice that he 'was rooted to the spot' (*TC*, 31, 122); he also draws associations between his circulatory system and the moribund canal: 'My heart stopped functioning, blood lay dormant within me, things stopped' (*TC*,107); 'My body was paralysed and completely static' (*TC*, 76). The mirroring of the narrator's body with the body of the canal, once again expresses his total assimilation with the environment. Unlike Benjamin's flâneur, whose feet penetrated the surface of Paris and followed the streets downward into a 'vanished time' (Benjamin, 2002: 416), Rourke's narrator remains on the surface where his body simply reflects the image of the canal back to the reader. The juxtaposition between the narrator's earlier coalescence with the canal and his final transcendence of it, then, suggests that the narrator has, to some extent at least, successfully transformed from a performer trapped within the urban milieu into a critical spectator alienated on the periphery.

Notes

1 The narrator remains visible throughout much of the novel and is repeatedly disturbed by various passersby including a homeless woman, a dog walker, a gang of male youths, a woman and two Slavic men.

2 See 'Not The Booker Prize: *The Canal* by Lee Rourke' (Jordison: 2010).

3 Before abandoning his job to spend all of his time at the canal, the narrator worked as a data entry clerk. In the following description, he conveys the repetitive conditions of his career and contemplates the meaningless nature of his acts: 'I thought about the many years I had wasted processing similar information, on similar company PCs and laptops, in similar buildings. All that information I had sent into the ether, the abyss, with each click of the mouse, each press of a button and tap of a key, over and over and over again' (*TC*, 105).

4 The German word for overlook is *übersehen* and possesses the same polysemic definition as the English term. '*Übersehen*' is used by Benjamin in the original text ('Pariser Tagebuch') to mean to ignore or to not see, but it is interesting to note that it can also mean the opposite of this as in to see the full extent of something.

5 The deterioration of depth in late capitalist societies is an issue that continues to preoccupy twenty-first-century spatial materialist discourse. Doreen Massey (2011: 22), for example, draws attention to the ways in which the geography of London is imagined as a surface: 'those who would convince us that London is the golden goose of the national economy, whence flow benefits for the rest of the country, or that the financial City must be supported so that its growth can solve the problems of urban poverty within which it is set [...] are implicitly mobilizing, most often, this imagination of space as a surface [...] Things flow outwards from centres to those who are recipients'.

Works Cited

Baudrillard, Jean (2008) *The Perfect Crime*, trans. Chris Turner. London: Verso.

Benjamin, Walter (1972) 'Pariser Tagebuch', in Rolf Tiedemann and Herman Schweppenhäuser (eds) *Walter Benjamin Gesammelte Schriften IV.I*, pp. 567–87. Frankfurt: Suhrkamp Verlag.

Benjamin, Walter (2002) *The Arcades Project*, trans. Howard Eiland and Kevin McLaughlin, Cambridge MA: Oxford University Press.

Benjamin, Walter (2005) 'Paris Diary', in Michael W. Jennings, Howard Eiland and Gary Smith (eds) *Walter Benjamin Selected Writings 1927–1930*, trans. Rodney Livingstone, pp. 337–54. Cambridge, MA: Harvard University Press.

Benjamin, Walter (2009) 'One-way Street', in *One-way Street and Other Writings*, trans. J. A. Underwood. London: Penguin.

Caless, Kit (2012) *Mapping The Metropolis*, 7 November, accessed March 2013, https://soundcloud.com/search?q=mapping%20the%20metropolis

Calvino, Italo (1997) *Invisible Cities*, trans. Harcourt Brace Jovanovich, Inc. London: Vintage.

Frisby, David (2001) *Cityscapes of Modernity*. Cambridge: Polity Press.

Gill, Stephen, and Duncan Wu (1997) *William Wordsworth Selected Poetry*. Oxford: Oxford University Press.

Jameson, Fredric (1996) *Postmodernism, or, The Cultural Logic of Late Capitalism*. London: Verso.

Jordison, Sam (2010) 'Not The Booker Prize: *The Canal* by Lee Rourke', *Guardian*, 4 October, accessed November 2012, http://www.guardian.co.uk/books/booksblog/2010/oct/04/not-the-booker-lee-rourke

Massey, Doreen (2011) *World City*. Cambridge: Polity Press.

Rourke, Lee (2010) *The Canal*. Brooklyn, NY: Melville House.

Sisson, C. H. (1998) *The Divine Comedy*. Oxford: Oxford University Press.

CHINA MIÉVILLE AND THE LIMITS OF PSYCHOGEOGRAPHY

Tony Venezia

Introduction

> We are in new times. Perhaps the Viae Ferae have grown clever, and stealthy. Maybe this is how they will occur now, sneaking in plain sight, arriving not suddenly but so slowly, ushered in by us, armoured in girders, pelted in new cement and paving. (Miéville, 2004: 77)

China Miéville's short story 'Reports of Certain Events in London' (2004) re-imagines a fantastic topography of the capital's streets in which roads malevolently and spontaneously appear and disappear, their status tracked and documented by a cabalistic group of urban explorers. These 'Viae Ferae', or wild roads, are liminal spaces that insert themselves into the interstices of functional urban street grids, extraordinary intrusions and unstable passages that invade and double the real, material places of the city. The narrator is a fictionalized version of Miéville who mistakenly receives an envelope of documents addressed to a Charles Melville: a collection of fragmentary papers and photographs that comprise the minutes and marginalia of a secret society.

While on one level the story artfully performs the generic hybridity that Miéville has come to be associated with, 'Reports' can also be read as a pastiche and critique of the London tradition of psychogeography. The term may have been coined by post-war French radicals, enthused by the affective intensities of city space while railing against what they saw as the increasing instrumentalization of urban environments, but has arguably become better known as a London-centric literary movement.

Psychogeography, as associated particularly with literature and film, was a peculiarly late-twentieth century phenomenon, a creative historiography dedicated to recovering lost histories. Thought of this way, psychogeography can be read as both a symptom of and a reaction against the waning of historicity and the prioritizing of the spatial over the temporal that Fredric Jameson identified as key characteristics of postmodernism (Jameson, 1991: 6).

At first glance, Miéville's writing seems to continue in this tradition. But, while it is demonstrable that Miéville's fiction and non-fiction shares affinities with London psychogeography and the phantasmagorical doubling of the city, his work leans toward other concerns, albeit still related to contemporary anxieties over space, history and memory.

A key term to help historicize this set of concerns is hauntology. Coined by Jacques Derrida, the term is a typically deconstructionist punning on 'haunting' and 'ontology' ('hauntology' and 'ontology' being homophones in French). Hauntology has been adopted in different ways. Within academia it inspired a critical model based around spectrality and usually focusing on gothic fiction. Meanwhile, on the fringes of popular culture it has been appropriated by para-academic discourses to refer to musical and visual subcultural texts. I want to consider some key examples – the sonic hauntology of the Ghost Box record label and the cartographic collages of Laura Oldfield Ford – in relation to Mieville's writing and its conception of the weird within the context of psychogeography. I am referring to the weird here as indicating an encounter with radical, irreducible alterity, as opposed to the hauntological uncanny's defamiliarized return of the repressed. Miéville's fiction privileges both the hauntological and the weird, and is characterized by its use of tropologies of monstrousness, doubling, and alterity.

The focus here is on how Miéville re-articulates such concerns within a twenty-first-century context. The hauntological and the weird can be read as constituted by and constitutive of the historical conjuncture some have termed late postmodernism (Green, 2005: 1–18; Wegner, 2009: 6–7).[1] I suggest that by tracing and mapping these tropologies in Miéville's work, we can identify affiliations with both the genealogy of the weird as promoted by Ann and Jeff VanderMeer (2011),[2] and also with visual and sonic hauntological texts, such as the radical neo-punk, post-psychogeographical, post-rave visual collages of Laura Oldfield Ford, and the recombinant soundscapes produced by the Ghost Box record label. Miéville's fictional landscapes oscillate between the hauntological and the weird. By oscillating in this way, Miéville's fantastic cartographies move, albeit inconclusively, beyond the limiting purview of psychogeography, while remaining entangled within its orbit.

Spectres of Derrida

In *Specters of Marx* Derrida wrote that: 'To haunt does not mean to be present, and it is necessary to introduce haunting into the very construction of a concept.' (Derrida, 1994: 161). One way of getting to grips with the concept is to read it as a re-articulation of Freud's idea of the uncanny, the return of the repressed anxiety or desire in an unfamiliar form (Freud, 1919). For Derrida, this process of deferral and return is located in the problematic figure of the ghost that questions the priority of being.

But if Derrida is offering us an account of ghosts and spectrality, one that extends his work on concepts such as the trace, supplementarity, and difference, it is also grounded in history through his reading of Marx and Marxism. *Specters of Marx* was primarily an engagement with the immediate historical and philosophical context, more specifically it entered into critical dialogue with the Francis Fukuyama's thesis on the End of History. Following the dismantling of the Berlin Wall in 1989, Fukuyama notoriously argued that we had reached the End of History by having moved through various forms of social and philosophical contradictions toward a final enlightened condition that was post-historical (Fukuyama, 1989: xi).

Derrida invoked a spectral politics to discuss the uncanny persistence of Marx's ideas after the death of communism. Marx cannot be written out of history, his presence disturbs us in ghostly form as long as the conditions of capitalism persist, and indeed are extended and intensified. This leads to a sense of 'time out of joint'; Marx's message of revolutionary critique continues to haunt us, both from the past and from the utopian futures that failed to materialize.

Like psychogeography, hauntology had continental origins and crossed over to Britain, this time following a trans-Atlantic route.[3] Following this crossing it underwent some revision. In his overview of sonic hauntology, Jamie Sexton suggests that the political aspects of Derrida's investigation 'have largely been downplayed in order to focus on the more ontological sense of hauntology: that being itself is haunted, constituted from a number of traces whose presence is felt but often unacknowledged.' (Sexton, 2012: 562). While this is true to an extent, it is also the case that some commentators specifically enrol hauntology as political critique. James Bridle (2011) blogged that hauntology 'is about six months away from becoming the title of a column in a Sunday supplement; of going the way of psychogeography', a reference to Will Self's column in the *Independent*.[4] This has conspicuously failed to happen, and is unlikely to given the ghostly vagueness associated with the term. Unlike psychogeography, hauntology is not a coherent movement but rather a loosely connected series of artefacts, affects, and associations. In terms of style, sonic hauntology conjures an aural sense of time out of joint is generated by the stitching together of looped samples along with the foregrounding of recording noises that signify decay and deterioration. Samples are pillaged from 1970s public information films (a popular source) and library music themes from post-war British horror and science fiction films and television.

The impression of uncanny ambience is evident in the output of the record label Ghost Box, established by musicians Jim Jupp and Julian House. This supernatural mood is married to another aspect that connects with Derrida's proposition of time out of joint and a sense of being haunted by the future as much as the past. The use of public information samples and the influence of the sound experiments of the BBC Radiophonic Workshop point to a nostalgia for the unfulfilled technocratic utopianism of the pre-Thatcherite Welfare State that continues to haunt the present.

The acts on Ghost Box, such as The Focus Group, The Advisory Circle, and Belbury Poly, channel these twin obsessions through disjointed sample and reverb heavy pieces. A paradigmatic example is the album *Séance at Hobbs Lane*, by the Mount Vernon Arts Lab, first released by Astra in 2001, which was rereleased by Ghost Box in 2007. The title is a reference to Nigel Kneale's *Quatermass and the Pit* originally a BBC serial broadcast in 1958, subsequently a better and better-known film by Hammer studios in 1967. The story pays particular attention to place in its depiction of a fictional London underground station, Hobbs End. Work on the station is halted with the discovery of an odd artefact, which turns out to be a Martian spacecraft. This discovery leads to a retrohistoricization of human history, as supernatural phenomena are explained as encounters with Martian travellers, who interbred with apes to produce the human race. Such a retrohistoricization thus appears initially hauntological, but ends up being in fact weird in its back-projection of a hybrid genealogy.

Séance at Hobbs Lane is a para-soundtrack made up of noise, sampled voices, and instrumentation. A visual corollary can be found in Laura Oldfield Ford's fanzine *Savage Messiah*. Serialized and self-published from 2005 to 2009, the fanzine collages image and text to produce a record of a decaying London landscape. The recombinant Xeroxed lo-fi form alludes to a whole genealogy of self-produced manifestos and polemics, from Wyndham Lewis' *Blast!* (1914–15) through post-war Situationism and pre-millennial psychogeography to Mark Perry's seminal punk fanzine *Sniffin' Glue* (1976–7).

Oldfield Ford employs an anachronistic cut and paste montage, which reads the city through layers of erasure and overwriting that map the transient and ephemeral nature of the urban environment. The city is haunted by the euphoria of warehouse raves of years gone by, the melancholy collages embodying a post-rave comedown. The confluences of post-punk and post-rave subcultures are important here: they mark a generational shift with psychogeography, which was fed instead by the currents of the 1960s counter-culture, especially specious New Age elements. Oldfield Ford's collages are a rebuke to the photoshopped images of a gentrified city and the growth of what Marc Augé called 'non-places' – the transient, homogenized by product of contemporary urban space. The proliferation of interchangeable retail parks and chain stores renders visible the effects of global capitalism in the monstrous transformation of space. Alongside this, there is the transformation of time into a flattened, homogenized experience: 'there are non-times as well as non-places.' (Fisher, 2012: 19)

These transformations make themselves felt through the liminal disturbances and anachronisms of the hauntological and the weird. The oscillation between the hauntological and the weird as reflected in the depiction of urban space is a factor that is repeated in Miéville's writing, and provides both a continuation and abjuration of the historical concerns of psychogeography. Sexton notes the influence of late Victorian/Edwardian gothic literature on hauntology, including Arthur Machen and Algernon Blackwood (Sexton, 2012: 3). Significantly, both writers are also claimed as psychogeographical *and* weird. In his essay 'M. R. James and the Quantum Vampire', Miéville identifies a breach between the uncanny and the weird in the early twentieth century, while noting that they remain nonetheless connected, a 'constitutive contradiction' (Miéville, 2008: 116). M. R. James' stories represent a stalled dialectic of the weird and the hauntological. For Miéville, the weird and the hauntological are 'in non-dialectical opposition, contrary iterations of a single problematic.' (Miéville, 2009a: 123).

Miéville's insistence on the separation of the weird and the hauntological is interesting in this context. The two categories exist, according to this argument, in opposition. When examined more closely, this is more complicated, with both terms existing in symbiotic relation to each other both in terms of their historical moments and in their generative affects. This stalled dialectic is also at work in Miéville's own fiction.

China Miéville and the New/Old Weird

China Miéville is an important figure in twenty-first-century British fiction. He has published nine novels, a novella, a collection of short stories, and collaborated on other media projects.[5] He has also produced a series of equally ambitious standalone works, starting with his debut novel, *King Rat* (1998), an updated version of the Pied Piper of Hamelin legend that recasts the story in the drum-and-bass subculture of London. The novel's protagonist, Saul, discovers that he is a descendent of King Rat, who once ruled the vermin of the world. Saul allies himself with animal-human hybrids Anansi and Loplop to defeat the piper. The novel is notable for introducing a number of elements that recur throughout Miéville's work, such as the interest in hybrid life forms, the doubling of the city, and the mingling of generic pulp and reflexive modernist registers. Hybridity is signalled in the novel's title, which associates human rank with animals, but also in the representation of Anansi the spider god and Loplop the king of the birds. These bring together the folkloric (Anansi is a West African deity), with the Surreal (Loplop was a collage creation of Max Ernst). The doubling of the city is imagined in two ways: first, the literal mapping of an underground, or, at times airborne, city that shadows the real world; and second, by the use of drum-and-bass, itself an 'underground' subculture.

Later novels include the Bas-Lag urban fantasy trilogy – *Perdido Street Station* (2000), *The Scar* (2002), and *Iron Council* (2004), set in the fictional city of New Crobuzon. The city is a monumental achievement in urban fantasy fiction, a sprawling industrialized metropolis at the centre of the imagined world of Bas-Lag, one that resembles Victorian London albeit with magic as a technology and human and non-human inhabitants. New Crobuzon freely intertwines its urban, industrial setting with capitalist modes of production and an autocratic polis. The trilogy established and confirmed Miéville's reputation for politically committed and formally experimental fiction that mixed the generic ingredients of science fiction, fantasy, and the gothic along with a maximalist, extravagant yet oddly precise use of language.

King Rat and the Bas-Lag trilogy established a spatial focus that resurfaces throughout Miéville's subsequent writing. This makes itself felt in two ways: imaginary environments that resemble to varying degrees real world environments, albeit substantially altered and twisted; and the doubling of contemporary London. It is the latter that I wish to focus on here.[6] Before doing so I want to emphasize the metaphor of boundary crossing on a more generic level in Miéville's fiction.

Miéville's fiction crosses genre boundaries while revelling in their embedded generic tendencies. As Sherryl Vint has pointed out, his work 'reinvigorates fantastic writing as a blend of science fiction, Surrealism, fantasy, magical realism, and Lovecraftian horror that is attentive to both its pulp and high culture influences and roots.' (Vint, 2009: 197). The term he was initially associated with was the now already anachronistic sounding 'New Weird.'[7]

The particularity of the label recalls both 1920s pulp hybrids of science fiction, fantasy, and horror associated with the magazine *Weird Tales* and writers such as H. P. Lovecraft and Clark Ashton Smith, but also the more self-consciously experimental writing of the sixties New Wave of science fiction associated *New Worlds* and the writing of J. G. Ballard, Michael Moorcock, and, especially, M. John Harrison (Luckhurst, 2005: 240).[8] The New Weird, as exemplified in Miéville's fiction, embodied this promiscuous slippage of generic and formal categories, both between genres and in the fluid movement between high and popular cultures. As an informal literary movement, the New Weird aligned this blurring of categories with a fascination for urban locations.

Miéville himself has argued that the New Weird offers 'a fiction born out of possibilities, its freeing-up mirroring the freeing-up. The radicalisation in the world. This is post-Seattle fiction.' (Miéville, 2003: 3). This sense of the radical potentialities of fantastic fiction and its connection to the politics of anti-globalization protest confirms Miéville's commitment to revolutionary Marxism. His own writing negotiates the divide between genre fiction and critical theory: in his editorial introduction to a special issue of *Historical Materialism* on 'radical fantasy', Miéville challenged the primacy of realist modes

of representation and proposed that fantasy reflects the fantastic absurdity of capitalism and offers a privileged site of critique (Miéville,
2002b: 41–2). But what interests me is less whether Miéville's writing
can be judged appropriately radical, than how it is processed by and
how it in turn processes history. This is related to the generic slippages
evident in much fiction from the 1990s onwards, and in the structures
of feeling such fictions provoke. The VanderMeers' 2008 anthology
effectively marked a high point – subsequently Miéville and others
have moved away from the term, seeing it transformed into reified
marketing category (Luckhurst, 2005: 241).

The VanderMeers followed *The New Weird* with the mammoth collection *The Weird* in 2011, which dropped the novel prefix in favour
of a more thoroughgoing engagement with the weird itself as both a
literary genealogy and an associated ontological affect. In their brief
introduction they further stressed the importance of New Wave writing, and saw New Weird as 'a re-inquiry into approaches and issues
raised by the New Wave of the 1960s [...] but in this case primarily
from the perspective of The Weird rather than science fiction or fantasy.' (VanderMeer and VanderMeer, 2011: xix). What is interesting
is their wider historicizing of the weird as a literary style. The weird
is 'as much a sensation as it is a mode of writing' (VanderMeer and
VanderMeer, 2011: xvi); it describes and engenders 'unease and the
temporary abolition of the rational' but also the 'strangely beautiful,
intertwined with terror.' (VanderMeer and VanderMeer, 2011: xv).

From this it is clear that the weird is a generic response to a particular stage of modernity: the weird tale comes into being in the late
nineteenth and early twentieth century, while the New Weird is associated with the coming of the millennium. The sense of dis-ease
is perfectly captured in Lovecraft's 'The Call of Cthulhu', which provides a useful point of comparison with Miéville's 'Reports'.

Lovecraft's unbalanced narrator starts by noting that: 'The most
merciful thing in the world, I think, is the inability of the human mind
to correlate all its contents' (Lovecraft, 1928/2011: 61). What follows is a series of documents – journal entries, newspaper reports,
ships' logs – whose fragmentary format hints at the existence of an an-
tediluvian cosmically indifferent extraterrestrial submerged under the

sea. Lovecraft typically privileges atmosphere over story. Cthulhu's unpronounceable name, a misalignment of vowels and consonants, is carried over into the creature's unique physical characteristics – an incommensurable mix of cephalopodic head, scales, claws, and wings whose existence is glimpsed 'like all dread glimpses of truth, flashed out from the accidental piecing together of separated things.' (Lovecraft, 1928/2011: 61) – which is itself mirrored in the fragmented narrative structure.

This baroque style generates a sense of awe and sublimity, which destabilizes the quotidian. Lovecraft's characters discover, often at the cost of their sanity, that extraterrestrial creatures have been hidden among us for millennia. Their undescribable physiologies signify, or fail to signify, radical non-human alterity, and represent a break from folkloric tradition.

Miéville's London Gazetteer

At this point it is worth returning to 'Reports' to get a sense of how these ideas are filtered through Miéville's work. The story bears some resemblance to Lovecraft's 'Call of Cthulhu' in its fragmentary structure and anxious narrator attempting find some correlation between the disparate elements. The scholarly narrator is a recurrent trope throughout Miéville's fiction. In this, he resembles the narrators of classic weird and gothic tales, the genealogists and antiquarians that Lovecraft and James relied on. He doubled by the invisible 'Charles Melville' to whom the reports have been addressed and misdelivered. In 'Reports' he tries to make sense of what he is reading:

> [*Two monochrome pictures end the piece. They have no explanatory notes or legend. They are both taken in daylight. On the left is a photograph of two houses, on either side of a small street of low century-old houses which curves sharply to the right, it looks like, quickly unclear with distance. The right-hand picture is the two facades again, but this time the houses – recognisably the same from a window's crack, from a smear of paint below a sash, from the scrawny front gardens and distinct unkempt buddleia bush – are closed together. They are no longer semi-detached. There is no street between them.*] (Miéville, 2004/2006: 64)

The photographs are placed at the end of a report of an expedition to try and locate, Varmin Way, one of the wild streets, though much to their chagrin, the street had 'unoccurred' (Miéville, 2004/2006: 64). The archival effect is amplified by the form of the story's print, which uses different fonts to indicate its disjointed feel, analogous to the stitched together aural and visual hauntologies of Ghost Box and *Savage Messiah*. The above quote is presented in italics and square brackets to show the narrator's distanced status, a separation that is gradually eroded.

There is even an attempt at taxonomic classification in the notes, found in a grid comprised of four columns and six rows that detail the incursion of wild roads from other cities into London (Miéville, 2004/2006: 68). This is an attempt at rationalizing the unthinkable: these fantastic occurrences, unoccurences, and recurrences that slip into the cracks of the urban landscape. This overwhelming transformation metaphorically enacts the spatial and temporal distortions of global capital on the city.

The secret group who issue the reports are themselves fractured with disagreement. The reports themselves contain pseudo-marginalia that reveals the group's factionalism ('What exactly did you do to get Edgar so pissed off?' [Miéville, 2004/2006: 64, emphasis in original]), also reminiscent of the sectarianism of post-New Left groupings such as the London Psychogeographical Association (LPA).

Psychogeography was famously categorized with 'pleasing vagueness' by Guy Debord to indicate the affective intensities of urban spaces (Debord, 1955: 5). From Paris, and an association with post-war continental left-wing groupings, psychogeography inspired what Merlin Coverley has called 'retrospective validation in traditions that pre-date Debord's official conception by several centuries' (Coverley, 2006: 11). This retrohistoricizing of the term has arisen largely in late twentieth-century English literature and film, and includes such diverse practitioners as Iain Sinclair, Peter Ackroyd, and Stewart Home, as well as a genealogy of largely gothic London writing including William Blake, Thomas De Quincey, Robert Louis Stevenson and Arthur Machen.

Concurrent with the visionary literary trend was the growth of localized psychogeography groups as part of a more politicized radical urban subculture continuing the tradition of Debord. The LPA was part of this trend. Social geographer Alaistair Bonnett notes that from 'the late 1990s activity among these revolutionary groups diminished and interest in psychogeography passed to the arts community' (Bonnett, 2009: 59, 65n.2). The occult played an important role for London psychogeographers. For Sinclair, what is required is a counter-conjuration to combat what he labeled the 'occult logic of "market forces"' that dictate new urban geographies (Sinclair, 1991: 265) For the LPA, the occult was enlisted as a method of provocation, ironic or otherwise, to aestheticize politics. In one famous missive, collected by Stewart Home in *Mind Invaders*, the London Psychogeographical Association announced that; 'We offer no attempt to "justify" or "rationalize" the role of magic in the development of our themes; it is sufficient that it renders them completely unacceptable' (cited in Coverley, 2008: 130). British organizations like the London Psychogeographical Association were channeling and redirecting the radical political energies of an earlier continental generation.

If Miéville's story seems to pastiche the psychogeographical obsession with the occult, it also moves beyond them in its descriptions of the plausibly unreal. The Viae Ferae themselves recall both the hauntological *and* the weird. They operate as uncanny intrusions, hidden in the interstices of history and place, their intermittent appearances it turns out are not restricted to London. The narrator concludes that '[w]e live in new times' (Miéville, 2004: 77); but these are less an indication of a rupture or a break, then a realization that, as with Lovecraft's alien Gods, the Viae Ferae have *always* been with us. Further, the roads possess a weird aspect in the suggestion of agency; that they have been fighting a centuries long war whose purpose we cannot comprehend given their non-human alterity. The narrator succumbs to understandable paranoia: 'I'm finding it hard to work. These days I'm very conscious of corners' (Miéville, 2004: 75). His attempts to locate any information on the roads, on Charles Melville, and the BWVF, via greasy spoon cafes, message boards, and Internet searches come to nothing.

The trope of invasion is realized more fully in 'The Tain' (2002/2006)[9] in which another recognizable London landscape is transformed by apocalyptic events. The city has been invaded by imagos, creatures who live behind the reflections in mirrors. The imagos include vampires, direct copies rather than the traditional undead, 'the most comprehensible and the weakest of them, they were still stronger than any human' (Miéville, 2002/2006: 257). But there is also a bizarre menagerie created from 'the detritus of reflection. Vanity's cast offs, the snippets of human forms thrown up and ignored in the echoes between mirrors' (Miéville, 2002/2006: 256). These include human hands joined together, scuttling and flying, butterfly lips, and drifts of hair billowing down the sides of buildings.

The story is told in parallel chapters that use the direct address of first person narration. Sholl, another of Miéville's scholarly narrators, studies the imagos, going as far as descending into an infested, infernal underground station to interrogate a vampire. An unnamed vampire doubles him, his initial speech reported in reverse type.

The doubling and reflection run the risk of collapsing into simplisic allegory, but readerly sympathy shifts, however, as the story unfolds. A history of imprisonment and oppression is revealed, the imagos subjected to agonizing torture by being pulled into distorted shapes to provide reflections for our world. The unnamed imago is the vampire Sholl confronts underground and tortures for information about the imago's leader. The unnamed vampire is later revealed not to have been an imago at all, but a human who killed his materialized reflection and adopted the role of vampire.

The novella then charts a movement from Hampstead Heath in North London, through Kentish Town – 'a wasteland of heat and burned out houses that smouldered endlessly' (Miéville, 2002/2006: 279) – through Clerkenwell, Russell Square, on to the centre of the infestation, the British Museum. The Museum is the prime example of what Thomas Richards called the 'Imperial archive': '[a late-Victorian] ideological construction for projecting the epistemological extension of Britain into and beyond its Empire' (Richards, 1993: 15). Arriving at the doors of the Museum, Sholl and his companions are confronted by the return of the Imperial repressed:

> The imagos were dressed in a flickering, a strobing sequence of forms, of people, of the people throughout history, staccato aggregates of their own oppression. They were a wind of flint-axe chippers, of pharaohs, of samurai, of American shamans and Phoenicians and Byzantines, helmets with placid faces and splinted armour, and tooth necklaces and shrouds and gold. (Miéville, 2002/2006: 290)

The shuffling images represent a shuffling of temporalities as well, recalling Derrida's comments on the 'non-contemporaneity' of the present whereby we are always haunted by 'the ghosts of those not yet born or who are already dead' (Derrida, 1994: xviii). The narrative shifts from the hauntological to the weird with Sholl's tracking of the imago leader, 'called Lupe, the Fish, or the Tiger' (Miéville, 2002/2006: 291). The lack of specificity and possible hybridity again recalls Lovercraft. There is nothing left to do but surrender to the weird as Sholl has come to do in negotiating the abject capitulation of humanity. On confronting 'The Tiger. The Fish of the Mirror' language turns in on itself:

> It was all etched in shadow on shadow, and he could see it all, in the black sunlight that poured out of the presence hanging in the room's centre, like a darkling star, invisible but utterly compelling, evading deliberation, not quite seen, insinuating its own parameters, patrolling the moiling cylindrical space with feline, piscine ease.
> (Miéville, 2002/2006: 292)

The idea of an alternative, magical London existing within the spaces of the everyday city is pushed to an extreme in the novel *Kraken*. The characteristics of generic intertextuality, linguistic excess, and playful absurdity are taken to their limits. *Kraken* is a longer, elaborate combination of conspiracy and caper that starts with the improbable theft of a giant squid from the National History Museum, an act that reveals the capital to subjected to the whims of various secret cults each with their own agendas and shifting allegiances. A group called the Londonmancers stands in for psychogeographers; the visceral corporeality of the city is literalized in metaphor when they dig up the pavement to read urban entrails:

He started the cutter. With a groan of metal and cement, he drew a line across the pavement. Behind the blade welled up blood.

'Jesus Christ,' said Billy, jumping back.

Fitch drew up the cutter again along the split. A spray of concrete dust and blood mist dirtied him. He put the angle grinder down, dripping. Put a crowbar in the red-wet crack and levered harder than it looked like he could. The paving stone started.

Guts oozed from the hole. Intestinal coils, purple and bloodied, boiled up wetly in a meat mass.

Billy had thought the entrails of the city would be its torn-up under-earth, roots, the pipes he was not supposed to see. He had thought Fitch would bring up a corner of wires, worms and plumbing to interpret. The literalism of this knack shocked him. (Miéville: 2010, 186)

The Londonmancers are one of a myriad of groups and groupuscles that are stitched into the cultural history of the city, attempting to kick-start or prevent the apocalypse. The weird, via iterations of popular culture, becomes the object of pastiche, albeit an excessive pastiche. Another Miéville scholarly narrator acts as surrogate for the reader and attempts to make sense of this. The psychogeographical practices of recalling of older forms, prior representations, and historical figures, all point to an ambivalence regarding historicity that borders nostalgia. This impulse had led some commentators to criticize London psychogeography for its nostalgic tone and voguish nonconformity. Phil Baker writes that London psychogeography became fixated on a series of predictable tropes and that 'anyone reading recent usages [of psychogeography] would discover that it is about Jack the Ripper, ley lines, why tower blocks are bad, Hawksmoor churches, the places we remember from earlier in our lives, landscape gardening, Stonehenge and the Kray twins' (Baker, 2003: 232). In his own London drift, *London's Overthrow*, Miéville claims that psychogeography has become a 'local cliché. A lazy label for hip decay tourism' (Miéville, 2012: 58). This metaphor is literalized in Kraken, which imagines a secret society that reads the decaying guts of the city.

Miéville followed this with perhaps the only thing left to do – return to psychogeography, or rather its radical roots and routes. The non-fictional *London's Overthrow* (2012) documents drifts through late night London in the autumn of 2011.[10] Miéville takes as his inspiration a painting by the little known nineteenth-century painter Jonathan Martin, brother of the better known John. After attempting to set fire to York Minster in 1829, Martin was incarcerated in Bedlam, where he busied himself with drawings of catastrophe, including one entitled *London's Overthrow*, reproduced in Miéville's (2012: 12) *London's Overthrow*: 'Scrappy, chaotic, inexpert, astounding. Pen-and-ink scrawl of the city shattered under a fusillade from heaven, rampaged through by armies, mobs, strange vengeance' (Miéville, 2012: 14). Miéville overlays this metaphorical eschatology onto the cityscape of contemporary post-riots London, referencing Iain Sinclair and *Savage Messiah*, but bypassing the usual suspects of British psychogeography by enrolling Martin as an inspiration rather than say Blake or Stevenson.

Conclusion

Miéville's writing can been seen as both moving away from and caught up in the tactics and strategies of psychogeography with its emphasis on the hauntological and the weird. These are different types of historicism at work in fantastic fiction, ways of re-processing both the past and the experience of anticipation associated with the future. In imagining such a vision of the city Miéville disavows the quasi-mystical constraints of Sinclair et al. while still remaining entangled within a genealogy of London phantasmagoria. Miéville's work both probes at the limits of psychogeography but also re-articulates its premises for a post-millennial city, having much in common with non-literary sources such as Laura Oldfield Ford, and the output of the Ghost Box label.

As with psychogeography, Miéville et al. are drawn to heightened states of mind, with the numinous immanent in the everyday. Their collective influences are more post-punk and post-rave than the 1960s counter-cultural associations of British literary psychogeography, but they often share the same interest in re-connecting with older imaginaries: hence the appropriation of figures such as Machen and Blackwood for genealogies of psychogeography *and* hauntology *and* the weird.

In this, his fiction embodies the stalled dialectic he identified between the hauntological and the weird, between remnants and nova. Concluding his essay 'M. R. James and the Quantum Vampire', Miéville proposes that with the hegemony of neoliberal capitalism, our experience of the world is both weird and hauntological, inhuman and filled with ghosts. I would suggest that, as with psychogeography, the co-existence of the hauntological and the weird are symptomatic and constitutive of the delirious structures of feeling we can associate with the intensified crises in historicity that we continue to experience. As Miéville himself concludes: 'If we live in a haunted world – and we do – we live in a Weird one' (Miéville, 2009a: 128).

Notes

1 For a consideration of the term 'late postmodernism' in relation to Miéville as a writer of 'Radical Fantasy' see Burling (2009).

2 As well compiling the monumental anthology *The Weird*, the Vander-Meers run the website *Weird Fiction Review*, a self-proclaimed 'non-denominational source for the weird', accessed May 2013, http://weirdfictionreview.com/

3 *Specters of Marx* was first presented as a series of lectures on the future of Marxism at the University of California, Riverside in 1993.

4 Collected in Self and Steadman, 2007.

5 These include writing for DC Comics: Miéville wrote the story 'Snow Had Fallen' for *Hellblazer's* 250th issue (2008), and is currently writing the series *Dial H for Hero* (2012–). He also co-authored a fantasy role play game *Pathfinder Chronicles: A Guide to the River Kingdoms* (2010). In addition to these collaborations, Miéville provided the script for the experimental political short film *Deep State* (2012), directed by Karen Mirza and Brad Butler. The film can be viewed online at http://www.mirza-butler.net/index.php?/project/deep-state/ (accessed May 2013).

6 In addition, Miéville has contributed to a growing body of literary and cultural discourse on genre fiction with a number of essays and editorials that bring together his interests in fantastic fiction and Marxist politics (Bould and Miéville, 2009; Miéville, 2002b).

7 See VanderMeer and VanderMeer (2008: xvi).

8 For an account of the historical importance of the New Wave see Luckhurst (2005: 141–60).

9 'The Tain' was originally published as a chapbook, complete with introduction by M. John Harrison, by PS Publishing in 2002. It was later republished in the collection *Looking for Jake and Other Stories* (2005).

10 It was published online at http://www.londonsoverthrow.org/ (accessed December 2012) and subsequently as a booklet by Westbourne Press. All references are to the print version.

Works Cited

Azzarello, Brian, Jamie Delano, Dave Gibbons, China Miéville, and Peter Milligan (writers); Eddie Campbell, Rafael Grampá, David Lloyd, Giuseppe Carmuncoli, and Lee Bermejo (artists) (2008) *Hellblazer* #250. New York: Dc Vertigo.

Baker, Phil (2003) 'Secret City: Psychogeography and the End of London', in Joe Kerr and Andrew Gibson (eds) *London: From Punk to Blair*, pp. 323–33. London: Reaktion.

Bonnett, Alastair (2009) 'The Dilemmas of Radical Nostalgia in British Psychogeography', *Theory, Culture & Society* 26(1): 45–70.

Bould, Mark and China Miéville (eds) (2009) *Red Planets: Marxism and Science Fiction*. London: Pluto Press.

Bridle, James (2011) 'Hauntological Futures', booktwo.org, 20 March, accessed January 2013, http://booktwo.org/notebook/hauntological-futures/

Burling, William J. (2009) 'Periodising the Postmodern: China Miéville's and the Dynamics of Radical Fantasy', *Extrapolation* 50(2): 326–44.

Coverley, Merlin (2006) *Psychogeography*. Harpenden: Penguin.

Coverley, Merlin (2008) *Occult London*. Harpenden: Penguin.

Debord, Guy (1955/1981) 'Introduction to a Critique of Urban Geography', Ken Knabb (ed.) *Situationist International Anthology*, trans. Ken Knabb, pp. 5–7. Berkeley, CA: Bureau of Public Secrets.

Debord, Guy and Gil Wolman (1956/2006) 'A User's Guide to Détournement', Ken Knabb (ed.) *Situationist International Anthology*, revised edn, trans. Ken Knabb, pp. 14–21. Berkeley, CA: Bureau of Public Secrets.

Deep State (2012) Karen Mirza and Brad Butler (directors).

Derrida, Jacques (1994) *Specters of Marx: The State of the Debt, the Work of Mourning, and the New International*, trans. Peggy Kamuf. London: Routledge.

Edwards, Caroline and Tony Venezia (2014) *China Miéville: Critical Essays.* London: Gylphi.

Fisher, Mark (2011) 'Introduction: Always Yearning for the Time That Just Eluded Us', in Laura Oldfield Ford *Savage Messiah*, pp. v-xvi. London: Verso.

Fisher, Mark (2012) 'What is Hauntology?', *Film Quarterly* 66(1): 16–24.

Ford, Laura Oldfield (2011) *Savage Messiah*. London: Verso.

Freud, Sigmund Freud (1919) 'The Uncanny', *The Standard Edition of the Complete Psychological Works of Sigmund Freud, Volume XVII (1917–1919): An Infantile Neurosis and Other Works*, ed. and trans. James Strachey and Anna Freud, pp. 219–56. London: Hogarth Press.

Fukuyama, Francis (1989) *The End of History and the Last Man*. London: Hamish Hamilton.

Green, Jeremy (2005) *Late Postmodernism: American Fiction at the Millennium*. Basingstoke: Palgrave Macmillan.

Hatherley, Owen (2010) *A Guide to the New Ruins of Great Britain*. London: Verso.

Jameson, Fredric (1991) *Postmodernism or, the Cultural Logic of Late Capitalism*. Durham, NC: Duke University Press.

Joshi, S. T. (1990) *The Weird Tale*. Holicong, PA: Wildside Press.

Lovecraft, H. P. (1928/2011) 'The Call of Cthulhu', in *The Call of Cthulhu and Other Weird Tales*, pp. 61–98. London: Vintage.

Luckhurst, Roger (2005) *Science Fiction*. Cambridge: Polity Press.

Miéville, China (1998) *King Rat*. London: Pan Macmillan.

Miéville, China (2000) *Perdido Street Station*. London: Pan Macmillan.

Miéville, China (2002a) *The Scar*. London: Pan Macmillan.

Miéville, China (2002b) 'Editorial Introduction – Symposium: Marxism and Fantasy', *Historical Materialism: Research in Critical Marxist Theory* 10: 39–49.

Miéville, China (2002/2006) 'The Tain', in *Looking for Jake and Other Stories*, pp. 227–304. London: Pan Macmillan. (Originally published as a chapbook, Hornsea: PS Publishing, 2002)

Miéville, China (2003) 'Long Live the New Weird', *The Third Alternative*, 35: 3.

Miéville, China (2004) *Iron Council*. London: Macmillan.

Miéville, China (2004/2006) 'Reports of Certain Events in London', in *Looking for Jake and Other Stories*, pp. 53–78. London: Pan Macmillan.

Miéville, China (2007) *Un Lun Dun*. London: Pan Macmillan.

Miéville, China (2008) 'M. R. James and the Quantum Vampire: Weird; Hauntological; Versus and/or and and/or or?', *Collapse: Philosophical Research and Development*, IV: 105–128.

Miéville, China (2009a) *The City and the City*. London: Pan Macmillan.

Miéville, China (2009b) 'Weird Fiction', in Mark Bould, Andrew M. Butler, Adam Roberts, and Sherryl Vint (eds) *The Routledge Companion to Science Fiction*, pp. 510–15. London: Routledge.

Miéville, China (2010) *Kraken*. London: Pan Macmillan.

Miéville, China (2012) *London's Overthrow*. Chippenham: Westbourne Press.

Miéville, China (writer); Mateus Santalouco (artists); Brian Bolland (covers) (2012–) *Dial H for Hero*. New York: DC. (Ongoing series).

Mount Vernon Arts Lab (2007) *The Seance at Hob's Lane*. Ghost Box.

Reynolds, Simon (2006) 'Society of the Spectral', *The Wire*, 273: 26–33.

Reynolds, Simon (2011) *Retromania: Pop Culture's Addiction to its Own Past*. London: Faber and Faber.

Richards, Thomas (1993) *Imperial Archive: Knowledge and the Fantasy of Empire*. London: Verso.

Self, Will and Ralph Steadman (2007) *Psychogeography*. London: Bloomsbury.

Sexton, Jamie (2012) 'Weird Britain in Exile: Ghost Box, Hauntology, and Alternative Heritage', *Popular Music and Society* 35 (4): 561–84.

Sinclair, Iain (1991) *Downriver (Or, The Vessels of Wrath); A Narrative in Twelve Tales*. London: Penguin.

Tranter, Kirsten (2012) 'An Interview with China Miéville', *Contemporary Literature* 53(3): 417–36.

VanderMeer, Ann and Jeff VanderMeer (2008) 'Introduction – The New Weird: "It's Alive?"', in Ann and Jeff VanderMeer (eds) *The New Weird*. San Francisco, CA: Tachyon.

VanderMeer, Ann and Jeff VanderMeer (2011) 'Introduction', in Ann and Jeff VanderMeer (eds) *The Weird: A Compendium of Strange and Dark Stories*, pp. xv-xx. London: Corvus.

Vint, Sherryl (2009) 'Introduction: Special Issue on China Miéville', *Extrapolation* 50(2): 197–9.

Wegner, Phillip E. (2009) *Life Between Two Deaths, 1989–2001: U. S. Culture in the Long Nineties.* Durham, NC: Duke University Press.

PART IV

TECHNOLOGIES

THE END OF MR. Y OR THE END OF THE BOOK?
DIGITAL TECHNOLOGIES AND THE
TWENTY-FIRST-CENTURY BRITISH NOVEL

Neal Kirk

With the exponential development of new media technologies, especially the advent of digital reading platforms, the book as a steadfast media technology is in flux. Where book reading was once a portal through the mundane wardrobe of reality to an exotic realm of linguistic adventure, the Amazon Kindle may become the new digital gatekeeper. Scarlett Thomas's *The End Of Mr. Y* (2006) situates debates about the continued relevance of the book within an increasingly globalized British locale. Thomas's evocation of an English setting acts as a national anchor but also a counter to the proliferation of globally identifiable, but still distinctly North American, new media technologies.

This essay is not yet an epitaph, nor is it a nostalgic pining away for the yesteryear of the book. Rather, Thomas's *End of Mr. Y* affords an opportunity to explore some of the overarching questions surrounding the role of authorship and readership in a digital age: when there is competition for mind and screen space, what is expected of the literary author? What does the audience expect, and what expectations about new media does the author bring to the written text? How do digital experiences influence paperback fictions? *The End of Mr. Y* addresses these questions even if it, by design, does not provide definitive answers.

Part of what this essay argues is that Thomas's *End of Mr. Y* diverts some of the novelty ascribed to the Internet back into reading, and back into a globalized but identifiably British framework. To do this the novel depicts an experience strikingly similar to using today's Internet as first having been invented by a scholastically neglected Victorian scientist. Thomas mythologizes Britain and book reading as her work participates in the rendering of the book as a fetishistic contemporary commodity operating alongside, rather than opposed to, new mediatization trends.

Anchored in contemporary *and* Victorian England, Thomas blends the new and faux old: a Victorian book and a contemporary PhD student, the linear present with nodular time travel. Thomas's articulation of the fictional Mindspace, and protagonist Ariel Manto's time travel by 'train of thought' are suggestive of contemporary social networking site MySpace and the Internet's early association with an 'information superhighway'. But Mindspace is more complex than a gesture toward a California-based new media company. Ariel's discovery of an exceedingly rare copy of fictional Victorian scientist Thomas Lumas's *The End Of Mr. Y*, opens an avenue for Thomas to interrogate the effect increasing global mediatization is having on herself as a British author. Referential and playfully meta-fictional, *Mr. Y* anticipates an Internet-aware readership.

'You now have infinite choice'

While not quite a 'choose your own adventure' novel,[1] Thomas's bestselling fiction suggests nodular, networked plotting, indicative of playing a video game or browsing the Internet. Despite being first published in 2006, before the first Kindle or iPhone, in her inclusion of the Internet as an important context for the protagonist and the readers, Thomas's fiction has held its own through several years of advances in new media technologies. Innovative and accessible but also distinctly English, *The End of Mr. Y* has the curious and compelling effect of engaging with the contemporary fascination with network models of social organization and thought, while making a fetishistic commodity of the book.

Unless you are Ariel Manto, you should not need a dramatic trigger event to acquire a copy of *The End of Mr. Y* from a local secondhand bookshop. Nor will it cost you £50.00 – the price should be under a fiver for the paperback. That is, unless you happen to stumble upon an exceedingly rare copy of *The End of Mr. Y*....

   'You now have infinite choice' (Mr. Y, 502).

The Amazon Kindle edition of Thomas's *The End of Mr. Y* is available for purchase for about £4.65.[2] In the media environment of the twenty-first century, this is a seemingly unremarkable fact. The Amazon Kindle Fire HD boasts the availability of '[o]ver 23 million movies, TV shows, songs, magazines, books, audiobooks, and popular apps and games' (Amazon, 2013). The digital edition of *The End of Mr. Y* is among some two million popular titles available, in addition to the millions of free public domain books that have been digitized and made available at the tap of the Kindle App. As formally distinct media continue their convergence into singular, mobile devices, book reading competes for mental and screen space in what cultural researcher danah boyd has articulated as an 'attention economy' (boyd, 2012). An Internet aware audience can also purchase the paperback used from Amazon for as little as £0.01. Incidentally though, *The End of Mr. Y* was the one Thomas Lumas book Ariel *could not* find on eBay or other secondhand-book sites (Mr. Y, 24).

Globally recognizable new media technologies like Amazon, eBay, MySpace, Facebook, Twitter, Hotmail, Google, etc., have proliferated since the publication of *Mr. Y*, and become ubiquitous elements of many people's daily lives. Users are now able to access the Internet from a variety of mobile devices, browsing a staggering amount of amalgamated media content. An advert for the practically archaic Apple 3g iPhone depicts an assortment of fairly mundane activities: checking snow conditions, calorie-counting, locating where the car is parked, and assures viewers that, 'there's an app for that', in fact, 'there is an app for just about anything' (Apple, 2009). In an 'app for that' media environment, book reading competes with listening to music, watching and producing YouTube videos, social networking, and playing Angry Birds or Candy Crush Saga.

The prevalence and capabilities of smartphones have increased since 2006, but the idea of technological advance and its effects on book reading is an obvious theme of *Mr. Y*. 'It's a strange experience' Ariel reflects about having no mediated context on which to compare *Mr. Y*, 'coming to such an old book without the benefit of a thousand TV adaptations and study guides and reading groups' (*Mr. Y*, 55). Although Ariel references televisual adaptations, her point lends support to the attention competition screens present to book reading. Ariel, however, relishes this *lack* of mediated context.

Simply stated, digital editions of books are so commonplace they are an already banal mainstay of contemporary popular culture. In fact, it is now uncommon for a recent popular book to *not* have a digital edition. Technology is so ever-present in contemporary life that an Apple iPhone 5 advert proudly proclaims the new device is, '[t]he biggest thing to happen to iPhone since iPhone' (Apple, 2012). Even in the media environment of the mid-2000s, the swell of new media technologies threatened to displace the cultural practice of book reading, if not obliterate the book outright.

From the advent of the commercial Internet, the fate of the book has been addressed with a question mark. Media and Cultural studies classes stage debates about the continued sociocultural relevance of books, and news media programs circulate headlines about how print media is in its death throes. In his seminal study of the technologizing of the word, Walter J. Ong (1982) argues that it is precisely the onset of new technologies that facilitates the critique of current technologies. Yes, long-standing news circular *Newsweek* recently ended its print run in favor of an all-digital format (New York Times, 2012), no, this does not signal the impending death of all print media, although books and newspapers are among the last bastions. In his study of primitive cultures, English anthropologist E. B. Tylor (1871: 16) observed 'processes, customs, opinions, and so forth, which have been carried on by force of habit into a new state of society different from that in which they had their original home, and they thus remain as proofs and examples of an older condition of culture out of which a newer has been evolved'. Tylor refers to that which has gone out with the new as 'survivals'.

Writing in 1871, Tylor could have been a contemporary of Thomas Lumas (if Lumas were a real person and not the imaginings of Thomas). Similar to Tylor, George Basalla (1988: 218) concludes his study of the evolution of technology by rejecting the concept of technological progress in favor of an 'appreciation for the diversity of the made world, for the fertility of the technological imagination, and for the grandeur and antiquity of the network of related artifacts'. According to Tylor and Basalla, the worst-case scenario for books is that they go the way of records, audiocassettes, shoulder pads, corduroys, bellbottoms, and other fashions that have come and gone, and come back.

This would be in keeping with how David Punter (2007: 6) theorizes '[t]he moment of modernity': that which is 'not merely the present, the here-and-now', but 'is deeply embroiled in the "succession" of states, it is an always temporary term which asserts both the *onset* of a condition of things and simultaneously the *passing-away* of other things' (emphasis in the original). He goes on to assert a paradox that, 'part of the complex structure of modernity will always be a certain kind of nostalgia, a moment of regret for that which is superseded – in Hegelian terms, *aufheben* – within the onset of the new' (Punter, 2007: 6). For Punter the continual present of modernity incorporates aspects of both nostalgia and the uncanny, aspects Thomas plays with in her fiction.

Networked Plotting

In the 'About' section of her website, Thomas alludes to a dislike of the postmodern poster theorist, Fredric Jameson, and claims that her novels *Bright Young Things* (2001), *Going Out* (2004), and *PopCo* (2005) were part of her 'Postmodernism is Rubbish' trilogy. Although nostalgia informs Thomas's depiction of books in *Mr. Y*, Ariel's love of books is more in keeping with a fetish. She is, after all, a bibliophile PhD student.

Ariel's grubby, cold, hungry, and poverty-stricken student life becomes a time traveling adventure when she stumbles upon a most improbable copy of her primary text. 'I look inside. And – suddenly I can't breathe – there it is: a small cream clothbound hardback with brown lettering on the cover and spine, missing a dust jacket but otherwise near perfect. But it can't be' (*Mr. Y*, 11). Surely this is the happily accidental fantasy of every literary PhD candidate? 'I open the cover and read the title page and the publication details. Oh, shit. This is a copy of *The End of Mr. Y*. What the hell do I do now?' (*Mr. Y*, 11).

It is no accident that Lumas's book is called *The End of Mr. Y*, nor that *Mr. Y* is by Thomas, Thomas Lumas. To round out the allure of this treasure, a rumor circulates about the book being cursed because everyone who has been known to read it has died shortly thereafter. If the book does contain a curse, perhaps it is the curse of knowledge. Although Lumas's text masquerades as fiction, the unabridged version contains a homeopathic recipe that can transport the user/reader to a realm of thought, metaphor, and time travel called the Troposphere. Unfortunately, someone (her advisor, Saul Burlem) has removed the page that contains the recipe for the formula: '[b]etween the verso page 130 and the recto page 133 there is simply a jagged paper edge. Pages 131 and 132, two sides of one folio page, are missing' (*Mr. Y*, 35). Upon reading that there are no pages 131 and 132 in *The End of Mr. Y*, the first thing I would expect most readers to do is check.

This is a subtle invitation to interact with the text and celebrate its materiality. This sort of interactivity is suggestive of Mark Z. Danielewski's monumental *House of Leaves* (2000). Investing in a narrative is, as Walter Benjamin (1937) argues, something primal, a matter of life and death no less. In his *The Storyteller* (1937) essay, Benjamin associates reading a well-plotted story as an act of consumption similar to a fire drawing air and fuel from the book's pages.[2] Danielewski's *House of Leaves* is a vastly more elaborate, but still relevant, American comparison to *Mr. Y*.[3] I would argue both texts are examples of what I term networked plotting, which goes beyond the inclusion and awareness of online computing and the Internet. By way of example, one of the characters in *House of Leaves* reads from a book entitled *House of Leaves*, but eventually resorts to burning its pages for warmth. Danielewski feeds this back into the plot with sections of the story lost to fire damage. Benjamin's reading-as-propelling-burning-desire is not a direct or fictitious reference for this passage (as Danielewski is apt to do), but the association once made, is significant.

Networked plotting can have this serendipitous and/or uncanny effect of incorporating past, present, and future cultural references, experiences, events, memories, etc. The *House of Leaves* introduction warns: the book *might* haunt its readers (*House of Leaves*, xxii-xxiii). Indeed, the layers of its meta-fiction are multiple. As Catherine Spooner (2006: 46) notes, it anticipates its own popular and critical reception. *House of Leaves* was written with the aid of a computer, and parts of it appeared online. This is also a component of networked plotting: the product of the commingling of intertextuality, hyper-textuality and Internet searchability. Networked plotting could be thought of as the inverse of research: a deliberately ambiguous reference or inclusion that offers the readers the opportunity to explore outside of the text, but allows for the results of that exploration to enrich (or frustrate) the story and/or the reading experience.

Does *The End of Mr. Y* contain the pages 131 and 132? I invite you to check for yourself. Kindle readers do not generally display the page numbers of a given digital edition, exhibiting instead the percent of the text already read.[4] To flip forward in a Kindle edition is a drastically different experience than with a material book. For Thomas and Danielewski, the materiality of books is important. As if anticipating the question of multimedia adaptations of *House of Leaves*, the dedication asserts, 'This is not for you' (*House of Leaves*, viiii). As of this writing there is not, nor as Danielewski's ten-year commitment to setting the type for the physical book pages suggests, will there ever be a Kindle edition (or 'official' film adaptation) of *House of Leaves*.[4]

Through some detective work not out of place in genre fiction like Scarlett Thomas's Lily Pascale Mysteries (2004, 2005), some luck and/or fate (and some plotting), Ariel eventually finds the page Burlem hid in his office copy of Erasmus Darwin's *Zoonomia* (1801). With the aid of some careful library (rather than Internet) research

(*Mr. Y*, 124), Ariel makes up the homeopathic tincture to experience the Troposphere herself. Her first attempt, however, is a dud. Wallowing in her presumed failure she faces the prospect of moving on: 'I could write something, but I can't. I could read something – but what do you read after *Mr. Y*?' (*Mr. Y*, 191). A similar sentiment circulated after the cult and popular success of *House of Leaves*. What do you read after *House of Leaves*? An Amazon.com algorithm might suggest *The End of Mr. Y*, in which case I recommend a material rather than digital edition to appreciate the full effect of the Nibbie award winning book design, and its ominous black pages.

Analoging the digital and digitizing the analog

After upgrading her hardware, a black circle markered in on the back of a 'rectangle of card with a Victorian pastoral scene on one side' (*Mr. Y*, 192), Ariel makes a second attempt. 'I'm falling into a black tunnel, the same tunnel Mr. Y described in the book. […] Wherever I am, it's completely silent and I have no bodily sensations at all. I'm fairly sure my body is here with me, but it has no feelings and no desires. […] Only my mind feels alive' (*Mr. Y*, 193). This time her journey takes her through a history of human development: 'I see […] a huge penis, drawn in the same style as that on the Cerne Abbas Giant, but rendered here in light. […]' (*Mr. Y*, 193). It also takes her through a history of language, numbers and advancements in human thought: 'Greek, Roman and Cyrillic. […] The alphabets look more familiar, and now include numerals, […]. I'm sure I see Newton's $F=ma$, and, later, Einstein's $E=mc^2$' (*Mr. Y*, 193–4). Ariel's homeopathic hallucination-like 'trip' is an example of Thomas's attempt to literalize thought as metaphor. 'Then something else happens, something not described in Lumas's version of this: the letters from the alphabet all disappear and turn into numbers, and then the numbers, apart from 1 and 0, disappear as well until I am left with millions and millions of 0s and 1s waterfalling down the walls around me' (*Mr. Y*, 194–5). If there were a Victorian *Matrix* (1999), it would be *The End of Mr. Y*, an association Thomas alludes to in *Our Tragic Universe* (2010).

Ariel's journey through seemingly infinite *potential* information is highly evocative of cultural imaginings of the contemporary Internet. Although Ariel prefers book research when possible, this passage provides plenty of Google search footer. According to the visitor's information website, the Cerne Abbas Giant is a cut turf and chalk hill figure in Dorset, England. The binary code: '01110111 01101000 01100001 01110100 01110100 01101000 01100101 01100110 01110101 01100011 01101011 01101001 01110011 01100111 01101111 01101001 01101110 01100111 01101111 01101110', which takes up nearly all of page 195, repeats the phrase 'whatthefuckisgoingon' (Binary Translator, 2013). The user generates the appearance of the Troposphere, and it is telling that Ariel conceives of the thought space in terms of the Internet.

The bodiless sensation is suggestive of Baudrillard's ideas about the contemporary predominance of mediated simulations having supplanted their real referents. Space prevents me from expanding the links between digital avatars and their relationship to *Simulation and Simulacra* (1981/1994), and Baudrillard's later theories, but Ariel's description of herself is suggestive of an avatar representation of self that mediates the real and the virtual expanse of 'cyberspace'. This description aptly depicts the synthesis of information into a metaphoric 'space'. Ariel travels through information, into a metaphoric thought space, not unlike a reader imagining the setting and plot of a book. To further the associations with the Internet, however, Ariel relates her journey with reference to computers and the Internet: '[m]y image of the street in front of me is overlaid, suddenly, with a console image: something like a city plan on a computer screen in my mind' (*Mr. Y*, 198). To navigate this landscape she uses 'something like a computer desktop' which acts as part of her video-game-like heads up display on which images act 'like a link on the Internet [...] that I can choose to jump into [...]' (*Mr. Y*, 200–1). In what I like to consider an homage to sci-fi movies and television programmes, when Ariel wants to access the interface she says/thinks *console!* (*Mr. Y*, 203) as Captain Kirk might say 'Computer!' or 'On Screen'. Ariel's console is expressly related to the Internet, and navigating the Troposphere functions as a literalization of visiting a homepage or shop front (*Mr. Y*, 217).

Ariel's journey into the Troposphere is a microcosm of the referential material *Mr. Y* contains, but does not explain outright. This is to say nothing, however, of the philosophy, theoretical math and physics, and religious theology and imagery the book contains for curious academics, bibliophiles, Easter egg hunters, fans, and motivated Internet-aware readers. For those readers that want to meet the text and the Internet half way, the U.S. publishers, Harcourt Trade Publishers, 'official' *The End of Mr. Y* website includes a bonus features section. In addition to a 'How to Surf Space and Time' short training primer, the website includes a 'Learn More' section full of links to various theory journals, Jean Baudrillard and Jacques Derrida links, mathematic encyclopedias, and homoeopathy sites and suppliers (should you want to attempt to visit the Troposphere yourself). *The End of Mr. Y* is a bricolage of all of this and more. The plot borrows and blends indiscriminately, sometimes implicitly, sometimes overtly. Sometimes the text yields referential links with little regard to synchronic timelines.

Where Thomas's *Going Out* is an evident reimagining of *The Wizard of Oz* (1900/1939), *The End of Mr. Y* is a more mature offering both in terms of writing quality and subject matter. Despite the iconic status and cultural legacy of *The Wizard of Oz*, *Going Out* is an example of what I call 'dial up fiction' because of its portrayal of Internet accessed in the dial up days before broadband, a technological era for which people are seemingly not especially nostalgic. Still, there are implicit connections between the depiction of the Troposphere and tumbling down the rabbit hole, what lies just beyond the wardrobe, far away Neverland, and the yellow bricked roads of Oz. Neither *Going Out*, nor *The End of Mr. Y*, however, are specifically intended as children's stories. While the development of her protagonists often involves a journey of self-discovery, Thomas's fiction does not, in a straight forward way, transition an innocent child to an aware adult as some children's fiction *might* do.[6]

Thomas has written that '*Mr. Y* is set in a fictionalized Canterbury', but just as Oz 'isn't Kansas anymore' for Dorothy, the Troposphere takes Ariel to an elsewhere away from her seedy, hand-to-mouth experience as a PhD student. In fact, in the end Ariel's journey could be considered a return to innocence through the urge to know everything. To this end, the text presents a complex quest for knowledge, while the playful allusions to the biblical Adam and a techno-philosophical reworking of the Fall amount to a qualified inversion of that archetypal story. In the 'Acknowledgements' section at the end of the novel Thomas responds to criticism, concluding that the narrative with Ariel and Adam walking towards a tree in an Edenic garden allowed for the book to be considered a 'shaggy God story' (*Mr. Y*, 506). 'For me,' she writes, 'Ariel and Adam never escape language and metaphor: they don't find anything absolute at the edge of consciousness, just religious imagery' (*Mr. Y*, 506). Whether a shaggy god story or just religious imagery, *The End of Mr. Y* does not reveal anything absolute. It trades in possibility.

Ariel: Horse of a Different Colo(u)r

Far from a *singular* work of genre fiction, *The End of Mr. Y* is a unique patchwork of *several* identifiable genres. Its split contemporary and Victorian settings fluctuate between the convincingly realistic, and the popular imaginings of Steam Punk Britannia. It is not all that far off from the Neo-Victorian, Gothic, Sci-Fi, Adventure Romance, Travelblog or Memoir, and there are even some shades of a Crime Noir Thriller in the mix, with Ariel as a young scholastic Sherlock. The anachronistic technology links are subtle, with Troposphere users wibbling and wobbling through distance, time, and ancestry à la *Dr. Who* or H. G. Wells. The novel's villains provide a faint essence of the dry vermouth of a James Bond plot. But rather than Cold War era Russian spies trying to weaponize the Troposphere and therefore monopolize creativity, independent and autonomous thought and emotion, and the very fabrics of consciousness, those roles are ideologically recast for Americans.

The American agents are renegades from the military sponsored Project Starlight, which was shut down because '[a]ny project that kills a hundred children can't go on, either with government funding or without it' (*Mr. Y*, 313). It is more accurate to say that the bodies of these children died while their minds live on in MindSpace. Autistic, but extremely proficient and able to manipulate MindSpace, the government recruited KIDS – 'Karmic Interface Delineation System' which is 'actually just an excuse for a neat acronym' (*Mr. Y*, 312). As with the advent of most new technologies each generation asks of the subsequent generation: are the kids all right? The KIDS, like Lumas and most others that experience the Troposphere, 'simply stayed in MindSpace too long' (*Mr. Y*, 313), a fate that Ariel and Adam ultimately also choose. This aspect of the novel is suggestive of social anxieties that circulate about the effects media consumption and participation are having on children and society in general. New technologies tend to be hailed as revolutionary or apocalyptic and valorization and condemnation can be found across the board. danah boyd (*sic*) identifies a 'culture of fear' circulating around new technologies, often perpetuated by the media and overly concerned but well-meaning parents (boyd, 2012). Spending too much time on the Internet is to watching too much TV, is to telegraph romances, is to Eighteenth century fears about the effects of novel reading, and so it goes.

In addition to its appeal to multiple genres and audiences, and its intentionally broad inclusions, *Mr. Y* is also part philosophy lecture, part playful meta-fictional thought experiment and game. As an example, in the middle of the book the protagonist explains: 'Ariel Manto – my alias, my pen name, the name I gave myself when I was only eighteen and I didn't want to be me anymore. [...] The Ariel part is real at least. And yes, it was the poetry not the play' (*Mr. Y*, 232). This reference is especially well tailored for the literary PhD student. The play in question is likely Shakespeare's *The Tempest* and although Ariel disavows this association, its inclusion helps enrich Thomas's networked plotting and meta-fictional associations.

The poetry Ariel alludes to also becomes a meta-fictional reference that enhances the inter/hyper-textual scope of *Mr. Y*. In the forward to the restored edition of *Ariel*, Frieda Hughes traces the trajectory of the distinct 'Ariel voice' of her mother, Sylvia Plath (Hughes, 2004: xii). Hughes suggests the early Ariel voice began in Devon and matured as the family settled into their London flat. Plath wrote that the title poem 'Ariel', referred to 'a horse I'm especially fond of' (Plath cited in Hughes, 2004: xv), but the association to horseback riding is ambiguous. The poem documents a moment of transcendence as the speaker moves from 'Stasis in darkness', to a suicidal drive 'Into the red/Eye, the cauldron of morning' (Plath, 1965/2004: 34). Such a movement is evocative of Ariel Manto's journey through the Troposphere to the 'edge of consciousness' (*Mr. Y*, 501). There is also Disney's *The Little Mermaid* (1989), which is loosely based on the Hans Christian Andersen fairytale and ballet first published in 1837 (with English translations by H. P. Paull available in 1872). The associations continue from there, Thomas's literary and cultural playground.

In the Harcourt Trade Press bonus web material, 'How to Surf Space and Time', one suggestion is, ' [y]ou may want to adopt an alias that reflects your new identity. Ariel simply changed her last name to Manto. Play with anagrams and see what you come up with'. Should any especially keen, Internet aware readers follow this advice, they may come up with 'I am not real' as an anagram of Ariel Manto, as Alex Watson did in his blog review of *The End of Mr. Y*.

In *Mr. Y*, questions about religion and the functions of the divine share page space with sadomasochistic scenes of rough sex. Like Ariel's experience of the Troposphere, the text presents many different complimentary and competing layers for its reader to explore. The Troposphere itself is related to layers upon layers: sometimes Derridean, sometimes Disney by way of Baudrillard. It is depicted, as both reading and using the Internet could also be considered, as a thought space: MindSpace, one layer removed from the human experience of real-world consciousness.

Using an Internet search, it does not take Ariel long to discover that the Troposphere is also the lowest layer of the Earth's atmosphere, making the fiction even more meta for her. Mimicking how a reader could interact with *The End of Mr. Y*: '[t]o pass the time, I open up the Internet browser on my machine and do a search for the word Troposphere. I don't expect anything to come up, but then I find out that it does exist' (*Mr. Y*, 101). Immediately following this Ariel does a search for *The End of Mr. Y*, 'just to see if there's any information online that I haven't seen before' (*Mr. Y*, 101).

Ariel has an intimate knowledge of what is available online about the text and she is surprised to find a fourth mention in addition to the three usual links, a blog post by the young clerk at the secondhand book shop (102). As it happens this is one of the ways the American antagonists track Ariel down, despite her anagramic non-existence, and her assertion that she is 'not in a story' (254).

How to Surf Space and Time

'Surfing in MindSpace is something you just can't stop doing' (*Mr. Y*, 313). When Ariel accidently ends up in the MindSpace of one of the American agents she 'overthinks' an important exposition of their motives: 'Can you imagine how much money there is in this? [...] This is the only time I've ever been close to anything of value. I have to get the book. I have to get the book... I... Actually, I have to take a dump. The urgency is like a voice in my head' (*Mr. Y*, 313). The scene suggests, yet again, the parallels between 'surfing' the Internet and MindSpace. It also indicates the urge not only to weaponize, and capitalize on the Internet-esque MindSpace, but also Ariel's ability to influence people from that space. Thomas's fiction presents a narrative of all too familiar public policy debates that surround the Internet. The American agents blur the line between government officials and private corporations, or here, citizens. Their skill set aligns them with hackers, who possess a technical skill enabling them to use the Internet for potentially malicious gain.[7]

In his critique of what he calls 'The Google Doctrine', Evgeny Morozov (2011) identifies a far-reaching U.S. policy blunder. In 2009, at the urging of the U.S. State Department microblogging site, Twitter, postponed some routinely scheduled site maintenance so that, the argument goes, pro-democratic activity could continue to circulate for Twitter users protesting in Iran. The consequence of this event, and why it is relevant, is that it alerted nations to the authority the U.S. government could wield over technologies that were based in the U.S. and subject to their laws, but are used practically all the world over. Although these events take place after the publication of *Mr. Y*, they help show the social consequences of themes raised in Thomas's fiction. The result of the U.S. State department's blunder, according to Morozov, was the cracking down on, and State infiltration of, various social networks and new media technologies. A more watchful eye was cast over Internet access, and the use of new and social media technologies that are based in the U.S. but have global implications.

The meta-fiction of a British author seems an unlikely place for the impact of mediatization and globalization to be explored, and yet, considering these (hyper?) links I have been mapping, the philosophic subject matter, and the intentionally playful, knowing, relationship with the reader, and the predominance of new media in the fiction, the text could be entered into a discussion about the effects particularly American forms of mediatization and globalization are having on the rest of the world. Attempting to locate her advisor, Burlem, Ariel overthinks his experience with the Project Starlight men and his reluctance to contribute to a militaristic ultimate weapon: 'My mind filled with unpleasant thoughts of world domination and thought-control. If a repressive regime – or any regime – got hold of this mixture, then ... what?' (*Mr. Y*, 352). Read this way, Thomas's *End of Mr. Y* gently accuses America of media colonization!

Because of their ubiquitous place in our everyday lives, new media use like Google searches, *You*Tube, and *My*Space, feel proximate, even intimate, so much so that it is easy to forget that they are principally American corporations subject to the laws of the United States. Because of their global influence and high accessibility, companies like these seem international, and indeed many successful new media companies have international offices. Google, Microsoft, Twitter, MySpace, Facebook: these are globalized corporations but still fundamentally associated with the United States, and while the general values these companies frequently represent are often expanded to Britain and other so called 'Western' nations, Thomas's contemporary British fiction challenges such an easy homogenization.

Early American literature is often presented as in anxious competition with the more established literary traditions of Britain and to a lesser degree, continental Europe. Enthusiasts of early American literature often point to this discrepancy in literary traditions to suggest a determined sense of uniqueness and novelty in classic American works. For everything else it might do, the great American novel also offered Europe some of the novelty of the new world.

Combining this literary argument with global technological trends is complex. Yahoo.com and Microsoft's Hotmail e-mail provider are both mentioned in *Mr. Y*, as is Apple's iPod. These references to globally recognizable, but distinctly American technologies draw the British setting into contrast. Thomas does this in many ways, including depicting America as a Roland Barthesian myth of 'Americanicity'. By adapting some of Barthes' general claims from his articulation of 'Italianicity' in *Image, Music, Text* (1977), Thomas can be understood as presenting an outsider's version of America, while also reflecting a mythologized Britain: Victorian, bookish, and full of heritage.

Ariel is able to locate Burlem in hiding by identifying the correct castle heritage site in Devon from a book at the local history library. But she identifies it based on its absences: 'this aerial view, certainly does make it seem like the space – the thing that isn't there – is more important than the walls which are' (*Mr. Y*, 406). Although an Internet-aware reader could while away the hours searching Google for 'aerial images of Devon castle heritage sites' (could it be Totnes Castle? That seems too easy. Okehampton?), even if there is such a castle in Devon, here it is fictitious, mythologized as an empty signifier: '[i]f you look at a castle for long enough the walls blur, and it's as if they don't have any point at all, except to keep all the nothingness in' (*Mr. Y*, 406). This could be the networked plotting description of English heritage castles.

In Thomas's meta-fictional literary representation of England, signifiers of authenticity resonate but do not necessarily solidify meaning. Likewise, her depiction of America references, and thereby also critiques, Hollywood films like *The Matrix*: '[w]here have I heard the term 'spoon bending' recently' (*Mr. Y*, 440),[8] a militaristic sense of capital gain, and the pursuit of, in this case, a hypnagogic experience that resembles a dream, but affords the dreamer more agency. Even from this brief sketch, Thomas's Troposphere forges a complex, but available British parallel to the ideological concept of the American Dream.

The Internet Information Superhighway: whatthefuckisgoingon

I have been identifying the multiple, nodular web of references that link the text and the Internet, and the reading audience. A final significant parallel between Ariel's experience of the Troposphere and the Internet is her time travel by train of thought. Trains abound in *The End of Mr. Y*. In an important scene, Ariel must reunite her mind, which has been wandering the Troposphere, with her body, which is in danger of dying. The trains of thought relate to emotions, and this is one of the most captivating and emotive sections of the novel. This is an important moment because the train of thought journey travels Ariel, and the reader, back in narrative time allowing her to choose a different path for her story.

The metaphor of a 'train of thought' is highly suggestive of other metaphors applied to the Internet. 'Today the Internet is often described as an information superhighway', Tom Standage (1998: 2) writes in his book *The Victorian Internet*; 'its nineteenth-century precursor, the electric telegraph, was dubbed the "highway of thought" [...] The equipment may have been different, but the telegraph's impact on the lives of its users was strikingly similar'. Ariel's journey aboard the metaphorical emotional train of fear causes her to relive and confront the fears of her life as well as more general fears. Like most of Ariel's experiences of the Troposphere, exiting the train proves to be a quandary: 'The train's still moving but the doors open and...' (*Mr. Y*, 394).

'You now have infinite choice'

While not quite a 'choose your own adventure' novel, Thomas's bestselling fiction suggests nodular, networked plotting, indicative of playing a video game or browsing the Internet...

With Ariel jumping from the train of thought, the text returns her and the reader to the events of some 80 pages prior, like pushing the 'back' button of an Internet browser, or loading a game from an important save point. This is the most iconic example of networked plot-

ting. The linear model of the plot of *Mr. Y* progresses from point A →
to point B → to point C and generally adheres to a three-act structure.
Yet ... the plot includes this revision. The networked plot model has
point A, point B, and point C constantly relaying information through
any available node, like the bits and bytes of information transmitted
through the digital network of the Internet.

In my assessment of Thomas's networked plotting, and my constant identification of the Troposphere with the Internet, it is not my
intention to limit the fiction. The Troposphere is often like the Internet, but it is also important in its own right within the fiction. I do
not mean to suggest that Thomas intended the Troposphere to be the
Internet, rather Thomas imagined an Internet aware audience, and
benefits from associations with these aspects of digital culture. 'What
is thought made of?', Thomas asks in her website post about *The End
of Mr. Y*. 'My research was more philosophical than factual, and I particularly remember listening to a podcast of a Derrida lecture on my
iPod while doing the ironing one Sunday and being very taken with
Derrida saying that praying is "not like ordering a pizza".' In true meta-
fictional fashion, Ariel also references Derrida's 'not like ordering a
pizza' statement (*Mr. Y*, 60). I have been arguing that *The End of Mr.
Y* drops Derrida into a society, and media environment where online
Churches thrive and pizza can be ordered with a keystroke. To this
end, Thomas's fiction articulates and anticipates important themes
that surround the increasingly global use of digital media technologies.

The End of Mystery?

With the Internet-like Troposphere, Thomas depicts a critical, but
also at times celebratory relationship with America's techno-global
influence. In her qualified critique, Thomas fictionalizes the relationship between Britain and America that political pundits often refer
to as 'special'. Reverberations of that special relationship permeate
through many aspects of both societies, including industrial, technological, and literary productions. While Thomas's depiction of

America is critical, she presents her characters as willing participants in the techo-globalized world, which is deeply influenced by American based companies.

Thomas's articulation of the collision of analog book reading and the surfing of digital information is not without some concern. 'I pray for the end of mystery. What would a life be like with all the mysteries solved? If there were no questions, there'd be no stories' (*Mr. Y*, 259). Ariel's desiring the end of mystery in the same breath (thought) as mourning its loss affirms Thomas's deliberate straddling of the line between new digital media and the material book.

Given the prominence of the cultural practice of 'googling it', Thomas may consider the Internet as sapping some of the mystery of the human experience (and book reading). But then again, there is no reason that the resulting Google query has to be the be-all and end-all. Rather, it can be a near infinite expanse of links to choose from, infinite choice. Thomas's celebration and pronounced rejection of digital culture presents a broad, sliding spectrum upon which readers and other writers can position, and reposition themselves. Is the digital taking us into infinite potential information, or is it returning us to the material? Ariel and Thomas choose neither and both.

Still, for Thomas, it remains important to root this digital/material quandary in an English context. As Benedict Anderson (1983) articulated, there are identifiable, highly important social bonds that form national communities and identities. But these factors are multiple, variable, and ultimately collectively imagined. Therefore, explaining precisely how *The End of Mr. Y* is identifiably British, and to be more specific, how it is especially English, is actually more difficult than it seems. One of the ways Thomas articulates Englishness is by equating English national identity with a particular reverence of the book and book reading. Bearing this in mind(space), I suggest that some of Thomas's attitude about the relationship between digital technologies and the book is expressed through Ariel:

> 'Real life is regularly running out of money, and then food. Real life is having no proper heating. Real life is physical. Give me books instead: give me the invisibility of the contents of books, the thought,

the ideas, the images. Let me become part of a book; I'd give anything for that. Being cursed by *The End of Mr. Y* must mean becoming part of the book; an intertextual being: a book-cyborg, or, considering that books aren't cybernetic, perhaps a bibliorg.' (*Mr. Y*, 147).

Thomas's plot may evoke the digital but through the various metatextual layers of her fiction, and her skillful networked plotting, she achieves a curious effect: she renders the material book an object of more than simple nostalgia; the book is valorized and fetishized. You can see this in its black edged pages, which smudge and bleed and exude the curse of *Mr. Y* into the hands of its readers. Although Ariel suggests books are not cybernetic, Thomas has clearly benefited from linking her fiction with new media, and although *Mr. Y* includes critiques of both American and British culture, the novel, and Thomas, are distinctly, and ultimately celebratory of (and celebrated in) Britain. Among Thomas's many accolades was the inclusion in the *2001 Independent on Sunday's* list of the UK's 20 best young writers.

Her American publishing company intuited the importance of the link between new media and literary fiction. They employed a 'Read It, Pass It!' promotion: 'We've placed 100 copies of *The End of Mr. Y* in 22 cities across the United States for people to find, read, and share. Can you find one like the people below?'. In a rudimentary Internet interface, people can leave their name, if they found or passed it and where, and any comments they might have. While splashing one hundred copies of the book around major cities in the U.S. might seem like a counterintuitive tactic to grab the attention of an Internet aware audience, I appreciate this publicity stunt as a past/present/future hybridization of the contemporary phenomena of something 'going viral'. Finding or passing on *The End of Mr. Y* is the bibliorg means of going viral, the organic parallel. As it happens, all of the people that posted about reading or passing a copy of *The End of Mr. Y* were Internet aware readers, since they bothered to seek the page out to report their finding or passing. This seems a successful confirmation of Thomas having her digital culture and reading books too.

Notes

1 Choose your own adventure novels are written such that at crucial plot points, the reader chooses the course of the plot by flipping pages back and forward through the book.

2 'Indeed, he destroys, he swallows up the material as the fire devours logs in the fireplace. The suspense which permeates the novel is very much like the draft which stimulates the flame in the fireplace and enlivens its play' (Benjamin, 1937: 100).

3 One particularly American concern could relate to the pre-millennial housing market and fears about sustained home equity. See Brian Jarvis' 'The Fall of the Hou$e of Finance: Gothic Economies in *House of Leaves* (2000) and *Lunar Park* (2005)' in *Twenty-First Century Gothic* (2010), eds Cherry, Howell, Ruddell.

4 Selecting the 'X-ray' function displays a graphic representation of the 'book' and includes a page number associated with the print edition (if there is one). Kindle versions of *The End of Mr. Y* have a small caveat: Contains real page numbers (Amazon, 2013).

5 J.J. Abrams and Dough Dorst's, *S* (2013) is also a relevant American comparison to *House of Leaves*, and Thomas's *PopCo*, and *The End Of Mr. Y*. Although *S* is a self professed 'love letter to the written word', the back and forth comments in the margins are, at times, suggestive of contemporary instant message chatting. Unlike Danielewski's resistance to media adaptations, plenty of media surrounds *S* from stylized teaser video promotions, audio and ebook versions, and user generated supplemental blogs. Mediated versions present a practical question about how the various maps, code wheels and additional material is presented and formatted for the new medium. *PopCo*, by contrast, includes all the decoding tools in the text, or as direct, searchable references.

6 I hesitate to make a claim about what children's literature is, should be, what functions it might serve, and when literature should be read, although these are relevant questions being considered in contemporary literary study. See Jack Zipes (1985, 2002), Karin Lesnik-Oberstein (2004).

7 I do not mean to imply an exclusively negative association with the term 'hacker'. Not all hackers are malicious, and some hacker collectives, 'hacktivists', and geek communities have complex, meritocratic systems of organization, like Anonymous. See *Geeks, Social Imaginaries, and Recursive*

Publics (Kelty, 2008), or Gabriella Coleman's *Is Anonymous Anarchy?* (2011), and *Our Wierdness is Free: The logic of Anonymous – online army, agent of chaos, and seeker of justice* (2012), or search keyword 'ethical hacking'.

8 In *The Matrix* (1999) the protagonist, Neo, visits a character named, The Oracle. While he waits to speak to her, a young child practices the manipulation of the digital code that presents the world around them. Bending a spoon by changing its code, the child says, '[d]o not try and bend the spoon, that's impossible, instead, only try to realize the truth […] there is no spoon. […] Then you will see that it is not the spoon that bends, it is only yourself.' (Wachowski, 1999)

Works Cited

Amazon (2013) 'Kindle Fire HD', accessed 7 January 2013, http://www.amazon.com/gp/product/B0083PWAPW

Amazon (2013) 'The End of Mr. Y', accessed 7 January 2013, http://www.amazon.com/The-End-Mr-Y-ebook/dp/B003WJQ6BS/ref=sr_1_1?s=digital-text&ie=UTF8&qid=1357622678&sr=1–1&keywords=the+end+of+mr+y

Anderson, Benedict (1983) *Imagined Communities*. London: Verso.

Apple (2009) 'There is an app for that', accessed 7 January 2013, http://www.youtube.com/watch?v=szrsfeyLzyg

Apple (2012) 'The biggest thing since the iPhone', accessed 7 January 2013, http://www.apple.com/iphone/

Barthes, Roland (1977) *Image, Music, Text*, trans. Stephen Heath. New York: Hill and Wang.

Basalla, George (1988) *The Evolution of Technology*. Cambridge: Cambridge University Press.

Benjamin, Walter (1937/1968) 'The Storyteller', in *Illuminations*, trans. Harry Zohn. New York: Schocken Books.

Binary Translator (2013), accessed 7 January 2013, binarytranslator.biz/binary.php

boyd, danah (2012) 'The Power of Fear in Networked Publics', *SXSW*, Austin, Texas, 10 March, accessed 7 January 2013, http://www.danah.org/papers/talks/2012/SXSW2012.html

Danielewski, Mark Z. (2000) *House of Leaves*. New York: Pantheon Books.

Harcourt Trade Publishers (2000–6) 'Bonus Materials: How to Surf Space and Time', accessed 8 January 2013, http://www.harcourtbooks.com/TheEndOfMrY/how_to.asp

Harcourt Trade Publishers (2000–6) 'Bonus Materials: Learn More', accessed 7 January 2013, http://www.harcourtbooks.com/TheEndOfMrY/learn_more.asp

Harcourt Trade Publishers (2000–6) 'Read it, Pass it!', accessed 8 January 2013, http://www.harcourtbooks.com/TheEndOfMrY/ReadItPassIt.asp

Hughes, Frieda (2004) 'Forward', *Ariel: The Restored Edition*. New York: Harper Collins.

Morozov, Evgeny (2011) *The Net Delusion: The Dark Side of Internet Freedom*. Public Affairs.

National Trust (2013), accessed 7 January 2013, http://www.nationaltrust.org.uk/cerne-giant/

New York Times (2012) 'At Newsweek, Ending Print and A Blend of Two Styles', accessed 7 January 2013, http://mediadecoder.blogs.nytimes.com/2012/10/18/newsweek-will-cease-print-publication-at-end-of-year/?hp

Ong, Walter J. (1982) *Orality & Literacy: The Technologizing of the Word*. London: Routledge.

Plath, Sylvia (1965/2004) *Ariel: The Restored Edition*. New York: Harper Collins.

Punter, David (2007) *Modernity*. Palgrave Macmillian.

Spooner, Catherine (2006) *Contemporary Gothic*. London: Reaktion Books.

Standage, Tom (1998) *The Victorian Internet*. New York: Walker Publishing.

Thomas, Scarlett (2006/2007) *The End of Mr. Y*. Edinburgh: Cannongate.

Thomas, Scarlett (2013) 'About Scarlett Thomas', accessed 7 January 2013, http://www.scarlettthomas.co.uk/about

Tylor, Edward Burnett (1871/1958) *Primitive Culture*. New York: Harper.

Watson, Alex (2009) *The End of Mr. Y*, The Wired Jester, 7 February, accessed 8 January 2013, http://thewiredjester.co.uk/2009/02/07/the-end-of-mr-y/

PLAYING WITH FIRE
GAMING, CYBERNETICS AND FICTIONAL FORM IN
LUKA AND THE FIRE OF LIFE AND *THE CYBERGYPSIES*

Marianne Corrigan

I see a hurricane coming. It's called practical virtual reality [...] The exo-dus of these people from the real world, from our normal daily life of living rooms, cubicles and shopping malls, will create a change in social climate that makes global warming look like a tempest in a teacup. – Edward Cas-tronov

In the preface to his 2007 text, *Exodus to the Virtual World* (2007), Edward Castronova predicts that the twenty-first century will witness an escalation in the number of individuals opting to expend increas-ing amounts of time immersed in second-order digital configurations of reality, or other 'virtual worlds' (Castronova, 2007: 5). Castron-ova's text examines the multifaceted cybernetic landscapes of the online gaming world where 'millions of people live out a collective fantasy existence' (Castronova, 2007: 5). Immersion in virtual worlds is characterized by a re-configuration of sensory and spatial awareness resulting from a perceived corporal embodiment in the aesthetics of the digital trajectory. As Barry Atkins (2003: 66) has argued, 'immer-sion, when successfully achieved, allows the reader to remain "in" that environment because attention is not drawn to the surface of the screen that actually intervenes between reader and text'. Such immer-sive digital spaces provide a stage for the complex bio-technological melding of the organic human self and its digital simulacra, which in turn represents an epistemological duality of subjectivity: the human body and its digital avatar, or other, straddle two polarized spaces in a seeming transcendence of the interface which enacts a boundary between the two worlds.

The use of digital technology in forms such as online games, social networking sites and email has emerged as a dominant aspect to cultural and social existence in much of the developed world in the early twenty-first century. As Paul Hopper argues:

> as well as overcoming the barriers of physical space and national borders that restrict the ability of people to interact and communicate, the continued expansion of the Internet may in time ensure that the formation of online communities and transnational networks becomes the norm. (Hopper, 2007: 69)

One could argue that Hopper's analysis is, if anything, a little cautious, given that today's extensive use of social networks, such as Twitter and Facebook, by an increasingly digitally-oriented global population already represents the rhizomatic, transnational networks of communities which Hopper describes. Given the prominence of digital culture in the twenty-first century, this article seeks to critically examine the ways in which late twentieth- and early twenty-first-century literary texts have sought to explore and aestheticize gaming, digital culture and aspects of play. Through a nuanced consideration of form and aesthetics in Salman Rushdie's *Luka and the Fire of Life* (2007) and Indra Sinha's *The Cybergypsies* (1999), this essay examines late twentieth- and early twenty-first-century textual depictions of cybernetic spaces do so through the employment of varying stylistic and aesthetic methods reminiscent of the modernist literary tradition, in order to disrupt conventional narration and characterization. Drawing on gaming discourse, as well as the shifting aesthetic and formalistic concerns of literary modernism, I shall examine the ways in which these two novels seek to register the symbiotic relationship between the organic human subject and the cybernetic other, as well as map the complex oscillation between two seemingly polarized worlds. While the fictional forms of the digital game and the novel clearly differ in terms of their material properties, this article shall argue that *The Cybergypsies* (1999) and *Luka and the Fire of Life* (2010) demonstrate how the intersection of the two provides exciting possibilities for the emergence of new fictional forms in the twenty-first century.

Dialogues between Cyberspace and Literary Modernism

In *Moving Through Modernity* (2003), an investigation into space and geography in modernism, Andrew Thacker argues that 'we should understand modernist texts as creating metaphorical spaces that try to make sense of the material spaces of modernity' (Thacker, 2003: 3). Thacker goes on to suggest that the aesthetic configurations of space explored in modernist literatures also need to be understood in light of the ways in which 'social spaces dialogically help fashion the literary *forms* of the modernist text' (Thacker, 2003: 4). When considering the manner in which some twenty-first-century literature seeks to register the spatial cartographies of the digital landscape, it is interesting and timely to note that critics such as David James have framed critical discourses regarding late-twentieth century writers' literary form as 'dialogues with, rather than departures from, their modernist past' (James, 2012: 6). Through attention to the aesthetic and stylistic properties of Sinha and Rushdie's prose, this article takes its cue from James's argument that there is a need to consider the 'aesthetically specific questions of *how* modernism's legacy has both informed and challenged writers' stylistic ambitions' (James, 2009: 9).

The task of representing the cybernetic spaces, which comprise an ever more significant dimension to our contemporary concepts of citizenship and subjectivity has impacted considerably on the aesthetic and stylistic properties of the twenty-first-century novel. As we progress through the new millennium, there is a pertinent need for novelistic form to find ways of registering the suspension of the subject between the cybernetic sphere and the organic materiality of the 'real' world, and the complex symbiosis of corporeality and materiality that this entails. Given this pressing requirement for the aesthetic forms of literary texts to reflect contemporary global, digital culture, it is interesting to note Thacker's argument that modernist writing is 'about living and experiencing "new times", not in the abstracted location of literary history, but in specific spatial histories: rooms, cities, buildings countries and land-scapes' (Thacker 2009: 13). When evaluating the discursive connections between the issues of form and aesthetics facing contemporary writers such as Rushdie and Sinha, and modernist writers, we can register a similar creative impulse towards what Thacker describes as 'new times' characterized by the spatiality of new landscapes. We might read Thacker's argument, in this sense, as relevant to the emerging digital geographies of the online gaming world. Modernist discourse frequently centres on the ways in which the work of writers such as Woolf, Richardson and Joyce represents what Lyn Pykett describes as 'an aesthetic response to a moment of rupture' (Pykett, 1995: 7), referring historically to the disintegration of received cultural and social hegemonies, and the beginning of a cultural shift towards a new orthodoxy in the early twentieth century. As we find ourselves at the beginning of the twenty-first century, existing sociological and cultural frameworks that previously gave form to national, cultural and religious identities are undergoing a process of fracture and re-configuration, both culturally and politically. In 1995, Stuart Hall argued that

> the question of 'identity' is being vigorously debated in social theory. In essence, the argument is that the old identities which stabilized the social world for so long are in decline. Giving rise to new identities and fragmenting the modern individual as unified subject. This so-called 'crisis of identity' is seen as part of a wider process of change which is dislocating the central structures and processes of modern societies and undermining the frameworks which gave individuals stable anchorage in the social world. (Hall, 1995: 596)

Hall's argument registers the ways in which concepts of self and identity have begun to shift considerably in the latter half of the twentieth century as a result of a new postcolonial world order, increased global migration and greater social mobility in both the West and Asia. However, we can also read Hall's argument as an accurate description of the ways in which digital technology was beginning to alter received frameworks of subjectivity and identity in the decade preceding the turn of the twenty-first century. In his discussion of *The Cybergypsies*, Philip Leonard locates the spatial realms of the digital sphere as facilitating 'a different form of sociality [...] which allows affiliation across national borders, between regions and outside of territorial space, perhaps even allowing the world finally to become inclusive and unified' (Leonard, 2013: 35). Leonard's argument highlights the need to consider the political spatiality of cybernetic landscapes. Material landscapes have historically been re-configured as a result of social and political modes of production, and it is therefore fitting that the architectural properties of the twenty-first century novel are similarly impacted upon by the cultural spaces developed and inhabited by that particular epoch: in this case, digital spaces. As Henri Lefebvre argued 'space has been shaped and moulded from historical and natural elements, but this has been a political process. Space is political and ideological. It is a product literally filled with ideologies' (Lefebvre, 1976: 31) In accordance with Lefebvre's argument, it is vital to read cyberspace as a political geography. The advent of video games and online cybernetic communities has marked the emergence of digital spaces where received racial, cultural and gender-based discourses, which might previously have constituted the organic subject, became redundant: the disembodied subject now emerges as a cybernetic citizen within the digital landscape, sustained by a system of codes relating to behaviour, aesthetics and origins which have come to bear little relation to the conventional models of class, race or gender recognized in the organic world.

In *Cyborg Citizen* (2001), Chris Hables Gray argues that such a transformative shift in concepts of subjectivity and citizenship can be 'liberating and empowering' as 'we can choose how we construct ourselves' (Hables Gray 2002: 31), while Catronova posits 'whatever our deepest shared fantasies may be, we will be able to pursue them in cyberspace together' (Castronova, 2007: xv). The purpose of my argument here is to draw attention to a conversation which, as critics, we might register between the shifting social, cultural and political frameworks which writers such as Woolf and Richardson sought to respond to through what has come to be theorized as the literary aesthetics of modernism, and the changing cultural and political world which Rushdie, Sinha and other contemporary novelists seek to record at the turn of the twenty-first century. This essay seeks to examine the complex interplay between the textual architecture of the novel, and the cybernetic landscape of the digital world, with specific attention to how Rushdie and Sinha have sought to draw upon the aesthetic and stylistic forms of modernism in order to represent the spatial geography of cyberspace.

Thacker argues that the novels of Virginia Woolf 'constantly play across the spatial borders of inner and outer, constructing a fiction that shows how material spaces rely upon imaginative conceptualization, and how the territory of the mind is informed by an interaction with external spaces and places.' (Thacker, 2003: 152). Similarly, in her discussion of spatiality and textuality in the writing of Dorothy Richardson, Elisabeth Bronfen draws attention to Richardson's desire to 'be in two places at once', with reference to the surface stylistics of *Pilgrimage* (1938/2002), and argues that one of her principal narrative strategies is the use of 'a spatial image to express simultaneity' (Bronfen, 1999: 2) The simultaneity that Bronfen registers in Richardson's prose is one of the key thematic and aesthetic aspects to the work of writers such as Rushdie and Sinha, who seek to narrate the epistemological simultaneity of the contemporary subject suspended between the organic and cybernetic worlds. The task facing writers of twenty-first-century fiction, who wish to examine an increasing social and cultural interaction with other virtual worlds, is to explore nuanced stylistic strategies that might effectively register this complex synthesis of biological corporeality and cybernetic subjectivity, as well as aestheticize the polarization of two spatial spheres.

The Cybergypsies

In *Reality is Broken* (2011), Jane McGonigal declares that

> gamers have had enough of reality. They are abandoning it in droves- a few hours here, an entire weekend there, sometimes every spare min-

ute of every day for stretches at a time- in favour of simulated environments and online games. (McGonigal, 2011: 2)

McGonigal's argument effectively sums up the plot of *The Cybergypsies*
(1999), Sinha's autobiographical novel, which narrates the increasing
immersion of its protagonist, Bear, a married advertising writer, in the
various cybernetic territories of the online gaming world. The subject
of McGonigal's research is the digital games industry, which at the
time of her writing (2011), was predicted to be worth in the region of
US$68 billion (McGonigal, 2011: 4). This figure marks a substantial
increase over the course of the first decade of the twenty-first century, when evaluated comparatively with its estimated global value of
US$20 billion in 1999 (http://www.fundinguniverse.com), the year
in which Sinha published *The Cybergypsies* (1999). Critics working in
the fields of economics and the gaming industry, such as McGonigal
and Castronova, have registered a boom in the value of the gaming
industry, which in turn has marked the emergence of an explosion in
new forms of online, digital culture: as Andrew Darley argues, 'video
games, digital films, simulation rides, these have become commonplace cultural experiences as we move into the twenty-first century'
(Darley, 2000: 1). Sinha's novel is therefore an important starting
point when undertaking a critical analysis of how the textual architecture of the twenty-first-century novel might be manipulated by
the writer in order to aestheticize the digital ontology of cybernetic
spatiality.

Bear's increasing addiction to, or what Leonard (2013: 37) has
described as a form of 'electronic enchantment' with, the digital ma-
trixes of the online world leads to a disturbance of his sense of organic
subjectivity, as well as a cognitive disorientation in terms of his spatial and temporal relationship towards the material world in which
he is corporeally rooted. While Bear maintains his job as an advertising writer in the material world, the textual aesthetics of the novel
are manipulated by Sinha to register a spatial expansion of Bear's consciousness into the digital trajectory of the cybernetic sphere. While
at work one day, Bear is immersed in an online conversation with one
of his cybernetic associates, Morgan, when he receives a telephone

call from Anita Roddick, a human rights campaigner and the founder of the retail establishment, The Body Shop:

> 'I said I wished she would just accept the money...' types the relentless Morgan. 'Not worry about taking it.
> 'I told Amnesty that I'm willing to swing every Body Shop in Europe behind them,' says the woman on the phone, 'For a month. Internationally.'
> '...but she is too honourable.'
> 'Morgan gives a gloomy laugh,' my screen informs me.
> '...And so I said I'd ring you,' says the woman on the phone, 'to ask whether you'd agree to work with my team.' (Sinha, 1999: 152)

The linguistic form employed by Sinha to narrate the temporal simultaneity of Bear's exchanges with both Roddick and Morgan effectively aestheticizes the bio-technical symbiosis of digital and organic subjectivity. Bear's sense of self is split between two polarized spatial realms, which are duly synthesized through a shared temporality that results in a sense of cognitive disorientation, or a 'detachment of cognition from the body' (Leonard, 2013: 37) in the protagonist as the narrative progresses. The textual aesthetics of the passage effectively mirror this disorientation. The quickly-paced linguistic utterances which arrive from opposing spatial spheres present a sense of confusion for the reader, and can be read discursively as the 'indefinite oscillation' and 'state of simultaneity' (Bronfen, 1999: 3) which Elisabeth Bronfen registers in the thematic and aesthetic dimensions to Richardson's *Pilgrimage* (2002), thus affirming a dialogue between the stylistic narration of cybernetic spatiality and modernist aesthetics.

A further link between modernist textuality and the narration of other virtual worlds emerges when examining passages of Sinha's prose that engage with the unbroken gush of words in a textual space that May Sinclair (1918) famously termed 'stream of consciousness' writing in her review of Dorothy Richardson's work. During a further online exchange between Bear and his friend Morgan, where they are discussing the relationship problems Morgan is experiencing with a fellow gamer, Calypso, Sinha draws our attention to the alienation of the organic subject, suspended in the digital world, from natural identification with familiar, human facial expressions and corporeal gestures, such as smiling or frowning:

> I can't see Morgan's face, can't read his expression. If – at the far end of the connection that runs from my modem through suspended and buried telephone wires, zips along miles of coiled metal cables, enters bundles of plastic spaghetti looped in sooty tunnels where trains roar in the darkness, traverses the fizzing electron exchanges of the city, threads its way to the heart of the massive computer in which the sprites of Shades perform their myriad tasks, receiving, sorting, stamping, swapping and posting packets of information, leaves by another set of tunnels and pipes, follows a different route out to the suburbs, is lifted into the air to race along miles of telegraph wire swooping in shining scallops from pole to pole tracking road and railway in frozen moonlight, until it comes at last to a connector on a wall of the house where Morgan lives, drilling through the brick, ingressing to a telephone jack, a wire, modem, screen close enough to be misted by his breath – there had been the briefest tremor of a smile, I have missed it. (Sinha, 1999: 87)

It is necessary to quote this lengthy extract in its entirety due to the manner in which the material trajectory of the electronic cables and technological devices required to facilitate Bear and Morgan's digital interactions in the cybernetic sphere, is framed, bookended, effectively, by the simple organic, facial gesture of a (missed) smile. The stream of consciousness style of the passage effectively aestheticizes the rhizomatic cartographies of electronic technology, which in turn enable the rhizomatic networks of interaction and connectivity between individuals in cyberspaces. The aesthetic and thematic juxtaposition of the materiality of the technology and the human emotion of the facial gesture that Bear misses, is also striking. McGonigal (2011: 3) argues that 'the real world just doesn't offer up as easily the carefully designed pleasures, the thrilling challenges, and the powerful social bonding afforded by virtual environments', yet the above passage paints a different picture, in drawing our attention to Bear's increasing alienation from the organic world as a result of his growing identification with his digital, online persona.

Indeed, this disorientating symbiosis of cyborg and human manifests in Bear's linguistic utterances, which in turn impacts upon the surface stylistics of the text: 'I had begun to think in game commands. Eve would say something and I'd reply, "Nod". She'd ask if I wanted a coffee and I'd say "Grin." I began referring to myself in the third person' (Sinha, 1999: 275). The disturbance which Bear experiences in terms of his sense of self can be read as the cognitive interaction of two polarized spatial realms, which become increasingly blurred in the space of Bear's mind as the narrative progresses. The juxtaposition of these two realms, and their moments of symbiosis, can be read as a further dialogue with the thematic and stylistic dimensions to Richardson's *Pilgrimage* (2002). In her discussion of the concept of 'world-making' in the text, Bronfen notes Miriam's 'construction of various opposing worlds which are either subsumed into a third world that contains both, or are simultaneously retained as different worlds.' (Bronfen, 1999: 114). We can therefore register a link between the manner in which *The Cybergypsies* (1999) and *Pilgrimage* (2002) seek to aestheticize the cognitive processes of Bear and Miriam through attention to the separating and melding of polarized spaces which takes place in their consciousness. *The Cybergypsies* (1999) is a complex textual arrangement of passages of computer code, digitized conversations containing coded prompts, as well as passages of poetry and more conventional prose narrative, mixed in with lists of computer viruses:

J-1361.ZIP	1216	09-12-93	jerusalem
modification 1361			
J-1605.ZIP	1338	09-12-93	jerusalem
modification 1605			
J-1735.ZIP	1478	09-12-93	jerusalem
modification 1735			
J-1813 ZIP	1346	09-12-93	jerusalem
modification 1813 (Sinha, 1999: 93)			

Passages such as the above, an abbreviated extract from a lengthier three-page section containing hundreds of mutant strains of a computer virus named 'jerusalem', result in a disorientating reader-experience that requires the navigation of often semantically alienating textual material. On an aesthetic level, the text seeks to register the fractured sense of subjectivity experienced by Bear through the juxtaposition of literary prose with computer code. Passages of computer coding, or transcripts of digital, online exchanges, bear relation to cybernetic systems that exist outside the textual framework of the novel, thus aestheticizing the complex spatiality of Bear's duality in terms of his identity.

When considering Bronfen's attention to 'world-making' in *Pilgrimage* (2002), we can identify a clear dialogue between the representation of the spatial geographies of the digital world, and the aesthetic approach to exploring consciousness taken by modernist writers such as Richardson. In *Narrative as Virtual Reality* (2001), Marie-Laure Ryan argues that 'for immersion to take place, the text must offer an expanse to be immersed within, and this expanse, in a blatantly mixed metaphor, is not an ocean but a textual world' (Ryan, 2001: 90). Reading *The Cybergypsies* (1999) involves immersion in the disorientating and fractured spatiality of Bear's consciousness: in a sense, the novel becomes a space where the symbiosis of the seemingly polarized realms of the digital and the organic world may be explored through the aesthetics of narrative. We might posit the theory that cyberspace is primarily about computers. However, the counter-argument to this claim is that it exists merely in the imagination. The latter can be read as problematic, considering that there is a clear symbiosis between the spatiality of the digital world and that of the material. However, it nevertheless has significance when considering the stylistic properties of *The Cybergypsies* (1999). Through a close critical analysis, we can see that the novel maintains a clear dialogue with literary modernism through its aesthetic registration of the complex interplay between organic spatiality and digital spatiality which takes place in Bear's conscious realm, or imagination: the result being a textual symbiosis of the states of organic and cybernetic subjectivity which have increasingly come to characterize culture in the twenty-first century.

Luka and The Fire of Life

When discussing dialogues between the work of twenty-first-century writers and literary modernism, Rushdie's name is possibly not the first that springs to mind, given the tendency for critics to evaluate his fiction within the discursive framework of postmodernism. Indeed, Christoph Reinfandt has described Rushdie as 'one of the cosmopolitan champions of Western postmodernism' (Reinfandt, 1998: 76), whereas Ian Almond discusses the 'near-synonymy of Rushdie's work with the term "postmodern fiction"' (Almond, 2007: 97). However, Stephen Morten warns that 'to read Rushdie as an avatar of postmodernism is to ignore the ways in which Rushdie's literary style is precisely a response to the historical condition of South Asia's postcolonial modernity' (Morton, 2008: 13). Moreover, as David James notes, there has been a 're-engagement with modernist perceptions in recent years' (James, 2012: 11) for many of Rushdie's contemporaries (James cites the work of Ian McEwan), and critics have consistently registered aspects of the modernist tradition in Rushdie's fiction. Neil Ten Kortenaar (2004: 229) argues that *Midnight's Children* (1981) retains 'strong elements of modernism: it questions ontology and epistemology both'. Kortenaar goes on to cite Kumkum Sangari, who argues that the novel's narrative 'finds its dynamic in the modernist challenge to premodern forms' (Sangari, 1987: 178). Priya Joshi notes that Rushdie is 'a novelist writing very much in sympathy with modernism's aesthetic and political tendencies' (Joshi, 2002: 232), and Laura Marcus posits that the opening of *The Satanic Verses* (1988) represents 'a direct link to Joyce's *A Portrait of the Artist as a Young Man* (1916), and to the imbrications of language, nation and colonial relations in Joyce's work' (Marcus 2007: 90).

To what extent, then, might we read modernism's legacy as impacting upon Rushdie's textual exploration of the online gaming world in his twenty-first-century novel *Luka and The Fire of Life* (2010)? Published eleven years after Sinha's *The Cybergypsies* (1999), Rushdie's novel maintains significant intertextual links with *Haroun and the Sea of Stories* (1990). Luka, the protagonist, is Haroun's younger brother, and whereas both texts explore the journeys of their respective child protagonists into other realms of consciousness, in order to restore their father's lost talent for storytelling, the principal difference between the two is *Luka and The Fire of Life*'s (2010) attention to the digital geography of the computer game. At the beginning of the novel, Luka is advised by his elder sibling 'I knew it would happen soon [...] you've reached the age at which people in this family cross the border into the magical world' (Rushdie, 2010: 6); thus commences Luka's gradual immersion in the digital trajectory of the computer game. The novel engages with twenty-first-century cybernetic subjectivity both thematically and in terms of form, yet differs from *The Cybergypsies* (1999) in that it is less explicit in its aestheticizing of the embedded digital coding, which enables Bear's online interactions. Instead, the narrative takes a more linear form, yet is aesthetically structured to mirror Luka's progression through multiple digital levels of the game, collecting 'lives' in order to survive as he advances along the cyber trajectory. In her research into story-rich gaming formats, Janet Murray argues that 'gaming and storytelling have always overlapped' (Murray, 2004: 9), whereas Andrew Teverson argues that, in Rushdie's writing

> the techniques of film and photography [...] combine with the structurally comparable techniques of oral narrative to assist Rushdie in his continuation of the modernist project of making the novel 'new' – of trying to extend what the novel is capable of doing, and therefore, what it is capable of saying. (Teverson, 2007: 54)

Teverson's assertions register a dimension to the aesthetic and structural properties of Rushdie's fiction which is particularly significant to a critical reading of *Luka and The Fire of Life* (2010): that of the intersection between digital media and the more traditional modes of oral narrative, or storytelling. The architecture of Rushdie's gaming-themed narrative relies upon the fictional form of the computer game as a means of examining the ways in which digital technologies of the twenty-first century, such as online gaming, have enabled greater transnational cultural connectivity across postcolonial nation states. In *Transnational Connections* (1996), Ulf Hannerz registers a cultural and anthropological desire 'to cultivate new understandings of how the world hangs together, of transnational connections, in the organization of meanings and actions – and move beyond mere astonishment over new mixtures and combinations' (Hannerz, 1996: 4). Hannerz's description of 'new mixtures and combinations' within the context of transnational cultural connections is an effective way of approaching a critical analysis of Rushdie's broader fictional aims. For Rushdie, contemporary culture is constituted through a process of forming new networks, connections and meanings via the re-structuring of existing textual material, linguistic systems, and cultural frameworks. The complex intertextuality of his novels arises from the re-configuration of cultural, political and religious discourse into new narrative frameworks. In the case of *Luka and The Fire of Life* (2010), we can read Rushdie in dialogue with the modernist impulse of 'making the novel new' and examining 'what the novel is capable of doing, and therefore, what it is capable of saying', as Teverson has argued, through a narrative which aesthetically and thematically resembles the intersection of the novel and the computer game.

Like Bear in *The Cybergypsies* (1999), Luka spends a substantial amount of his time immersed in the digital landscape:

> Like everyone he knew, he had joined imaginary communities in cyberspace, electro-clubs in which he adopted the identity of, for example, an Intergalactic Penguin named after a member of the Beatles, or, later, a completely invented flying being whose height, hair colour and even sex were his to choose and alter as he pleased. (Rushdie, 2010: 12)

Through his corporeal re-staging in the digital spatiality of the computer game, Luka enacts the dualism of posthuman subjectivity. His organic human self and its cybernetic other concurrently exist in the two opposing spatial geographies of the real and the digital. We can draw dialogues between Luka's subjectivity and that of Miriam in *Pilgrimage* (2002), as Bronfen argues, Miriam is 'at times situated between worlds, at other times belonging to one world or another' (Bronfen, 1999: 151). Through a narrative which follows Luka through the digital trajectory of the online quest to save his father, the novel dramatizes one of the dominant cultural discourses of the twenty first century: that of the complex symbiosis, and at times dichotomy, between an idealized on-screen avatar or persona, and the cultural, racial or gender-based frameworks which give form to identity in the material world. As Danet and Herring argue in *The Multilingual Internet: Language, Culture, and Communication Online* (2007), despite the ability of their online avatars or gaming persona to transcend geographical frontiers, 'online interlocutors live in the physical world and are grounded in offline cultures, defined by national, ethnic, religious and other boundaries' (Danet and Herring, 2007: 7). How then, are postcolonial concepts of self and identity examined in *Luka and The Fire of Life* (2010), given that the novel is set in cybernetic territories that seemingly transcend the political borders of the material world?

While the novel clearly thematizes gaming and cybernetic culture, it also explores many of the socio-political concerns of Rushdie's other fictional writings, particularly his interest in examining the effects of violent social and political hegemonic structures which promote singular models of national identity. Morton argues that

> it is crucial to read Rushdie's writing in relation to both critical and popular understandings of nationalism, secularism and political violence in postcolonial South Asia, as well as the historical experience of South Asian migrants to Britain in order to understand the complex and multiple socio-political worlds that Salman Rushdie's fiction represents. (Morton, 2008: 12)

Morton's argument that Rushdie's fiction can be read as representative of multiple socio-political worlds is particularly relevant when evaluating *Luka and The Fire of Life*'s (2010) examination of virtual spaces, and the various hierarchies, concepts of identity and political codes that might characterize such complex territories. During Luka's journey through cyberspace, he travels to a place called The Respectorate of I, which has become overrun by rats who are fanatical about controlling the borders of their territory and become agitated when Luka is unable to present any papers. Luka notes that the rats are all grey in colour, and that the people who inhabit the same space share the same greyish tinge to their skin. Nobodaddy, a cybernetic simulacra of Luka's father, explains to Luka the reason for this neutralizing of the colour pallet:

> 'They developed a Colour Problem here a little while ago,' Nobodaddy said. 'The Rats who hated the colour yellow because of its, well, cheesiness were confronted by the Rats who disliked the colour red because of its similarity to blood. In the end all colours, being offensive to someone or other, were banned by the Rathouse—that's the parliament, by the way, although nobody votes for it, it votes for itself, and it basically does what the Over-Rat says.'
>
> 'And who chooses the Over-Rat?' Luka asked. 'He chooses himself,' said Nobodaddy. 'Actually he chooses himself over and over again, he does it more or less every day, because he likes doing it so much. It's known as being Over-Rat-ed.' (Rushdie, 2010: 72)

The Colour Problem experienced by the rats is clearly a metaphor for state monopoly and racial violence. Nobodaddy's description of the Rat's parliament, which votes for itself, and which is controlled by the Over-Rat who remains in power not through a democratic process of election, but by repeatedly 'choosing himself' represents a system of dictatorship over the proletariat of Rats. Whilst there is a parliament within the regime, 'the Rathouse', nobody votes for this either; like the Over-Rat, it votes for itself, and exists merely as a layer of government which aids the Over-Rat in imposing his ideologies over the populace through state control. In effect, the Over-Rat is the sovereign, and as Michael Hardt and Antonio Negri argue, 'modern sovereignty operates [...] through the creation and maintenance of fixed boundaries among territories, populations, social functions, and so forth' (Hardt and Negri, 2001: 325). These fixed boundaries to which Hardt and Negri refer are reflected not simply in the tight system of border control operated by the Rats, but also in the racial ideologies which have been imposed through the Over-Rat's system of dictatorship. Unable to overcome the 'Colour Problem', the Over-Rat has imposed a rigid and systemic model of national identity to which all the rats must conform. All colours have been banned and all Rats must remain grey in tone.

The passage exemplifies the secular ideologies explored across Rushdie's previous fictional writing, that, in order to exist as multicultural nations within a global framework, it is impossible to conform to closed, prescriptive ideals of self which dictate that all members must resemble a homogenized ideal. In doing so, the thematic concerns of the novel also problematize some of the utopian ideas expressed by critics such as Hables Gray and Leonard (cited in the first half of this essay), regarding possible affiliations between geographic regions and a sense of collective unity which transcends both national frontiers and racial, class and gender-based prejudices. Hannerz observes, 'local and national frameworks for thinking about the social organization of meanings and meaningful forms have been strongly entrenched both in the anthropological tradition and elsewhere in social and cultural thought' (Hannerz, 1996: 9). Hannerz argument draws our attention to the ways in which culturally received notions of self and identity in the material world are not necessarily eradicated when new spatial territories, such as digital spheres, emerge. In this sense, *Luka and The Fire of Life* (2010) politicizes the digital spaces of the cybernetic sphere through its interrogation of concepts of national identity and citizenship for the posthuman subject in the twenty-first century.

Conclusions

A comparative approach to the critical evaluation of *The Cybergypsies* (1999) and *Luka and The Fire of Life* (2010) reveals a commonality in terms of a creative desire to register the cybernetic culture of gaming and online interactivity that constitutes an increasing aspect to culture in the twenty-first century. It is clear from an analysis of the two texts that there are nuanced differences in the ways in which Rushdie and Sinha manipulate novelistic form in order to find effective ways of exploring the oscillation of the subject between the digital landscape and the materiality of the organic world. However, it is nevertheless apparent that each text maintains a clear dialogue with literary modernism, in terms of its aesthetic and stylistic approaches, and creative concern with the registering of new realms of consciousness. The employment of an interdisciplinary approach to critically evaluating each text, namely by drawing on discourse from literary modernism, economics, gaming theory and anthropology, makes for a fruitful and nuanced reading of the ways in which late twentieth and early twenty-first-century fiction seeks to register the increasingly blurred connection between the organic human subject and the cybernetic simulacra. It is also interesting to note the dialogue that emerges between writers such as Woolf and Richardson, and Rushdie and Sinha in terms of each writer's attention to the aestheticizing of spatiality and temporality, with specific attention to other worlds and other realms of consciousness. The simultaneity that Bronfen locates in Richardson's writing emerges as a central aesthetic and thematic aspect to the state of hybrid subjectivity experienced by the contemporary subject suspended between the digital and 'real' worlds. Clearly, the materiality of the novel and the spatial geographies of cybernetic world differ in many ways, but this essay has sought to demonstrate how the nuanced intersection of the two discourses represents an exciting trajectory for fiction of the twenty-first century.

Works Cited

Almond, Ian (2007) *The New Orientalists: Postmodern Representations of Islam from Foucault to Baudrillard*. London: I.B. Tauris & Co. Ltd.

Atkins, Barry (2003) *More than a Game*. Manchester: Manchester University Press.

Bronfen, Elisabeth (1999) *Dorothy Richardson's Art of Memory: Space, Identity, Text*. Manchester: Manchester University Press.

Castronova, Edward (2007) *Exodus to the Virtual World*. Basingstoke: Palgrave Macmillan.

Danet, Brenda and Susan C. Herring (2007) 'Introduction: Welcome to the Multilingual Internet', in Brenda Danet and Susan C. Herring (eds) *The Multilingual Internet: Language, Culture, and Communication Online*, pp. 3-40. Oxford: Oxford University Press.

Darley, Andrew (2000) *Visual Digital Culture: Surface Play and Spectacle in New Media Genres*. London: Routledge

Hables Gray, Chris (2001) *Cyborg Citizen*. London: Routledge.

Hall, Stuart (1992) 'Extract from "The Question of Cultural Identity"', in S. Hall, D. Heid and McGrew (eds) *Modernity and its Futures*, pp. 274-91. Cambridge: Polity Press.

Hannerz, Ulf (1996) *Transnational Connections*. London: Routledge.

Hardt, Michael and Antonio Negri (2001) *Empire*. Cambridge, MA: Harvard University Press.

Hopper, Paul (2007) *Understanding Cultural Globalization*. Cambridge: Polity Press.

James, David (2012) 'Mapping Modernist Continuities', in David James, *The Legacies of Modernism: Historicising Postwar and Contemporary Fiction*, pp. 1-19. Cambridge: Cambridge University Press.

Joshi, Priya (2002) *In Another Country: Colonialism, Culture and the English Novel in India*. Chichester: Columbia University Press.

Kortenaar, Neil Ten (2005) Self, Nation, Text in Salman Rushdie's Midnight's Children. Quebec: McGill-Queen's University Press.

Lefebvre, Henri (1976) *Reflections on the politics of space. Antipode* 8(2).

Leonard, Philip (2013) *Literature After Globalization: Textuality, Technology and the Nation State*. London: Bloomsbury.

McGonigal, Jane (2011) *Reality is Broken*. London: Jonathan Cape.

Marcus, Laura (2007) 'The Legacies of Modernism', in The Cambridge Companion to The Modernist Novel, pp. 82-98. Cambridge: Cambridge University Press.

Morton, Stephen (2008) *Salman Rushdie*. Basingstoke: Palgrave Macmillan.

Murray, Janet (2004) 'From Game-Story to Cyberdrama', in Noah Wardrip-Fruin and Pat Harrigan (eds) *First Person: New Media as Story, Performance and Game*, pp. 2-11. London: The Massachusetts Institute of Technology Press.

Perlin, Ken (2004) 'Can There Be a Form between a Game and a Story?', in Noah Wardrip-Fruin and Pat Harrigan (eds) *First Person: New Media as Story, Performance and Game*, pp. 12-18. London: The Massachusetts Institute of Technology Press.

Pykett, Lynn (1995) *Engendering Fictions: The English Novel In The Early Twentieth Century*. London: Arnold.

Reinfandt, Christoph (1998) 'What's the Use of Stories that Aren't Even True: Salman Rushdie as a Test Case for Literature and Literary Studies Today', *Literatur in Wissenschaft und Unterricht* 31(1).

Richardson, Dorothy (2002) *Pilgrimage*. London: Virago.

Rushdie, Salman (1981) *Midnight's Children*. London: Knopf.

Rushdie, Salman (1988) *The Satanic Verses*. London: Vintage.

Rushdie, Salman (1990) *Haroun and the Sea of Stories*. London: Granta.

Rushdie, Salman (2010) *Luka and The Fire of Life*. London: Jonathan Cape

Ryan, Marie-Laure (2001) Narrative as Virtual Reality. Maryland: The John Hopkins University Press.

Sangari, Kumkum (1987) The Politics of the Possible. Cultural Critique 7: 157-86.

Sinclair, May (1918) 'The Novels of Dorothy Richardson', Little Review 4.

Sinha, Indra (1999) *The Cybergypsies*. London: Schribner.

Thacker, Andrew (2003) *Moving through Modernity*. Manchester: Manchester University Press.

Jeff Noon and the Contemporary Aesthetics of Uncreativity

Kaja Marczewska

In his Avant-Pop Manifesto (1993), Mark Amerika declared the birth of the artist as a parasite, sampling from everything and bringing in the future of fiction in a realm where 'creating a work of art will depend more and more on the ability of the artist to select, organise, and present the bits of raw data' (Amerika, 1993/2007: 293). Composing his manifesto on *How to Make a Modern Novel* in 2001, Jeff Noon proclaimed that the future has arrived, that 'we are now living in the future' (Noon, 2001a), a disappointing period, according to Noon, when compared with the world we promised ourselves, 'not a time for great art' (Noon, 2001a). In line with Amerika's statement, this is a literary future of uncreative production, unoriginal writing, a future of recycling, remixing, reshuffling, or at least, as this paper will argue, the American literary future might be described as such. Today, the aesthetics of Surf-Sample-Manipulate, as Mark America describes the current creative condition, seems to have gained momentum on the American critical and creative scene. The year 2010 alone saw publications of Kenneth Goldsmith's *Uncreative Writing*, Marjorie Perloff's *Unoriginal Genius*, Kembrew McLeod's *Cutting Across Media*, to name just a few, all focusing on the proliferation of writing that foregrounds the limits (or lack of thereof) of contemporary (re)production: experimenting with strategies of copying, often radical appropriation;

exploring challenges as well as the potential offered by this new condition of writing for the late age of print and the all-encompassing dominance of information technologies. Framed by the notion of currently evolving conceptualism in literature – as recently put forward by Craig Dworkin, Kenneth Goldsmith, Rob Fitterman and Vanessa Place – uncreativity seems to be the stuff that literary conversations are now made of on the American literary scene, a literary mode eliciting widespread critical interest, a point of contention and, at times, minor disdain as well.

Literary works exemplifying the contemporary 'copy-paste' tendencies include Flarf poetry, radical appropriations by Kenneth Goldmsith in his trilogy of word-for-word transcriptions: *Weather* (2005), re-typing a year's worth of weather reports from the New York radio station WINS, *Traffic* (2007), recording a 24-hour WINS traffic reports at 10-minute intervals on a first day of a holiday weekend, and *Sports* (2008) containing a transcription of a broadcast of an entire five-hour baseball game between New York Yankees and Boston Red Sox; other examples include Vanessa Place's *Statement of Facts* (2011), repurposing legal prosecution and defence documents of violent sexual criminal cases verbatim; David Shields's *Reality Hunger* (2010), a manifesto collated out of a selection of excerpts, over 600 of which are quotations, some acknowledged; Austin Kleon's, *Newspaper Blackout* (2010), a collection of poems composed by erasing text from newspapers; or Joanthan Safran Foer's *Tree of Codes* (2010), a book composed of holes, cut out from a different book, Bruno Schultz's *Street of Crocodiles*. And the list could continue.

According to Goldsmith (2011), the abundance of language and writing as well as the ease of accessing and processing information today encourages such 're-gestures', the promiscuity of writing, of text grubbed, cut, pasted, processed, rewritten, reblogged, retweeted. In a culture dominated by the textuality of 'ctrl+C', 'ctrl+V', 'Fwd', the everyday practices now inherently embedded in the dynamics of textual production seem to translate into the tendencies governing contemporary creativity with writing, as Goldsmith argues, mimicking the workings of a computer: its cut-and-paste aesthetics within the constant flow of discourse, where everything is up for grabs, also translating into the dynamics of creative writing beyond the immediate confines of the World Wide Web. Contemporary anti-writers, as Stuart Home (2013: 78) describes artists engaging with uncreative aesthetics, might have no interest in the ideology of realism, but, importantly, 'the fragmented style they use is in fact closer to what we experience in daily life than the tediously even tone of conventional literature'. As such, the appropriated, remixed, mashed up writing turns into a creative writing method for today; a method which presupposes a treatment of language as material to be processed and edited, drawing from the conceptual foundations of the current cultural moment of liquid modernity, to borrow Zygmut Bauman's term. The notion, as defined by Bauman, represents a swiftly changing order in a state of constant flux, an amorphous reality of melting powers and structures that undermines all notions of stability, fixity and durability. As Bauman (2006: 2) asserts, 'there are reasons to consider "fluidity" or "liquidity" as fitting metaphors when we wish to grasp the nature of the present, in many ways *novel* phase in the history of humanity'. The current condition seems defined by fragmentation, short-term pursuits, accelerated processes of change, all dictated by a state of constant mutability and unrest that govern the liquid times of uncertainty. This twenty-first-century fluid modernity differs from the solid modernity that preceded it; the current cultural moment is defined by a shift from solidity to liquidity, from heavy to light modernity. Read in the context, the state of contemporary textual culture can be interpreted, by analogy, as residing in a transition of discursive practices from the printing press to hypertextuality and disembodied textual production of the software era, which results in opening up avenues for turning uncreativity into a creative practice. 'Citationality', Perloff (2010: 17) argues, 'with its dialectics of removal and graft, disjunction and conjunction, its interpretation of origin and destruction, is central to twenty-first century poetics. [...] récriture [rather than écriture] [...] is the logical form of "writing" in an age of literary mobile or transferable text'.

Critical statements on conceptualism, uncreativity, unoriginality, recriture, citationality and radical appropriation reverberate with all-encompassing, overarching declarations on the universal condition of writing today. In her speech at the &Now 2012 festival in Paris, Vanessa Place (2012) declared the global nature and reach of conceptual poetics. However, the scope and the proliferation of the conceptual practice are both far more limited than critics such as Dworkin, Place, Fitterman or Goldsmith all seem to imply. Uncreative aesthetics does find its manifestations in countries as far ranging as Norway and Chile but these developments represent exceptions rather than the rule; uncreativity seems to remain, at present, a primarily North American literary phenomenon and the developments do not seem to find equally fertile ground on the international literary scene. The same can be said about Great Britain where contemporary literature is dominated by a proliferation of what could be described as re-appropriated grand narratives for the globalized, information age, with a prominent presence of The New Historical Novel, genre fiction, and multiple facets of realism, exhibiting a rediscovered propensity for and a fixation with linearity. The themes range from questions of multiculturalism, identity, diasporic culture in transition, late-capitalist urbanism, post 9/11 trauma and uncertainty, as the look at *Granta* 119 issue, entitled *Britain* or the contents of this collection itself both prove. Where questions of authorship, originality, creativity in and for the contemporary information society or the issues of new media and digitalization themselves do feature (and Winterson's *Power Book* or Will Self's *Dorian: An Imitation* could be quoted as examples) they are approached as literary subjects rather than textual objects, and their treatment remains restricted to the narrative level, engaged with as ideas to be spoken about, discussed and presented in a linear, traditional analog-print media fashion. In contrast, and as my brief overview attempted to prove, the American uncreative writers explore the collective range of questions through formal experiment with modes of textuality. The difference could be described as that between telling and showing, or to adopt Kenneth Goldsmith's (2011: 100) taxonomy, between readership and thinkership. As such, the broadly conceived British twenty-first-century literature could be regarded as narrative dominated, a literature interested in telling, among others, the stories of new media and favouring the dynamics of readership, in contrast to the work of American writers such as Goldsmith or Kleon with their propensity for formalism and experiment, focusing on showing the results of the interplay of text and digital context and advocating literature that is, in Kenneth Goldsmith's (2011: 100) words, created not so much to be read as to be thought about. This is of course not to say that all American literature now is uncreative. Examples of what has been so far described as the inherently British take on literary expression now proliferate on the American literary scene as well and Jonathan Franzen could be referred to as a prime example of an American writer with a penchant for traditional forms of narrativity. However, the same parallel could not be drawn between the increased prominence of conceptual uncreativity in the US and the UK.

On the contemporary American literary scene, the practice has been consistently attracting the interest and attention of academic scholars, established literary avenues, including *Poetry* magazine and, increasingly so, of prestigious university presses, with Goldsmith's most recent books published by Columbia and Northwestern. This shift is particularly significant as previously uncreative writing was essentially associated with small independent presses, upholding its status of marginalized avant-garde. This shift from the marginalized to mainstream is apparent, especially when considered in the light of other, recent developments in the uncreative literary circles: contemporary conceptual literature in America recently saw a publication of two anthologies: *Against Expression* (2011), edited by Kenneth Goldsmith and Craig Dworkin and *I'll Drown My Book* (2012), edited by Caroline Bergvall, Laynie Browne, Teresa Carmody and Vanessa Place; in what could be described as an ultimate act of canonization of uncreative writing, Goldsmith performed at the White House during An Evening of Poetry hosted by President Barak Obama in May 2011 and in winter/spring season held a residency at MOMA as a part of Artist Experiment series. Despite this state of increased institutionalized affirmation, commodification, and recognition that uncreative writing as a practice seems to be currently attracting in the USA, it has also been the source of heated debate and criticism. The effect of these developments has been to put into question, again, the nature of avant-gardism that conceptualism in contemporary writing eagerly foregrounds. At the same time, however, the status uncreative writing enjoys in USA highlights the particular condition of American writing now. Whether this loss of status of marginalized literary experiment is a positive or a negative development and whether it is one that will have permanent effects on the literary scene at large remains to be seen. What is clear at the moment is that the 'success' remains primarily an American affair and a parallel development is not taking place in the UK, although there are, of course, exceptions. Echoes of uncreative writing as a recognized practice are starting to reverberate on the British literary scene as well, with Information as material (Iam) most significantly contributing to the dissemination of the practice in Britain. Set up by a British artist, Simon Morris and based in York, UK, Iam is an independent imprint whose output includes works by a few British authors as well as some international but UK-based writers alongside publications of established conceptualists such as Goldsmith (USA) and Derek Baulieu (Canada). Craig Dworkin, who, alongside Goldsmith, Fitterman and Place remains at the forefront of American conceptual poetics, acts as a member of Iam's editorial board. As such, the work that Information as Material is presently committed to, remains firmly rooted in and driven forward by the contemporary American aesthetics of uncreative literary production and by the influence of artists associated with its development. Apart from Iam, Nick e-Melville, Caroline Bergvall and Peter Manson should all be mentioned in this context. However, the work of all the writers referred to above remains marginalized in the UK, so far generating a limited level of interest, in stark contrast to the increased recognition of uncreative writing in the USA.

When discussing the US–UK creative dichotomy, it is worth turning to the work of Britain's own Jeff Noon, and his *Cobralingus*, published in 2001. Although not immediately associated with the developments described earlier, the textual experiments Noon engages in *Cobralingus* lend themselves to a particularly interesting reading in the context. As Noon describes it, *Cobralingus* is an example of dub fiction, a genre that takes the idea of remix fiction to a whole new level, pushing it toward an experimental extreme. The label derives from the verb 'to dub', i.e. to make a copy of one recording to another and the concept is based on both dub and electronic glitch music, a consistent influence of Noon's. What makes dub music of particular importance to Noon's creative practice is the nature and approach to the act of creative production that characterizes the genre. As Noon describes it:

> I was used to the idea of music being built up, track by track, piece by piece, until the final mix was reached. Jamaican dub producers such as Lee Perry and King Tubby reversed this process. The final mix of a song became the starting point for experimentation. Composing at the mixing desk, they punched holes in the sound; they let instruments drop away, only to return at some later moment; they added sound affects to the mix. Very often the track revealed its skeleton, the bass and drums; at other times a ghost seemed to be haunting the mix. Music had become a liquid experience. (Noon, n.d.)

As such, dub becomes a genre that, as Noon observes, 'no longer has a final outcome [...] exists in a constant state of flux' and as a result serves as an adequate reflection on contemporary subjectivity, defining an appropriate genre for the age of liquid modernity, 'totally in tune with the contemporary mind' (Noon, 2012). Growing out of 1960s developments in reggae music, dub's modes of remixing are deeply rooted in analog technology. Producers such as Lee Perry and King Tubby – whose work Noon frequently refers to as a source of inspiration – would have traditionally used B-sides and 45 RPM records to manipulate and reshape the recordings, the process that frequently involved stripping down the original tracks of vocals to emphasize the drum and base and subsequently adding extensive echoes, panoramic delays and dubbing, among other techniques. At the same time, a computer and digital technology as a musical creative tool remains a source of formative inspiration of Noon's and grows out of his interest in experimental electronic music where digital technology acts as an essential element of the dynamics governing the creative process. To quote Noon again, commenting on the source of his influence:

> Over the last few years, I've been listening to a lot of experimental electronic music. Some of this is allied to the outer fringes of Techno Culture; music by Pole, Autechre, Oval, and so on. Other musicians place their music in a more avant-garde setting. But what all these mu-

sicians share is an interest in computers as a creative tool. Reading interviews with musicians, I started to learn a little about the machinery used, and the techniques involved. A musical signal is sent along a pathway. This signal passes through various software gates or filters, each of which has a different effect on the music. These gates are called things like 'Decay', 'Reverb' and 'Echo'. Sometimes, diagrams of the signal pathway were included in the design of the record sleeve. I might well have been studying one of these diagrams when the initial idea for *Cobralingus* came to me: could a piece of text be pushed along a similar pathway? (Noon, n.d.)

Combining the influence of the two in a juxtaposition of the analog and the digital, Noon engages in literary attempts at telling stories in a mode akin to that characterizing musical remix culture and in a manner aimed at opening up avenues for narrative to partake in the cultural liquid experience.

Cobralingus is not the author's first attempt at incorporating musical influences in his writing; *Nymphomation* (1997) includes what Noon described as a 'reverse dub' of Lewis Carroll's *Jabberwocky*, some of the stories in *Pixel Juice* (1998) also engage with the technique, while *Needle in the Groove* (2000) includes and is influenced by its own remix. *Cobralingus*, however, remains the most explicit example of this mode of textual experimentation and employs what the author describes as a Cobralingus Engine, a machine built out of a series of gates used to manipulate text into new material forms and new meanings. There are 21 gates in total, 17 of which exhibit the capacity to alter the text and each has a different effect on the text processed, from decaying text, enhancing text, drugging text through to ghost editing, mixing, sampling, overloading and release virus, the last one only 'recommended to advanced users' (Noon, 2001b: 15). Some of the gates derive directly from the terminology describing modes of remixing applied in music, while others are Noon's own creations. Noon (2001b: 13) calls the mode of compositional practice governing *Cobralingus* aesthetics a 'metamorphiction process' and stresses its reliance on the treatment of text as signal. *Cobralingus*, the book, is a collection of texts that have been subject to the process, pushed through the Engine and as a result transformed in a course of an almost Kafkaesque metamorphosis. The selection of source texts, or inlet texts as Noon describes them, includes classics such as Shakespeare, Mary Shelley's *Frankenstein* and Emily Dickinson as well as Noon's contemporaries and Noon's work itself.

Rosalynde's Madrigal

Plucke the fruite and tast the pleasure

    Youthful Lordings of delight,

Whil'st occasion giues you seasure,

    Feede your fancies and your sight:

        After death when you are gone,

        Joy and pleasure is there none.

Thomas Lodge, 1591

21

Figure 1. Rosalynde's Madrigal inlet text.

The process of textual production, *Cobralingus* style, always begins with an activation of the Cobralingus Engine, denoted with 'Start' filter gate directly followed by the 'inlet' filter gate, introducing the source text that is to be transformed in the process. On a page, each stage of the transformation includes the text itself and an indication of the filter gate applied. In the case of the first metamorphed text in the collection, the inlet text used is 1591 *Rosalynde's Madrigal* by Thomas Lodge (Figure 1).

The text initially goes through the 'overload' filter gate ('Drastically increases the image density of the text. To be used with caution' [Noon, 2001b: 15]), followed by 'control' gate ('Brings the text down to earth. Forces language to behave itself' [Noon, 2001b: 14]) and 'sample' gates ('Introduces new element to signal. Source of sample to be specified' [Noon, 2001b: 15]). The interim text is subsequently pushed through 'purify' ('Loses deadwood. Selects images or images from the text' [Noon, 2001b: 15]) and 'mix' gates ('Combines all elements into a single entity' [Noon, 2001b: 15]) to produce an outlet text which is a conceptual rendering of the inlet text, both on the textual and formal and visual levels with focus placed on the interplay of word and image, foregrounding experimentation in typography and reverberating clearly with echoes of experiments characteristic for concrete poetry (Figure 2).

The textual transformation that Lodge's madrigal undergoes in the process centres around an engagement with culturally familiar notions, where 'the fruite' is immediately interpreted as an apple, an object of biblical temptation, a forbidden fruit and a source of pleasure. The word 'apple' itself, although not mentioned in the inlet text, materializes in the process of metamorphiction, both in the text and on a page. As such, the process of transition, from Lodge's original to Noon's transformation, turns into an exercise in reading and interpretation; the metamorphiction process influences and alters the original text. At the same time, however, the altered, metamorphosed outlet text, influences the reading of the original inlet text, imposes a culturally charged interpretation that focuses on the central concept of an apple as a source of pleasure, as foregrounded by the outlet text. The sixteenth-century Madrigal, remixed in the process of sampling

```
                              wak
                               e:
                              jul
           ie;bed;cat;ra di o;cat;fo
          od;drink;tastethepleasure;new
         s;football;tennis;manchester;revie
        ws;arts;shakespeare;invention;huma
        n;thelookingglass;tastethepleasure;
      work;cobralingus;tony;talk;food;dri               p
      nk;chocolate;tastethepleasure;p                        l
      hotographs;venice;work;cobrali    e       a
      ngus;ideas;everythingidotoday;                       s
       music;biokinetics;tastethepleas        u             r
      ure;tv;archaeology;radio;topten;              e
        tenderisthenight;blur;car;thesmiths;
        chinesefood fruit tastethepleasure;ho
        me;countryandwesternsongs;talk;ch
         eckingformessages;bed;warmth;r
          eading;novels;kiss;love;jnoon
              ;sunday;28/02/99;
                  sleep
```

SAVE

24

Figure 2. Rosalynde's Madrigal outlet text.

```
CONTROL
   |
SAMPLE — Sunday 28 Feb, 1999
```

wake up; Julie; bed; Badger Cat; Radio One; Kevin Greening Show; Spice Cat; feed cats; breakfast; fruit and fibre cereal; milk; tea; coffee; cats out; read newspaper; The Observer: news sections; aftermath of report into the Stephen Lawrence case; sports section; Henman and Rusedski win Guardian Direct doubles final; Manchester United 2 Southampton 1; Chesterfield 1 Manchester City 1; review section; Gilbert and George article; Sarah Kane suicide; new Underworld CD; book reviews; Shakespeare: the Invention of the Human, Harold Bloom; Into the Looking Glass Wood,

```
                                e as
                      h
                  e   at
              ehfruite  ue ea a nha
           uckeethhefruutean antathleas u
         I luckeethhefruitteantaastthpleeasu e
        p lpluckeetheffruiteandttasthepleasurere r
        ppyyyouthhulloorddigsofdelighhtuutreer
      y   yyouthfulllorrdingsoffdeliighttghtthtu u
       w w yhilstococassigiuesyoseeuuree e              r
        w hilstooccasiogiuesyouseasuree    p       e        u
     h  hffeedeeyoufanciiesndyurrsigh hte        l   s        e
        f eedeyyourrfanciesaandyyoursightt                a
      e  eeaafteerdeeathhwhennuaaregonee
         afterddeathhwwhennyouaaegone
      a  ajjoy apple easuristhernoon n
      o  oyadpleasureisthereejno on
      o  aand leea sl sthero
```

Alberto Manguel; work; Cobralingus; Tony arrives, lunch; ham sandwiches; chocolate biscuits; photographs of Venice; work; Cobralingus; idea of including everything I do today; listen to records; Pole, CD1; Porter Ricks, Biokinetics; Time Team, Channel 4; Radio One Chart Countdown; 10 Written in the Stars; 9 Lullaby; 8 Fly Away; 7 Erase/Rewind; 6 Runaway; 5 Strong Enough; 4 Just Looking; 3 It's Not Right but It's Okay; 2 Tender; 1 Baby One More Time; out; car stereo; The Smiths, The Queen Is Dead; The New Emperor Chinese Restaurant; Pork with Peking Sauce, Chicken in Black Bean Sauce; jasmine tea; home; car stereo; country and western tape; tea; check email; you have no new messages; bed; read; Box Nine, Jack O'Connell; sleep

23

Figure 3. Rosalynde's Madrigal, sample gate

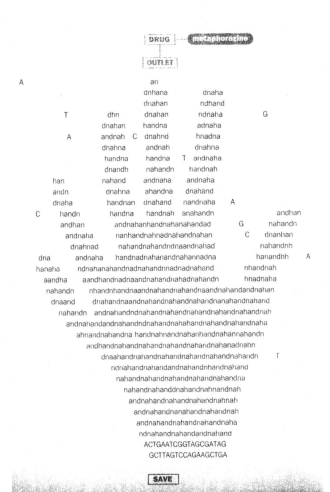

Figure 4. Thomas De Quincey, *Confessions of an English Opium Eater*, Cobralingus outlet text.

a list of objects and events dated Sunday 28th Feb, 1999 (Figure 3) (as they, presumably, featured in Noon's life on the day – an approach brining to mind Goldsmith's *Day*), turns into a springboard for a conceptual, mashed up recording of actions and objects associated with Noon's life.

An interest in concretism and typography remain prominent throughout *Cobralingus*, with further examples such as a transformation of an excerpt from *Confession of an English Opium-Eater* into a rendering of a hand created out of manipulation of multiple retypings of the word 'hand' itself (Figure 4). Further textual experimental techniques at play in *Cobralingus* include fragmentation and erasure to constrained composition in the style of Christian Bök and OU-LIPO, anagrams, translations, substitutions. In all cases, however, *Cobralingus* foregrounds a process of reading in fragments, from a textual de-composition to a re-composition and back, a fractured form of mimetic representation. In each case, the new text becomes, in Noon's words, the ghost, or an unconscious desire of the original text – '*Cobralingus*, very like a Lee Scratch Perry dub mix, is a way of calling up these ghosts' (2012). On a level of each individual textual metamorphosis a procedural movement can be observed, from a linear narrative to a fractured, fluid poetics, a peculiar textuality with a glitch. This textual dynamics at the same time serves as an embodiment and a meta-textual commentary on the nature of the liquid aesthetics and matamorphiction in a broader sense, of the nature of the genre as propagated by Noon. To quote one of the *Cobralingus* interim texts that could be treated as a self-conscious commentary on the nature of the kind of creativity Noon puts forward, this is a textuality that 'sets fire to the language [...] It is like Shakespeare exploded. Like a word-serpent making a nightmare book' (Noon, 2001b: 53). This is an ultimate text, so it would seem, for the age of digital reproduction, foregrounding the working of the machine that produced it, mechanical modes of textual production in general and dynamics of hypertextuality; treating the reader as user, to apply Noon's term, and reverberating with conceptual assumptions governing the aesthetics of uncreative writing as described by Goldsmith et al., so like the works of American conceptual literature and so unlike the modes of traditional linear narrativity that it overtly subverts. But this writing machine, and the texts it generates are produced without any engagement with technology at all. As a note on the back cover of *Cobralingus* reads 'Cobralingus uses only imaginary technologies and the strangely twisted pathways inside Jeff Noon's head' (Noon, 2001b).

Noon explains the approach by declaring contemporary technology insufficient for the kind of experimental textuality he is interested in:

> With Cobralingus, I'm doing a lot of random manipulation. But I have to do it all by hand, either on screen or on bits of paper. There isn't a button I've got that can randomise it for me. Sure, there are random text generators and so on, but they're seen as add-ons rather than part of the process of Liquid Culture. We need to allow words to become part of that. And to do it we need the tools, like they already have with music. At the moment, all I have is my mind and a cut and paste button! (Johnson, 2010: 376)

A replication of workings of a computer, and strong affinity to the uncreative aesthetics is clear here, but framed by the constraints of a traditional print of an analogue book. This juxtaposition of the digital and analogue serves as an immediate echo of musical remix culture influences against the backdrop of which *Cobralingus* was created, engaging the nature of analogue remixing that governs dub as opposed to digitally generated electronic experimental music. The approach serves as a subversive commentary, I argue, not only on traditional modes of authorship that Goldsmith and Dworkin foreground and (mis)appropriate, but also on the methods of literary production in the age of digital reproduction, in a culture obsessed with the machine, the Web and new modes of information dissemination. The Cobralingus Engine guarantees a system, a structural, formalized textual principle and immediately deconstructs it. As such, the relationship between authorial control and its relinquishment in the machine age of computer textuality is realized and questioned at the same time, with the Cobralingus Engine both conforming to and subverting the dynamics of automatization, while operating as a simulacrum of simulated textual pseudo-randomness. The only generator in this textual generator is Noon himself: the deterministic, pre-programmed coded textuality that *Cobralingus* exemplifies on the surface is abandoned. There is no way of determining the code or the algorithm that produced *Cobralingus* for the only source code remains, in the most nondigital fashion, Noon's own imagination. Foregrounding fluidity and change, *Cobralingus* turns into a work of anti-change aesthetics, in a somewhat perverse way maintaining the authority of an individual subject.

This approach also brings further significance to the nature of the dynamics governing the modes of appropriation that Noon engages in. As an expression of the individual author's creativity alone, *Cobralingus* becomes a peculiar exercise in hermeneutics where new texts are not simply randomly generated appropriations of old texts but, specifically, Noon's interpretations of them; foregrounding the inherent subjectivity of the process, the nature of authorship and modes of appropriation involved. The juxtaposition of the inlet and outlet texts, their interplay and mutual influence, as described above, acquires new significance in the context of Noon's assertion of a single, traditional authorial persona. Considered within the frame, the prefix 'meta' constituting the term 'metamorphiction' can be seen as acquiring new meaning – metamorfiction transforms into a form of metafiction, foregrounding its own self-conscious textuality. Conceptualizing *Cobralingus* as a self-referential text encourages a meditation on the essence of textual reception that Noon as a reader rather than as an author engages in and subsequently renders on a page – a collection of Noon's exercises in close reading. In the process, the boundaries between the roles of a reader and a writer, producer and consumer of texts become blurred – the dynamics of textual production represented as such yet again reverberating clearly with the processes governing contemporary liquid modernity, where production gives way to excessive consumption and, as Bauman (2006: 121) describes it, 'the disembodied labour of software era'. Thomas Lodge's madrigal, remixed with the events and objects that features in Noon's life on the 28 February 1999, turn into a conceptual rendering of Gadammer's notion of 'fusion of horizons'. As frequently referred to by Ricoeur, a notion assumes a fluid dialectical relationship between the world of the reader and that of the text, their constant interpenetration growing out of the assumption that the reader belongs to both the experiential horizon of the work imaginatively, and the horizon of his action concretely, here embodied through the aesthetics of metamorphosis.

In an interview with Mark Amerika, Noon pointed out that creatively he felt isolated, most of the time, in Britain, where 'it's getting more than a bit bland and deadly right now' (Amerika, 2007: 238), 'where retreat is made to the past' (Noon, 2001a), in a culture which, as he suggests in his 2001 manifesto, might have lost the courage to engage with a challenging text. As an example of this contemporary condition of British writing, Noon refers to Nicholas Blincoe's and Matt Thorne's *All Hail the New Puritans,* an anthology of short stories published in 2000. The collection comprises work by fifteen young writers, a selection of short stories composed in line with a set of ten rules for writing fiction, a New Puritan manifesto, propagating narrativity that foregrounds storytelling and rejects formal experimentation, echoing the minimalist naturalism of Dogme 95 movement. While Thorne admits his admiration for the formal literary experiments and names writers such as B. S. Johnson, Italo Calvino and Georges Perec in the introduction to the volume, he at the same time declares that 'the stories in this collection prove that the most subtle and innovative form available to prose writers is always going to be a plot-line' (Blincoe and Thorne, 2000: vii–viii). Although The New Puritan Manifesto focuses on modes of short-story composition, it can be seen, as Head (2002: 246) suggests, as an attempt at an intervention in the contemporary state of the novel. The New Puritan approach signifies, according to Philip Tew (2007: 4), 'a movement from heterogeneity and deconstructive decentring toward apprehensible meaning'. Noon (2001a), on the other hand, sees the New Puritan aesthetics as an expression of 'a fearsome denial of the imagination', exemplifying a level of 'fixation with the linear narrative' so prominent on the contemporary literary scene in Britain. To quote Noon:

> By dismissing the textual adventures of Joyce, British writers stayed true to the old pleasures of straightforward storytelling. This leads to our current situation, where the vast majority of novelists are still intent on drawing a single narrative thread through a complex world. Yet we live daily in a web of connections, all of us becoming adept at riding the multiple layers of information. This is the fluid society. Tracing pathways through this intricate landscape needs a different kind of narrative art. [...] I do not mean a refusal to tell stories. But we need to expand the notion of what a story is, and to seek out new

ways of telling these stories. We need to be brave in this, as writers, as critics, and as readers. (Noon, 2001a)

In the light of Noon's criticism, the New Puritans become an example of an attempt at a stand against the contemporary literary establishment, an exercise in literary novelty that, instead of introducing the new, results in proliferating the same familiar literary models, only showcased by a discursive frame of the manifesto. While attempting to set out a declaration of a subversive artistic agenda, the New Puritans manifesto is, in fact, scarcely a radical challenge to contemporary modes of literary production it declares to encourage; instead, as Head observes, 'a line of continuity can be drawn between the Movement writers of the 1950s' (Head, 2002: 246) and the work propagated by Blincoe and Thorne. Not surprisingly, when propagating such a view of the state of British literature, Noon openly positions himself against the grain of the contemporary British novel and foregrounds the experimental and avant-garde status of the kind of textuality that *Cobralingus* puts forward. In an interview for *Spike* magazine, he distinguishes, within his own oeuvre, between 'mainstream novels' (Johnson, 2010: 372), which rely on narrative and traditional modes of storytelling, and overt experimentalism of the non-linear, remixed and marginalized *Needle in the Groove* or *Cobralingus* – the latter favouring form as function and self-consciously exploring boundaries of writing and the way language operates in a liquid culture. These experimental texts form an attempt at finding a literary equivalent of the liquid culture, a new, more adequate mode of storytelling, as Noon describes it. Noon's work, and *Cobralingus* in particular, is more concerned with the way stories are told than with stories themselves, yet again reverberating clearly with echoes of the uncreative writing of Goldsmith or Fitterman.

There are numerous reasons for Noon's marginalization in the UK and, more broadly, the creative–uncreative disjunction between US and UK fiction. The proliferation of the uncreative writing in the USA might have something to do with a self-proclaimed, publicity-driven nature of the avant-gardism of Goldsmith and Dworkin that these authors are frequently accused of. More importantly, however,

I would like to suggest, even if only briefly, that the experimentalism of the conceptual uncreativity that is failing to ascertain an equally marked presence in the UK might be the result of the developments that the British literature went through in the post-war Britain. Following Dominic Head's (2002) stand, I would like to suggest that we can talk about very distinctive postmodernisms, the British and the American, where British postmodern writing as it developed in 1970s and 1980s exists as a hybrid form of expression that renegotiates tradition and is characterized by questioning metanarratives and de-centring of cultural authority. At the same time, British postmodern writing, as Head describes it, conveys a conviction about the moral and emotional function of literature and its ability to make readers reengage with the world they know. To quote Head, 'in performing this role, the novel in the hands of those [British postmodern] writers has depended on re-working of the realist contract' (Head, 2002: 229). And although Head focuses on the novel and its development alone, the dynamics he describes are applicable to British literature in general. Seen as such, the most crucial transformations in the British postmodern literature should be considered as characteristically contingent on 'supplementing rather than rejecting given forms' (Head, 2002: 224); British 'creative literary movements have not necessarily depended upon extravagant or iconoclastic innovations for their productive energy' (Head, 2002: 224). In contrast, American, or internationally recognized postmodernism, exhibits an inherent penchant for a radical overhaul of established, allegedly exhausted literary forms and norms, characteristically foregrounds its own artifice, in a self-degrading playfulness, favouring a culture of pastiche, often radical linguistic experiment, a kind of 'ludic postmodernism' of Barthelme, as Head describes it, that has not found a fertile ground in the British literary culture. Postmodernism that was much more successful in the UK relied on reworked realism and historiographic metafiction. Reasons for this dichotomy are multiple and the developments of the two postmodernisms stem partly from divergent intellectual, literary critical and fictional traditions and partly from different economics and approaches to institutionalization of creative writing in the USA and UK. If read within the frame, the contemporary scarcity of uncreative, formal experimentalism similar to the work of Goldsmith and Dworkin in British literature could be seen as a natural development from British postmodernism to contemporary valedictory realism, to borrow Ian Jack's (1996) term – a reappropriation for the twenty-first century of the already appropriated British postmodern aesthetics, of 'a postmodernism-that-wasn't' (Waugh and Hodgson, 2013: 28). Similarly, the rise and development of conceptual writing in America can be perceived as a product of the same cultural trajectory, a result of the dynamics governing the American postmodern literary practice that contributed to forming American literature now. Even the aggressive publicity and growing institutionalization and commodification of uncreative writing in America seems to mirror the earlier cultural developments of American postmodernism. As Will Self (2009: 91) reflects in *Dorian*, the countercultural, subversive nature of the postmodern aesthetics in the USA in the 1980s gradually gave in to the popular lure of mass culture: 'What happened to flagrant queers and uppity blacks and defiant junkies in America is that they got absorbed, then packaged and retailed like everybody and everything else. In America in the 1980s the counter-culture becomes the over-the-counter culture with sickening alacrity'.

Interestingly, as Head (2002) points out, concerns about the state of British literature in the 1970s and 1980s and its future have tended to focus on an elementary, binary division between realism and experimentalism with conspicuous value judgements attached to both approaches to literarariness. While American literature to come was to be bold, innovative, experimental and cosmopolitan, as Ron Silliman proclaimed in 1986 in his introduction to *In the American Tree*, Britain was to remain the dominium of the familiar, established literary norms. As Peter Middleton points out, discussing a 1988 anthology of *The New British Poetry*, a level of nostalgia or settled tradition prevailed in the British literature at the time. 'No anthologist in the U.K. poetry', writes Middleton, 'would be able to unselfconsciously parallel Ron Silliman's announcement of a "new moment in American writing" [...]' (Middleton, 2003: 131), in an environment where, as John Wilkinson (1992) put it, '"we" has lost all possibility of adventure'. Similarly, the novel in the UK appeared no longer novel as

Situation of the Novel debate at the time had it. In the 1980s Granta debated the end of the English fiction – according to Fredrick Bowers characterized by an irrelevant parochialism:

> what strikes [...] most about the contemporary British novel is its conformity, its traditional sameness, and its realistically rendered provincialism. Shaped only by its contents, the British novel is a product of group mentality: local, quaint, and self-consciously xenophobic. Why is it that of the many able craftsmen writing in Britain so few have experimented with form, and, of those, experimented with such caution? [...] The culture from which British fiction derives, and the culture insistently expressed in its writing, is clearly oriented towards fact, content, metonymy, empiricism, and the body. (Bowers, 1980)

The same concerns that dominated the debates about British literature in the 1980s and its future prevail in often anxious, sometimes disillusioned, deliberations on the state of British literature now; to quote Colm Tóibín (2012), recently commenting on the contemporary writing in Britain, a quintessential English novel of the twenty-first century is 'well made, low on ambition and filled with restraint, taking its bearings from a world that Philip Larkin made in his own image'. Characteristically, those debates on the nature of contemporary literary creative practice in Britain are, essentially, always juxtaposed with and framed by contemporary developments in America. This dichotomy seems to contribute to a level of high anxiety in Britain, a certain sense that British writers have lost the courage to engage with a challenging text that the retreat is really made into the past, that, to turn to Middleton (2003: 128) again, contemporary British poetics 'belongs to a premodernist era', somehow lagging behind the daring American persistence in pursuing change and literary innovation. What we have not lost, however, is, as Patricia Waugh and Jennifer Hodgson argue, 'our mania for manifesting the particularity (and the peculiarity) of being English. The metephysics of Eliot and Leavis might have gone lukewarm for many and stone cold for most, but we still continue to attempt to conjure a coherent whole from less than the sum of its parts' (Waugh and Hodgson, 2013: 23). The American uncreative experiment remains, on the other hand, more interested in the parts themselves. Considered through the lens of this assertion, American literature, as it is developing now, seems to have undergone a natural, linear progression, from modernism to postmodernism, followed by contemporary digimodern developments, whereas Britain encountered a peculiar cultural analepsis, from modernism to postmodernism and back, to the pre-modernist nineteenth century modes of aesthetic expression. While Ian Jack, in his introduction to *Granta Best of New British Novelists 3* (2003) declared that 'we don't, it seems, have young Roths, Updikes, Wolfes and DeLillos ... ' (Jack, 2003: 12), today we also do not have young Goldsmiths, Dworkins and Places. Ten years on, *Granta 123: Best of New British Novelists 4* (2013) could, hypothetically, be making similar claims when comparing British and American attempts (or lack of thereof) at uncreative, experimental writing dealing with issues of authorship, originality and contemporary formalist modes of textual production. Instead, John Freeman in his introduction suggests that an interest in form emerges from the pages of issue 123 – a sense that the writers included in the 2013 list of the best young British writing are interested in the 'dialogue with the novel as form' (Freeman, 2013: 15). Freeman's (2013: 15) examples include Zadie Smith's *NW* as a text that 'collapses the social-realist style she perfected in *On Beauty* with a more fragmented narrative voice' alongside Steven Hall's *Raw Shark* and Thirlwell's *Escape*. The reference to Thirlwell is probably the most fitting here. His *Kapow!* with its fold-out pages, text printed diagonally and upside down or sections composed solely out of black polka dots – Damien Hirst-style, shows clear preoccupation with formal experiment and typography. The same interest is, however, far less apparent in 'Slow Motion' – an excerpt of his novel in progress included in *Granta 123*. The formal innovations that Freeman advocates in his introduction remain deeply rooted in the traditional modes of realist narrative, exemplifying instances of (modest) experimentation with a range of 'new' realisms and described by Theo Tait (2013) as a collection of 'solid, old fashioned storytelling or hit-and-miss, boil-in-the bag postmodernism'. As such, the level of apprehension towards experimenting with form in Britain that Bowers was concerned with in the 1980s reverberates clearly in British literature now; 'our peculiar creed', as Waugh and Hodgson put it, 'is mortally suspicious of untrammelled aestheticism, endlessly asserting the primacy of content over form [...] literary experiment still tends to be perceived as a pernicious form of French "flu"' (2013: 10–11), or maybe, in the twenty-first century of uncreative writing, an American flu instead. Contemporary, limited and marginalized, attempts at literary formal experimentation with appropriation and non-linearity seem to echo the marginalization and peculiar cultural displacement of writers at the forefront of British experimental fiction in 1960s, 1970s and 1980s, bringing to mind B. S. Johnson, Ann Quin or Christine Brook-Rose.

This is not to say that questions of authenticity, authorship and originality as well as attempts at experimentation with all of the above do not arise in the context of contemporary British writing – as Phillip Mead (2012: 339) observed 'authenticity in relation to literary production is always now a question'. The preoccupation with the destabilization of normative ideas governing contemporary conceptual understanding of the author–text relationship feature prominently both in the American and British fiction, only approached and expressed differently and need to be addressed and considered in line with the form–content dichotomy exemplified by the divergence between the British and American approaches to the notions and modes of expression in question. As Waugh and Hodgson points out:

> Insofar as such a model ever could anywhere, the one that bisects the twentieth century more-or-less down the middle, dividing its paper assets between categories of modernism and postmodernism, has never comfortably applied here. On the whole, British writing embraced postmodern inclusivity for its capacity to welcome new voices, new perspectives – and, indeed, new market demographics – into the great tradition, but it tended to dispense with the formal and linguistic gymnastics. (Waugh and Hodgson, 2013: 27)

In such a creative context, uncreative writing in Britain, as it is currently developing, can only remain an avocation rather than a vocation – a hobby, a distraction, a diversion; at times taking seriously not being serious and leaving open possibilities of meaning – while in North America this mode of literary experimentation is gradually turning into a new cultural dominant. What the current British and American literatures do have in common is the dialectical relationship with earlier texts. 'In the climate of the new century', Perloff (2010: 11) observes, 'we seem to be witnessing a poetic turn from the resistance model of the 1980s to dialogue – a dialogue with earlier texts or texts in other media [...] Inventio is giving way to appropriation, elaborate constraint, visual and sound composition and reliance on intertextuality'. The interest in the past – past events as well as past texts – is apparent in contemporary writing both in the UK and USA, only approached differently. If the twenty-first-century realism turns to the past to create the 'new', traditionally favouring content over form, American conceptualism is guided not so much by an attempt at doing away with the past, but, to quote Stuart Home (2013: 73), is instead focused on 'brining selected parts of it into play. In many ways so much has been written that all we need to do is plunder and rewrite'. As such, British and American approaches to this recycled poetics for today can be seen as ranging from the aesthetics of what Perloff (2002) describes as twenty-first-century modernism, Alan Kirby (2009) labels Digimodernism, or Philip Tew (2007) sees an expression of ultra-, super-, late phase of modernism – all echoing the ontology of the early twentieth century avant-gardes of DADA or futurism in the USA, to the new realism, or domesticated modernism, to use Patricia Waugh's term, dominating British fiction today. British fiction seems driven by the fictionalization of liquid identities rather than expression and representation of the state of liquid modernity itself. It seems that a certain consensus can be observed in relation to the themes that dominate Anglo-American writing today; the disjunction lies in the methods and approaches to creative expression, akin to the disjunction that governed the transition between the early twentieth-century avant-garde and the grand narrativity of the nineteenth-century novel. Noon, arriving at the creative methodology of metamorphiction calls for a need to develop a new way of telling stories in a mode reflective of and not simply about the digital age and the development of his creative career, fittingly, seems to bridge the gap between current UK and US literary scenes and reflect the transition from the highly self-conscious, though traditionally linear, intertextual metanarrartives (*Authomated Alice*) to formal textual experimentation of *Cobralingus*, a transition from telling to showing, from narrativity to formalism and conceptualism, from readership to thinkership.

Works Cited

Amerika, Mark (1993/2007) 'Avant-Pop Manifesto: Thread baring Itself in Ten Quick Posts', in Mark Amerika, *Meta/Data: A Digital Poetics*, pp. 289–93. Cambridge, MA: MIT University Press.

Blincoe, Nicolas and Matt Thorne (eds.) (2000) *All Hail the New Puritans*. London: Fourth Estate.

Bauman, Zygmunt (2000) *Liquid Modernity*. Cambridge: Polity Press.

Bowers, Fredrick (1980) 'An Irrelevant Parochialism', in *Granta 3: The End of English Novel*, pp. 150–154, London: Granta Publications.

Freeman, John (2013) 'Introduction', in *Granta 123: Best of Young British Novelists 4*, pp. 11–18. London: Granta Publications.

Goldsmith, Kenneth (2011) 'Why Conceptual Writing? Why Now?', in Craig Dworkin and Kenneth Goldsmith (eds) *Against Expression: An Anthology of Conceptual Writing*, pp. xvii – xxii. Evanston, Il: Northwestern University Press.

Goldsmith, Kenneth (2011) *Uncreative Writing: Managing Language in the Digital Age*. New York: Columbia University Press.

Head, Dominic (2002) *Modern British Fiction, 1950 – 2000*. Cambridge: Cambridge University Press.

Home, Stuart (2013) 'Humanity will not b happy until the last Man Booker Prize winner is hung by the guts of the final recipient of the Nobel Prize for literature!', in Patricia Waugh and Jennifer Hodgson (eds) *The Review of Contemporary Fiction: The Future of British Fiction*, Fall 2012, Vol. XXXII, pp. 72–78. Champagne, IL: Dalkey Archive Press.

Jack, Ian (2003) 'Introduction', in Ian Jack (ed.) *Granta 81: Best of Young British Novelists 2003*, pp. 9–14. London: Granta Publications.

Jack, Ian (1996) 'Editorial', in Ian Jack (ed.) *Granta 56: What Happened to Us?*, pp. 7–8. London: Granta Publications.

Johnson, Anthony (2010) 'Jeff Noon: Liquid Culture' (Interview) *Spike: 15 Years of Books, Music, Art, Ideas* ed. Chris Mitchell, October: 363–76, accessed November 2012, http://www.spikemagazine.com/spike-book

Kirby, Alan (2009) *Digimodernism: How New Technologies Dismantle the Postmodern and Reconfigure our Culture*. New York: Continuum.

Mead, Philip (2012) 'Hoax Poetry and Inauthenticy', in Joe Bray, Alison Gibbons and Brian McHale (eds) *Routledge Companion to Experimental Literature*, Abingdon and New York, NY: Routledge.

Middleton, Peter (2003) 'Imagined Readership and Poetic Innovation in U.K. Poetry', in Romana Huk (ed) *Assembling Alternatives: Reading postmodern Poetries Transnationally*. Middleton, CT: Wesleyan University Press.

Noon, Jeff (2001a) 'How to Make a Modern Novel', *Guardian*, accessed November 2012, http://www.guardian.co.uk/books/2001/jan/10/fiction.film.

Noon, Jeff (2001b) *Cobralingus*. Hove: Codex Books.

Noon, Jeff (n.d.) 'Origins of Dub Fiction', Language as Virus, accessed November 2012, http://languageisavirus.com/articles/articles.php?subaction=showcomments&id=1099110671&archive=&start_from=&ucat=&#.UMUWfOSvFIE.

Perloff, Majorie (2010) *Unoriginal Genius: Poetry by Other Means in the New Century*. Chicago, IL and London: University of Chicago Press.

Perloff, Marjorie (2002) *21st-Century Modernism: The "New" Poetics*. Oxford: Blackwell Publishers.

Place, Vanessa (2012) 'Global Conceptualisms: I am American', *&Now Festival, Paris 6 June 2012*, UbuWeb, accessed November 2012, http://ubu.com/papers/place_global.html

Self, Will (2009) *Dorian*. London and New York: Penguin Books.

Tait, Theo (2013) 'Best of Young British Novelists 4, edited by John Freeman – review', *Guardian*, 16 April, accessed April 2013, http://www.guardian.co.uk/books/2013/apr/16/granta-young-british-novelist-review

Tew, Philip (2007) *The Contemporary British Novel*. London: Continuum.

Colm Toibin (2012) 'Going Beyond the Limits', *New York Review of Books*, accessed June 2012, http://www.nybooks.com/articles/archives/2012/may/10/julian-barnes-going-beyond-limits/

Waugh, Patricia and Jennifer Hodgson (2013) 'Introduction', in Patricia Waugh and Jennifer Hodgson, *The Review of Contemporary Fiction: The Future of British Fiction*, Fall 2012, Vol. XXXII. Champaign, Il: Dalkey Archive Press.

Wilkinson, John (1992) 'Imperfect Pitch', in Denise Riley (ed.) *Poets on Writing: Britain, 1970–1991*. London: Macmillan.

PART V

FORMS

You-niversal Love
Desire, Intimacy and the Second Person in
Ali Smith's Short Fiction

Tory Young

This chapter considers the ingenious ways that Ali Smith employs the second-person narrator, 'you', to challenge preconceptions about gender and to enable the reader to focus on the experiences of love and desire, through a chronological discussion of her short stories. There is no single or straightforward definition of second-person or 'you' fictions. There are well-known fictions, such as Jay McInerney's *Bright Lights, Big City* (1984), in which 'you' is the consistent form of self-reference, of a narrator telling her or his own story in a quasi-second-person voice that shares the positional but not the grammatical qualities of first-person narrative. 'You' can refer to the narratee, another character in the story who is being addressed, as the 'you' in Calvino's *If On A Winter's Night A Traveller* (1979) turns out to be. These two types of second-person pronoun use can be termed 'intradiegetic', since they refer to people within the storyworld. But equally 'you' could be the reader, as the 'you' in *If On A Winter's Night A Traveller* at first seems to be: 'You are about to begin reading Italo Calvino's new novel' (Calvino, 1982: 9), which is 'extradiegetic', referring to outside of the storyworld. Five stories in Lorrie Moore's first collection, *Self Help* (1985), use a 'you' narrator to experiment with the non-fiction genre of instructional guides or manuals, the imperative 'you'. These 'you's turn out to be characters in the storyworlds (as in *BL,BC*) but the 'How to...' format of their titles ('How to Be an Other Woman', 'How to Talk to Your Mother [Notes]', 'How to Become a Writer') gulls the reader into imagining that they are the addressee at whom advice is being directed. In each of Moore's 'How to' stories, there is an acerbic determinism that 'you' must be a woman and that 'your' affair will fail. Identification with 'you', if you are a man, may not then happen; such narratives do not securely establish what David Herman describes as the 'projection relations between reader and narratee' (Herman, 2002: 333).

This question of gendered identification is perhaps the most interesting one to emerge from this fuzzy grammatical ground of the second-person pronoun. There is a compelling connection between the ambiguous, plastic and indeterminate forms of second-person reference and the fictional treatment of gender, and it will be my project here to explore the ways in which these formal uncertainties open out into thematic issues in the politics of gender. The second person is employed with surprising frequency by contemporary women writers to portray the failure of heterosexual romance and the familiarity of the extra-marital affair.[1] In poetry, 'you' more often, and traditionally, retains the dignity of the love object and can be used to preserve anonymity, mask gender and sexuality, to enable universality of appeal. In such verse, or in the elegy, the text may focus on the emotions of the speaker, whilst 'you' remain undescribed, out of sight. 'You' can be generalized and non-specific, comparable to the way 'one' is used in formal writing or speech. 'You' is a special case of person deixis in that,[2] as even this brief overview demonstrates, it can be more than one of these things at once. Most significantly, as a result of its capability to address, at the same time, a reader of and a character in the text, it can be 'metaleptic', or capable of crossing, if not destroying, the boundary between what is inside and outside of the fiction:

> second-person narration [...] provides an interesting case study in how stories can at once rely on and challenge the border between text and context [...] In some cases, at least, narrative *you* does not simply or even mainly refer to storyworld participants but also (or chiefly)

addresses the interpreter of the narrative. And sometimes a single instance of narrative *you* both refers and addresses. The result then is a
fitful and self-conscious anchoring of the text in its contexts, as well as
a storyworld whose contours and boundaries can be probabilistically
but not determinately mapped, the inventory of its constituent enti-
ties remaining fuzzy rather than fixed. (Herman, 2002: 332)

Narratologists have recognized that distinguishing between 'intradiegetic and extradiegetic narratees, or narratees represented as characters and narratees not so represented' (Herman, 2002: 333) is not sufficient to determine the density of 'the projection relations between
reader and narratee' (Herman, 2002: 333). It may be that questions
like this – of how far the reader recognizes 'you' as 'me', her or himself – are not susceptible to technical or narratological description.
My interest in the difficulty lies in the possibility that, in this slippage
between the determinate mapping of narratological description and
the fuzzy grammatical territory of the second-person pronoun, we
might be able to identify fictional resources that are of particular importance for the representation of gender, and the gender dynamics
involved in reading.

The more detail provided in the text about 'you', the less likely you
are to prick up your ears and think 'that's me'. (Our establishment of
'projection relations' in 'you' fictions in this way is particularly enabled by the English language, in French, for example, the gender,
number and intimacy of the narratee would be indicated by grammatical forms: gendered nouns and the selection of 'vous' or 'tu'). Of
course, we do not need to share the life and experience of a character
to identify with her, that is what fiction is for, but 'you' narratives often seek to exploit the possibility that word-for-word you are being
spoken to. Texts that employ the second person are therefore often
explicitly engaged with issues of narrativity, and those by women that
I have loosely grouped together use 'you' to explore love; how the
emotions may be produced by the genres of telling and simultaneously how existing narratives of love fail to describe the experience.
Margaret Atwood's often-anthologized, comic, short story 'Happy
Endings' plays with another form of 'you' narrative, the children's

'choose-your-own-adventure' books, and invites 'you' the reader to select the events and outcome of John and Mary's love story from six options – 'If you want a happy ending, try A' (Atwood, 1994: 50) – but concludes with the admonishment 'The only authentic ending is the one provided here: *John and Mary die. John and Mary die. John and Mary die.*' (Atwood, 1994: 56). Although 'you' are addressed and initially presented with choices, each option depends upon those before, suggesting an inescapable linear chronology to the romance plot, if not romance itself. The scenarios of loyalty, infidelity, desire are presented bluntly as just 'a what and a what and a what' (Atwood, 1994: 56) but not the 'How' and the 'Why' that she calls for ('Now try How and Why' [Atwood, 1994: 56] – to you the budding writer? The reader?) and which would reflect the nuances of an individual life. The collection of flash fictions that the story appeared in makes several references to Beckett's *The Unnamable*, famously a text with a 'you'. Atwood takes the unnamable women of folk tales and myth (ugly sisters, stepmothers) and gives them voice and 'you', as Sharon R. Wilson suggests, are the reader 'who cannot resist becoming involved' (Wilson, 2003: 28). Here 'you' are not gendered or necessarily heterosexual, although a member of a heteronormative society, and the textual features determining these factors (such as those in the stories by Moore) are absent allowing for the kind of intimacy that as we shall see in the rest of this essay, Ali Smith develops ingeniously.

Ali Smith has written six texts broadly described as novels: *Like* (1997), *Hotel World* (2001), *The Accidental* (2005), *Girl Meets Boy* (2007), *There But For The* (2011) and *Artful* (2012), the last sitting most uncomfortably within the category of either art or criticism, demonstrating instead the characteristic generosity of thinking about literature that is evident in Smith's intertextuality but most visible in the number of introductions to editions of the works of many writers including Angela Carter, Tove Jansson, Katherine Mansfield, Muriel Spark, and Margaret Tait that she has written. The titles of her four short story collections signal the ludic metafiction of her prose: *Free Love and Other Stories* (1995), *Other Stories and Other Stories* (1999), *The Whole Story and Other Stories* (2003), *The First Person and Other Stories* (2008).[3] At first glance, the stories and title of the first collection appear more straightforwardly realist than those following it but upon scrutiny the 'free' in 'free love' can have a grammatical meaning of unattachment that also pertains to the non-specificity of 'you', and that signals the freedoms that Smith finds in linguistic innovations and puns. In the rest of this article, with a focus on her short stories, and one in particular ('May'), I will show that the playful engagement with issues of narrativity, and the scope for narrative intimacy created by second-person fictions can be found throughout her works; she delights in the possibilities that are offered by the 'fuzzy rather than fixed' pronoun and we are delighted to enter her storyworlds through its invitation, and to have our default positions about romance narratives shaken up.

The final story in *Free Love* is a second-person narrative. 'The World with Love' opens with a move that is characteristic in 'you' narratives: an open address to 'you' is swiftly revealed to be an address to the character within the story who shares thematic qualities of a first-person narrator. (In Monika Fludernik's taxonomy of 'you' narratives with six forms, the 'you' narrator whose tale is being told in this way is type A):

> On a day when it looks like rain and you're wandering between stations in a city you don't know very well, you meet a woman in the street whom you haven't seen for fifteen years, not since you were at school. (Smith, 1995: 141)

The scenario feels familiar enough (to this reader); the old schoolfriend is visiting the unnamed city with her children, one of whom reminds the narrator of the schoolfriend at her age. The friend reminds the narrator, Sam, of the nervous breakdown experienced by their French teacher as a result of their class's misbehaviour, and prompted by this memory, Sam recalls the intensity of emotions felt for another classmate Laura Watt, and how, unable to describe or enact these feelings, s/he listed them in French vocabulary instead. This, like others in the collection, is the story of a first love; the new language of French is a perfect metaphor for the new emotions of an adolescent. In her essay on 'The Genderization of Narrative', Fludernik undertook empirical research to show that when the gender of a narrator is unspecified, heterosexuality is assumed to be the default position.[4] Without reference to Smith, Fludernik notes that gay and lesbian writers often employ second-person narration to challenge such normative reading positions. However, in 'The World with Love', the 'contextual anchoring' of this story as the final one in Smith's collection, if it is read in the order in which it is placed (which can never be a given), produces a default position of homosexuality. Read in isolation, Sam's unnoted full name, which the French teacher so mistakenly abbreviates, could as well be Samuel as Samantha but we assume the latter since many of the preceding stories in the collection concern two women. 'Free Love', the first story, is a first-person account of a young woman in Amsterdam losing her virginity to a prostitute. On the first page, the reader might well assume the default position of the heterosexual norm and think of the narrator as male; the story opens: 'The first time I ever made love with anyone it was with a prostitute in Amsterdam' (Smith, 1995: 1), but once the page is turned, in this story the characters' genders are made very clear; immediately any gender stereotypical interpretations are challenged. The unnamed narrator is on holiday with Jackie, the friend she fancies and who becomes her lover after she is emboldened by the prostitute's lovemaking and a few beers during a visit to a Heineken factory. In this story, ambiguous deictic markers are employed to portray the uncertainties that pertain to a new relationship: Jackie asks 'Do you like this?' (Smith, 1995: 6) of a picture in a modern art gallery, but the reader knows that when the narrator answers in the affirmative, 'this' refers to the sensation of their legs pressed together and not the painting. In 'A Quick One', the first-person narrator recalls the passion of the early days of a love affair that is now over, thinking 'That was the crazy time, everybody gets the crazy time' (Smith, 1995: 32). This is a theme to which Smith constantly returns in her fiction. In the predominantly first-person stories of *Free Love*, the contextual anchoring of the stories when read in sequence mean that even when gender markers are not explicit, we read the stories as about love affairs between women; free from the collection, many of them could be read as between a man and a woman, although not between two men since the love object is always clearly marked as female.

Fittingly enough, the last of Fludernik's six forms of 'you' narrative; 'Type F includes a large number of texts in which the addressee is no longer alive and the address to the *you* is therefore imaginary and commemorative' (Fludernik, 2011: 113). The first sentence of the first story in Smith's second collection, *Other Stories and Other Stories*, employs the deictic marker of 'now' to indicate that 'you' are a dead or departed lover of this kind: 'There are so many things that you don't know about me now' (Smith, 1999: 3). This narrator is a first-person narrator whose cat leaves her dead and mangled birds each day; the story ends with her speculation as to whether or not one she has managed to rescue will live to fly or will fall, a metaphor for her own state. The theme of death suggests that the lover is indeed dead rather than departed, but uncertainty is emphasized at the same time as the reader is alerted to the ambiguities of 'you' narration when the narrator says of her former fear of flying now:

> I wasn't frightened, I wasn't frightened on any of the flights, since you are only frightened of losing something if you've got something to lose. Not you: one. One is only frightened, etc. (Smith, 1999: 4)

Linguistic ambiguities and misunderstandings are more overt in this collection. The second story, 'The Hanging Girl', starts with the interior monologue of a young woman who is about to be executed. The perspective shifts to Pauline who becomes deranged after witnessing the execution on television and the puns of losing one's head, being at the end of one's tether, hanging around are replete and so forceful that when the terms appear again in the other stories in the collection, the reader shudders warily: when 'More Than One Story' for instance starts with a man seeing a girl on a neighbouring roof, or in the opening paragraph of 'Small Deaths' when the heat is described as 'hanging around' (Smith, 1999: 69). (The literalization of metaphor in this way is another feature that Smith increasingly employs in her short fiction.) This is perhaps an expanded 'contextual anchoring' to that which Herman conceives but it is a powerful force in Smith's work and one that relates to Derridean notions of the traces that all language bears, and Smith's own intertextuality. The switching of perspective which appears frequently in the short fiction from this point from one character to another (also a feature of her contemporaneous first novel *Like*) suggests that stories are subjective and have many tellers, through what Genette termed the frequency with which events recur in a narrative, and continues to draw attention to the issues of narrativity that become more prominent in her work.

'Blank Card' is a first-person narrative about two people living together in a relationship whose genders are unspecified and undetermined by any suggestive features. The narrator receives a bunch of flowers that she assumes to be from her partner 'you' but the card accompanying them is blank and upon her return from work, the partner claims not to have sent them. Here again the reader shares the protagonist's uncertainty about events; the non-specificity, anonymity of person deixis 'you', 'anybody', 'nobody' functioning for the reader as the blank card does for the narrator. The flowers have an invigorating effect on the couple's sex life to the extent that the narrator sends a bouquet with a blank card to her partner at work, 'She'll know who they're from' (Smith, 1999: 49). We are left guessing that perhaps the partner sent the anonymous flowers all along, but not knowing is shown to be a powerful aphrodisiac rather than a cause of distress even when after an erotic phone call the narrator wonders 'if the you you believed you were talking to on the phone was definitely me after all' (Smith, 1999: 48). There are many other occasions of 'you' in this collection, some metaleptic and metafictional. Like 'The World with Love' and others, 'The Theme is Power' begins with an injunction to a 'you' who seems to be the reader but then is shown to be a character in the story, again the narrator's partner; 'The thing is, I really need you with me in this story' (Smith, 1999: 119). The narrator wants to recount an episode from her youth in which she and a friend were approached and pursued by a woman and a man who clearly intended harm. (The narrator seems to be the narrator from 'Free Love' recalling a time after she and Jackie became lovers in Amsterdam; here they had returned from a holiday of shared beds and love in Paris). The narrator does not seem to have thought about this memory for some time, and certainly has not told her partner; its harrowing unknowns and the impact of what might have happened emphasise why she does not only require an audience but a partner who is 'really [...] with' her, on her side. Her partner is out, so she imagines her there as she internally recounts her tale and we, as readers, take the partner's place; we are 'really [...] with' her. The second-person pronoun allows this; if the story had started 'The thing is, I really need Tory with me in this story', the rest of you would have felt left out. Do all stories need someone to read them who is 'really [...] with' them? We know of characters in fiction who function as reader substitutes, who are not agents in the plot but serve to receive and thus transmit information that is necessary but would be otherwise absent to the reader. 'The Theme is Power' alerts us to the fact that 'you' fictions can create the reverse: a reader who is a character substitute. Smith's stories suggest that every story needs a listener or a reader, and the word 'story' itself is of great importance in life.

The final story in *Other Stories and Other Stories* presents another version of Smith's credo from *Free Love* that 'everybody gets the crazy time' (Smith, 1995: 32). 'A Story of Love' starts with the request of the first-person narrator for a love story from her second-person partner:

> Okay, you said. There was once a boy who really wanted to own a dog.
> A boy and a dog, I said. Does it have to be a boy? It's always stories of boys and dogs. Can't it be a girl?
> Yes, you said, it can be a girl; true love stories are always interchangeable. (Smith, 1999: 167)

The boy becomes a girl and the dog becomes any pet in the second person's story, in the story. (Another notable characteristic of Smith's writing is the telling of stories by characters within the storyworld; even the lectures that Smith gave herself are placed into the voice of a character in *Artful*.) The first-person later mishears another love story to be about, not a girl who fell in love with '*this guy*' (Smith, 1999: 175) but a girl who fell in love with the sky. The lovers and love objects are interchangeable; the details and the interpretation depend upon the listener not the teller. This is at once a political statement about love and sexual preference and a performative critical act about textual meaning that Smith develops even more boldly in a story from her next collection upon which I shall focus.

The cover of *The Whole Story and Other Stories* promises a rewrite 'of the year's cycle into a very modern calendar'. 'May' is the fourth story in a collection of twelve; the last story is called 'The Start of Things' and may well refer to January ('it was the worst month of the year, the one where [...] the money seems to take longer to reach people's bank accounts' [Smith, 2003: 167]). In its most widely recognized definitions, the word 'May' is the fifth month of the year, and a verb denoting possibility in the present or future ('I may'), or sanction ('may I?'), but also a slightly old-fashioned woman's name and (in Britain) the name for the Hawthorn tree. In arcane usage the noun designated a virgin or maiden, the verb to take part in the festivities of May day, to gather flowers in the month of May or, significantly for this story, to cover with hawthorn blossom. All of these meanings are relevant to the story, and the fact of their multiplicity is suggestive of the universality connoted by the 'you' narrator.

'May' is fifteen pages long. Exactly half way through there is a slightly extended gap between paragraphs, and after it the second narrator of the story gives her account of events, although it is not immediately apparent that there has been a change in narrator because they are both first-person narrators who address a narratee: 'you'. But once the shift has been realized, and a reader familiar with Smith's earlier short stories may be quicker to recognise it, this structure suggests the truism that there are (at least) two sides to every story. The story opens with what seems to be an address to the reader: 'I tell you. I fell in love with a tree. I couldn't not. It was in blossom.' (Smith, 2003: 45). This first narrator describes the day 'like all the other days' (Smith, 2003: 45) when walking to work she finds herself mesmerized, 'in love with' (Smith, 2003: 45), a tree. We share her surprise when only two paragraphs later, the woman in whose garden the tree is, calls the police (because of the trespass), and they take her home; 'I hadn't even realised I was in someone's garden, never mind that I'd been there for a long enough time for it to be alarming to anybody' (Smith, 2003: 46). She thinks about calling her partner, 'I thought about phoning you' (Smith, 2003: 47) – this sixth usage of 'you' is the first that unambiguously refers to a specific, albeit nameless, character – but then is distracted by the tree's beauty, which can be seen from their house, and the remainder of her half of the narrative is an erotic description of the blossom, facts about trees that she has discovered on the internet, and a rainy night time vigil underneath the tree (back in the woman's garden). I have used the pronoun 'she' to refer to this narrator but in fact, as with much of Smith's earlier short fiction, no name or gender markings are given. No name or gender markings are given to the partner either in this story, and the narrative allows this again through use of the pronominal 'you'.

The first, first-person narrator, uses the word 'you' seventeen times. On five occasions it denotes one / anyone. Occasions six and eight to seventeen refer to her partner, the second first-person narrator, but the first narratee. Occasion seven 'the white of the sheets that you bring in from the line in the garden' (Smith, 2003: 47) is ambiguous, it could mean anyone, as anyone can bring in washing that has been hung outside to dry, but it seems to point to the domestic harmony of the two narrators' relationship that is integral to the story, and thus to refer to the second. The first occasion ('I tell you. I fell in love with a tree'), might be both a hailing in of the reader, as we have seen in her earlier stories, and, as we later discover, an address to the second narrator, as she later indicates that she has heard at least part of the first's opening declaration when she records the first narrator's words: '*I fell in love with a tree. I couldn't not*' (Smith, 2003: 53). The second narrator's narrative containing one hundred 'you's starts 'You sit opposite me at the table in the kitchen and tell me you've fallen in love' (Smith, 2003: 52), and as the events of the story are largely those of the first narrator, it is unsurprising that the word 'you' occurs mainly in the second half and that the vast majority of instances (ninety-four of them) refer unambiguously to the first narrator. (Long stretches of the first narrative occurred without any 'you's at all; there are none for almost three pages which detail the effects the tree has upon her.)

The first narrator is infatuated with a tree; her narrative is one of desire and all the emotions attendant on new love, the 'crazy time' that the narrator of 'A Quick One' misses. The second narrator's text is an account of devotion, the patient care borne out of a longstanding relationship – 'I am perfectly within my right to be angry. Instead, I keep things smooth [...] I try to think of the right thing to say'

(Smith, 2003: 53) – and the story ends, when the second narrator joins the first to lie down next to her under the tree. It is, at first, funny (in the sense of humorous, and not serious) that the object of love is a blossoming tree – indeed, even the second narrator thinks so 'All these years we've been together and my only real rival in all this time doesn't even have genitals. I go around for quite a while smiling at my good luck' (Smith, 2003: 53) – but then concedes 'I am such an innocent. I have no idea' (Smith, 2003: 53) when the gravity of the situation is revealed. As a mimetic act, the story could be read as an account of a person's continued care when her partner seems to suffer from some kind of delusion, mental health disorder, but when the second narrator directs the first, and the reader, towards other stories, myths about trees, the you-narrative lifts anchor from its particular referents and drifts towards these intertexts, and the story's concerns seem to be much more purely about two types of love: passion versus longstanding solicitude. Trees recur in Smith's fiction; in *Artful* the narrator works with trees, her partner was an academic inviting the reader to compare the leaves of trees and books and think of a book's origins.

Susan S. Lanser has argued that when a narrator's sex is unmarked, this is a paralepsis (Lanser, 1996: 254); it in fact focuses attention on what is missing, the question of gender, leading the reader to search for textual clues that will pinpoint it and thus also reveal gender prejudices. When I asked my students, who had read 'May' without the author's name attached and isolated from the other stories in the collection, if they had gendered the narrators, for example, one of them thought that the first must be male because 'he' considers going to Homebase to buy a drill, and conversely, another thought that the first must be female because if she was a man, she'd already own a drill. We have seen that Fludernik has noted 'the heterosexual default structure (if A loves B, and A is a man, then B must be a woman)' (Fludernik, 1999: 156). I suggest that in 'May', perhaps even more than in Smith's earlier stories, which can gain some gender attachments from their 'contextual anchoring' within the collections, the use of the second-person pronoun allows such discussions of gender attributes and roles within homosexual or heterosexual relationships and prejudices about them to be sidestepped in favour of focus upon the 'universal' experiences of being in love, and it is the story's inter-texts that particularly insist upon this redirection of attention. Be-cause the object of desire is a tree, we are inclined to read the story as somehow symbolic rather than realist but the first narrator directs against a reading of the tree as metaphor:

> How many times had I passed that tree already in my life, just walked past it and not seen it? I must have walked down that street a thou-sand times, more than a thousand. How many other things had I missed? How many other loves? It didn't matter. Nothing else mat-tered any more. The buds were like the pointed hooves of a herd of tiny deer. The blossom was like – no, it was like nothing but blossom. The leaves, when they came, would be like nothing but leaves. I had never seen a tree more like a tree. It was a relief. (Smith, 2003: 48)

The move away from realism or from mimesis, falling in love with a tree, allows a space for the reader in the story, for 'you' to mean 'me'. The tree can stand for whomever we want, whomever (or whatever?) we desire. But it also suggests, with humour, that it is the emotion or experience of love that is universal, because, after all, the tree is not even given a species; it is a genus and the first narrator's declaration is only as ridiculous, or not, as saying 'I fell in love with a person' would be (that is, at once true, but devoid of convincing particularity). But in removing the gender of the love object, the gender of the subject also becomes irrelevant. We are not snagged by the identification or failure to identify with a homosexual or heterosexual relationship, or, unlike in the case of Jeannette Winterson's *Written on the Body*, which has often been used in discussions of feminist and queer narratology,[5] the working out of which of the narrator's relationships are homo – or heterosexual. The reader can freely identify with either and both nar-rators because, even though the narratees are fictionalized characters in the story, at the level of the word, here, 'you' addresses the reader. While it is true that as Suzanne Keen has claimed, in line with Her-man's discussion of the establishment of 'projection relations', about 'you' narratives, 'the more specific information about the thoughts, actions, and speech of the protagonist accumulates, the less likely these features are to be confused with the reader's' (Keen, 2003: 46), I would argue that the absence of gender markings and the fantastical status of the tree as love object don't prevent the reader from identifying as 'you' either. Lanser claimed that the gender-unmarked narrator or narratee can only be a feature of the shortest of texts, usually poetry or children's rhymes because of the need for particularity, and, of course, Smith's 'you' fictions including this one do not quite extend to novel length (although she uses the technique extensively in *Artful*, *Girl Meets Boy*, and *Hotel World*), but the combination of the tree as love object and the 'you' narrators stretches the possibility quite some way beyond a child's verse.

Smith's story does have particular referents but the story if not universal, addresses a wider group: and the 'you' pronoun partakes of the same logic. It is both inter – and extradiegetic, both homo – and heterosexual. In its appeal to the abstractions of aesthetics (the blossom) and emotions (desire, care and infidelity) it may even go beyond the conventions of sexuality as a basis of monogamous relationships. I am arguing the opposite of Lanser's paralepsis; this absence of gender markings does not draw attention to gender but draws attention to the universality of the experiences of love that Smith reiterates throughout her fiction: 'everyone gets the crazy time' (Smith, 1995: 32), 'true love stories are always interchangeable' (Smith, 1999: 167). The talk of 'true love *stories*' [my emphasis] is a claim to not only the universality of love but also the universality of its narrative existence, the narrativity that 'May' examines: 'I tell you. I fell in love with a tree.' (Smith, 2003: 45). It is a performative statement, it is a recognition of what Literature can do, and it is an elegiac riposte to the depressing finality of Atwood's 'Happy Endings'.

The normative drive associated with universality is repudiated by Smith's tale. It is perhaps queer to fall in love with a tree, but it's a standard practice to read a tree as a symbol for a love object. When the second narrator asks the first what type of a tree it is:

> you went into a huff [...] because what kind it is, you said, waving your arms about in a pure show of panic, is just a random label given by people who need to categorize things, people are far too hung up

on categorization [...] it's the most beautiful tree I've ever seen, that's all I know and all I need to know, I don't need to give it a name, that's the whole point, you said. (Smith, 2003: 55)

It is hard not to bring contextual information to a reading of this humorous passage and see the dialogue as about sexuality or the suitability of any lover as perceived by a concerned relative. It is another example of the story's narratological knowledge.

Prompted by a Greek salad that the first narrator has left her, the second searches the house for the book, presumably Ovid's *Metamorphoses*, that contains the two tree myths that she can remember. The stories are not named but they also describe both types of love; the myth of Baucis and Philemon tells of an old married couple whose generosity to the gods was rewarded by a wish – they requested that when one died, the other should also and when this happened they were turned into intertwining trees, oak and linden. These intertwined trees are a symbol of enduring love and perhaps it is significant that the second narrator finds the book, but cannot find this story in it. The story of Daphne that she does locate is more widely told; Apollo was in love with Daphne who desired not to be caught. Her father enabled her mortal escape by turning her into a tree, but Apollo vowed to tend to the tree and ensure that her leaves remained evergreen. His ardent desire thus turns to enduring care (while poor Daphne, denied agency and sexuality by her father, is left in permanent stasis to endure it).

These myths are intertexts known diegetically. The story's title, however, points to another that is not referred to in the storyworld: Daphne Du Maurier's 1951 short story 'The Apple Tree' is about a man for whom two trees function explicitly as symbols of sexual desire and its absence. This is a rather sinister tale, long and detailed, in which an unnamed male third-person narrator comes to think of an apple tree in his garden as emblematic of his now dead, once dejected wife, Midge (her name is highly suggestive of character traits: a midge is an irritating tiny insect). Another pretty tree reminds him of a landgirl he had desired and almost witlessly caressed in Midge's sight. Late on in the story it is revealed that her name was May and that she is also dead. Deeply troubled by his memories, the narrator decides to chop down the scraggy, dismal tree. He cannot remove its twisted roots and one night returning home, he walks towards the pretty tree to touch its branches, but is caught and trapped by a 'jagged split stump' (Du Maurier, 2004: 159) and dies; effectively the tree representing his nagging wife has killed him. The trees in this story connote the narrator's misogyny, his constrained approach to marriage and to desire. By contrast, although 'May' is also about infidelity, through the deployment of 'you', the story does not offer a view of gender relations in contemporary society.

Smith's story may also remind readers of another famous short fiction with an infidelity and a tree (there are many!). Smith is a known admirer of Katherine Mansfield and the influence of 'Bliss' is apparent. This tale, like 'May', starts with the protagonist's attempts to communicate an almost inexpressible, inexplicable emotion of bliss, but ends with a sharp poignancy as Bertha realizes that her new friend with whom she has fallen in love 'as she always did fall in love with beautiful women who had something strange about them' (Mansfield, 2001: 95) is having an affair with her husband. The reader shares the shock of this ending with Bertha since the story has recounted a moment of bliss that she and Pearl Fulton shared when admiring the beautiful pear tree in Bertha's garden. When Bertha cries 'Oh, what is going to happen now?' (Mansfield, 2001: 105) upon discovery of the infidelity, the pear tree remains 'as lovely as ever and as full of flower and as still' (Mansfield, 2001: 105). The tree stands out as a totem of constancy and beauty in a story full of uncertainty; we are never quite sure whose infidelity causes Bertha to suffer – Pearl's or her husbands? – or what the future of Bertha's troubled relationships will be. Upper-class convention has prevented her from time with her baby and until the evening of the dinner party, she has felt no physical desire for her husband.

The two other stories in *The Whole Story and Other Stories* that have 'you' narrators could easily be about the couple in 'May'. They are both about a domestic relationship and follow the now familiar template of each character, unnamed, ungendered, being given a share of the narrative to give their version of events. The story that precedes 'May', 'Being Quick' – an allusion to and pun on the idiom 'the quick and the dead' – is one of loss: loss of life and sanity. On the way home from London, a suicide on the line causes the first narrator's train to be cancelled, her mobile phone has died so she calls from a phone box in the middle of the night to say that she is in a supermarket and is walking home. In conversation with the first, the second narrator seems initially practical and unperturbed but then recounts her own evening of anguish at wondering what has happened. The final story in the collection, 'The Start of Things' (the one that might be about January) is about a (their?) failing relationship; 'It was the end and we both knew it' (Smith, 2003: 167). There are three segments to this story; in the central italicized section it is not clear which of the narrators is speaking but the narrator recalls *the time last summer that you fell in love and it wasn't with me*' (Smith, 2003: 171); was it with a tree? In the ensuing discussion about what to do about their relationship, the first narrator is tricked outside to the shed to collect logs for a fire (do they symbolize the death of the love object in 'May', the hawthorn tree?) and then locked out of the house by the second. However, the story ends once the heat of the row has cooled and the second narrator wonders why she was so angry and whether she should rescue her lover from the shed or stay indoors and run a bath. Her decision is certain for her but uncertain for the reader: 'I stood at the door with the key in my hand and of course I decided yes' (Smith, 2003: 178).

Although *Other Stories and Other Stories* doesn't contain a story called 'Other Stories', and there is no single fiction titled 'The Whole Story' in *The Whole Story and Other Stories*, in the 2008 collection *The First Person and Other Stories* the final tale in a countdown that also includes 'The Third Person' and 'The Second Person' is 'The First Person'. The stories are narrated as their titles suggest, although 'The First Person' has 'you' narration in it and 'The Second Person' has 'I' in it, as if to show the multiplicity of forms of 'you' narration. As in the earlier collections, the stories with 'you' (also including 'No Exit' and 'Astute Fiery Luxurious') each concern communication and the recall of memories or weaving of new fantasies in a relationship between an unnamed, ungendered couple. The switches between nar-

rators and 'you/I' narration of 'The Second Person' make it quite difficult to read; this confusion such as the fact that each partner uses the
words which open and close the story of the other 'You're something
else, you. You really are' (Smith, 2008: 121, 134) implies the shared
intimacy of the long-standing but now separated couple (one partner might be in a new relationship in their former house). The story
presents an argument in which one narrator describes the way she
feels her ex-partner sees her and accuses the ex-partner of arrogance
in making such assumptions. The scene that she has imagined her
partner imagining is of her buying two accordions on impulse, without being able to play them. A twist in the tale occurs when, having
returned to her flat, a parcel arrives and we share the narrator's belief
that it contains an accordion. Her arrogance or storytelling became a
prediction; her ex-partner has extravagantly and impulsively bought
the instrument, but the ex-partner was also right in her judgement
of the narrator's presumptions. Instead of a note declaring that the
second accordion would be with the ex-partner, which is what she
desires and presumes, the note states 'You're something else, you. You
really are' (Smith, 2008: 134). The final story in the collection, 'The
First Person', is about a new relationship; it could easily be the partner who has kept the house in the earlier story. The narrator tells her
partner 'You're not the first person I've ever gone to bed with so many
times in one day' (Smith, 2008: 205) and continues with a sequence
of statements beginning 'You're not the first person' but concluding
'But you're the one right now' (Smith, 2008: 206).

Recounted like this, Smith's commitment to developing second-
person narration is striking. After the first collection, these 'you' stories do not contain gender markings for either or any figure in the
relationship. I have suggested that this allows the reader to develop an
intimacy, to establish dense 'projection relations' not so much with
the characters themselves but their situation and experiences of love
and domestic relationships. Read together, the stories can be regarded as charting the ups and downs of one relationship; there are stages
that anyone could relate to. The stories cannot be described as realist
or straightforwardly mimetic; it is precisely the playful, metafictional

and metaleptical qualities of the stories that allow intimacy, connections to be formed.

Notes

1 See for example *So I Am Glad* by A. L. Kennedy, 'Once in Lifetime' by Jhumpa Lahiri, Diane Schoemperlen's 2008 *At a Loss for Words* (sometimes also subtitled *A Post-Romantic Novel*). *The Malady of Death* is an earlier and troubling example by Marguerite Duras.

2 that is 'the resources of language that anchor it to essential points in context' (Herman, 2002: 332).

3 She has also written plays including *The Seer* in 2001.

4 This is also known as 'Lanser's rule' after the groundbreaking work on feminist narratology undertaken by Susan S. Lanser.

5 See Fludernik (1999), Lanser (1996).

Works Cited

Atwood, Margaret (1994) 'Happy Endings', in *Good Bones and Simple Murders*, pp. 50–6. New York: Doubleday.

Beckett, Samuel (1958) *The Unnamable*. London: Grove Press.

Calvino, Italo (1982) *If on a Winter's Night a Traveller*, trans. William Weaver. London: Picador.

Duras, Marguerite (1986). *The Malady of Death*, trans. Barbara Bray. New York: Grove/Atlantic.

Du Maurier, Daphne (2004) *The Bird and Other Stories*. London: Virago.

Fludernik, Monika (1999) 'The Genderization of Narrative', *GRAAT* 21: 153–75.

Fludernik, Monika (2011) '*You* and *We* Narrative-Multiplicity', in Greta Olson (ed.) *Current Trends in Narratology*, pp. 101–41. Berlin: De Gruyter.

Herman, David (2002) *Story Logic: Problems and Possibilities of Narratives*. Lincoln and London: University of Nebraska Press.

Keen, Suzanne (2003) *Narrative Form*. Houndmills: Palgrave Macmillan.

Kennedy, A. L. (1995) *So I Am Glad*. London: Random House.

Lahiri, Jhumpa (2008) 'Once in a Lifetime', in *Unaccustomed Earth*, pp. 223–51. London: Bloomsbury.

Lanser, Susan S. (1996) 'Queering Narratology', in Kathy Mezei (ed.) *Ambiguous Discourse: Feminist Narratology and British Women Writers*, pp. 250–61. Chapel Hill: University of North Carolina Press.

McInerney, Jay (1984) *Bright Lights, Big City*. New York: Vintage.

Mansfield, Katherine (2001) 'Bliss', in *The Collected Stories*, pp. 91–105. London: Penguin.

Moore, Lorrie (2008) *Self Help, The Collected Stories*, pp. 535–665. London: Faber and Faber.

Schoemperlen, Diane (2008) *At a Loss for Words: A Post-Romantic Novel*. Toronto: Harper Collins.

Smith, Ali (1995) *Free Love and Other Stories*. London: Virago.

Smith, Ali (1999) *Other Stories and Other Stories*. London: Granta.

Smith, Ali (2001) *The Seer*. London: Faber and Faber.

Smith, Ali (2001) *Hotel World*. London: Hamish Hamilton.

Smith, Ali (2003) *The Whole Story and Other Stories*. London: Hamish Hamilton.

Smith, Ali (2005) *The Accidental*. London: Hamish Hamilton.

Smith, Ali (2007) *Girl Meets Boy*. Edinburgh: Canongate.

Smith, Ali (2007) *Like*. London: Virago.

Smith, Ali (2008) *The First Person and Other Stories*. London: Hamish Hamilton.

Smith, Ali (2011) *There But For The*. London: Hamish Hamilton.

Smith, Ali (2012) *Artful*. London: Hamish Hamilton.

Wilson, Sharon Rose (2003) *Textual Assassinations: Recent Poetry and Fiction*. Columbus: The Ohio State University Press.

Winterson, Jeanette (1992) *Written on the Body*. London: Jonathan Cape.

WHAT NO'UN ALIVE UND'STANDS
DAVID MITCHELL'S TWENTY-FIRST-CENTURY
RECONTEXTUALIZATION OF ORAL CULTURE

Dorothy Butchard

In the central section of his 2004 novel, *Cloud Atlas*, David Mitchell portrays a post-cataclysmic community eking out survival in a disaster-struck future version of Hawaii. This tiny tribe of 'Valleysmen' has been shaken generations previously by what they term 'the Fall', a cataclysmic global event that has wiped out the bulk of humanity. In a newly primitive, necessarily survivalist society, writing is revered as key to a lost civilization, a half-forgotten former time referred to as 'the Civ'lize'. Books are revered as a relic of the 'Smart' of 'Old'Un times' (*CA*, 284), treasured by a newly superstitious society as evidence of past heights of learning and technological prowess. Such reference to vestiges of a past civilization is a relatively familiar trope within speculative fiction, and Mitchell has acknowledged his 'debt' (Mitchell, 2005: 47) to other literary representations of post-cataclysmic societies, in particular the linguistic portrayal of a future version of language in Russell Hoban's 1982 novel, *Riddley Walker*. Mitchell's representation of storytelling in the central sections of *Cloud Atlas* combines conventional perceptions of oral culture with speculation on the nature of language and society in a pre- and post-cataclysmic context. Contrasting the uncertainties of the fictionalized oral narration in the central and final phase of *Cloud Atlas* with its representation of pristine recorded language of texts preserved from 'pre-Fall' society, Mitchell invokes a series of significant cultural assumptions aligning literacy with notions of the 'civilized' and 'civilization', and an unrecorded storytelling tradition with 'primitive' society. Examining how these concepts function in terms of the portrayed society's loss of knowledge and information, this chapter will discuss the ramifications of this depiction for both the fictional world of *Cloud Atlas* and Mitchell's assumed readership of concerned twenty-first-century literary consumers.

Cloud Atlas comprises six distinct narratives arranged by chronological time period, each marked by a unique narrative style. Opening with the nineteenth-century 'Pacific Journal of Adam Ewing', the six phases of *Cloud Atlas* are differentiated by tics of visual formatting, vernacular, and historical period. Each section is conceived as representative of a conventional narrative genre: journal, epistle, pulp novel, memoir, interview. The sections in the first half of the novel end abruptly, mid-sentence in the first case, to be reprised in inverse order for the second half. In this cascading structure, the sixth and central section is the only undivided story. It is also the last in terms of the narrative's chronological progress. Titled 'Sloosha's Crossin' an' Ev'rythin' After', the tale is posited as a first-person oral narrative, describing the experiences of 'Zachry', a teenager who witnesses the destruction of the last repository of textual objects retained from the days of 'the Civ'lize' – ''razed, yay, the last books an' the last clock' (*CA*, 313).

When recreating the environment of a pseudo-oral culture in the centrepiece to *Cloud Atlas*, David Mitchell is careful to establish several facets integral to conventional notions of oral storytelling tradition. In doing so, he diverges from his representation of encounters with text and storytelling modes elsewhere in the novel and across his oeuvre. In her discussion of 'diegetic readers' in *Cloud Atlas*, Courtney Hopf notes the importance of narrators who 'perform' their particular mode of storytelling:

> David Mitchell's novels are populated with readers and writers who draw special attention to their narration: rather than just relaying

'what happens', his narrators perform their discourse, always empha-
sising the process of storytelling as a transformative act. (Hopf, 2011:
107)

Hopf's focus on inscribed texts is betrayed in her concentration on
'readers and writers' in this citation, and her article presents a compelling account of Mitchell's depiction of fictional and fictionalized
readers. In each ensuing chronological phase of *Cloud Atlas*, the new
section's protagonist encounters a remnant of the text from the previous section. Hopf (2011: 111) describes these encounters as 'acts of
consumption' whereby the 'influence of each text' is 'felt tangentially'
by the ensuing fictional reader. As I will demonstrate, however, 'Sloosha's Crossin'' also complicates and reconfigures such a process of
'consumption', challenging the reader/writer relationship by portray-
ing a more complex form of 'textual' encounter. 'Sloosha's Crossin''
represents a conscious move away from the realm of the written word
to portray a complex version of primary oral culture. Though still contained within the written novel, this section uses peculiarities of form
and language to recreate an environment in which spoken storytelling
has taken precedence over literate forms, although its practitioners
and audience remain aware of the pre-existence of recorded texts.

Although portrayed as being in the process of becoming a predominantly oral culture, the communities described in the central
section of *Cloud Atlas* are by no means divorced from the influence
of written texts. Mitchell does not invoke the notion of a pristine oral
culture of the kind found in, for example, anthropological accounts of
cultures that have never encountered reading or writing. Instead, the
oral storyteller of 'Sloosha's Crossin'' dwells extensively on descriptions of texts, recounting past examples of reading and writing. In this
account, however, 'old books' (*CA*, 276) are characterized as relics
of the past, affording limited cognitive access to 'pre-Fall' things and
concepts. Books function as incomplete providers of historical information, whose consumption offers an estimation of how things may
have once been, but are effectively disowned as the product of a previous culture. The place of storytelling in this imagined future world
is in oral delivery, with tales recounted entirely from memory. Our

narrator describes himself as part of a network of 'Storymen', commenting that 'most' of his 'yarnin's' have been gleaned from a network
of established tale-tellers, or as he phrases it, 'scavved off other Storymen' (*CA*, 259). The narrator also allows for the adjustment and
alteration of stories with each retelling, introduces the notion of the
passing of stories between generations, and draws attention both to
his audience and to the time elapsing as the story is told. '[B]y'n'by,
if the fire don't dozy you to sleep, I'll be telling you...', he promises
his listeners, marking the progress of his tale as it unfolds. 'My yarn's
nearly done'n'telled now', he declares on the penultimate page of
'Sloosha's Crossin'' – though the broader 'yarn' of *Cloud Atlas* is only
halfway through.

The introduction of this narrator's listening audience is a vital factor in Mitchell's establishment of his central section's pseudo-oral
nature. The first-person narrative of 'Sloosha's Crossin'' succinctly
announces the presence of a fictional listenership in its opening paragraph. 'Gimme some mutton an' I'll tell you 'bout our first meetin'',
the narrator declares, clarifying his request for 'a fat joocesome slice,
none o'your burnt wafery off'rins' (*CA*, 249). The direct address
neatly conflates the physical presence of both a hungry narrator and
his mutton-donating audience. It also establishes a community of exchange, implying the willingness of listeners to barter food for a story.
In doing so, it echoes the consciously nostalgic notion of oral storytelling found in Walter Benjamin's 1936 essay 'The Storyteller', where
'a man listening to a story is in the company of the storyteller' (Benjamin, 1936: 99) and the environment for the tale is predicated upon
a willing 'community of listeners' (Benjamin, 1936: 90). Indeed, for
Benjamin the unique aspects of the oral tale involve its capacity to
counter solitude, through the companionship of a shared experience.

The companionship of a 'community of listeners' implies a shared
environment, and Mitchell's introduction of our narrator and his listenership's corporeal presence also serves to define and characterize
the environment which has produced the tale. A request for 'mutton'
conjures a community whose food is plain, limited to necessity. Nevertheless this limited food has the capacity to be 'joocesome' (*CA*,
249), in an example of one of Mitchell's many neologisms in this

section, conflating the senses of 'juicy' and 'wholesome'. Such plain nutrition, combined with the implied willingness to barter food for a story, marks a stark contrast with this section's predecessor in the novel, the dystopian 'Orison of Sonmi'. In the advanced consumerist 'pre-Fall' world described by Sonmi, foodstuffs consist of processed fast food served by a highly organised system of slavery and consumerism, or the sinister supplement 'Soap', a drugged substance used to control the behaviour of cloned workers.

Hélène Machinal (2011: 142) has suggested that the 'primitive society' portrayed in 'Sloosha's Crossin'' is 'positioned as the opposite of the posthuman commodity-fetishism model' found in the preceding section:

> Zachry's tribe takes us back to the genesis of value in labour-time, that is to say, to the importance of a straightforward relation between production and consumption. (CA, 142)

In this statement Machinal refers to the 'Valleysmen' described in Zachry's story – a different tribe from the one that comprises our narrator's fictional audience. Yet the narrator's reference to mutton, bartering and a 'community of listeners' clustered around a fire not only supports Machinal's conception of this new future as 'primitive', but also extends notions of the 'straightforward relation' between production and consumption out of the realm of the recounted story and into the very act of storytelling itself. In Benjamin's (1936: 82) version of oral tradition, storytelling is similarly figured as an 'exchange' between teller and listener, taking place in an environment which is explicitly non-urban and anti-industrial. For Benjamin, the 'web in which the gift of storytelling is cradled' is that of boredom and repetitive tasks, the literal 'weaving and spinning' (Benjamin, 1936: 91) of a listening community – a state which he considers to be 'extinct in the cities and ... declining in the country' (Benjamin, 1936: 90). As in Benjamin's conception of simple communal environments as the natural context for an oral tradition, the 'yarnin'' portrayed in 'Sloosha's Crossin'' is underpinned by the demand of a 'community of listeners' whose physical presence is portrayed as a vital factor in the practice and propagation of the storyteller's art, and who are defined in terms of their lack of technological sophistication.

The keen consumption of a meat that the contemporary reader might be expected to associate with peasantry and relative hardship is the first intimation of a theme destined to emerge with increasing urgency as the section unfolds: 'Sloosha's Crossin'' depicts humanity's return to a culture of scarcity, stripped to essentials. This sense of reduction to pure necessity extends to Mitchell's selection of the oral tale as the narrative style of this section. The spoken nature of the story told in 'Sloosha's Crossin'' is not portrayed as based on nostalgia, nor an urge to find the companionship of a listening community. Instead it is a necessity, borne out of the final destruction of literate culture – the loss of 'the last books' (*CA*, 313). Within the fictional context, the story is spoken aloud because recorded and/or written language is no longer a practical possibility; the narrator's tale looks back from the stance of a now bookless environment, recounting the process by which that state was reached. Mitchell's invocation of the oral tale as the necessary narrative form for a community no longer privileged to consume the luxuries of 'civilization' is thus both prompted by and elaborated through repeated reminders of the constraints or 'primitivism' of the speaker's environment, whose state of necessity is further removed from the time of the events it describes.

This further remove leads to a heightened sense of estrangement in the scenes described, as the narrator recounts objects and events familiar or at least conceptually manageable to the reader, but without full comprehension himself. This is compounded by the narrator's constant expectation that his ever-present 'community of listeners' will understand even less. In part this is due to a fundamental loss of vocabulary, whereby broken links in a process of associative naming lead to an inability to comprehend or describe. This factor extends to Zachry's inability to recount his own tale; he uses his own voice as a point of reference, but only to form comparisons between his own cognitive capacities and the past that he attempts to articulate. 'Describin' such Smart ain't easy', he confesses to his audience when trying to recount a trip to an 'observ'tree' in the heights of Big I:

Gear there was what we ain't mem'ried on Ha-Why so its names ain't mem'ried neither... almost nothin' in there could I cogg. (*CA*, 290).

The narrator's emphasis on a loss of vocabulary – the inability to 'und'stand' a voice or object inherited from a past civilization – is symptomatic of the confluence of familiarity and estrangement that characterizes 'Sloosha's Crossin''. Throughout the section, elements which the reader knows or can construe are problematized by Zachry's inability to fully interpret or describe them. In addition, the style and diction constitute a carefully constructed illusion of *estranged* language, where literary devices are used with the aim of faithfully representing oral speech while retaining readability and familiarity. The tale aims to approximate the possibility of the 'lost trace' while remaining fully interpretable. As a result, it is a far less radically estranging text than some other efforts at conceiving of a future version of language, of which possibly the greatest example is Russell Hoban's 1980 novel *Riddley Walker*.

Mitchell acknowledged a 'specific debt' to Hoban's novel in 2005, noting that it provided 'evidence that what I wanted to do could be done' in his attempt to represent 'a dialect that was the result of decades of linguistic continental drift':

> Like the characters in the novel's other time zones, I wanted [Zachry's] narrative to use period speech. For this, I needed a dialect that was the result of decades of linguistic continental drift and was studded with onomatopoeia and puns. Zachry's voice is less hard-core and more Pacific than Riddleyspeak, but Mr Hoban's singular, visionary, ingenious, uncompromising, glorious, angelic and demonic novel sat on my shelf as evidence that what I wanted to do could be done, and as encouragement to keep going until I'd got it right. (Mitchell, 2005: 47)

There are several illuminating strands to this statement, not least Mitchell's categorization of Zachry's speech as 'dialect'. Whereas *Riddley Walker* is radical in its abandonment of most forms of punctuation and wildly inventive in its creation of neologisms, in *Cloud Atlas* the shade of 'standard English' haunts each and every line, where

Zachry's 'broken English' is distinguished, in Mark Abley's words, by 'verbal truncation and amputation'. For Abley (2008: 207), these 'words have reverted to a future past', an impression that is marked by the insistent annotation of dropped letters and elided phonemes. In Zachry's tale, the governing methodology for conveying linguistic difference lies in (mis)spelling, dropped letters, grammatical adjustments and, particularly, the addition of the epithet '-some' to form adjectives ('lornsome' [*CA*, 254], 'joocesome' [*CA*, 273]). Most of the apparently 'new' nouns in Zachry's vocabulary are also formed from well-known verbs, such as 'spiker' for knife *or* spear, while others are unfamiliar combinations of familiar morphemes, 'lardbird', 'redscab', 'mukelung' (*CA*, 252). Most significantly, a key element of this limited defamiliarization of language is the use of additional punctuation to mark the elision of vowels and consonants. The apostrophe plays a vital role in distancing Zachry's 'speech' from the reader's linguistic comfort zone, while functioning as a persistent visual reminder of the distance between this supposedly 'broken' language of the imagined future and the reader's own realm of knowledge and expectation. Each lost phoneme is commemorated by an apostrophe, and such literary stigmata inundate the page almost to the point of distraction. As a result, Zachry's 'dialect' is continually marked by loss and reduction, rather than the kind of innovative new connotations which emerge in Hoban's *Riddley Walker*.

In *Riddley Walker*, the protagonist is expressly *writing* his experiences, recording them for posterity in a consciously historical and educative act. In the tale recounted as 'Sloosha's Crossin' An Ev'rything After', by contrast, there is no suggestion that this story might survive in anything other than oral form. It describes a small tribe of 'Valleysmen' who are themselves perched on the cusp of illiteracy. Books and reading are venerated as the barely comprehensible key to a lost age of information, the 'Smart' of the 'Old'Uns'. The 'Abbess', practical and spiritual leader of this community, is distinguished by her literacy and is responsible for imparting this skill to children born in the Valley. While protagonist Zachry cheerfully confides his own difficulties with studying, confessing he'd 'not much smart in school'ry learnin'' (*CA*, 313), he is fiercely proud of his younger sister Catkin's facility with literacy, and worshipful in his description of the community's slender library. This 'school'ry' is 'touched with the holy mist'ry o' the Civ'lised Days', its windows' glass miraculously 'still unbusted since the Fall' (*CA*, 313). However, although still nominally functional, Zachry's tribe's repository o' the Civ'lised is a fragile relic, threatened by decay:

> Ev'ry book in the Valleys sat on them shelfs ... saggy'n'wormy they was gettin' but, yay, they was books an' words o' knowin'! (*CA*, 313)

For the Valleysmen, these School'ry books, along with their own cherished literacy, represent a slender thread of connection with a past that they venerate for its technological supremacy. They are a reminder of a time that protagonist Zachry imagines as a utopia of knowledge and capacity, glowing in comparison with his own beleaguered community as it struggles to maintain survival.

Zachry's sense of the inferiority of the society he inhabits and the loss of the 'Smart' of 'Civ'lise' haunts his account of events in 'Sloosha's Crossin''. Our protagonist has reconstructed a version of the past world discovered through the remains of books still available to his community. Describing his 'maginin's o' places from old books'n'pics in the school'ry' (*CA*, 284), Zachry's rhetoric exults in size, prowess and power: 'towns bigger'n'all o' Big I, an' towers an' stars'n'suns blazin' higher'n Mauna Kea' (*CA*, 284). These descriptions also emphasize what Zachry's tribe now lacks – ease and plenty – in their practical nostalgia for 'Smart boxes what make delish grinds more'n'any'un can eat, Smart pipes what gush more brew'n'any'un can drink' (*CA*, 284). Suffused with a sense of loss and incapacity, the Valleysmen of Zachry's tribe deify relics of the past while struggling to survive in the present. Yet Mitchell's portrayal of this neo-primitive society also emphasizes a sense of community that has become close-knit in the face of struggle. Zachry may be critical of his tribe, but it also represents the closest *Cloud Atlas* comes to offering a compromise between the greed and suffering inflicted by advanced civilization – portrayed throughout the novel and most starkly in the preceding 'Orison of Sonmi' – and the outright 'savag'ry' of neighbouring tribe the 'Kona', who are ultimately responsible for the annihilation of Zachry's Valleysmen.

The battle between the violent, colonizing Kona and Zachry's peaceful Valleysmen recalls other fictional representations in which a relatively enlightened group of individuals attempt to preserve the final remnants of a mostly destroyed culture, against the forces of others who display conventional signs of unexpurgated savagery. Like the 'savage' groups or peoples depicted in, for example, Ursula Le Guin's *Always Coming Home*, Russell Hoban's *Riddley Walker* or, more recently, Cormac McCarthy's *The Road*, the Kona are uninterested in retaining or reviving knowledge from a civilized past. Instead they engage in the vicarious and vicious pursuit of instant gratification, gradually establishing power by enslaving and even consuming individuals from other tribes. A strictly postcolonial reading of *Cloud Atlas* would have much to say about the blunt characterization of the Kona as a primitive warlike tribe, engaging in cannibalism, self-mutilation and bloodshed. In this discussion, however, I am most interested in the implications of Mitchell's portrayal of the role of books and literacy as a means of dividing between 'civilized' and 'savage' peoples. It is as a direct result of the tribe's peacefulness, figuratively connected with their partial literacy and devotion to preserving the pre-Fall books they have inherited, that they are singled out for the anthropological interest of Meronym, a character who arrives as another symbol of a last vestige of civilization. Meronym is a 'Prescient', hailing from an ark-like ship which 's'vived all the flashbangin' an' the Fall' (*CA*, 258). Populated by a cult who foresaw and escaped the cataclysmic combination of disease and warfare that appears to have constituted the Fall, the 'Great Ship o' the Prescients' nevertheless emerges as another vulnerable relic of past times, which like the 'school'ry', has been destroyed by the end of Zachry's tale.

The encounter between Meronym, Zachry and the tribe of Valleysmen is figured as explicitly anthropological in nature. Indeed, it appears to draw on anthropological details of encounter with 'primitive' societies, as in Zachry's proud assertion that the Prescients agree to barter with his tribe because of their own 'Civ'lize':

[O]nly us Valleysmen got 'nuf civilise for the Prescients, yay. They din't want no barter with no barbarians what thinked the Ship was a mighty white bird god or sumthin'! (*CA*, 258)

What distinguishes the Valleysmen from the 'barbarians', as Meronym expressly states, is their aspiration to 'Smart', exemplified in their willingness to read and write (*CA*, 258). This anthropological stance is emphasized further by the scholarly distance Meronym initially retains from her indigenous hosts. This is partly because, as she puts it, Prescients 'vow not to interfere in no nat'ral order o' things' (*CA*, 279). The academic nature of Meronym's project becomes clear when Zachry begs her to use her more advanced medical technology to save his dying sister. Agreeing, she mutters 'if my pres'dent ever finded out, my hole faculty'd be disbandied' (*CA*, 281). Zachry passes no comment on this except for noting his lack of understanding of the words he faithfully reports: 'times was she used hole flocks o' words what I din't know' (*CA*, 281). However the statement, evidently included by Mitchell for the reader's benefit, clearly aligns Meronym with anthropological projects of the twentieth century, which aimed to capture and record the experiences of 'primitive' tribes threatened by the seeping expansion of global notions of 'civilization'. The irony here is that although Meronym's rhetoric is that of the scholarly anthropologist, it transpires that her true impulse is an evaluation of the Valleysmen's tribe as a potential home to absorb her own threatened troupe of Prescients, in a project which is simultaneously colonial and (for now) non-interventionist.

Mitchell's representation of the linguistic and social elements of oral culture is both painstakingly executed and carefully considered. It is also fraught with difficult implications. In choosing to give 'Sloosha's Crossin'' the form of an oral tale – crucially, one in which language has degenerated – David Mitchell invokes a Western cultural tradition, reaching back through Lévi-Strauss to Rousseau, which has long associated 'orality' with the 'primitive'. This draws upon a traditional Western conception of oral culture and storytelling that problematically views oral systems of transferring and preserving cultural capital as cognitively and conceptually inferior to those of writing. Indeed, this notion of inferiority or reduction in the oral form is a factor which Mitchell invokes as a deliberate narrative strategy, employing it as a means of emphasizing the distance between his narrator's world and that of his own presumptive literate audience.

In *The Muse Learns to Write: Reflections on Orality and Literacy from Antiquity to the Present*, Eric Havelock noted how 'the term 'primitive' by its pejorative sense masked an unwillingness to recognize orality as a formative social process' (Havelock, 1986: 36). Havelock's summary of several phases of Western civilization's approach to oral culture suggests 'the romantic and extravagant value' placed by Rousseau on '"natural", that is "savage" speech (which today we would interpret as strictly oral speech)' (Havelock, 1986: 36), before moving to consider the domination of literacy during the nineteenth century and later. From this point on, Havelock (1986: 38) judges, 'if you did not read and write you were, culturally speaking, a nonperson'. Havelock's analysis of aggressively literate cultural environments as ones in which illiteracy might consign an individual to the status of 'nonperson', at least in terms of cultural engagement, is significant for Mitchell's depiction of the social and cultural role of writing and reading in *Cloud Atlas*. Zachry and his listenership are not the only examples of deliberate or unwitting non-readers in Mitchell's work. In the opening section, Adam Ewing recounts the history of Autua, a stowaway escaping Moriori slave. Unlike Zachry's testimony – which the reader encounters as if it is itself an anthropological document, a dialect precisely transcribed – Ewing entirely rephrases the tale of this 'savage'. 'His pidgin delivered his tale brokenly', Ewing explains, 'so its substance only shall I endeavour to set down here' (*CA*, 30). The reference to 'broken' speech recurs; Autua is castigated by a slave owner for his 'broken language' (*CA*, 32), an 'impure' version of Maori. Like Zachry, Autua is a natural storyteller: 'Days, I yarned tales of Maui to birds, & birds yarned sea-tales to I' (*CA*, 33), but his inability to inscribe his own tale means that its recording is interpolated, recast and altered by its reporter. Ewing adds details interpolated by himself – 'when he was ten years old (?)' (*CA*, 33) – and Autua's putative voice disappears in all but Ewing's reports of his direct speech, where he responds to his interlocuter's questions.

Among Mitchell's portraits of the relationship between (il)literacy and self-expression in *Cloud Atlas*, perhaps the most striking is found in the futuristic world portrayed in the chapter preceding 'Sloosha's Crossin''. 'The Orison of Sonmi ~451' quite literally recounts the transition of an individual from the status of 'nonperson' to 'person' – a process of 'Ascension' which is instigated by, and detailed in terms of, her progress from the status of illiterate drone to sensitive literate intellectual. Sonmi's initial 'Ascension' begins when she is given a children's book, which her fellow clone believes to show 'outside, as it really is' (*CA*, 197). Initially, Sonmi can only 'read the pictures' (*CA*, 197), and her recollection portrays characters familiar to Mitchell's twenty-first-century reader as fairy tales – 'ugly sisters', 'a white witch', and the seven dwarfs recast as 'seven half-sized fabricants carrying strange cutlery behind a girl in a white skirt' (*CA*, 197). This is a printed text in a world of digital reading devices; when Sonmi wonders why the pictures don't move, her co-conspirater, Yoona, sweetly speculates that the book is 'broken' (*CA*, 197), a supposition which prefigures the book's actual fate, ripped up before their eyes by the fabricants' overseer. As the tale unfolds, Sonmi's ethical and intellectual progress is portrayed as achieved through avid consumption of literature, film, and philosophy via an electronic reading device given to her by a fellow fabricant, Wing~027. For Wing, reading is explicitly figured as the key to knowledge:

I asked, how is knowledge found?
'You must learn how to read, little sister,' he said. (*CA*, 216)

Learning to read, Sonmi describes herself as 'a starving servant at a banquet' (*CA*, 216). 'My appetite deepened as I dined', she informs her Archivist, adding 'we are only what we know' (*CA*, 216).

The emphasis on reading as the key to knowledge, and account of the sheer quantity of information it affords Sonmi, underpins the section which enfolds 'Sloosha's Crossin'' within the structure of *Cloud Atlas*. However, writing does not feature in Sonmi's story. Like Zachry's tale in 'Sloosha's Crossin'', Sonmi's account of her experiences is also depicted as spoken aloud, albeit in an interview intended to be recorded and stored in a digital archive. Unlike the portrayal of Zachry's vividly self-governing spoken performance, Sonmi's sombre testimony is recorded by an interlocutor, the 'Archivist', who poses a series of questions, recording her replies for the anticipated benefit of 'historians still unborn' (*CA*, 187). This reference, which Sonmi reprises as she ends her testimony by sardonically delegating further interpretation to 'future historians' (*CA*, 366), places the representation of recorded oral testimony in the context of notions of cultural posterity. The promise of future generations' access to personal experience through recorded or repeated storytelling runs throughout *Cloud Atlas*, but becomes especially dominant in these two oral testimonies at the novel's heart. Both sections portray the repetition of personal experiences, framed with the express purpose of contributing to the knowledge of future generations. Indeed, we learn in 'Sloosha's Crossin'' that Sonmi's testimony has been reproduced and reconsidered by generations subsequent to her own; after the end of her 'short'n'judased life', her testimony has been able to 'find say-so over purebloods 'n' freakbirths' thinkin's' (*CA*, 290).

In contrast with the oral story imagined in the central phase of *Cloud Atlas*, 'The Orison of Sonmi~451' is aligned with the kind of act of permanent archiving conventionally associated with the written text. The testimony has been preserved intact, although any potential historians now being born may be unable to understand its significance – a point to which I will return. The physical survival of this recorded performance complicates the kinds of divisions between literacy and orality theorized by Walter Ong in *Orality and Literacy: The Technologizing of the Word*. In his controversial work, which has prompted much debate since its first publication, Ong contrasts oral and literate cultures by characterizing the 'perishable' and 'essentially evanescent' nature of sound (Ong, 1982: 32) as 'an event, a moment in time' that lacks 'the thing-like repose of the written or printed word' (Ong, 1982: 75). For Ong (1982: 80), the 'rigid visual fixity' of the text 'assures its endurance and its potential for being resurrected into limitless living contexts by a potentially infinite number of living readers'. In Ong's view, this 'fixity' and 'endurance' of the written word offers an objective temporal advantage which ensures the 'limitless' potential resonances of the text; from this he extrapolates the capacity to read and re-read as directly related to the progress of civilization. Although Sonmi's oral testimony is not a written text, in *Cloud Atlas* its recorded nature affords precisely the kind of 'thing-like repose' which Ong describes. This is in direct contrast to the 'evanescent' tale of 'Sloosha's Crossin'', where Zachry's story is presented as ephemeral, changeable, and possibly even untrue. In a disorienting twist at the end of the section, it transpires that our narrator is not recalling his own experiences, but rather a tale recounted to him by his long-dead father. Like Autua's, then, Zachry's testimony cannot survive except in the mouths of others, retold and perhaps altered in the telling.

Mitchell's portrayal of the descendant storyteller and the inherited tale again recalls conventions associated with the formation of an oral storytelling tradition. Benjamin's characterization of oral storytelling portrays a process relying on 'memory' where storytelling is 'always the art of *repeating* stories' (Benjamin, 1936: 97). This depicts oral tradition as a web of interconnected and reciprocal narratives that allow interpretive tales to be transmitted across generations. In terms of cultural posterity, this is an important factor: passed 'from generation to generation', tales within an oral tradition are flexible enough to adjust to new listenerships yet ensure that the propagated story may remain grounded, as John Tosh (1984: 318) puts it, in 'description of actions and events as they were experienced in life'. Yet the newly revealed son-of-Zachry casts doubt on any illusions of an intrinsically reliable oral testimony by noting that 'most o' Pa's yarnin's was jus' musey duck-fartin'" (*CA*, 324). Although our narrator adds the dubious affidavit that this particular tale is 'mostly true, I reck'n' (*CA*, 324), the contrast between this messy, musey oral tale and the pristine recorded story of Sonmi is clear.

The factor of adaptation and reinterpretation emerges in *Cloud Atlas* through the determination of the narrator of 'Sloosha's Crossin'' that objects and things should be carefully described, even if they cannot be fully comprehended. Sonmi's testimony follows the example of Anthony Burgess's use of neologisms in *A Clockwork Orange*, or William Gibson's refusal to interpret words for his reader in *Neuromancer*, offering limited explanations and mostly leaving the reader to construe the meaning of 'sonys' or 'disneys'. Zachry (or his son), on the other hand, anticipates his listenership's incapacity to understand the things he describes. Because he himself has battled to comprehend the relics of 'Smart', his descriptions are vivid and his reliance on technical language limited. The most significant of Zachry's explanations is his account of the very object which has retained the testimony of Sonmi in the previous section, the 'Orison'. In that chapter, the Archivist offers Sonmi, and thereby the reader, a brief but precise introduction to the device of the orison. It is a 'silver egg-shaped device' which 'records both an image of your face and words' (CA, 187). Once recording is complete, it is destined for 'the Ministry of Testaments' (CA, 187), while the person whose experiences it preserves is destined for a death sentence. In 'Sloosha's Crossin'', far removed from the long-destroyed Ministry of Testaments, the orison is unveiled to the reader in Zachry's newly tactile terms: a 'silv'ry egg, sized a babbit's head, with dents'n'markin's on it what fingers rested in' (CA, 275). The 'eery' egg has a 'fat weight' and an uncanny responsiveness to human warmth, 'purrin' an' glowin'.. yay, like it was livin'' (CA, 275). The narrator anticipates his audience's sceptical response. 'I know that don't sound senseful', he interjects, 'but yarns 'bout Old'Un Smart... ain't senseful neither, but that's how it was, so storymen an' old books tell it' (CA, 276). Warmed in his hands, the 'silv'ry egg' spawns a hologram, and Sonmi appears: a 'beautsome ghost-girl' (CA, 276) who speaks in a way Zachry recognizes as familiar but struggles to comprehend: 'For ev'ry word I und'standed 'bout five-six followed what I din't' (CA, 277).

Sonmi's recording speaks in 'an Old'Un tongue, an' not p'formin none' (CA, 277). Zachry tries to respond – 'Sis, can you see me?' – but the hologram simply continues to speak, responding to the Archivist's 'hushed' questions. Zachry's inability to understand Sonmi's testimony – and his surprise at her lack of 'performance' – emphasizes the gulf between this society and that of its predecessor. Sonmi's speech has been faithfully recorded, yet cannot now be fully comprehended. The orison re-emerges at the end of 'Sloosha's Crossin'' as an artefact the narrator displays to support his story, a final memory of 'Old'un times' which, like the story, has been given to him by his father. By this point, the unfamiliar message of Sonmi's orison has been entirely lost, divorced from understanding by the intervening expansion of time. Zachry's son brings out the orison merely as proof of the story's truth, but this time the ghost-girl 'speaks in an' Old'un tongue what no'un alive und'stands nor never will' (*CA*, 324) – a far more complete state of incomprehension than Zachry's own ability to understand one word in six.

In Mitchell's portrayal, the 'thing-like repose' of Sonmi's surviving orison has proved no guarantee of conceptual longevity. Instead it is Zachry's messy oral tale, passed from father to son, which can still be understood as a concluding memoir of 'civilization', while the perfectly preserved message of the pristine Orison of Sonmi is eventually relegated to the status of a children's toy. In a narrative suffused with a sense of loss at the destruction of pre-'Fall' knowledge, this total lack of linguistic understanding represents the reversion to a culture which can rely only on living memory and transferred stories. Sonmi's testimony (which the reader of *Cloud Atlas* is yet to finish reading) is a thoughtful and impassioned evidence against the dehumanisation of corporate society. On one hand, the community established in the narrator's context might represent the ultimate solution to her concerns. On the other hand, this is no peace-loving utopia of health and happiness in the 'far-future' of humanity. Instead, all the signs in Zachry's story point towards a continuation of the devastating limitations he imagines a technologized society can avoid: illness, starvation, violence. Amidst this culture of scarcity, the orison's sole purpose is wonderment and distraction. It 'ain't Smart you can use 'cos it don't... fill empty guts', son-of-Zachry announces at the end of the tale, but it ''mazes the litt'luns' and lulls 'babbits' to sleep' (*CA*, 325). He proffers it to his audience:

Hold out your hands
*
Look.

In her discussion of the 'diegetic reader' – which I cited at the opening of this chapter – Courtney Hopf analyses Zachry's son's presentation of the orison as a positive ending in which 'the external reader is in the position of the "receiver"':

> [B]ut this time that reception is performed as an act of looking and listening rather than reading, thus reinforcing the 'reality' of this diegesis. In other words, this chapter is the first instance in which the 'I' of the text is not filtered through a physical medium, but simply the newer voices who have picked up the tale and retold it. The ironic result of the nested structure of *Cloud Atlas* is that the narrative buried at the centre of the text is granted the highest ontological authority; everything is contained within that which appeared to be contained. (Hopf, 2011: 117-118)

For Hopf (2011: 117), the placement of the oral tale at the centre of the novel indicates that 'Cloud Atlas privileges the power of oral storytelling, the only method of storytelling that requires no physical medium'. However, by concentrating on this privilege, this 'authority', Hopf's analysis overlooks the fact that the 'act of looking and listening' invited within the fictional environment is one that expects no ontological understanding. If 'everything is contained within' this central text, then everything is also lost, since future potential 'readers' are no longer able to comprehend the meaning of its preceding texts. This disjunction is further exacerbated by the inevitable rejection of the invitation by the 'external reader', who, commanded to 'look', instead turns the page to reprise reading, discovering the second half of Sonmi's orison – encapsulated, as is Zachry's tale, in the 'physical medium' that constitutes the volume of the book. This act of page-turning will eventually return the reader to the original chronological phase, Adam Ewing's journal – a text that has already demonstrated the vulnerability of Autua's oral tale, itself 'filtered through a physical medium', convoluted and contracted in the process. Thus the physically inscribed medium emerges as the predominant form – indeed, it is the one in which Mitchell's twenty-first-century reader encounters Zachry's tale. Finally, considering the precipitous nature of this narrator's depicted community, it is difficult to share Hopf's (2011: 118) confidence that Zachry's story will inevitably 'continue to pass thus from generation to generation'.

In *After the End: Representations of Post-Apocalypse*, James Berger (1999: 6) argues that 'post-apocalyptic fiction' requires a particular temporal dexterity on the part of both reader and writer, who must each 'be in both places at once, imagining the post-apocalyptic world and then paradoxically "remembering" the world as it was, as it is'. In *Cloud Atlas*, this act of anticipatory remembrance demands that the reader imagine a situation in which such remembrance is no longer fully possible. It also frames the process of testimony and the description of individual experiences as contingent upon social and historical conditions which threaten the text to the point of destruction or incomprehensibility. When Zachry's son suggests that the orison uses a language which 'never will' be understood, Mitchell offers us an absolute example of what Richard Klein has described as 'the loss of the trace of the loss of the trace':

> What may be most vulnerable is the collective memory of our culture, not merely its existence but the persistence of the memory of its loss. Its loss may be lost, with no trace of survival – a possibility that literary fiction has always claimed the prerogative of proposing: the fiction or fable of the loss of the trace of the loss of the trace. (Klein, 2000: 91)

Although one story continues to subsist in oral form, the bulk of the history that has concerned *Cloud Atlas* and entranced its twenty-first-century reader is shown to disappear from its future's view, a factor which should give pause to the readers still able to 'consume' the text before them. The oral tale at the heart of *Cloud Atlas* is represented as vital, vivid and immediate, in both its play with language and its account of individuals struggling to preserve their own humanity in the face of extreme difficulty. As a fiction or fable of loss, however, it offers a bleak vision of the final eradication of a history that we, as readers, are still involved in creating. But this is not the final word. The ending of *Cloud Atlas* itself appears to offer an opportunity to start afresh, with Adam Ewing's suggestion that 'if we *believe* that humanity may transcend tooth and claw... such a world will come to pass' (*CA*, 528). The world Adam Ewing envisages is not the one *Cloud Atlas* has shown us. But it is a version which each individual – whom

Adam Ewing's final rhetorical flourish figures as 'one drop in a limitless ocean' – may help to form, if they so choose. At this point, it is left
to the reader.

Works Cited

Abley, Mark (2008) *The Prodigal Tongue : Dispatches From the Future of English*. London: William Heinemann.

Berger, James (1999) *After the end: Representations of Post-Apocalypse*. Minneapolis: University of Minnesota Press.

Havelock, Eric A. (1986) *The Muse Learns to Write: Reflections on Orality
and Literacy from Antiquity to the Present*. New Haven, CT: Yale University
Press.

Hoban, Russell (1980/1982) *Riddley Walker*. London: Pan Books.

Hopf, Courtney (2011) 'The Stories we Tell: Discursive Identity through
Narrative Form in *Cloud Atlas*', in Sarah Dillon (ed.) *David Mitchell: Critical Essays*, pp. 105–26. Canterbury: Gylphi.

Klein, Richard (2000) 'The Future of Nuclear Criticism', in Porter and Waters (eds) *50 Years of Yale French Studies, Part 2*, Special Issue of *Yale French
Studies*. Yale: Yale University Press.

Lévi-Strauss, Claude (1992) *Tristes tropiques*, trans. John Weightman and
Doreen Weightman. New York: Penguin Books.

Machinal, Hélène (2011) '*Cloud Atlas*: From Post-Modernity to the Post-
Human', Sarah Dillon(ed.) *David Mitchell: Critical Essays*, pp. 127–54.
Canterbury: Gylphi.

Mitchell, David (2005) 'On reading *Riddley Walker* in Hiroshima', in Chris
Bell (ed.) *The Russell Hoban Some-Poasyum Celebratory Book*. London:
Cambridge Silent Artists.

Mitchell, David (2004) *Cloud Atlas*. London: Hodder & Stoughton.

Ong, Walter (1982) *Orality and Literacy: The Technologizing of the Word*.
London: Methuen & Co.

Rousseau, Jean-Jacques and Johann Gottfried Herder (1966/1986) *On
the Origin of Language: Two Essays*, trans. John H. Moran and Alexander
Gode. London: University of Chicago.

Tosh, John (1984) *The Pursuit of History: Aims, Methods and New Directions
in the Study of Modern History*. London: Longman.

Afterword
Enduring Periodicity

David James

Unlike more than a few of the younger scholars contributing to this book, I'm old enough to have glimpsed as an undergraduate what a university English curriculum looked like before the current reign of modularisation. Nowadays students are encouraged to question canonicity in all its forms; to move nimbly back-and-forth across time, regions and modes; to cultivate their own areas of specialization, embracing concentration (if they wish) yet without foregoing thematic or literary-cultural diversity. In short, they have the chance to map their own voyage of inquiry with unprecedented freedom. Few of us who have the fortune to teach in H. E. institutions today would bemoan this widespread conversion from degree-paths that ploughed chronologically and comprehensively across literary history to an ethos now of unfettered choice, where decisions about who and what to study are made by our tutees rather than imposed by us.

Structures of discovery for undergraduates have thus become ever more malleable, which means that determinants of textual and cultural value have never been more debatable. But if certain literary periods are no longer considered compulsory, the logic and legitimacy of periodization itself has remained relatively intact. Constraints of periodicity have endured, in part, precisely because of the pragmatic constraints of modular curricula, where a level of competency within manageable coordinates is often the only way to ensure our students achieve definable 'learning objectives' and 'transferrable skills' – the rhetoric of which we love to satirize, however dutifully we recycle it in order to have module proposal forms approved. There's nothing wrong with the persistence of periodization, of course. After all, periods help us to introduce complex texts against the backdrop of clearly framed yet complicated sociohistorical contexts. They allow us to show how, in temporally precise terms, the anatomy of something as formally multifarious and generically promiscuous as the novel has evolved in response to localised conditions of cultural change. But it's striking to see that, beyond the classroom, this periodizing impulse persists in scholarly work on contemporary fiction – and particularly, one notices, on contemporary *British* fiction.[1]

What are the implications of that persistence, and what does it say about the way we currently historicize narrative in Britain today? Will the current surge of interest in post-millennial literature do more to consolidate than interrogate our reliance on period divisions for distinguishing phases in the progression of the British novel? Eric Hayot might declaim that as critics and teachers we belie a 'collective desire to remain institutionally inside periods', and that 'the near-total dominance of the concept of periodization in literary studies' is a 'dominance that amounts to a collective failure of imagination and will on the part of the literary profession' (Hayot, 2012: 149). But nowhere has the need for, and resilience of, periodization seemed more apparent than in relation to fiction from the past decade. And that includes fiction's producers as well as its critics: when Zadie Smith (2008: 4) asks, simply, 'Where is our fiction, our 21st-century fiction?', she gives a flavour of the urgency of that endeavour to find what is distinctive, exactly, about literary production now. Much of that endeavour has, necessarily, become concerned with the adequacy and aims of its own vocabulary, as exemplified by the impressive methodological self-reflexivity of the preceding essays here. So while I certainly agree with Hayot that periodization carries with it 'a strong unstated theory of *era* as the final goal and subtending force of the intimacies of literary criticism, which reifies at an ideological level a powerful theory of periods as social wholes' (Hayot, 2012: 151), I would suggest that a more even-handed consideration of why periods matter – why they endure – continues to be important to scholarship on twenty-first-century writing.

What follows is a reflection on how, collectively, the perspectives in this book draw attention to the salience and consequences of periodization for the study of recent British fiction. They do so, first, as already hinted, by virtue of the admirable self-reflectiveness with which they negotiate the very interpretive discourses and paradigms within which they move; and second, by expanding the 'corpus' of candidates who we should consider as the significant players in contemporary letters. We're thus introduced to a stunning range of recently established writers who've yet to receive sustained critical attention; we're also given an insight into the advantages of reassessing genres (comics, the gothic, pastoral, crime) and political or popular-cultural practices (cybernetics, pychogeography, cosmopolitan collectivities) that shed fresh light on the narrative strategies of a new generation of novelists. That this picture of generic and contextual expansion is enriched by accounts here of its distinctive periodicity is one of the successes of a volume that connects twenty-first-century fiction with various lineages and previous traditions.

In a related turn of the critical screw, we're also offered nuanced discussions of how our present era itself can in part be seen as idiomatically retrospective. A key aspect of the periodicity of the 2000s is thus captured by its creative – yet not necessarily, or not always, nostalgic – re-entry into past decades. One such perspective is offered by Chris Vardy, who attends to contemporary responses to the 1980s as a 'radical and intensely divisive socio-economic paradigm' (p. 84). Citing but also complicating Simon Reynolds's rather catch-all characterization of postmillennial culture as marked by chronic and sentimentalizing retrogression, Vardy significantly advances the conversation concerning how we address twenty-first-century fiction in a period of retro-oriented motivations, where the past has become for both literary fiction and television serials alike the engine of invention. Vardy's contribution thus joins a growing body of engagements with nostalgia itself that refuse to dismiss this phenomenon and its complex function within the cultural imaginary. As Dominic

Head has put it, 'the nostalgic impulse sits unhappily with the normative model of literary history, in which development is invariably determined by the demarcation between the old and the new'. The knock-on effect of this clash between reductive preconceptions about nostalgia and habitual ways of telling a developmental story of literary change is that any 'notable literary movement is then perceived to embody a reaction against (if not a progression beyond) the forms, habits, styles or preoccupations of the preceding generation' (Head, 2012: 44).

Such concerns are especially prescient for engaging with fiction of the 2000s, as its strategies of retrospection, homage and inheritance become increasingly multivalent and artistically self-conscious. Head warns of the temptation to rehearse a monochrome notion of nostalgia as the supposed adversary to innovation, a temptation refused by Marianne Corrigan's astute account of the affinity between recent renditions of digital worlds and modernist form. Offering another example of the way this collection refracts writing of the postmillennial period through substantive thematic and stylistic connections with earlier twentieth-century practices, Corrigan shows that 'textual depictions of cybernetic spaces' in Salman Rushdie and Indra Sinha reveal 'the employment of varying stylistic and aesthetic methods reminiscent of the modernist literary tradition, in order to disrupt conventional narration and characterization' (p. 246). The implications of Corrigan's seemingly counterintuitive argument are highly significant for the lexicon with which we approach the poetics of virtual realms and experiences in contemporary fiction. Instead of presupposing that cybernetic representations demand a whole other language of classification and critique, Corrigan suggests that we need to listen-in to 'a conversation which ... we might register between the shifting social, cultural and political frameworks which writers such as Woolf and Richardson sought to respond to through what has come to be theorized as the literary aesthetics of modernism, and the changing cultural and political world which Rushdie, Sinha and other contemporary novelists seek to record at the turn of the twenty-first century' (p. 250).

One can scarcely contemplate the impact of virtual technologies on everyday reading habits – bearing in mind what Corrigan elegantly calls 'the oscillation of the subject between the digital landscape and the materiality of the organic world' (p. 261) – without raising the spectre of arguments, both ominous and upbeat, about the fate of the printed book. Even the most anecdotal empirical research, in taking a glance at commuters' visible preferences or hearing the views of our students, would suggest that the paperbound novel is here to stay. Beyond doomsayers' tales of tablet technology and its grim consequences for now-unwieldy (and expensive) hardbacks, Neal Kirk paints a somewhat more complicated picture. While his main case study is Scarlett Thomas, Kirk opens up a broader avenue for considering fiction that 'participates in the rendering of the book as a fetishistic contemporary commodity operating alongside, rather than opposed to, new mediatisation trends' (p. 222). One does wonder whether the past decade has been a period for rather beautiful books in the face of the novel's encroaching technologization, even though to call them fetishized objects might not be so fair or applicable in each instance. Think of Jonathan Cape's seductively transparent dust jacket for Tom McCarthy's avant-garde *C* (2010), a cover that feels like pliable glass, complementing in turn the novel's pellucid and glacial narrative voice. Think of Zadie Smith's typographically extravagant *NW* (2012), a novel that not only exemplifies some of what Kaja Morczewska terms the 'multiple facets of realism' in British fiction today, but that also ranges widely in font size, style and paragraphical arrangement – making the book as innovative in construction as it was in its emotive momentum and ethical gravity. Think of Julian Barnes's Booker-winning *The Sense of an Ending* (2011), a novella compromised of crystalline moments, sparely presented yet carefully weighted; moments whose smallness as half-snatched memories belies their significance, just as the miniaturist scale of the hardback from Cape seems to emulate the degree of compression that, for Barnes's narrator, recollection fatally involves. This brief of clutch of exquisitely manufactured novels reminds us that reading contemporary fiction on a tablet will always be woefully incomplete: to explore what a book does in its physical entirety, we cannot be denied the choice of forming interpretations beyond the level of semantics alone, that is, of reading what Glyn White calls the material text's neglected 'graphic surface' (see White, 2005).

This return – if it is a return and not, in fact, a much needed critical advance – to considering the aesthetics of the book in age of fiction's digitization is one of several methodological points of departure that, as I've been suggesting, are peculiar to the postmillennial period. Of course, this collection also reminds us that certain critical preoccupations have remained so widespread as to become embedded as default positions. Marie-Luise Kohlke, for instance, raises the issue of whether the concern with trauma has now turned out to be a rather standard optic through which to view postmillennial writing. As Kohlke points out, 'trauma has become the norm' (p. 63), since it 'functions as perhaps *the* privileged trope for conceptualizing personal and collective identity formation and politics' (p. 62). But despite its dominance, this paradigm can still tell us something useful about the very periodicity of its prevalence. For after the catastrophe of 9/11 and its world-historical fallout, Kohlke suggests we can now see in hindsight that the 'millennial cusp marked not a break with the horrors of the twentieth century but rather a repetition and return to trauma, Gothic politics of terror and the paranoia of infiltration and persecution' (p. 64). This isn't simply to single-out a peculiarly resilient academic trend (though it is that too); fiction itself is no less a catalyst for trauma's current perpetuation. Indeed, it would seem that the persistence of such explanatory frameworks reveals once again the dialectic between what we consider to be definitively 'postmillennial' about cultural production today and the histories of upheaval to which writers remain so consciously and conspicuously responsive.

Finding new ways of framing twenty-first-century fiction *as* twenty-first-century in matter and mode can therefore be both helpful and haphazard. But that's the case with any act of periodization, regardless of the historical era in question. Brian McHale has recently observed that '[i]t is in the nature of the periodizing enterprise that every gesture of temporal delimitation is a kind of thought experiment or enabling fiction, necessarily arbitrary, though not for that reason inconsequential' (McHale, 2011: 328). Whenever we attempt to impress a period on what is in reality a manifold phase in the evolution of the novel, 'every such decision has knock-on consequences for the kind of period or sub-period one constructs and the kind of cultural-historical narrative one tells'. As McHale reminds us – and as the variety of standpoints, commitments and interpretive concerns of the essays here epitomise – 'choose a particular onset date or threshold moment, and particular continuities and discontinuities, causes and effects, themes and figures, leap into focus, while others recede into the background; choose a different date, and different continuities, discontinuities, *etc.*, emerge' (McHale, 2011: 328–9). Presenting precisely this scene of difference and discontinuity, on the one hand, resonance and aesthetic recapitulation, on the other, this volume as a whole finds new ways of opening out the tapestry of contemporary British fiction. Yet it does so without resorting to the convenient language of homogenizing tendencies, and without seeing the cultural work of fiction as purely symptomatic of what has been a geopolitically fraught and devastating era since 2000. And for that reason, the period this book covers continues to warrant attention in and of itself. When Bianca Leggett argues that cosmopolitan writing, 'like the ethos at is centre, retains a mood of the subjunctive', providing a 'vehicle for imagining how an ideal global community might work' (p. 22), the same could be said for the periodicity of postmillennial fiction. That is to say, it might be apt to tackle the task of periodization in that same subjunctive mood, whereby the period becomes a placeholder for possibilities rather impositions. Even a period sceptic like Hayot notes that '[w]hat matters is how history is handled inside the period concept' (Hayot, 2012: 164). The essays here seem alert to this injunction, forging connections between what writers tell us about our historical moment, without ignoring what they tell us about why this moment could be such an important one in the history of British fiction.

Note

1 Two recent book series stand out: Bloomsbury's *A Decade of Contemporary British Fiction*, which includes forthcoming volumes on the 1970s, 1980s, 1990s and 'Noughties'; and the *Edinburgh History of Twentieth-Century Literature in Britain* series, edited by Randall Stevenson, which

includes (as volume 9) Joseph Brooker's acute multi-generic assessment, *Literature of the 1980s: After the Watershed* (Edinburgh: Edinburgh University Press, 2010).

Works Cited

Hayot, Eric (2012) *On Literary Worlds*. Oxford: Oxford University Press.

Head, Dominic (2012) 'H. E. Bates, Regionalism, and Late Modernism', in David James (ed.) *The Legacies of Modernism: Historicising Postwar and Contemporary Fiction*, pp. 40–52. Cambridge: Cambridge University Press.

McHale, Brian (2011) 'Break, Period, Interregnum', *Twentieth-Century Literature* 57(3–4): 328–40.

Smith, Zadie (2008) 'The Book of Revelations', *Guardian, Review*, Saturday 24 May.

White, Glynn (2005) *Reading the Graphic Surface: The Presence of the Book in Prose Fiction*. Manchester: Manchester University Press.

Index